Business and the Risk of Crime in China

Business and the Risk of Crime in China

Roderic Broadhurst   John Bacon-Shone

Brigitte Bouhours   Thierry Bouhours

assisted by Lee Kingwa

ASIAN STUDIES SERIES MONOGRAPH 3

ANU

THE AUSTRALIAN NATIONAL UNIVERSITY

E PRESS

ANU

E PRESS

Published by ANU E Press
The Australian National University
Canberra ACT 0200, Australia
Email: anuepress@anu.edu.au
This title is also available online at: http://epress.anu.edu.au/

National Library of Australia Cataloguing-in-Publication entry

Title: Business and the risk of crime in China : the 2005-2006 China international
              crime against business survey / Roderic Broadhurst ... [et al.].

ISBN: 9781921862533 (pbk.) 9781921862540 (ebook)

Notes: Includes bibliographical references.

Subjects: Crime--China--21st century--Costs.

              Commercial crimes--China--21st century--Costs.

Other Authors/Contributors:

              Broadhurst, Roderic G.

Dewey Number: 345.510268

Cover design and layout by ANU E Press

Cover image: The gods of wealth enter the home from everywhere, wealth, treasures and peace
beckon; designer unknown, 1993; (Landsberger Collection) International Institute of Social
History, Amsterdam.

Contents

Foreword vii
  Lu Jianping

Preface ix

Acronyms xv

Introduction 1

1. Background 25

2. Crime and its Control in China. 43

3. ICBS Instrument, Methodology and Sample 79

4. Common Crimes against Business 95

5. Fraud, Bribery, Extortion and Other Crimes against
   Business 111

6. Predictors of Business Victimisation. 133

7. Reporting Crime Victimisation and Satisfaction with Police
   Response. 143

8. Perceptions of Business Environment and Crime Trends 171

9. Summary, Implications and Future Directions 189

Appendix A. World Governance Indicators 215

Appendix B. Review of Business Victimisation Surveys 221

Appendix C. Media Sources Used in Chapter 2:
   Crime and policing in Shanghai, Shenzhen and Xi'an 231

Appendix D. Hong Kong ICBS Pilot Survey, 2003 235

Appendix E. Schematic Overview of the ICBS China
   Questionnaire, 2004–05 239

Appendix F. ICBS China Questionnaire, 2004–05:
   Hong Kong version. 241

Appendix G. Victimisation by Common Crime by City,
      Business Sector and Size 273

Appendix H. Victimisation by Non-Conventional Crime by
      City, Business Sector and Size 277

Bibliography 279

Foreword

Lu Jianping[1]

It is a great pleasure to introduce for the public the results of the 2005–06 China International Crime against Business Survey (China ICBS) conducted by the team of ANU professors and researchers in Hong Kong.

The general aim of the China ICBS is to enhance our understanding of the extent and nature of crimes against business, and their impact on business and confidence in China. As the first large-scale survey of crimes against business undertaken in Chinese cities, the China ICBS shows that it is possible to obtain useful data about crime risks, prevention practices and reactions of business enterprises through empirical studies such as fieldwork, surveys, questionnaires, and so on. It also makes possible valid comparisons of the prevalence of crimes against business in Chinese cities (Hong Kong, Shenzhen, Shanghai and X'ian) with others cities similarly surveyed in both emerging economies and developed countries.

China's economic growth since 1978 is no doubt a miracle both at the domestic and the global level. At the same time, crime (common crimes and economic crimes including crimes against business) is also soaring. It is a fascinating terrain for criminologists to verify classical theories, to explore the reason for this phenomenon and possibly to find new explanations.

A privilege once reserved for state power or enterprises in command economies, doing business is becoming fashionable for everybody in China today, and the so-called 'socialist market economy' has been established. But China is still developing its market economy and problems such as distinctions (or discrimination) in status between public and private market actors and conflicts between state monopolies and marketisation still exist in China. The policy of opening and reforming has triggered profound changes in the economic system of China today, while economic changes in turn bring up new situations and changes in the social interest structure, class status, culture, mentality, human behaviour and governmental functions. This social transformation aggravates the phenomenon of institutional shortage. In this context of economic development and social change, business enterprises suffer (as victims) from the differences in status, in policy and in the competitive environment between the public and private sectors, and from bureaucracy and monopolies, but, at the same

---

1   Lu Jianping is Professor of Law, PhD, Vice-President of the Chinese Society of Criminology, a member of the Board of Directors of the International Society of Criminology, and Vice-Dean of the College for Criminal Law Science, Beijing Normal University, China.

time, they are more inclined towards using bribery and organised crime. Crimes against business in China today reflect not only prominent features of a society in transformation, but also conflicts of interest between public and private, freedom and control, market and government, and civil society and state power.

This book is of great value not only to experts in criminal justice, criminology and sociology who are willing to increase their knowledge about China's economic development, social transformation, crime control and rule of law, but also to businesspeople who just want to do business in or with China.

Preface

This book reports the results of the first large-scale survey of crimes against business in China. We believe that the survey provides vital benchmark estimates of the risks and costs of crime for businesses operating in various economic sectors in China. These costs are worth monitoring and the survey can play a role in the development of both private and public policy responses, as well as crime prevention. As the first comprehensive attempt to measure the risks of not only common crimes such as robbery and fraud but also newly emergent crimes such as cyber crime, credit card fraud and intellectual property theft, our work will, we hope, encourage further investigations based on the same broad victim-centred methods described here. Our view is that despite the usual difficulties of obtaining the cooperation of business leaders and their reluctance to engage with researchers on such a sensitive topic, large-scale independent prevalence surveys of crimes against business are effective in identifying risks, including those involving bribery and organised crime. They also have much to offer in assisting businesses in the reduction of both the direct and the indirect harms that flow from crime. Such surveys provide public police and private security with an understanding of the nature and impact of crime on business—an impact that ultimately falls adversely on everyday consumers.

The data collection for the study we report in this monograph was completed in May 2007. Although some years have elapsed, preliminary results were reported at the twentieth annual conference of the Australian and New Zealand Society of Criminology in Adelaide, 24–27 September 2007, and selected final results at the sixteenth Congress of the International Society of Criminology conference in Kobe, Japan, 5–9 August 2011. Even allowing for the considerable time needed to clean and check raw data, conduct analysis and re-check data and results, we have taken longer to finalise the work than intended. In part, this delay arose from the usual time pressures upon the research team amplified by changes in post and location, illness, as well as the additional complexities of working across different locations. Yet this research had its genesis even further back, when in 2003 a small grant from the University of Hong Kong with further support from that university's Centre for Criminology enabled us to conduct a small pilot survey of crime against businesses in Hong Kong and also in Shenzhen. The pilot was undertaken in July–August 2003 by the survey team of the Social Science Research Centre at the University of Hong Kong and reported by the first author at the Societies of Criminology first Key Issues Conference, held in Paris on 13–15 May 2004. With the feasibility of the research ensured, the principal investigators (Roderic Broadhurst and John Bacon-Shone) in conjunction with the Institute of Crime Prevention, Ministry of Justice of the People's Republic of China (then under the direction of Professor Guo J. H.), were able to secure competitive funding from the Research Grants Council of the Hong Kong Special Administrative Region (7204/04H) in 2005 to conduct the survey in four key cities in China. We are grateful to the Research Council for their support and assistance, especially for extending the time to complete the research.

The survey adapted the relatively untried UN protocol for measuring crimes against business provided by Dr Anna Alvazzi del Frate, then at the UN Office of Drugs and Crime (UNODC). In 2004, Dr Alvazzi del Frate was in the process of completing the analysis of an earlier version of this survey conducted in Eastern Europe in 2000 and she gave us invaluable assistance and advice. We draw on the results of that and other similar surveys of crimes against business in the pages that follow.

Given the scale of the project and the numerous challenges encountered in collection and analysis, we owe many debts for the support we have received from the funding committees, our respective universities and the work of our survey teams based at the Social Sciences Research Centre. We also note the support of the Australian Research Council Centre of Excellence in Policing and Security and its Australian National University (ANU) node for their support, without which the final product would have been much less comprehensive. Such support enabled Brigitte Bouhours to assist the project at a crucial time, and she was instrumental in helping to bring the work to its conclusion. Thierry Bouhours became engaged with the project in 2008 and again in the later stages, notably in the final analysis and our interpretations of the results.

Among those who have helped this project, in particular, we thank Lee Kingwa who was the initial research officer and was responsible for oversight of the data collection. Lennon Chang Yaochung, our colleague at the ANU, was also a wonderful aid who, in addition to his comments on an early draft of the manuscript, provided much-needed assistance with finding as well as translating otherwise invisible references and web sites. We gratefully acknowledge the help of Zhong Yueying and Aris Chan for the translation from the English to the Chinese (both Cantonese and Mandarin) versions of the interview protocol and subsequent modifications after the pilot survey. We thank Eduardo Ramirez and Nishank Motwani from the ANU who, in the final stages of producing this monograph, helped us put together the references and appendices.

At various times we also benefited from the help of colleagues T. Wing Lo, Susan Trevaskes and Børge Bakken on specific matters. We also acknowledge the generous support and interest of our colleagues at the ANU, especially John Braithwaite and Peter Grabosky, who encouraged us to produce a book-length version of this research. Their encouragement along with the interest and support of Craig Reynolds, of the ANU E Press Editorial Board (Asian Studies), were important parts of the drive to complete this book. We acknowledge the kind interest of Margaret Thornton, also of the ANU E Press (Law), who gave the idea the attention and support needed to bring the work to fruition. Finally, we thank the reviewers whose thoughtful comments and suggestions we readily incorporated into this work.

Roderic Broadhurst
Australian National University
Canberra
September 2011

Map 1 Map of the four cities surveyed in the China UNICBS

Source: <http://chinapage.com>

Acronyms

ADB	Asian Development Bank
AIC	Australian Institute of Criminology
BPI	Bribe Payers Index
CATI	computer-assisted telephone interviewing
CCBS	Crime and Corruption Business Survey
CCP	Chinese Communist Party
CCTV	closed-circuit television
CIA	Central Intelligence Agency
CNY	Chinese yuan
ComVS	Commercial Victimisation Survey (UK)
CPI	Corruption Perception Index
CTS	United Nations Survey on Crime Trends and the Operations of Criminal Justice Systems
CVS	Crime Victimisation Survey (Hong Kong)
GDP	gross domestic product
GNP	gross national product
HK	Hong Kong
HK$	Hong Kong dollar
HK SAR	Hong Kong Special Administrative Region
ICAC	Independent Commission Against Corruption (Hong Kong)
ICBS	International Crime against Business Survey
ICCS	International Commercial Crime Survey
ICVS	International Crime Victims Survey
IP	intellectual property
KPMG	global professional services firm

MPS   Ministry of Public Security (Mainland China)

OECD   Organisation for Economic Cooperation and Development

PAP   People's Armed Police

PCCW   Hong Kong's leading communications provider

PPP   purchasing power parity

PRC   People's Republic of China

PSB   Public Security Bureau

PWC   PriceWaterhouseCoopers

SAR   special administrative region

SEZ   special economic zone

SOE   state-owned enterprise

UK   United Kingdom

UN   United Nations

UNICRI   United Nations Interregional Criminal Justice Institute

UNIDO   United Nations Industrial Development Organisation

UNODC   United Nations Office on Drugs and Crime

USA   United States of America

USD   United States dollar

USSR   Union of Soviet Socialist Republics

Introduction

Commercial activity entails many risks with the potential to 'shrink' profit margins. Losses arising from wastage, damage, fraud and theft are an integral part of the cost of doing business. Crime is a ubiquitous factor in commercial life, a 'cost' to avoid, minimise and manage. Losses from theft and fraud can sometimes be fatal to business survival, but usually losses are absorbed or passed on to clients or consumers. Drawing on the experiences of more than 5000 businesses, the research reported here seeks to understand the scale and impact of crime on business in the People's Republic of China, exploring both conventional or common 'street' crimes, such as burglary, robbery and theft, and crimes that specifically target business such as fraud, counterfeiting, bribery and extortion. We estimate that in the year of the survey, our sample of 5117 businesses suffered a total annual loss to crime of US$20.35 million, most of which was due to fraud by either employees (US$7.45 million) or outsiders (US$7.56 million). We were able to extrapolate these losses to all Hong Kong companies and estimate that annual losses reached approximately US$1.52 billion in 2004; however, data about the size and nature of the population of businesses in the mainland cities of Shanghai, Shenzhen and Xi'an are insufficient to determine the representativeness of our sample. At best, we offer a 'guesstimate', based on untested assumptions, that suggests that about US$4.9 billion is lost to crime annually in these three mainland cities.

A vast literature addresses street crime and the social impact of crime but much less has been written about crimes against business. Apart from interest in 'white-collar' and corporate crime and crime perpetrated by business against employees, customers or society in general, little is known about business as a victim of crime. The relationship between crime in the broader society and crime against business is a matter little explored. The available evidence suggests that businesses are at much higher risks of theft than households or individuals and their losses can have a significant impact on investment and growth. Crimes such as robbery, theft, fraud, extortion, bribery and criminal damage form a significant cost impost in certain high-risk business activities. Significant financial and psychological costs are reported for small business, and crime victimisation is not randomly distributed (Gill 1998; Shury et al. 2005; Taylor and Mayhew 2002; van Dijk and Terlouw 1996). Crime can also damage brand reputation, the value of shares, staff morale and companies' standing with government regulators and police. In addition, a real or even a perceived high rate of crime can have unwanted consequences and incur additional costs for individual behaviour (risk avoidance), business investment, the price of products, tax revenues and tourism.

Like ordinary citizens, businesses rely in part on the public police to protect their property and activities from crime. They might even seek to influence the role and deployment of public police, who are key actors in crime prevention and crime detection. Unlike street crime or public-order offences, however, to which state or public police are normally expected to respond, some crimes against business might attract little interest from public police (for example, copyright violations, shop theft). Police resource and capacity limitations might also result in inadequate support for businesses that are victims of crime. Major fraud cases often require specialist expertise and often involve complex deception that could easily overwhelm the available law-enforcement expertise. The costs of crime and its prevention represent a considerable burden on state revenues, and police, like other public services, are subject to rationing. In these circumstances, some of the burden of policing will increasingly need to be shared with community and business 'partners' (see Ayling et al. 2009).

As a consequence, and given that the risks of crime are seen as a normal feature of commercial activity, businesses have adopted countermeasures—often at the industry/sector level—to minimise exposure to crime. They typically respond to the risks of crime by improving their internal controls over loss mitigation, applying external or internal auditing schemes, training staff and providing company governance and ethics guidelines, rotating personnel and duties and participating in crime-prevention initiatives. Investment in private security services and in risk mitigation is widely practised by large businesses, but smaller ones tend to rely more on public police and some forms of collective protective security practices, such as the hiring of security guards or the installation of CCTV for common areas and activities. This tradition of self-help, however, has limits, and businesses, like other institutions and activities, are part of society, and societies can experience wide fluctuations in the rate of crime. Indeed the People's Republic of China (PRC) has experienced, in the language of its security officials, several crime 'waves' and 'high tides' of crime since 1949 (Dutton 1997) and recognises that it is currently going through a wave of economic crime that is yet to peak (Jiang 2004; Lu 2011). The extent and nature of crime will, therefore, have a bearing on how businesses cope with its consequences, but social forces beyond the control of business and governments will play a significant role in the actual risk to business.

Perspectives on Crime

The character and extent of crime in a particular time and place are often treated as proxy measures of a society's virtue and social cohesion. The frequency and severity of criminal events and the effectiveness of the response of the state, via its police and courts, are also a reflection of the quality of governance and fidelity to the rule of law. Since Durkheim's seminal analysis of the impact of rapid economic and cultural change on crime in the nineteenth and early twentieth centuries, shifts in patterns of crime have been seen as emblematic of social and cultural strain. Durkheim's concept of 'anomie' or normlessness captures the uncertainty and ambiguities of social conduct and the rules of everyday life that arise in complex modern societies. Modernity, especially in the economic sphere, necessitates tolerance of difference but also creates the circumstances for deviance because as social integration and regulation falter, adherence to social rules becomes more a matter of choice than compulsion. Crime, then, is a normal (functional) outcome of social and economic change when social integration and regulation are weakened by a focus on individuality, but crime is also a focus for social solidarity around moral and legal rules (Durkheim 1964, 1997).

Durkheim anticipated the impact of the cult of individualism in modern society and the decline of religious or moral solidarity in creating social order (Marks 1974; Rock 2002). In a society faced with uncertainty about its social or religious values, or in the case of China, with a shift from austere communism to a socialist market economy, social control would have to rely more on the state and its legal apparatus than on social conventions, gossip and traditional forms of social hierarchy. Merton (1968), reflecting on the rapid social and economic changes in American society in the 1920s and 1930s and the associated widespread corruption, used the concept of anomie (in his adaptation of the term, arising from the disconnect or strain between cultural goals of success and the institutional means of achieving these goals) to explain the increases in crime as the innovative response to inadequate opportunities in a supposedly merit-based, equal society. The criminal deviance of the notorious gangster of this period, Al Capone, was, in this sense, that of an arch innovator seeking out the best means to achieve the American dream of success through wealth (cf. Merton 1938). In Chapter 2, we examine in greater depth how theories of modernisation and crime fit the context of China's economic opening and modernisation.

The functionalist approach to crime suggested by Durkheim, Merton and others provides an account of macro-level conditions conducive to crime but offers little guidance on the specific risks for individuals and businesses, except for broad policies designed to mitigate disadvantage or strain. From a crime-prevention perspective, routine activity theory offers a more prescriptive approach to criminal incidents resulting from the convergence of three factors: a motivated offender and his/her resources (for example, skills, contacts), attractive targets and the absence of capable guardians (Cohen and Felson 1979).[1] Routine activity

---

1   These authors and others have written extensively about routine activity theory or situational crime prevention, and incorporate ideas of crime prevention through environmental design (see further Clarke 1995; Clarke and Felson 1993; Felson 1998; Felson and Clarke 1998).

posits both instrumental and rational decision making as key offender attributes, and does not rely on pathologies to explain criminal motivation, although individual pathologies might lead to irrational decisions. These 'situational' crime-prevention approaches do not focus on the offender but on the offence, and propose making potential targets of crime less attractive and strengthening guardianship as preferred solutions; what matters is the reduction of criminal opportunities rather than attempts to change offenders. Many businesses and industry bodies have successfully applied this approach to crime prevention, and the systematic adoption of such strategies in partnership with police still holds great promise in reducing the impact of crime on small and large business operations (Clarke 1995).

These perspectives on crime were developed in Western capitalist economies. We do not know how well they would apply in socialist nations or transitional economies. The abrupt transition to a market economy that followed the collapse of the Soviet Union has resulted in widespread lawlessness, the rapid expansion of organised crime groups who took over legitimate enterprises, and intense corruption. The rule of law was not implemented; instead the legal structures and state-control apparatus disintegrated and organised crime merged with the political leadership (see, for example, Karstedt 2003; Ledeneva and Kurkchiyan 2000; Sergeyev 1998; Shelley 1995a, 1995b). Shelley points out that 'Russia, unlike China, tried to simultaneously create a free market and a democratic society. Therefore, citizens have been unable to determine whether their present criminalised economy is a result of the difficulties encountered in creating capitalism or forming democratic institutions' (Shelley 1995b:245). The International Crime against Business Survey (ICBS) is able to shed light on some of the consequences of the Chinese transition from a command to a market economy and its opening to Western markets. Throughout the book, we present comparisons between the results of the China ICBS and that of a similar survey conducted in Eastern Europe in the post-Soviet period (Alvazzi del Frate 2004).

Economic Transformation and Crime

China's 'open-door' policy was instigated under the premiership of Deng Xiaoping in the late 1970s as the principal means of modernising China after the destructive impact of the 'Great Leap Forward' and the Cultural Revolution. Deng's vision was that if China's socialist modernisation was to succeed it had to engage the latent entrepreneurship and productivity of the people with the idea that 'poverty is not socialism—to be rich is glorious', as he famously put it in his 1992 southern tour.[2] Deng's essential pragmatic approach of 'seeking truth from facts' ('it does not matter what colour a cat is as long as it hunts mice') and of assessing what works by trial and error ('cross the river by feeling for the stones with your feet') formed the basic ingredients for unleashing the economic potential of China.[3] Discarding class struggle as the key party strategy for socialist modernisation to concentrate on the development of China's productive forces was critical but only in the context of firm government leadership.[4] Social disorder, including crime, was to be kept in check by political unity.

The economic renaissance of China was nevertheless guided by the 'Four Cardinal Principles' of the Chinese Communist Party (CCP)—namely: 1) the socialist path; 2) the dictatorship of the proletariat (the people's democratic dictatorship); 3) the leadership of the Communist Party; and 4) Marxist-Leninism and Mao Zedong thought.[5] The Twelfth National Congress in September 1982 confirmed the open-door policy, and Deng affirmed the classical Marxist position that China makes its own history, building socialism with Chinese characteristics. Thus began one of the great social transformations of modern history. As Golley and Song observe, the results were spectacular:

> Within just three decades, China has succeeded in transforming itself from a centrally planned closed economy into one of the world's most dynamic and globally integrated market economies. The dynamics unleashed by Deng Xiaoping's reforms, open-door policies and institutional changes have unleashed enormous entrepreneurial energy and propelled continuous capital accumulation, productivity gains and trade and income growth on a scale the world has never seen before. During this period, China's total gross domestic product (GDP), industrial output, foreign trade and, importantly, its per capita income

---

2   During the 1992 southern tour, the famous phrase 'to be rich is glorious' seemed to be a catchcry of the press (see Deng Xiaoping 1994; Zhao 1993).

3   The Sixth Plenary Session of the Eleventh Central Committee adopted the 'Resolution on Certain Questions in the History of Our Party Since the Founding of the People's Republic of China', which condemned the Cultural Revolution and re-evaluated Mao's role, affirming his contributions but acknowledging his mistakes in later years. The 70 per cent correct (in respect to the official view of Mao's legacy) resolution helped unify the Communist Party of China and permitted an orderly transition under stable government. (See *People's Daily*, online English version, undated and reproduced in 'The life of Deng Xiaoping', *Chinabusinessworld. com*, viewed 5 February 2011, <www.cbw.com/asm/xpdeng/life.html>).

4   Deng's goals for China were: first, to quadruple the 1980 gross national product (GNP) by the end of the century to raise the people's standard of living; and second, on the basis of that achievement, to again quadruple GNP over the following 30–50 years, to reach the level of the moderately developed countries. He argued that China would have pointed the way for all the people of the Third World and demonstrated to humankind that socialism was superior to capitalism.

5   According to Deng Xiaoping, the approach was about achieving socialist modernisation: 'to carry it out and make China prosperous we must, first, carry out the policies of reform and opening to the outside world, and we must, second, adhere to the Four Cardinal Principles, the most important of which are to uphold leadership by the Party and to keep to the socialist road, opposing bourgeois liberalisation and a turn to capitalism. These two points are interrelated' (Deng Xiaoping 1987, cited in the Deng hagiography in *People's Daily* online n.d.).

increased respectively by factors of 16, 27, 124 and 12. As a result, the incidence and severity of poverty have declined dramatically in China. (Golley and Song 2010:1)[6]

With annual growth rates often exceeding 10 per cent per annum over the past 30 years, China's economy has been rapidly restructured and modernised with significant impact on everyday life, but has remained based on the pragmatism advocated by Deng and the strategy of retaining political control to ensure economic and social transformation. This approach was vindicated by the instability and eventually the failure of Gorbachev's *glasnost* and *perestroika* that relied on a top-down approach in the Soviet Union (Evans 1997). The legacy of Deng's socialist market economy has been spectacular economic growth, but it also encountered numerous problems such as unprofitable state-owned enterprises, regional imbalances and urban–rural wealth disparity. Economic expansion came at a cost to social cohesion, and, like many emerging/developing market economies, China has had to confront problems of crime and corruption.

The liberalisation of labour mobility so critical to rapid economic growth led to the accelerated urbanisation of Chinese life: in the 1970s, 20 per cent of the population lived in towns and cities compared with 47 per cent in 2009, when the 'floating population' of urban migrant workers was estimated at 160 million (Cai and Wang 2010). Urbanisation was not, however, accompanied by effective public infrastructure development and social welfare measures. Large numbers of mobile peasant workers in pursuit of work in the cities quickly transformed into a mass of disconnected and disaffected workers, radically increasing both the pool of potential offenders and the opportunities for crime.

Urbanisation is one of the major general drivers of crime, combining both opportunity for crime through the presence of attractive targets and the enhancement of anonymity and anomie (Newman 1999; Shelley 1995b). The impact of broad economic change on social cohesion has not escaped the attention of Chinese authorities, particularly the potential disorder that could result from millions of internal economic migrants who might transform into a 'dangerous class' worthy of special policing and regulation.

'Although some areas and segments of society were notably better off than before, the re-emergence of significant inequality did little to legitimise the Communist Party's founding ideals, as the Party faced increasing social unrest' (*People's Daily* online n.d.). Growing inequality, the collapse of the Soviet Union and other communist states, and the pressure for political reform within

---

6   Although the massive restructuring of the economy created a new urban poor—the so-called 'floating population' of rural migrants—'between 1981 and 2004, the fraction of China's population consuming less than US$1 a day in today's purchasing power fell from 65 per cent to 10 per cent and about half a billion people were lifted out of poverty' (World Bank 2009:iii, cited in Golly and Song 2010:1).

China (as illustrated by the 4 June 1989 Tiananmen Square incident) ushered in important regulatory transformations to the political and policing arms of the state. The 1987 Thirteenth National Congress endorsed reforms that sought to separate the functions of the party and the Government, delegating powers to lower levels, reforming government institutions and oversight of party cadres, and improving grassroots consultation (for an overview of legal reforms post 1980, see Zou 2000).

Given the contradictions between the ideal of socialism and the pragmatic politics of market socialism, significant cultural and ideological changes were needed to support economic prosperity. In short, a capitalist China could not modernise society in isolation and political disunity would undermine the prosperity engendered by economic reform. Currently, China faces a new transitional phase, which could pose even greater challenges as labour costs rise and consumption falls in response to a rapid decline in the Chinese population. In this context, policing as a key function of an authoritarian state might have limited capacity to manage threats and social differences. Golley and Song observe:

> [I]ncome inequality and widening regional disparities, along with uneven access to health services and social welfare systems, are some of the most undesirable outcomes associated with the rapid economic growth of the past. Failure to deal with these issues could pose the greatest threats to social stability, which in turn could become a serious obstacle for growth and development in the decades ahead. (Golley and Song 2010:5)

China's next transition from an export-driven economy to one that is focused on domestic consumption and growth might indeed highlight inequality within cities and between the cities and the countryside, and increase crime (Shaw 2006). Thus, the problem of social disorder remains a major risk in maintaining China's exceptional economic growth, and could threaten China's millions of businesses. Under the Government's 'harmonious society' slogan, high expectations and demands for policing are created—often stimulated by an actual and/or a perceived increase in crime (Trevaskes 2010a). The close ideological association between crime and the problem of political stability also creates additional problems in the legal reform process and the modernisation of police (Dutton 2006). The costs of domestic public order have grown rapidly in China, even rivalling defence, and the legitimacy of the police will depend increasingly on their efforts to curb crimes such as fraud, corruption and organised crime (Sun et al. 2010; The Economist 2011b). From our perspective, therefore, the legitimacy of China's police and courts will be crucial given the presence of two powerful drivers of crime: inequality and urbanisation. The role public police play in producing order should be of interest to households and business since effective policing engenders both stability and legitimacy, which are cornerstones of effective crime prevention.

Social Change, Crime and Policing

As we remarked earlier, the Chinese Government and its public security apparatus have long acknowledged the impact of economic development on the emergence of illegitimate opportunities, including opportunities for economic crime. In 1989, the Ministry of Public Security (MPS) Research Unit Number Five produced an influential assessment of crime titled *The Basic Character of Crime in Contemporary China* (see Dutton 1997). This confidential report highlighted the seriousness of the crime situation and the loss of the old order and control over a once stable population managed by the household registration system, work units and neighbourhood committees. It also unwittingly depicted the police in 'crisis management mode' driven to campaign-style or *yanda* (strike-hard) policing (Dutton 1997:160). The report acknowledged that crime stemmed from social contradictions, but that these had been deepened by the commodity economy and the transition from an old system to a new one with more conflicts and 'loopholes' in social administration (Dutton 1997:161). It also noted the changes in the offenders' demography, especially the increasing number of offenders from among the unemployed ('idlers') and the emergence of gangs. The imperfect nature of the legal response was recognised as well as the weaknesses in the ability to control and guard against crime. The rapid rise in property crimes, including crimes against business and state-owned enterprises, and a clear expectation that such crimes would continue to rise were explained in terms of rapid changes in values.

> Many factors account for the large increase in criminal cases involving property, but all are closely linked to the present social and economic situation in China. In recent years, there has been vigorous development of the socialist commodity economy. The commodity economy is a powerful lever for improving social development, but it is also a major inducement to crime. With the development of a commodity economy, money has functioned as a 'battering ram', knocking down traditional values and concepts. As a result, there have been great changes in people's ideology. The historical tradition of looking down on trade has disappeared. In its place has emerged a new craze for trade and running businesses. What many people now want is simply to make money. At the same time, there has been one wave after another of consumerism that has engulfed the country. The huge gap between the high consumption lust and existing buying power of the people has

resulted in a serious contradiction emerging. Stimulated by the above factors, some people who cannot fulfil their personal desires for material enjoyment through legal or proper means have taken the other route—namely, getting money through criminal activity (MPS Research Unit Number Five, cited in Dutton 1997:165).

The situation described in the quote above illustrates a typical Mertonian[7] 'innovative adaptation' and suggests that in the context of China's rapid economic and social changes, functionalist theories of crime as a form of adaptation to strain enhanced by institutional anomie are relevant (Bernburg 2002; Messner and Rosenfield 2009). Institutional or regulatory weakness occurs alongside Mertonian anomie when the 'rules of the game' are unclear, such as in a transitional economy or a colonial order of dubious legitimacy. In these circumstances, a permissive environment for crime emerges, exacerbated by the limited capabilities of police and other forces of law and order (capable guardians in routine activity theory). As a consequence, China's policing agencies have embarked on an extensive process of modernisation and adaptation to the new social problems presented by the unremitting economic transformations that followed Deng Xiaoping's open-door policies. In Chapter 2, we outline some of the criminal justice reforms implemented by the Chinese Government to boost police effectiveness in controlling crime and corruption, and enhance the legitimacy of the police with the Chinese people.

The rise of economic crime (broadly defined in China as money laundering, deceptive contracts, fraudulent tax evasion, false cheques, fake trademarks, food and medicine counterfeiting and infringements of intellectual property rights) has also attracted the attention of the Government. In 2004, the Ministry of Public Security convened a national conference on economic crime in response to concerns about another potential crime wave. At this forum, Premier Wen Jiabao, stressed the dangers of such crimes not only to the interest of the people but also to economic and financial order, and the Minister of Public Security, Zhou Yongkang, warned of the destructive impact of economic crime and its connection with corruption (Jiang 2004). Chen Anfu, Director of the Department of Economic Crime Investigation of the Ministry of Public Security, reported that since 2000 his department had investigated 277 000 cases of economic crime, arrested 262 000 suspects and recovered CNY67 billion (US$8.1 billion or an estimated US$2 billion annually).[8] Chen noted that many of those arrested were well educated, had special skills or knowledge and usually operated from within their work units. According to the Ministry of Public Security, illegal

---

7   As in reference to Robert Merton's 'strain theory' interpretation of Durkheim functional theory in the context of American capitalism and the role of unintended consequences (see Merton 1968).

8   Compare these estimated losses with those reported in 1987 by the Public Security Bureau when the cost of property crime was estimated at CNY530 million (US$64 million) and that of exceptional fraud cases at CNY240 million (US$29.6 million) (Dutton 1997:164, 167).

pyramid selling had become 'an economic cult', involving the jobless, laid-off workers and farmers, university students, soldiers and even public servants. Chen also predicted that intellectual property (IP) infringement cases would increase rapidly in the future and noted that 'the police should also improve capability through team building and resist corruption' (Jiang 2004).

Reforms of the Chinese Public Security Bureau (PSB), especially the adoption of police beat or foot patrols in the major cities such as Shanghai in the early 1990s, and more proactive methods of policing were fundamental to the expansion and professionalisation of policing (Fu 1990, 2003). They were equally fundamental for crime-prevention practices based on the establishment of closer relations with local businesses and households. Other changes have included improved training, specialisation (in traffic, forensics, and so on), modernisation of equipment (for example, vehicles, radios, databases), reorganisation of detective or judicial police functions, integrity oversight functions and versions of 'community policing' (Wong 2001, 2011). At the same time, following a reorganisation after the Tiananmen Square incident, reforms to the People's Armed Police (PAP) under State Council and Military Commission supervision augmented the policing apparatus by providing a *garde mobile* for the control of crime and domestic disorder (Cheung 1996). This was followed by concerted efforts from 1998 under Minister of Public Security, Jia Chunwang, in accord with Premier Zhu Yongji's general reforms of the civil service, to modernise policing practices. These reforms included the removal of unqualified officers, a focus on clearing crime (with less focus on crime reports, which are prone to manipulation), a central inspection and supervision system, attempts at the reduction of corruption among police (reinforced with an open telephone [110] call service), and reorganisation of the Ministry of Public Security (Dai 2001). In short, many police reforms have focused on 'reassurance' and public-order policing, especially in urban areas where great concern existed over the criminal potential of the floating population of internal migrants (Bakken 2004; Nielsen and Smyth 2009).

These police reforms seem to have had some impact on the rise of common crimes but the effect on crime prevention within the business community has been limited. Campaign-style policing ('strike hard') and harsh and swift punishment, which had been the bedrock of policing strategy until recently (Trevaskes 2010a, 2010b), are possibly effective against street crimes and more visible forms of deviance in authoritarian contexts but seem inept means of uncovering financial fraud. These 'strike-hard' mass campaigns bolstered by bonuses for police (a process of commodification; cf. Dutton 2006) and a compliant judicial process seldom focused on 'white-collar' or 'cadre' crimes such as fraud. Tax evasion and counterfeit products featured in campaigns between 2000 and 2007 and economic crime in 1982 but there has not been the sustained attention given to 'non-conventional' crime that has been given to common or street crimes such as robbery (Trevaskes 2010a). The Hong Kong Police have a dedicated crime-prevention unit and Shenzhen police have undertaken crime-prevention campaigns (Zhong 2009a). As we report in Chapter 8, however, only a minority of the businesses in our study was interested and had engaged in cooperative action with the police, and there is considerable room to further develop collective crime-prevention approaches. Chinese police in general have yet to engender the co-production of crime control and prevention within the community or within economic units in the sense that *reassurance policing*[9] is understood as the police response to public demands through a combination of 'soft' and coercive 'hard' policing practices (Innes 2005).

Corruption and Organised Crime

Low crime rates, low levels of fear of crime and high levels of public safety are theoretically associated with good governance, while high crime levels, particularly when they involve criminal organisations, are associated with poor standards of governance and corruption (Chin and Godson 2006). The scale of corruption has intensified since the mid-1990s and involves many more high-level party officials, whose punishment has become the focus for the development of a culture of clean government (Li 2010). Although since the economic reforms corruption has worsened, it has not become rampant or out of control, but nevertheless remains a serious issue for ordinary Chinese and a threat to government legitimacy (Li 2010; NBS 2007; Gong 2010; Wedeman 2004, 2008). Corruption in government and corporate affairs is largely seen as a consequence of lack of transparency and weak regulatory practices inherent in a state where party and government are intertwined and checks and balances fail because the all important political and legal oversight institutions are not independent (Gong 2004, 2008; Wedeman 2004, 2006, 2008). There is, however, little evidence that such corruption has hindered economic growth. Wedeman's (2004) analysis of corruption in China addresses the apparent contradiction between continued economic success and increases in corruption.[10] He argues that anti-corruption campaigns have impacted on low-level 'anarchic' corruption

---

9   Reassurance policing is defined as 'an approach that integrates the delivery of formal social control with other local sources, rather than automatically privileging the role of the police; thereby, at least partially countering increasing expectations of and dependency on the state' (Innes and Roberts 2008:242).

10   'If corruption increased in gross quantitative terms during the initial phase of reform and intensified in the later phases, then simple assumptions about its negative economic consequences clearly need to be critically re-examined and the apparent contradiction between rising corruption and rapid growth in China resolved' (Wedeman 2004:920).

while the negative consequences of organised high-level corruption have lower transaction costs, because they are more predictable and less likely to involve the risk of exposure; thus:

> [T]he apparent contradiction between 'worsening' corruption and China's extraordinarily high rate of growth might be, in part, a function of reductions in low-level corruption and the forging of a collusive relationship between high-ranking cadres and the emerging business community, wherein those with political power have material incentives to facilitate profit-making by their 'business partners.' (Wedeman 2004:920)

Tanner and Green (2007) also note the high degree of public security decentralisation practised, despite its unitary structure, by the Chinese state, which largely stems from fears of a Soviet-style centralised police force of the kind that led to abuses in the 1930s Chinese Soviet.[11] Thus, ordinary police have no jurisdiction over the CCP, which is reluctant to have public security work monopolised by professional state agencies—a situation that undermines the assertion of the rule of law over the rule of man. Public security 'is to be handled by the mass…The mass line principle…is to transform public security work to be the work of the whole people'.[12] Given the authoritarian character of the state and police, the mass-line approach is essentially top down and, as noted earlier, not the kind of co-production of policing that engages communities in priority setting or cedes power away from police (per Innes and Roberts 2008). Other factors—such as the difficulty of monitoring police work and the limited nature of oversight of police by Beijing or provincial heads of the Ministry of Public Security—are equally relevant to corrupt party officials' relative impunity. The high degree of autonomy occurs because in the main the PSB is funded by local governments, who in turn look to the local CCP legal and political committees to govern the PSB and resolve disputes between the courts, police and other law-enforcement/regulatory agencies (Tanner and Green 2007). The local political committees include the head of the PSB, so this structure is unlikely to provide sufficient independence to investigate police misconduct or corruption among officials, and the courts remain second in status to the police (Clarke 2007). So the problem of who guards the guardians (*quis custodiet ipsos custodes*) can be acute at the local county and township levels, but stems from the same structure at the centre (Trevaskes 2010a). Widely publicised corruption cases such as the one that occurred in Chongqing in 2009 involving entrepreneur

---

11   The Chinese Soviet Republic or the Jiangxi Soviet was established in late 1931 by Mao Zedong and General Zhu De but was eventually overrun by the Kuomintang in October 1934, precipitating the famous Long March of the Chinese communists. The Chinese Soviet was officially dissolved in September 1937 as part of the united-front strategy of the communists and nationalists in response to the outbreak of the Sino–Japanese war.

12   Minister of Public Security, Lui Ruixing, 1994, cited in Wong (2001:1).

Li Chian, who through intimidation and bribery gained control over transport in the city, illustrate the growing sophistication of criminal activity and the weakness of local institutional oversight. Li had on his payroll a large number of officials, including the Deputy Chief of the PSB. He was sentenced to 20 years' imprisonment and fined CNY2.5 billion (US$376 million) (Dai 2010). China's internal and foreign intelligence service, the powerful Ministry of State Security, which is responsible to the State Council, is also responsible for revenue protection and the prevention of threats to China, and could therefore play a decisive role in matters involving corruption especially if foreign interests are involved, as in the Rio Tinto bribery case noted below.

Much of what has been written about crime in China has focused on corruption and what might be done to overcome its corrosive and persistent influence. In addition to its political impact in terms of legitimacy and stability, corruption in China has also received sustained attention from economists and business analysts. This is not surprising as 6 per cent of the businesses in our survey reported incidents of bribery in the past year. The risks were higher in mainland cities than in Hong Kong,[13] and in large businesses, particularly those engaged in manufacturing (see Chapter 5). Businesses which had been the victims of corruption revealed that instigators were as often the managers or employees of other companies as state officials. Although corruption involving government agencies is cause for alarm, corruption among corporations and other private business actors is equally damaging (Kaufman et al. 2009).

Much of Chinese business remains within the sphere of state-owned enterprises, and company officers are indeed as likely to be involved in corrupt practices as state officials. Illustrating that point is the case of Australian Rio Tinto executive Stern Hu, arrested in July 2009 along with three Chinese colleagues and sentenced in March 2010 to a total of 10 years' imprisonment for bribery and for stealing business secrets. The case centred on Hu's role in Rio Tinto's negotiations with Chinese steel producers over the price of iron ore—then in high demand. Hu had obtained, by paying lavish bribes to officials in the Chinese steel industry, highly detailed and sensitive information about Rio's customers, including storage levels and sales plans, which gave him insider knowledge about the kinds of prices that might be sought. He was also in receipt of unlawful commissions provided by Chinese steel executives hoping for preferable treatment in obtaining the ore (Sainsbury 2010). A number of China's trading partners are regulated by extra-territorial laws criminalising such corrupt conduct even if it occurs overseas. Another recent example involved

---

13   Throughout this book, for brevity, we use Hong Kong when referring to the Hong Kong Special Administrative Region (SAR) of the People's Republic of China and, to distinguish geographically the PRC from its islands, including Hong Kong, we use the term mainland or mainland China.

the US firm IBM, which was fined for breach of the US Foreign Corrupt Practices Act for providing gifts and entertainment to Chinese officials in order to secure preferential treatment in government contracts (China Economic Review 2011).

The US Foreign Corrupt Practices Act of 1977 and the Australian Commonwealth Criminal Code Amendment (Bribery of Foreign Public Officials) Act 1999 are examples of legislative attempts by a growing number of states that wish to ensure fair access to overseas contracts, untainted by bribery, and have endorsed the Organisation for Economic Cooperation and Development (OECD) 1997 Anti-Bribery Convention (Hill 2000). As of 2010, 38 countries have adopted the Convention on Combating Bribery of Foreign Public Officials in International Business Transactions. Japan and South Korea are, however, the only parties from Asia. The Convention observes in its preamble: 'bribery is a widespread phenomenon in international business transactions, including trade and investment, which raises serious moral and political concerns, undermines good governance and economic development, and distorts international competitive conditions.'[14] Wilder and Ahrens (2001) note that corruption in international business transactions has significant negative effects, including, for businesses that engaged in bribery, the risk of being threatened by extortionists with public disclosure and contract cancellations. They list many harmful consequences such as distorted tendering processes and priorities for government contracts (for example, encouraging 'white elephant' or redundant investment projects); drawing funds away from the public to the private sector with a disproportionate impact on the very poor who are more dependent on government funds; undermining equity, efficiency and integrity in the public service; undercutting aid programs; and adding uncertainty and extra costs for businesses.

As part of a raft of reforms to the Criminal Law of the PRC in 2011, the bribery of foreign officials was also criminalised (Article 164 as amended), in recognition of the growing role of Chinese business abroad and the inherent risks illustrated by cases such as the Rio Tinto example. These reforms (the Eighth Amendment passed at the nineteenth meeting of the Standing Committee of the Eleventh National People's Congress on 25 February 2011) focused on enhanced punishment and redefined laws in respect of food adulteration, bogus medicines and corruption of officials, which had been at the forefront of public scandals that had threatened political stability and the legitimacy of police and judicial organs (College for Criminal Law Science of Beijing Normal University 2011). The extensive revision of Article 294 that redefined organised crime or 'black

---

14 Convention on Combating Bribery of Foreign Public Officials in International Business Transactions: see <www.oecd.org/dataoecd/4/18/38028044.pdf>

societies' more clearly and addressed the role of public officials or 'umbrellas' in the spread of such crime was belated recognition that more needed to be done about the penetration of business by organised crime.

Another source of potential corruption has been the rapid expansion of Chinese stock markets where some government officials have fraudulently disclosed confidential market information. Chinese equity markets have, over eight years (2002–10), reportedly lost US$30 billion, of which only US$4.5 billion has been recovered, despite efforts by the State Council to improve regulatory controls, especially over insider-related trading. Since 2008 (up to late 2010—details not reported), the securities regulator reported 295 insider cases or 45 per cent of all cases pursued. The scale of such losses appears to be modest when compared with the pervasive money laundering and estimated US$120 billion reported by the Bank of China[15] to have been taken out of the country by 16–18 000 corrupt officials between 1994 and 2008 (Lewis 2011). The prominent case of Huang Gangyu of Gome Electronics who was convicted of insider trading and related offences, including links with triads and corruption, is another illustration of the collusive connections between private business and corrupt officials to the disadvantage of competitors and consumers (Dasgupta 2010). Lo (2010) provides an example of market manipulation by the triad Sun Yee On that was able to exploit close contact with government officials and dubious state-owned enterprises (or shell companies). Such crimes may result in the death sentence, which was, for instance, imposed on insider trader Yang Yanming, convicted in 2005 for defrauding US$9.52 million and executed in 2009 (Fay 2009).

Economic Crime in China

As we show in Chapter 2, the paucity of reliable data on crime and the absence of victim surveys have made the study of the impact of crime in China speculative. This has not, however, prevented self-help action by many crime victims, who, thanks to social media and the Internet, can publicise crime incidents online and alert social networks about crime. For example, a 2005 news report from the *China Daily* (2005a, citing a *Shanghai Star* story) told about a 'netizen' who had published a 'thief map' on the Internet that showed more than 10 places 'haunted by thieves' in Shanghai's downtown areas and transport hubs. Drawing from the *Jiefang Daily* and the *Shanghai Morning Post*, the report pointed out that between 21 and 31 December, 2456 thefts had occurred in Shanghai, most of them in locations noted on the map, and that more than 60 thieves were caught in only one day in December 2004. Citing Yu Pinghua, a police officer

15   See Bank of China 2008, 'A study of the methods of transferring assets outside China by Chinese corruptors and monitoring methods for this problem', unavailable at the original URL but a translated source available in Lewis (2011). The authors thank Peter Reuter for bringing this document to our attention.

of the Public Transportation Sub-Bureau of the Shanghai PSB, the report noted that the PSB had caught 762 thieves on public transportation in a 15-day action, recovering more than CNY120 000 (US$14 510) and 272 mobile phones (*China Daily* 2005a).

While the extent of crimes against business in China might not be well understood, such crimes do receive considerable media attention. For example, in July 2007, the *China Daily* reported an increase in waterside theft from Shanghai's ports, which the Shanghai Hongkou District Prosecutors' Office attributed to the widespread use of fake business licences that made possible the theft of cargo. About the same time, 52 people were charged with trading in fake government documents, mostly business and driving licences. The fakes often originated from Hunan and Henan Provinces (Cao and Zheng 2007). Large-scale banking fraud is also commonplace, and the Bank of China, along with other domestic banks, has often been required, after a series of high-profile scandals, to review procedures and strengthen controls to prevent fraud (as noted above). For example, the Beijing Huayuanda Real Estate Development Company allegedly colluded with staff at the Bank of China's Beijing branch to obtain CNY645 million (US$77.7 million) in fraudulent mortgage loans for its Senhao Apartments, while an official of one of its sub-branches in Heilongjiang Province disappeared with CNY290 million (US$34.9 million) (*China Daily* 2005b). Public Security Bureau sources quoted by *China Business Daily* estimated direct losses through Internet fraud arising from nearly 30 000 cases of Internet crime reported in 2005 by everyday domestic users at more than CNY100 million. Attacks on commercial activities and financial systems were, however, estimated to have cost about CNY1 billion. Most of the 72 836 incidents of malware identified in 2005 targeted commercial web sites or business activities.

The recurring problems of counterfeit medicine and tainted food have also been widely reported. The contaminated milk scandal of 2008 resulted in at least six deaths and thousands of hospitalised children (Associated Press 2010) and led angry parents to demand better government controls and policing. Further cases of contaminated milk (involving the addition of melamine and more recently nitrates) continued to surface in 2010 and 2011 (Stone 2011) despite the conviction and execution of a dairy farmer and a milk salesman over the melamine contamination and other crackdowns on breaches of product safety regulations. Some of these cases have led to mass protests and a decline in confidence in key government agencies, and naturally in the case of contaminated milk to a substantial loss of business for the Chinese dairy industry. Although there are many examples of counterfeit medicines, one from 2005 will suffice. It involved three counterfeited medicines of well-known household brands: the cold medicine Contac NT, the painkiller Fenbid and the antibiotic Cefalexin, on sale in suburban pharmacies in Beijing (*China Daily* 2005c). All three products were taken off the shelves when the Beijing Municipal Drug Administration found out that the medicines looked like the authentic ones but did not contain the active ingredients. Trademark violations are common in China. In 2004, the administrative authorities for industry and commerce registered 40 171 trademark[16] infringement and counterfeiting cases, of which 5401 were related to foreign trademarks. Only 96 of these cases were transferred to the police and courts.[17]

An element in the pervasive nature of white-collar crime and a relevant aspect of crimes against business has been the widespread use of fake credentials. It is also a serious problem in academia where plagiarism and data fraud are of significant concern—prompting *The Lancet* (2010), a leading medical journal, to call for improvements in China's scientific integrity, especially given Premier Hu Jintao's goal of making China a research superpower. The sheer boldness of some cases is staggering. Zhang Wuben, an untrained traditional Chinese medicine practitioner, amassed wealth by faking credentials from Beijing Medical University to sell treatments based on mung beans, and the former head of Microsoft China, Tang Jun, boosted his status with a fake doctorate from the California Institute of Technology (Jacobs 2010).

Measuring Crimes Against Business

The general aims and objectives of the research reported in this book are to enhance our understanding of the extent and nature of crimes against business and their impact on business costs and confidence in China. The China United Nations Crime against Business Survey (UNICBS) is the first large-scale survey of crimes against business undertaken in Chinese cities. The results of the survey show that it is possible to obtain useful data about crime risks, prevention practices and the degree of corruption/crime tolerance of business enterprises. Given the relatively limited crime data from official and other sources, the survey allows for the monitoring of crime risks, including corruption, in a country well advanced in its rapid transition from a command to a market-based economy. It also makes possible valid comparisons of the prevalence of crimes against business in Chinese cities with other cities similarly surveyed in both emerging economies and developed countries. Because the UNICBS (hereinafter the ICBS) uses a protocol that is similar to the United Nations International Crime Victims

16   In 1983, China's annual trademark applications were less than 20 000, among which only 1687 were foreign applications. By 2004, the number of applications had reached 588 000, some 60 000 of which were foreign trademarks. By the end of June 2005, China's accumulated number of registered trademarks had reached 2.37 million, among which 422 000 were foreign trademarks (see China Internet Information Centre News 2005).
17   See ibid.

Survey (UNICVS), comparisons between business and individual victimisation within and between jurisdictions are also feasible. This book, therefore, also contributes to comparative studies of crime and its causes.

The ICBS extends studies of criminal victimisation against individuals and households by including business activity or corporate victims. The ICBS focuses on crimes *against* business—that is, when a commercial entity is the victim of crime. Crime against business might be perpetrated by individuals (for example, employees, customers), other businesses (for example, competitors, suppliers), officials (for example, in the case of bribery) or criminal groups (for example, extortion). The ICBS, therefore, excludes crimes committed *by* businesses or corporations against customers (for example, faulty products), employees (for example, work safety violations), the environment (for example, pollution), the public at large (for example, accidents caused by negligence such as the Bhopal disaster in 1984) and other businesses (for example, price collusion). In the ICBS, businesses are the unit of victimisation analysis, not the individuals who operate and work in these businesses, although it is clear that crimes against business can have severe effects on individuals when, for example, losses to fraud or other crimes force a business to close or to lay-off workers, or when staff members are injured or killed.

Household and personal crime victim surveys have been carried out regularly in Hong Kong since the late 1970s, but have rarely been used in the mainland. In Hong Kong, the Government Census and Statistics Department has so far conducted seven sweeps of the Crime Victimisation Survey (CVS), in 1979, 1982, 1987, 1990, 1995, 1999 and 2006. For the first time, in 2006, the University of Hong Kong conducted the UNICVS (Broadhurst et al. 2010). While the CVS and UNICVS have measured only crime against individuals, Hong Kong businesses have since 2001 participated in the PriceWaterhouseCoopers' biennial Global Economic Crime Survey, which estimates the extent of global economic crime against business. In contrast, the first rigorous study of crime victimisation in modern mainland China took place in 1994 with the Beijing survey, conducted as part of the UNICVS (Zhu et al. 1995).[18] Ten years later, in 2004, the Tianjin survey built upon and extended the earlier ICVS (Zhuo et al. 2008). In 2005, the Taiwan National Police Agency undertook the Taiwan Areas Criminal Victimisation Survey, which also focused on personal and household crime (Shieu et al. 2005).[19] No substantive attempt to measure the prevalence of crimes against mainland businesses had been made prior to the UNICBS reported in this book. The survey protocol assumes that businesses will be the targets of both

---

18 A repeat survey was conducted in Beijing in 1996; unfortunately, the data and findings of that survey have never been released.

19 A unique feature of the Taiwan survey was that, in addition to the randomised survey, it also interviewed 2025 victims of crime who had reported a burglary, robbery, vehicle theft or fraud to the police in 2004. An earlier study of a smaller sample of Taipei respondents was reported by Mon (2003).

common crime[20] and crimes that manipulate business practices, and accounting and payment procedures. Thus, business crime surveys include so-called 'white-collar' crimes such as fraud—often neglected or poorly captured by household surveys—and also help plan the cost and distribution of government and private-sector crime-prevention initiatives (Doerner and Lab 1998; Eigen 2002; Kaufman et al. 2000; van Dijk 1999).

A basic requirement of a prevention-oriented approach to crimes against business is the availability of extensive and reliable data and, as noted, this is generally not the case for China or indeed for many countries in the developed and developing world. The value of crime victim surveys lies in measuring the 'hidden' or 'dark' figure of unreported crime.[21] Van Dijk, a leading researcher on crime victimisation, argues that crime victim surveys constitute 'a better indicator of the level of crime than the numbers of crimes reported to, and recorded by, the police' (2000:97). The reporting behaviour of victims directly affects the size of the hidden crime figure and, in turn, the official crime rate. Thus, victim surveys can contribute to policy assessment by overcoming the limitations of official crime statistics (Carach and Makkai 2002; van Kesteren et al. 2000). Official police data are usually inadequate in identifying incidents involving repeated victimisation; yet, we know that 'some people and places are targeted more frequently than others, such that a small proportion of victims experience a large proportion of all crimes' (Taylor and Mayhew 2002:4). The limitations of official data might lead to inefficient expenditure on crime control and prevention and misinformation about the risks of crime amongst the general public, adversely affecting criminal justice policies. For example, a 1999 Australian survey showed that police statistics based on recorded crime misled policy about the prevalence of burglary and robbery compared with other types of crime in the business community (Taylor 2002). In the case of business, it might lead entrepreneurs to rely on inaccurate estimates about the risks and cost of crime when they consider investing in a particular country or industry.

The UNICVS has highlighted that residential locality and town size, self-exposure to criminal opportunities, target attractiveness and the strength of guardianship are significant factors in the risk of individual victimisation (van Kesteren et al. 2000) and it is likely that they also play a role in crimes against business. The ICVS also showed that more than 40 per cent of crime victims were victimised more than once in the course of a year and one-third were victims of multiple incidents (Wittebrood and Nieuwbeerta 2000). British experience

---

20 Street or common crime refers to offences such as burglary, car theft, threats, common assault, robbery, sexual assault, criminal damage and other personal theft that directly affect individuals and households.

21 For example, the 2009 US National Crime Victimization Survey estimated that only 49 per cent of the 4.3 million violent crimes were reported to the police (Truman and Rand 2010) and the Hong Kong UNICVS showed that nearly 70 per cent of personal and household victims did not report their victimisation to the police (Broadhurst et al. 2010).

indicates that businesses have higher risks of crime victimisation than both individuals and households, and businesses located in city/town centres tend to be more at risk than those in smaller towns (Hopkins 2002). Chapter 6 explores these risk factors and attempts to identify businesses at greater risk of criminal victimisation, including those vulnerable to corruption.

The 1999 sweep of the UNICBS in Central Eastern Europe challenged conventional views about the reasons businesses do not report their victimisation to the police. Few victims cited negative publicity or company policies as reasons; however, the rates of refusal to answer a question and 'don't know' responses were elevated for some offences—notably, employee fraud (Alvazzi del Frate 2004). Even in developed countries businesses are often unwilling to report crime, in part because of perceived high transaction costs, especially if the losses are not deemed large enough to warrant the involvement of police and there is a risk of reputation damage. A 2002 KPMG survey of 351 large Australian businesses found that 55 per cent had experienced a fraud (average loss AU$1.4 million), but only 64 per cent of the victimised businesses alerted the police or regulatory agencies (KPMG Forensic 2003).[22] Through questions that explore the willingness of business to report crime and their reasons for calling the police or not, we seek to identify factors that inhibit or encourage the reporting of crime to police and test previous findings that businesses might be more prone to certain crimes than households but less willing to report crime than households. Although it is often assumed that reporting crime is both a public duty and an effective response to crime, Chapter 7 discusses how in some contexts or in regard to certain crimes it might be an unwelcome and onerous duty.

Our study in part falls within the field of 'victimology', defined by van Dijk (1997:3) as 'the scientific study of the extent, nature and causes of criminal victimisation, its consequences for the persons involved and the reactions thereto by society, in particular, the police and the criminal justice system as well as voluntary workers and professional helpers'. It also, however, has cross-disciplinary relevance to economics, management, finance and law (Shahid 1991). It provides a tool for improved risk assessment of investment strategies and enables detailed comparisons of crime as a business risk relative to market development. The negative and distorting role of crime, corruption and insecurity on business performance is a priority focus of national, provincial and municipal crime-prevention and enforcement strategies. The ICBS permits the estimation of business risks and identification of vulnerable sectors to assist investment, trade and management decisions; facilitates the policing of

---

22   Smith and Urbas (2002) in another Australian survey of fraud against business found that that 5–10 per cent of online consumer transactions were fraudulent but few incidents of cyber crime were reported to police.

the business community not only by the public police but also by regulators and professional bodies; and helps prevent crime and corruption in one of the fastest-growing economies of the world.

Our research addresses some broader questions, particularly the extent to which the 'rule of law' creates an advantageous context for business. The survey estimates the prevalence and severity of crimes against business in Chinese cities of varying levels of economic and legal development, and differential risks of common street crime. Our underlying assumption is that the prevalence and severity of crimes against business will co-vary with regional levels of legal and economic development. We hypothesise that the presence of strong legal institutions will reduce the likelihood of crime and increase confidence in policing and government. The four cities included in the survey (Hong Kong, Shanghai, Shenzhen and Xi'an) were chosen because to some degree they might be representative of the relative differences in economic and legal development found between Chinese cities. For example, in comparison with Hong Kong, which is a free-trade port long wedded to capitalist market economics, an inland city such as Xi'an has been less open to market reforms and its industrial and commercial sectors remain dominated by state-owned enterprises.[23] Shanghai, on the other hand, has been restored to its traditional role as the commercial centre of China and has overtaken Hong Kong as the major port for Chinese trade. Shanghai might not have yet fully developed its legal institutions or a thoroughly independent system of rule of law usually considered essential for a modern market economy, but it has been the most progressive city in reforming commercial law (Mako 2006). Shenzhen exemplifies the 'open-door' policy advocated so successfully by Deng Xiaoping. In 1979, the 'overnight city'—as Shenzhen is now known—was the first of many 'special economic zones' (SEZs) allowed to experiment with 'market socialism', and it has been a revealing laboratory for the governance of the reform process and other problems caused by rapid change. While official data on the prevalence of crime, especially against business, in Chinese cities are scarce, there is sufficient information to conclude that Hong Kong has a relatively low level of 'street crime' at least compared with Shenzhen (see Chapter 2), and a more developed capitalist economy and legal institutions than other Chinese cities. Hong Kong also ranks much higher on World Bank governance indicators such as rule of law, voice and accountability, political stability and violence, government effectiveness, regulatory quality, and corruption control (Kaufman et al. 2009; see Appendix A). We acknowledge, however, that limited resources also influenced the selection of the four cities (the next chapter provides further background details about the cities included in the survey).

---

23   The absence of a direct question as to whether the business was state or privately owned was a significant omission in respect to mainland cities. The aim was to reduce the survey burden and raise the response rate. Moreover, such a question was not part of the original ICBS protocol.

Our research also sought to: 1) extend the scope of crimes measured by the UN business crime survey by including new or emergent crimes such as cyber crime, credit-card fraud and intellectual property (IP) crimes; 2) estimate the risk of organised crime to legitimate business through bribery, corruption and 'protection/extortion' in anticompetitive business practices and other distortions in market development; 3) assess the effectiveness of countermeasures and the potential of crime-prevention initiatives; and 4) estimate the direct and indirect costs of crime and crime prevention.

We aim to provide a benchmark for subsequent surveys and encourage longitudinal research on changes in business crime risks, which could be undertaken via periodic surveillance of crimes against business in selected Chinese cities. Unlike the UNICVS, the ICBS has not been extensively applied nor have the repeated sweeps—which could make assessments of change possible—been conducted. Further ICBSs are planned in Eastern European countries under the auspices of the UN Office on Drugs and Crime (UNODC) and follow on from large-scale surveys of the prevalence of corruption in the western Balkans.[24] A low-cost reliable instrument can routinely monitor crime against business by type of business activity and scale of enterprise (that is, small, medium and large business operations in various sectors: manufacturing, transport, communications, retailing, service and construction). Such monitoring could prove essential in emerging and transitional economies where police and other official sources of data are incomplete and often unavailable. At present, a number of business consultants (for example, PriceWaterhouseCoopers, KPMG and Kroll) undertake surveys of fraud and other business-related crimes, sometimes drawing on their client base for participants. They often suffer, however, from limitations of scope and many small business operations are not included. These industry-sponsored surveys have included Chinese businesses (see Chapter 2) but, as noted, scope and samples have been relatively small in spite of their global and regional focus.[25] Private industry-sponsored surveys of business crime risks are useful tools (albeit often used as marketing material) that attempt to collect information that is absent from official data sources, but they might lack the crucial independence that is essential for credible influence on policy. While victim surveys are not immune to sampling error and under-reporting (in the UNICVS, for example, assaults between intimates), they have had a substantial impact on policy development, notably in improving services to victims. Surveys of crimes against business have generally suffered from low response rates and reluctance to disclose information about income, profits and losses. We have also encountered these problems, which we discuss in Chapter 9 along with other limitations of the China ICBS.

---

24 Personal communication with Enrico Bisogna, Statistics and Survey Section, UNODC, 19 August 2011.
25 In some cases, the survey methodology is not detailed and response rates, interview methods and the exact number of respondents are not disclosed (for example, see Economist Intelligence Unit 2010).

Structure of the Book

This book has nine chapters that report in detail the findings from the large-scale survey of the prevalence of crimes against business in four Chinese cities. Chapter 1 briefly reviews research that examined the victimisation of business and outlines the development of the ICBS. Chapter 2 provides further background on the overall crime situation in China and the response of crime-control institutions in the context of China's transformation from a socialist to a market socialist economy. This chapter also summarises the general pattern of crime in China since the 1970s. Chapter 3 outlines the methodology of the survey, the structure of the questionnaire and the lessons learnt from the initial pilot survey conducted in Hong Kong in 2003. This chapter concludes with a description of the characteristics of the sample, an assessment of the response rate and the limitations of the survey protocol and its implementation. Prevalence and incidence rates of victimisation by common crimes against business are presented in Chapter 4, where we compare our results with other survey findings on crimes against business and the Hong Kong UNICVS. This is followed by an analysis of the correlates of victimisation by common crimes. We also highlight variation in the rates of victimisation on four criteria—by city, business sector, business size and location—and estimate the cost of these crimes. Chapter 5 examines victimisation by 'non-conventional' crimes such as fraud (by insiders and outsiders), Internet fraud, bribery, extortion, intellectual property (IP) infringements, and computer-related crime. We disaggregate the prevalence of non-conventional crimes along the same criteria selected for common crimes, estimate the cost of fraud, and compare our results with the findings of other business victimisation surveys of non-conventional crimes. In Chapter 6, we present our statistical analysis of the predictors of business victimisation and show how sector and size of business are associated with certain crime risks. In Chapter 7, we analyse businesses' responses to their crime victimisation, their reasons for reporting or not to police, and their level of satisfaction with the ways in which police responded to their complaint. This chapter also examines all respondents' attitudes about the effectiveness of the police in their area, and their engagement in collective crime prevention. Chapter 8 analyses attitudes to crime and corruption, particularly as an obstacle to doing business, but in the context of attitudes to other factors that might also inhibit business growth. We investigate respondents' perceptions of crime trends and compare Hong Kong and mainland cities' attitudes to various obstacles to business. Finally, Chapter 9 outlines our conclusions and recommendations for future research in light of the findings from this first attempt to measure the prevalence of crimes against business in China.

1. Background

Development and Findings of Business Victimisation Surveys

The United Nations International Crime against Business Survey

Since its inception in 1989, the United Nations International Crime Victims Survey (UNICVS) has provided comparative information on the victimisation of individuals, but there is limited comparable information at the international level on crime and corruption affecting business, particularly in terms of direct experiences as opposed to perceptions. A new focus on business crime arose from a growing concern about the impact of crime, especially organised crime and corruption in developing economies, and the rising costs of crime prevention for government and the private sector (Doerner and Lab 1998; Eigen 2002; Kaufman et al. 2000; van Dijk 1999). The first national victimisation survey—conducted among a sample of businesses in the Netherlands in 1990—confirmed that businesses were the victims of a range of crimes, from common crimes to extortion and fraud (van Dijk and Terlouw 1996). Crime increases operating and insurance costs and causes significant damage to business in terms of reduced profit, increases in prices paid by consumers and loss of jobs and income. Persistent and serious crime can also result in the loss of trust in business and confidence in the economy, and at worst lead to financial instability. Exposure to crime affects business investment strategies and can slow economic development. As potentially attractive targets, many businesses have evolved strategies that seek to minimise the risk of crime from external and internal offenders. The relative success of such prevention efforts, however, and the costs involved are less well understood. Prevalence studies such as the ICBS provide contextualised baseline information about the scale and nature of such risk-minimisation strategies. The development of a strong crime-free business community needs reliable knowledge about the nature of crime risks that vary with the situational and socioeconomic environment in which businesses operate.

During the 1992 Rome Conference on the International Crime Survey, the possibility of extending studies of crime victimisation from individuals and households to businesses using an international survey mirroring the ICVS was raised. The first International Commercial Crime Survey (ICCS) was conducted in

1993 in Australia and in 1994 in eight European countries:[1] the Czech Republic, France, Germany, Hungary, Italy, the Netherlands, Switzerland and the United Kingdom. Surveys based on the ICCS questionnaire were also conducted in Finland (1994–95; see Aromaa and Lehti 1994), Estonia (1997) and South Africa (1998; see Naudé et al. 1999). The ICCS explored experiences of crime, perceptions of safety and pollution, security precautions and their cost, and attitudes towards police. Common crime and crime by staff surfaced as the main problems for businesses, but only a small proportion of respondents mentioned incidents of corruption.

Using a comparable methodology, surveys focusing on issues of security (particularly that of foreign investors) were conducted between 1995 and 1999 in St Petersburg, Latvia and Lithuania. There, corruption and extortion emerged as major problems. To explore these problems further, the UN Office on Drugs and Crime (UNODC) and the UN Interregional Criminal Justice Research Institute (UNICRI) revised the questionnaire to include new questions that measured the extent of corruption, extortion and fraud, and assessed whether these were seen as obstacles to doing business.[2] In 2000, the survey was renamed the International Crime against Business Survey (ICBS) and carried out in the capital cities of nine Central Eastern European countries.[3] Alvazzi del Frate (2004) argues that the ICBS instrument offers great potential to study business victimisation. Her study showed that despite some reluctance by businesses to discuss and disclose events that might damage their public image, there was great interest among businesses which participated in the survey. Limited funding constrained the scope of the Central Eastern Europe ICBS—for example, data collection was restricted to capital cities and sample sizes were small. Most of the resources available for the ICBS were spent on fieldwork rather than on analyses and the publication of a comprehensive report, and few researchers and policymakers are aware of the survey and its results (Alvazzi del Frate 2004).

In 2005, following a cooperative agreement between the UN Industrial Development Organisation (UNIDO) and UNODC, work began on developing the ICBS further to produce the standardised International Crime and Corruption Business Survey (CCBS). The questionnaire addresses bribery, corruption, fraud, extortion and several other forms of crime against business and industry. Pilot studies were carried out in Bulgaria and Canada in 2005–06, with small samples of businesses, and the revised CCBS was conducted in Cape Verde (2006; see Alvazzi del Frate 2007) and Nigeria (2007; see Nigerian NBS 2009, 2010).

---

1   For details on the development and methodology of the ICCS, see van Dijk and Terlouw (1996), and Walker (1995a, 1995b) for Australia.

2   Questions on perceptions of institutional obstacles to doing business, including crime, and corruption and bribery practices, were taken from the World Bank's Private Sector Survey (Alvazzi del Frate 2004).

3   These were: Albania (Tirana), Belarus (Minsk), Bulgaria (Sofia), Croatia (Zagreb), Hungary (Budapest), Lithuania (Vilnius), Romania (Bucharest), Russia (Moscow) and Ukraine (Kiev).

Other Business Crime Victimisation Surveys

At the same time as the ICBS was being developed, a number of other surveys and studies focusing on the victimisation of businesses took place (see AIC 2004 for a review). The majority was conducted in the developed world by academic institutions, criminal justice organisations and private companies. In the United Kingdom, there were small local surveys on crimes against business (Hopkins 2002). The scope and wording of the questionnaires varied, but the most comprehensive ones, such as the Australian Crimes Against Small Business Survey (Perrone 2000) and the British Commercial Victimisation Survey (Shury et al. 2005), tended to include similar questions to the ICBS. Others focused on a single type of crime—for example, fraud (Ernst and Young 2010), economic crime (Global Economic Crime Survey: PWC 2007a, 2009), or a single economic sector, most often retail (for example, US National Retail Security Survey: Hollinger 2010; British National Survey of Retail Crime: Centre for Retail Research 2000; Global Retail Theft Barometer: Bamfield 2010).[4] All the studies found that criminal victimisation was a significant problem for business, with serious consequences in terms of costs and loss of profitability. They also indicated that generally businesses were victimised at a higher rate than individuals or households. Few of these surveys looked at bribery and corruption; those that did reported a low prevalence, which is perhaps not surprising since most were conducted in Western Europe and other industrialised countries where high standards of governance and the rule of law tend to prevail. It was an assumption of this study that, because of the long-established English common-law system in Hong Kong, a similarly low level of bribery and corruption would also be found in Hong Kong when compared with mainland cities. (See Appendix B for a list of business victimisation surveys identified by our research.)

Findings of Business Crime Victimisation Surveys

Table 1.1 presents the findings from three business victimisation surveys with a similar design to the China UNICBS and a comparable sample size. Two were conducted in developing countries—the Central Eastern Europe ICBS, in 2000 (Alvazzi del Frate 2004), and the Nigeria CCBS, in 2007 (Nigerian NBS 2009, 2010)—and one in Western Europe (in 1994) and Australia (in 1993), which,

---

4   The ICBS and many of these other studies also included a section on workplace violence. Workplace violence is not examined in the China UNICBS. The prevalence of and problems associated with violence at work are fully discussed by Chappell and Di Martino (1999), who reported the results of a 1996 EU survey about violence at work. With a sample of 15 800 respondents, the research showed that 4 per cent of workers had been subjected to physical violence in the previous two years; 2 per cent to sexual harassment; and 8 per cent to intimidation and bullying. The survey showed, for example, that young women engaged in precarious work were at high risk of workplace violence.

for brevity, we call the Western Europe ICBS (van Dijk and Terlouw 1996).[5] The lowest prevalence of victimisation by common crime during the 12-month reference period was recorded in Eastern Europe (27 per cent) and the highest in Western Europe (at least 60 per cent for theft by customers, employees and outsiders).[6] While the overall prevalence of victimisation in the Nigeria CCBS was lower than in the Eastern Europe ICBS (48 per cent and 27 per cent respectively), rates of victimisation by specific crimes were consistently higher than those of both sweeps of the ICBS. This indicates that businesses in Nigeria were particularly prone to multiple victimisations by different types of crime, during the same or different incidents. The three surveys found that larger firms (that is, those with a larger workforce) were more likely to be victimised than smaller ones.

The prevalence of corruption was much lower in Western Europe (3 per cent; this figure included incidents of extortion as well as bribery) than in Central Eastern Europe (19 per cent) and Nigeria (34 per cent).[7] In both Nigeria and Eastern Europe, businesses were often asked to pay bribes to obtain services from officials as a way of 'greasing the wheels'. Nigerian businesses were most likely to pay a bribe when dealing with the police or with customs. About 8–9 per cent of businesses in Eastern Europe and Nigeria reported incidents of extortion or intimidation.

The proportion of criminal incidents that was reported to the police varied greatly depending on the type of crime and the seriousness of the incident. In the three surveys, theft of a vehicle and burglary had high reporting rates, which were linked to insurance requirements. The main reasons invoked by respondents for not reporting to the police were that the incident was too minor or that it was an internal matter. Overall, theft by employees had the lowest reporting rates and businesses were more likely to deal with such incidents through disciplinary rather than judicial measures.

5　Although the Western Europe survey was conducted just more than 10 years prior to the China ICBS, we expect that in countries with a stable political and economic system, crime rates have changed relatively little over this time. The survey was also conducted in the Czech Republic and Hungary, but we do not include these countries.

6　When comparing the results of these surveys, variations in rates of victimisation might also be partly due to the composition of the samples (for example, business sectors and size), the mix of crimes that was included, the way in which questions were asked and the survey methodology. For example, the proportion of retail businesses in the Western Europe ICBS was more than 68 per cent, but only 25 per cent in the Eastern Europe ICBS.

7　The measurement of corruption differed between the ICBS and the CCBS. In the ICBS, respondents were asked whether someone had tried to obtain bribes from the company. In the CCBS, respondents who had contact with public officials/agencies were asked whether the company did pay a bribe.

Table 1.1 Selected Findings from Three Business Crime Victimisation Surveys

	ICBS Western Europe	ICBS Eastern Europe	CCBS Nigeria
Year of victimisation	1993	1999	2006
Mode of survey	Telephone	Telephone/ face-to-face	Face-to-face
Sample size (N)	7558[a]	4322	2203
Victimised at least once per annum by:			
Any common crime (%)	-	27	48
Burglary (%)	29	9	30
Vandalism (%)	10	4	10
Theft of vehicle (%)	6	4	7
Theft from vehicle (%)	13	7	11
Theft by employees (%)	} 60	4	22[b]
Theft by customers (%)		5	-
Theft by outsiders (%)		13	17[b]
Robbery (%)	3	3	12
Assault and threats (%)	9	1	14
Corruption and bribery (%)	} 3	19	9[c]
Extortion/intimidation (%)		9	8
Reported to police[d] (%)	>90 (burglary) to 33 (crimes by employees)	19 (employee theft) to 67 (burglary)	46 (outsider theft) to 85 (robbery)

Sources: International Crime against Business Survey (ICBS), Central Eastern Europe (Alvazzi del Frate 2004); International Crime against Business Survey (ICBS), Western Europe (van Dijk and Terlouw 1996); Crime and Corruption Business Survey (CCBS) (Nigerian NBS 2010).

Notes: [a] This figure includes businesses in the Czech Republic and Hungary; except for Australia (N = 1000), sample size by country was not provided; [b] includes theft as well as fraud; [c] this is the percentage of businesses that did pay a bribe to an official; it does not include requests for bribes that were not paid; [d] for all common crimes except theft of a vehicle.

It is worth mentioning the PriceWaterhouseCoopers (PWC) Global Economic Crime Survey, conducted in 2007 in 40 countries from all regions of the world (PWC 2007a), although it focuses only on economic crime.[8] The economic crimes that were surveyed covered similar acts to the ICBS but were categorised differently. They included

---

8   The PWC survey has been conducted every two years since 2001 and has included an increasing number of countries. The latest survey was carried out in 2009 but we use the results of the 2007 sweep, as it is the closest in time to the China ICBS. The companies surveyed are selected randomly and for each country the sample size is determined according to the country's GDP. The 2007 sample included 47 per cent of respondents from Western Europe, 16 per cent from the Asia-Pacific, 15 per cent from Central and Eastern Europe, 11 per cent from North America, 6 per cent from South and Central America, and 5 per cent from Africa.

- asset misappropriation: the theft of company assets such as monetary assets, cash, supplies and equipment by company directors, others in fiduciary positions and employees
- accounting fraud: the falsification or misrepresentation of the company accounts in such a way that they do not truly reflect the value of the company or its activities
- corruption and extortion: the unlawful use of an official position to gain an advantage and the use of intimidation or blackmail
- money laundering: acts intended to legitimise the proceeds of crime by disguising their origin
- IP infringement: illegal copying, counterfeiting and illegal distribution of fake goods in breach of patent or copyright.

Of the global sample of 5428 companies, 43 per cent of companies reported suffering at least one type of economic crime in the two years prior to the survey. The prevalence of economic crime was lowest in Western Europe (38 per cent) and the Asia-Pacific (39 per cent) and highest in North America and Africa (52 per cent). The most prevalent type of victimisation was asset misappropriation (mentioned by 30 per cent of respondents), followed by IP infringement (15 per cent) and corruption and extortion (13 per cent).

Consistent with other business surveys, the PWC survey found that larger companies were at greater risk of economic victimisation. Globally, 62 per cent of companies with more than 5000 employees reported one or more instances of victimisation, but only 32 per cent of companies with fewer than 200 employees did so. Rates of victimisation also varied by sector of activity. The insurance and the retail sectors reported the highest prevalence of economic crime (57 per cent) and the pharmaceuticals sector the lowest (27 per cent). Economic crime in the financial services sector was slightly above average (46 per cent) while it was close to average in the manufacturing sector (42 per cent).

The total direct monetary loss reported by respondents over two years was in excess of US$4.2 billion. PWC estimated that nearly one-third of that amount was lost through asset misappropriation; 15 per cent was due to IP infringement, 13 per cent to bribery and extortion and 12 per cent to accounting fraud. Adding to these direct losses were 'crime-management costs' such as the cost of litigation, reallocation of management time and potential fines from regulators. Companies also faced less tangible kinds of loss such as damage to the company brand, a drop in share price, decline in morale and impaired relations with other businesses and regulators.

Before we outline the design and methods of the ICBS, we briefly describe the four cities that were surveyed, which provides a background to better understand the ICBS results in each city.

The Four Cities: Hong Kong, Shanghai, Shenzhen and Xi'an

These four Chinese cities were chosen because of their different administrative status and geographic location. Initially, we considered running the survey in Beijing where the UNICVS had been conducted in 1994. We also considered Tianjin where in 2004 a similar omnibus crime victim survey had been conducted by local and overseas researchers (see Chapter 2). Beijing and Tianjin are, however, located close to each other on the east coast of China and we decided not to include them to maximise administrative and geographical variation.[9] Table 1.2 presents selected characteristics of the four cities.

Hong Kong

The Hong Kong Special Administrative Region (HK SAR) of the People's Republic of China (PRC) comprises a peninsula and more than 200 islands located in the South China Sea at the mouth of the Pearl River, covering an area of 1104 sq km.[10] Hong Kong borders the Shenzhen Special Economic Zone of the PRC's Guangdong Province. A British colony since 1842, Hong Kong was handed back to China on 1 July 1997 under the 'one country, two systems' principle agreed in the joint Sino–British declaration of 1984. The 'one country, two systems' allows Hong Kong to continue to follow English common law and maintain its autonomy in all domains except foreign affairs and defence. Article 5 of the Hong Kong Basic Law states: 'The socialist system and policies shall not be practised in the Hong Kong Special Administrative Region, and the previous capitalist system and way of life shall remain unchanged for 50 years.' Hong Kong SAR has a two-tier system of government, headed by the Chief Executive. The Legislative Council comprises 60 members elected every four years, of whom 30 are elected directly by geographic district and 30 are elected by so-called functional constituencies (that is, comprising various sectors such as labour, industry and professional associations), and 18 District Councils (also elected) that manage local affairs. The Legislative Council reviews government policy, approves budgets and endorses the appointment or dismissal of the appellate judges and the Chief Judge. The two official languages of Hong Kong under the Basic Law are English and Chinese, although the language policy is 'biliterate and trilingual', meaning that Cantonese is acknowledged as the de facto official spoken variety of Chinese in Hong Kong, while the use of Mandarin is also accepted.

---

9   Funding constraints also limited the range of cities, but apparent sensitivity at the time to social and other surveys conducted in Beijing was also a factor.
10   This section draws mainly from Census and Statistics Department, Hong Kong (2007b, 2007c).

In 2004, the population was estimated at 6 882 600 people, with few non-permanent residents (0.3 per cent) (Table 1.2). Following the trend in most industrialised countries, here, the rate of population growth has been slowing—from an annual rate of about 3 per cent in the mid-1970s to just more than 1 per cent in 2000–05. Because of a decline in the fertility rate, the proportion of youths under fifteen years is decreasing, while the proportion of the population aged sixty-five and over is growing. The population median age has been rising, from thirty-four years in 1996 to thirty-six years in 2001 and 38.6 years in 2004. People of Chinese descent constitute 95 per cent of the Hong Kong population; Filipinos (1.6 per cent) and Indonesians (1.3 per cent) form the largest ethnic groups and this is mainly due to the large numbers of migrant workers (mostly domestic helpers) from the Philippines and Indonesia.

Hong Kong is one of the world's leading financial centres. It continues to have a capitalist economy based on free trade, low taxation and minimum government intervention. In 2006, it was the twelfth-largest trading entity in the world, with the second-largest stock exchange in Asia in terms of market capitalisation after Tokyo. About half of Hong Kong's total trade value is with mainland China. Four key industries contribute to Hong Kong's economic success and employ nearly half the workforce: trading (wholesale, retail and import/export) is the largest (29 per cent of GDP), followed by financial services (13 per cent), various professional services (11 per cent) and finally tourism (3 per cent). In 2004, Hong Kong's gross domestic product (GDP) was US$192 billion—one of the highest among Asian as well as Western countries (Figure 1.1, top). The GDP was overwhelmingly driven by the tertiary sector, which accounted for 88 per cent of GDP. More than 60 per cent of the population was in the labour force. At 6.8 per cent, the rate of unemployment was slightly higher than in neighbouring countries (Singapore, 3 per cent; Taiwan, 4 per cent; Japan, 4.5 per cent), and closer to rates in the United States and Australia (5 per cent). Although Hong Kong's GDP has more than doubled since 1988, Hong Kong also has the greatest level of income inequality as measured by the Gini coefficient.[11] Hong Kong's Gini coefficient (53.3) is relatively close to Singapore's (48.1), but much higher than Seoul (31.3), Taiwan (33.9) and Tokyo (38.1) (Figure 1.1, bottom).

---

11   The Gini coefficient is a measure of equality that varies from 0 to 100. Zero represents perfect equality (everyone has the same income) and 100, perfect inequality (one person has all the income). Numbers closest to zero indicate countries with smaller income disparities.

Table 1.2 Selected Characteristics of Hong Kong (2004) and Three Mainland Cities (2005)

	Hong Kong	Shanghai	Shenzhen	Xi'an
Total population (million)	6.88	17.78	8.28	8.06
Percentage of non-permanent population	0.3	33	75	9
Percentage of population aged:				
Under 15 years	15	8	11	21
15–64 years	73	80	88	73
65 years and over	12	12	1.3	6
Average annual population growth, 1985–2005 (%)[a]	1.9	2.5	10.6	2.8
Average annual disposable income for household (US$)	-	2293	3394	2171
Average annual income for employees (US$)	16 082	3299	3345	2180
Unemployment rate (%)	6.8	4.4	2.6	4.3
GDP per capita (US$)	24 400	6331	7171	1951
Sector of economy, percentage of GDP:[b]				
Primary (agriculture & mining)	0.1	1.0	0.5	5.0
Secondary (manufacturing)	12.0	48.6	61.5	42.0
Tertiary (services)	87.9	50.4	38.0	53.0

Sources: Census and Statistics Department, Hong Kong (2005); Government of Shenzhen (2006); Government of Xi'an (2006); Shanghai Municipal Statistics Bureau (2006).

Notes: [a] Estimated from United Nations Secretariat (2006); [b] CIA (2005).

Shanghai

Shanghai is located on the coast of eastern China, at the heart of the Yangtze River Delta, but extends beyond urban areas into the surrounding rural hinterland, covering about 7000 sq km. Strategically located as a centre for international trade, but also as a key point of entry into the China market, particularly the eastern regions, Shanghai is the largest city in China, and one of the largest in the world. It is one of four municipalities, along with Beijing, Tianjin and Chongqing, under direct administration of the Central Government, with administrative status equal to that of a Province. As a result, national policies have much influence on the city, but the Mayor of Shanghai also has political support to run the city, and several National Government officials, such as former President Jiang Zemin, have risen in Shanghai.

The Shanghai municipality comprises 17 districts and one county. While the central district including the Old City remains Shanghai's political, economic and cultural centre, urbanisation has shifted focus from the central area to the outskirts, with the creation—on the basis of industries—of new urban towns with planned layouts and favourable conditions for economic development. From a population of about 5.3 million in 1950, Shanghai's resident population reached 17.78 million in 2005—that is, just more than 1 per cent of China's population (of 1.33 billion). One-third of this population comprised non-permanent residents. The proportion of the permanent population aged under fifteen was only 8 per cent—suggesting an ageing population trend. Of the total workforce, 42 per cent was employed in state-owned or collective-owned enterprises, 26 per cent in privately run businesses, 10 per cent in foreign investment companies and the rest in various other forms of business. Shanghai's GDP totalled US$112 billion with a per capita annual disposable income for urban households of US$2293 in 2005 (an increase of 11.8 per cent from 2004). Annual wages for staff and workers averaged US$3299, with an unemployment rate of 4.4 per cent in urban areas (Shanghai Municipal Statistics Bureau 2006). Not everyone, however, has benefited from the city's phenomenal growth. Guang (2002) remarks that the distribution of socioeconomic and infrastructural resources is uneven and shanty areas coexist with the best-quality residences. Large-scale migration from the countryside to the city has resulted in problems of social disorganisation such as traffic congestion, inadequate transport and water supply, homelessness, and lack of training opportunities for unemployed and low-skilled workers. According to the United Nations, Shanghai's Gini coefficient for 2004–05 was 32.[12]

Already a major trading port in the seventeenth and eighteenth centuries, Shanghai grew rapidly following the Treaty of Nanking, in 1842, which settled the First Opium War (1839–42) fought against the British to prevent the importation of opium. The treaty opened Shanghai (and Canton, Ningbo, Xiamen and Fuzhou as well as ceding Hong Kong Island) to international trade and granted foreigners the right to live and trade in Shanghai. The foreign concessions (the 'unequal treaties') and settlements were administered under the laws of the French, English, Americans and later the Japanese in the colonial period before World War II (Jones 1939:34). Foreign banks, factories and trading houses were established, along with international shipping routes to Europe, the United States, Japan, Hong Kong, South-East Asia, India and Australia. From the end of the nineteenth century until the mid-1940s, Shanghai accounted for about half of China's foreign trade and became the main banking, financial, industrial and shipping centre in China (Yan 1984:101). Shanghai during this period also became known for its crime problems and the role of organised crime groups such as the Green Gang in the city's government and illicit markets (Wakeman 1995).

---

12   Other sources, however, suggest that the Gini index for Pudong, Shanghai's new economic zone, is much higher and rose from 37 in 1994 to 45 in 2001 (Chen 2009). The Gini index is typically based on the resident population, which excludes many migrant workers. Therefore, for Shanghai and other mainland cities, these indices could be biased.

Figure 1.1 GDP and Gini Coefficient for Selected Cities

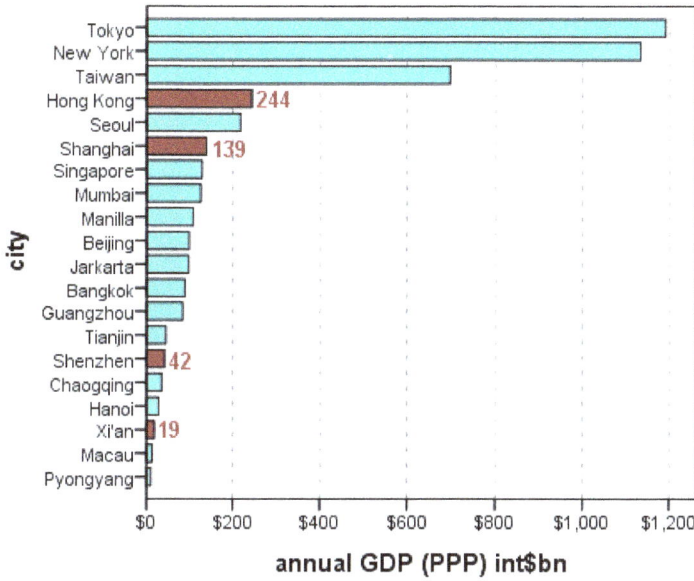

Sources: Hawksworth et al. (2007:24–6); for Taiwan, CIA (2005).

Note: GDP at purchasing power parity (PPP) is based on the international dollar, a hypothetical unit of currency with the same purchasing power as the US dollar within the United States. It is a useful measure to compare various countries' standard of living in space and over time; the GDP for Taipei was not available so we use that of Taiwan.

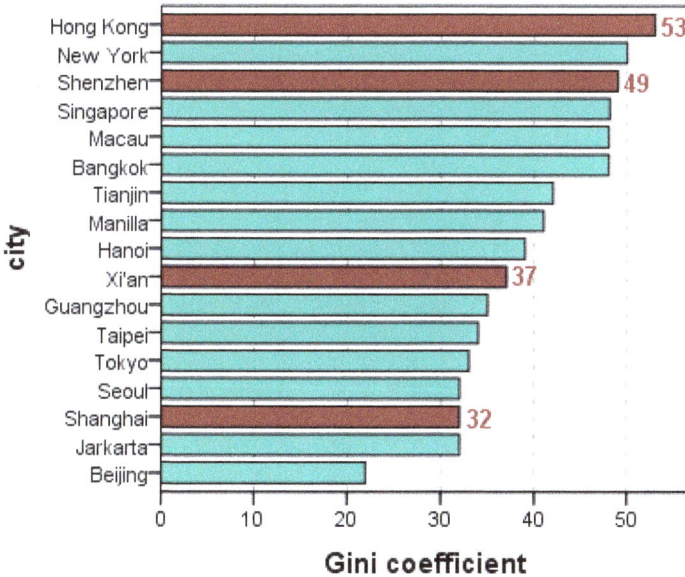

Sources: UN-HABITAT (2008); for Taipei, ADB (2007).

Note: The Gini Coefficient was calculated for various years ranging from 2001 to 2006; for Hong Kong, the year is 2001; for mainland cities, it is 2004–05.

In 1949, the Communist People's Liberation Army took control of Shanghai. Most foreign companies moved their offices and headquarters out of Shanghai and many relocated to Hong Kong. During the next two decades, Shanghai became an industrial centre and one of the main contributors to the Central Government's tax revenue. For this reason, despite high economic growth, Shanghai's infrastructure and capital development was slow until the municipality was permitted to initiate economic reforms in 1991. Starting with the creation of the Pudong New Economic Zone in the early 1990s and an influx of foreign and domestic investments, Shanghai experienced a period of fast economic development, with an annual growth rate between 9 and 15 per cent. Major industrial restructuring led to a decrease in low value-added manufacturing but spectacular growth in the tertiary sector—finance, insurance, trade, retail and wholesale, transportation, communications, real estate and information technology—the total GDP of which exceeds that of both the agricultural and the industrial sectors. In 2005, the tertiary sector contributed 50.4 per cent to Shanghai's total GDP; the secondary sector, 48.6 per cent; and the primary sector, just 1 per cent. Shanghai has, in addition to the tertiary sector, a diverse economy comprising a range of manufacturing industries (electronics, communication, information, automotive, and iron and steel), a sophisticated petroleum and chemical industry, biomedicine, and tourism.

Shanghai is considered China's first commercial and financial centre for both domestic and international trade. The independent Shanghai Stock Exchange, opened in 1990, is the largest in mainland China in terms of the number of listed companies and total market value, and the world's fastest-growing stock exchange. Shanghai hosts branches of most international banks, insurance and securities companies, and 325 of the world's top-500 companies have investments in Shanghai (Guang 2002). With several districts designated as special economic zones (SEZs), the non-state sector has grown to now generate 42 per cent of Shanghai's GDP. Shanghai occupies only 0.1 per cent of the land area of the country, yet supplies more than 12 per cent of the municipal revenue and handles more than one-quarter of total trade passing through China's ports. In 2005, container traffic through Shanghai's port overtook that of Hong Kong, making Shanghai the second-busiest port in the world behind Singapore (American Association of Port Authorities 2005). Hong Kong provided the largest source of overseas investment in Shanghai, mostly in infrastructure, real estate, food catering and retail trade. Supported by rising income levels and a large inflow of tourists, Shanghai is the largest consumer market among all the mainland cities, and is considered a trendsetter for fashion and lifestyle. Major foreign retailers, department stores and franchised chain stores are present in Shanghai's shopping malls, but supermarkets and convenience stores are mostly locally owned.

Shenzhen

Shenzhen is located on the Pearl River Delta at the southern tip of the Chinese mainland, about 100 km south-east of Guangzhou, the capital city of Guangdong Province, and adjoining Hong Kong SAR on its southern border.[13] The city covers roughly 2000 sq km with access to 230 km of coastline. Shenzhen has the status of sub-provincial city—that is, it is governed by Guangdong Province but it administers its economy and law independently. Shenzhen has jurisdiction over six districts and two zones. For most of its history, Shenzhen had been a fishing village with fertile agrarian land and a relatively small population, estimated at 30 000 in 1979. Shenzhen's landscape and status changed radically when it was chosen to be China's first SEZ in May 1980. Under Deng Xiaoping's policies of economic reform and liberalisation known as 'socialism with Chinese characteristics', Shenzhen was opened to foreign investment, restrictions on business development were reduced or lifted, and several free-trade processing zones, where imports and exports were exempt from the usual duties, were established. The city was promoted to prefecture level with the right to draft local laws and set local regulations and was granted special economic management status and flexible governmental measures conducive to business and economic growth. Since then, Shenzhen has been one of the fastest-growing cities in the world and has become a major centre for foreign investment and trade, importing more goods than any other city in China. In 2006, among 120 mainland Chinese cities, Shenzhen was ranked second-best in terms of investment climate for foreign firms by the World Bank, ahead of Shanghai (ranked 17) and Xi'an (ranked 70), and third-best in terms of the Government's effectiveness towards foreign firms, ahead of Shanghai (ranked 26) and Xi'an (ranked 57) (Mako 2006).

Since 1980, Shenzhen has experienced a population explosion, with average annual population growth of more than 10 per cent fully justifying its reputation as the 'overnight city' (Table 1.2). The population increase was particularly high during the 1990s when it reached nearly 20 per cent annually (UN Secretariat 2008). Ninety per cent of the population growth has been fuelled by the large-scale influx of migrant workers from China's interior (Chen 1987). In 2005, Shenzhen's resident population reached 8.28 million; however, less than one-quarter was registered under the *hukou* (household registration system), the majority being 'floating' workers registered elsewhere but mainly from rural areas of China. The household registration system, *inter alia*, entitles those registered in urban areas to low-cost government services and benefits (health, education and housing), but without such registration many migrant workers must pay fees even for access to local services such as a bus pass. Millions of poor rural workers have

---

13   Unless otherwise indicated, information in this section is from Shenzhen Government Online:

been drawn to rapidly developing cities such as Shenzhen. Efforts to reform the *hukou* system and to reduce the negative consequences of no registration have yet to reduce the disadvantages experienced by many migrant workers (Chan and Buckingham 2008).[14] Many of China's social problems, including crime in urban areas, have been attributed to the impact of the large floating population of unregistered peasant workers drawn to low-skilled jobs in the cities (Roberts 2002; Zhong 2009a).

Because of the large migrant population, both Cantonese, the language spoken in Guangdong (and eastern Guanxi Province), and Mandarin are used in Shenzhen. Shenzhen's population is young, with an average age of about thirty years. More than 88 per cent of the population is aged between fifteen and fifty-nine years, including 20 per cent aged twenty–twenty-four years, with only 1.3 per cent aged sixty-five and over. At the end of 2004, Shenzhen's GDP was US$42 billion and the per capita annual disposable income of urban households was US$3394. Shenzhen's employees' annual wages averaged US$3345 and unemployment in urban areas was 2.6 per cent—lower than in the other cities.

Shenzhen's economy is oriented mostly towards exports. In 2005, its import and export volume represented one-seventh of the country's total import/export volume and ranked first in the Mainland. The major share of exports from Shenzhen goes to Hong Kong (44 per cent, with most of it re-exported), then to the United States (22 per cent) and Europe (11 per cent), with a growing market developing with India and Russia. Shenzhen has three free-trade zones reserved for foreign businesses, where no taxes or duties are levied on imported and exported goods. These special zones are attractive to foreign investors, who can cheaply produce goods that are exported back to the West. More than 150 000 companies have premises in Shenzhen: 60 per cent are privately owned, 26 per cent are state or collective owned and 14 per cent are funded using foreign investments. Thirty per cent of workers are employed in the private economy sector, which contributes to half of Shenzhen's total revenues. The majority (70 per cent) of foreign investment in Shenzhen comes from Hong Kong; the rest comes from a variety of countries including investments by more than 100 of the largest multinationals.

Hong Kong firms have long outsourced manufacturing and other business activities to Shenzhen where labour and other costs are much lower. In more recent times, labour and service costs have risen and many manufacturing enterprises have relocated to cheaper locations in the interior. It is commonplace for Hong Kong business to operate in both Shenzhen and Hong Kong, and

---

14 Chan and Buckingham (2008:583) note: 'the hukou system is a cornerstone of China's infamous rural–urban "apartheid", creating a system of "cities with invisible walls". It is a major source of injustice and inequality, perhaps the most crucial foundation of China's social and spatial stratification, and arguably contributes to the country's most prevalent human rights violations.'

increasingly for companies from Shenzhen and other mainland cities to operate or establish branches in Hong Kong. These dual operations are reflected in the format of the questions asked in the survey.

Shenzhen's economy is driven by the secondary sector (manufacturing, 61.5 per cent of GDP) supported by the tertiary sector (38 per cent of GDP). Industrial development is based on low-input/low-consumption and high-input/high-efficiency industries. High-tech production is prominent in Shenzhen and accounts for half of the city's gross industrial output value. Key industries include information technology and computers, software, communication equipment, light machinery, microelectronics, video and audio products, electro-mechanical goods, chemicals and plastics, and modern energy-producing technology. The development and production of pharmaceuticals, medical equipment, biotechnology and new materials are increasing. Shenzhen is also a manufacturing and trade centre for textiles and clothing, as well as jewellery, clocks and watches. In 1990, the Shenzhen Stock Exchange opened and helped Shenzhen develop as a centre for finance, commerce and trade. Real estate, the legal and accounting sectors, insurance and tourism are key tertiary industries that contribute to Shenzhen's economy, and 38 foreign banks have branches in Shenzhen.

As the fastest-growing city in China for the past 30 years, Shenzhen is characterised by rapid industrialisation, urbanisation, migration and population growth, with its associated problems. Qi and Liu (2008) remark that land scarcity might restrict Shenzhen's future sustainable development and that urban sprawl has led to increases in petrol consumption and vehicle-related pollution. The economic liberalisation of the early 1980s has changed the status of land from collectively owned public property to an economic asset and a source of profits (Hang 2008). In a fast-developing city such as Shenzhen, the high demand for land and housing has led to skyrocketing land prices and, because of the extraordinary number of migrant workers, there has been a great need for rental housing that could not be filled by government housing. In contrast with many Western and newly developing countries, however, in Shenzhen, slums and shanty towns have not spread and the housing needs of low-paid migrant workers have been provided by urban 'villages'. Originally, urban villages were rural settlements that have been incorporated into the built-up areas by the growing city. Cheap housing has been developed by farmers on their land and rented out. In this way, urban villages provide an income to the traditional village population who manages these villages, and supplies affordable accommodation, near the city centre and industrial areas, to migrant workers. Shenzhen urban villages share some characteristics of shanty towns, such as overcrowding, lack of infrastructure, and social and environmental problems, but basic services such as water, electricity and sewerage systems are provided and the housing is of relatively better quality than that of slums (Wang et al. 2009a, 2009b).

According to the Shenzhen Government's description of life in Shenzhen, 'the population structure polarises into two opposing extremes: intellectuals with a high level of education, and migrant workers with poor education'. The Shenzhen Government makes it relatively easy for people to obtain *hukou* (residence permits) if they are highly educated, but this does not apply to the low-end migrant factory workers. While average wages tend to be higher in Shenzhen than in the rest of mainland China, inequality is also high. With a Gini coefficient of 49 in 2004–05, Shenzhen approximates the high level of inequality in the United States (Figure 1.1).

Xi'an

Xi'an is the only surveyed city located in central China, on the Guanzhong Plain, between the Huang He (Yellow River) and the Yangtze River. It is the capital of Shaanxi Province and has the status of a sub-provincial city, with jurisdiction over nine districts and four counties. It is governed by Shaanxi Province but, like Shenzhen, it independently administers its economy and law. As one of the Four Great Ancient Capitals of China, Xi'an has a long and rich history dating back 7000 years. Because of its strategic location on the Silk Road, it has been the capital of some of the most important dynasties in Chinese history. Xi'an is best known as the site of Emperor Qin's mausoleum and its Army of the Terracotta Warriors (247–208 BC). Xi'an's (or Chang'an as it was known at the time) political influence declined in the second century AD, when the empire's capital was moved to Luoyang, Henan Province, but it remained an economic centre at the starting point of the Silk Road. Under the Tang Dynasty (618–907), Xi'an was re-established as the capital and became one of the largest international cities of the time. After the fall of the Tang Dynasty, Xi'an's prestige declined although it still played an important role as a regional capital and a trade centre on the Silk Road. In December 1936, the Xi'an Incident,[15] which led the Nationalists and Communists to cooperate and fight the increased threat posed by the Japanese invasion, was a significant event in Chinese recent history (see Crossland 1987; Tuchman 1971).

The city of Xi'an is located about 1000 km south-west of Beijing. It covers nearly 10 000 sq km and is surrounded by fertile arable lands and several rivers and streams. In 2005, the resident population was 8.06 million, including 9 per cent

---

15   The Xi'an Incident involved the capture of the Nationalist leader, General Chiang Kai-shek, by Marshal Zhang during the civil war and led to the formation, among otherwise bitter political opponents, of a united front just prior to the outbreak of the second Sino–Chinese war (see Garver 1991; Tuchman 1971).

who were non-permanent residents. Nearly three-quarters of the population (73 per cent) was aged between fifteen and sixty-four, and 6 per cent was sixty-five and over. Since the 1980s, Xi'an has experienced an economic revival and has re-emerged as an important cultural, industrial and educational centre for the central region, with facilities for research and development, national security and China's space-exploration program.[16] In 2005, the GDP of Xi'an totalled US$15 billion, with a per capita annual disposable income for urban households of US$2171. Xi'an's employees' annual wages averaged US$2180 and unemployment in urban areas was 4.3 per cent. The city's GDP nearly doubled between 2000 and 2005, and in 2005 Xi'an's GDP accounted for one-quarter of the Province's total GDP. Tertiary industries (service and tourism) contributed 53 per cent to GDP, followed by the secondary sector (industry and construction, 42 per cent), and the primary sector (agriculture and mining, 5 per cent). The land that surrounds Xi'an is fertile with easy access to irrigation and consequently large yields of farm produce are obtained. The area is also rich in mineral resources and is close to the sources of relatively cheap energy of the north of Shaanxi Province (coal, oil, and natural gas), which ensures an adequate supply of energy for industries and residents.

With three state-level development zones (economic and technological development, hi-tech industries, and export processing), Xi'an is the largest industrial centre in China's mid and north-west and receives large amounts of direct foreign investment. The level of import/export activity achieved by the industrial sector makes up more than 60 per cent of the city's total trading value. Equipment manufacturing is a key industry including aviation equipment, railway equipment, motor vehicles and heavy and light machinery. The city is a pioneer in the software industry including a significant export trade in software applications. The hi-tech sector is at the heart of Xi'an's economic development and includes electronics and microelectronics, mechanical and electrical integration, bioengineering, pharmaceuticals, new materials, and energy-saving devices. Several national and multinational telecommunication companies also have factories and research centres in Xi'an.

Xi'an is, in addition to manufacturing, a major scientific and technological research centre in China with about 500 research institutions, laboratories, and engineering and industry research and testing centres. With many higher education institutions, it is also a leading centre for engineering training. Significant scientific achievements such as the first Chinese engine for carrier rockets and the first satellite-borne computer were designed and developed in Xi'an. The city is home to several state-owned military industries and is a leader in the development of science and technology for national defence, as well as a major centre for missile production. With its rich cultural history, Xi'an is one

---

16   Information in this section was drawn from *Xi'an Statistical Yearbook 2006* (Government of Xi'an 2006).

of the nation's key tourist destinations, and tourism (primarily internal) forms the basis of the service industry, along with service outsourcing from overseas. A financial and commercial sector is now also emerging as an important element of Xi'an's growth.

Xi'an presents many advantages that encourage companies and professionals to relocate there. Because the city is a leader in aeronautics, aerospace software and other high-value industries, the proportion of technical personnel in Xi'an is the highest in China, providing substantial numbers of skilled technicians and workers. In addition, labour and human resources costs are much lower than on the eastern coast and this has benefited the city in more recent times as such costs (and associated inflation) have led to increasing labour costs in established coastal cities. For example, in 2005, 19 of the world's top-500 companies, such as Mitsubishi, Coca-Cola, Boeing and Toshiba, had established branches in Xi'an. State and public ownership of businesses is still dominant, but foreign capital enterprises and private companies are also rapidly developing a presence. The Gini coefficient of Xi'an is 37—that is, the second-lowest after Shanghai, suggesting lower inequality in Xi'an than in Shenzhen or Hong Kong.

2. Crime and its Control in China

Both Hong Kong and the mainland have experienced profound social, political and economic changes in the past 30 years, which have influenced crime rates and the responses to crime. Research on crime and victimisation is well developed in Western industrialised countries, but less so in developing countries and new economies. In Hong Kong, official crime and justice statistics as well as data from victimisation surveys are readily available. Information from the mainland is becoming more accessible, particularly in the English language; however, crime statistics are limited, by and large, to aggregate national data. Although the extent and nature of crime in communist China are still subject to speculation, there is a tendency towards a more open discussion of crime problems, and a growing body of empirical (albeit small-scale) and criminological studies is appearing in the relevant scholarly and police journals. Generally, experts agree that crime rates were traditionally very low, but rose dramatically in the 1980s (Bakken 2005; Messner et al. 2007a). In this chapter, we review data and trends for crimes against both persons and businesses to contextualise the results of the ICBS. We argue that the general climate for criminal activity will be relevant to the risks of crimes against business. We also provide an overview of policing and crime-control mechanisms, first looking at Hong Kong and then at the mainland, including what is known about crime problems in Shanghai, Shenzhen and Xi'an. We compare crime and victimisation rates in Hong Kong and the mainland with a number of selected countries in Asia and the rest of the world, drawing from both official data and victimisation surveys. Finally, we discuss how well these data fit with theories of modernisation and crime.

Crime and Policing in Hong Kong

Crime Trends and Common Crime

Despite its economic success and 'safe city' status, Hong Kong has experienced several crime waves and major crises in the past half-century. Industrialisation after World War II produced social problems—notably, a class of urban poor, aggravated by the continuous influx of migrants. Long-held anti-colonial feelings and social discontent led to riots in 1966 and 1967, to which the Government responded by implementing social reforms regulating working conditions and funding public housing to accommodate the influx of migrants from mainland China. Yet, crime continued to increase and official figures of police-recorded crime feature a rapid rise during the early 1970s, which was maintained from 1974 (1294 per 100 000) until 1995 (1493 per 100 000). From the mid-1990s, crime rates started to decrease. For example, the rate of homicide stood at 0.79 per 100 000 population in 1961, which rose to 2.79 in 1972 and 2.4 in 1990. By 2005, it had fallen to 0.49—a lower level than in 1961. The pattern for other crimes followed that of homicide (see Broadhurst et al. 2007 for details).

The Asian financial crisis of 1998 triggered a recession in the Hong Kong property market and the 2003 SARS (Severe Acute Respiratory Syndrome) epidemic further depressed the already weakened Hong Kong economy. These events intensified social instability and might have been reflected in an increase in the overall crime rate in 1999 and 2003, but the effect was temporary because crime rates returned to the previous lower level in the late 2000s. The drop in crime since the mid-1990s matches a reduction in the population group with the highest risk of offending—that is, those aged fifteen–twenty-nine years (Broadhurst et al. 2008).

Table 2.1 Hong Kong: Police-recorded crime, 1999 and 2004, and Crime Victimisation Survey, 2005 (rate per 100 000)

	Police-recorded crime[a]		Hong Kong CVS[b]
	1999	2004	2005
All crime	1162	1199	5250[c]
All violent crime	238	205	1070
Homicide	0.9	0.7	-
Wounding and serious assault	112	105	290
Robbery	55	33	250
Criminal intimidation	17	17	250
Burglary	139	103	1520
Deception/fraud	52	59	280
All theft	441	551	-
Shop theft	-	135	-
Triad-related crime	44	37	525[d]

Sources: Census and Statistics Department, Hong Kong (2007a); Hong Kong Police Force (2009a).

Notes: [a] Rates are per 100 000 population and are calculated based on population data from the Census and Statistics Department; except for homicide, rates have been rounded to the nearest whole number; [b] except for 'all crime', rates are per 100 000 population *aged twelve and over*; to enable comparisons, we have converted the rates per 1000 reported by the CVS to rates per 100 000; [c] overall rate estimated by adding up total N household crime + N personal crime/total population; rate is underestimated because the CVS sample consists of people aged twelve and over; [d] in the CVS, 10.2 per cent of crime victims believed the incident might have involved triads, but this is not directly comparable with police definitions of triad-related crime.

Table 2.1 presents official crime statistics for 1999 and 2004 (the reference year for the ICBS), and rates of victimisation reported in the Hong Kong Government's own victimisation survey for 2005. Not surprisingly, victimisation rates are much higher than those in official records because not all crimes are reported or come to the attention of the police. In addition, the Hong Kong UNICVS showed that rates of reporting to police tended to be relatively low, particularly for less serious offences (Broadhurst et al. 2010). For example, the official rate of burglary represents less than 10 per cent of the estimates from the UNICVS, but for wounding and serious assault, the official record accounts for 35 per cent of the UNICVS estimate. In both 1999 and 2004, homicide rates were less than 1 per 100 000 population—about the same level as in the early 1960s. At 1199 per 100 000, the 2004 overall rate of crime was similar to that of 1999 (1162).

Crimes against Business, Non-Conventional and Organised Crime

It is difficult to know the extent of crimes against business because official crime statistics typically do not report the characteristics of victims. For example, police record the number of frauds reported to them, but the monetary amount of the fraud and details about perpetrators and victims are rarely available. Since fraud can be perpetrated by businesses against consumers or other businesses, or by suppliers, consumers and other persons against businesses, official statistics are inadequate to study the fraud victimisation of businesses. Studies and surveys that specifically target business (like those reviewed in Section 1.2) are more useful; we found only two studies that had been conducted in Hong Kong and one in the mainland.

In 2009, seven large retail corporations located in Hong Kong took part for the first time in the Worldwide Shrinkage Survey or Global Retail Theft Barometer, which examines the cost to retailers of 'shrinkage'—that is, loss of stock due to theft by customers, employees and suppliers, and loss due to errors.[1] Across the 41 countries surveyed, shrinkage was estimated to represent 1.43 per cent of global retail sales in 2008–09. In Hong Kong over the 12 months of the survey period, shrinkage cost US$294 million to the retail industry and represented 0.9 per cent of total retail sales. One-quarter of the loss was due to pricing and accounting errors; three-quarters to theft and fraud: 52 per cent was attributed to theft by customers and shoplifting, 19 per cent to theft by employees, and 9 per cent to fraud by suppliers. Consistent with Hong Kong's generally low rates of all types of crime, Hong Kong ranked second-lowest among the 41 countries included in the survey, just ahead of Taiwan. India reported the largest shrinkage (3.2 per cent of retail sales); Singapore, China and Japan (1.2 per cent, 1.1 per cent and 1 per cent respectively) ranked lower than Western countries such as the United States (1.6 per cent) and the United Kingdom (1.4 per cent) (Bamfield 2009).

Hong Kong companies have participated in three sweeps of PriceWaterhouseCoopers' (PWC) Global Economic Crime Survey, which every

---

1   The survey has been conducted globally since 2001 by the British Centre for Retail Research. The 2009 sweep surveyed 1069 large retail companies across 41 countries. The data period was one year: 1 July 2008 to 30 June 2009. In 2009 and for the first time, the survey included companies in four Chinese cities: Hong Kong, Beijing, Guangdong and Shanghai.

two years since 2001 has examined the prevalence of and perceptions about economic crime against businesses in 40 countries from all regions of the world.[2] In 2007, PWC contacted the representatives of 100 Hong Kong companies and asked them about their experiences of asset misappropriation, accounting fraud, corruption and bribery (including extortion), money laundering, and intellectual property (IP) infringement (PWC 2007b).[3] As Table 2.2 shows, of the 100 companies surveyed, just more than one-quarter (26 per cent) reported that they had been victims of economic crime in the past two years, which was much lower than the global average of 43 per cent. Yet, this figure was 4 percentage points higher than in the 2005 survey. Nearly half (N = 46) the companies surveyed also conducted business activities in mainland China and those were asked about their experiences of victimisation and perceptions of economic crime in the mainland. For them, the rate of victimisation was slightly higher, at 29 per cent, and the type of victimisation was different. Bribery and corruption were reported more frequently in the mainland (14 per cent—close to the global average) than in Hong Kong (9 per cent), and the prevalence of IP infringement (21 per cent) was much higher than in Hong Kong (7 per cent) and globally (15 per cent).

Asked about the likelihood that, in the next two years, their company would become a victim of economic crime, only 4 per cent of Hong Kong respondents thought this was likely or very likely to occur within Hong Kong, but 11 per cent believed it could happen in mainland China. Respondents from the rest of the world generally perceived that corruption was a major obstacle to doing business in the mainland.

In contrast with the mainland, Hong Kong is perceived as one of the least-corrupt countries in the world, but this was not always the case. During the colonial period and particularly in the 1950s and 1960s, when Hong Kong experienced rapid economic and population growth, corruption was extensive and endemic in all government agencies, including the police force. In 1973, revelations that Chief Police Superintendent, Peter Godber, had accumulated great wealth through receiving bribes and had managed to flee Hong Kong led to a public outcry. In 1974, the Independent Commission Against Corruption (ICAC) was established (Lethbridge 1985). The ICAC is independent of the police and proactively fights corruption through law enforcement, prevention and education, and is often represented as a model anti-corruption agency.

---

2   The companies surveyed are selected randomly and for each country the sample size is determined according to the country's GDP. The 2007 sample included 47 per cent of respondents from Western Europe, 17 per cent from North and South America, 16 per cent from the Asia-Pacific, 15 per cent from Central and Eastern Europe, and 5 per cent from Africa.

3   Although the survey has been conducted every two years and Hong Kong participated in the 2003 and 2005 sweeps, disaggregated (by city) results were not available, so we draw only from the fourth sweep, conducted in 2007 and covering crimes that occurred in the previous two years.

Table 2.2 Economic Crime Victimisation of Hong Kong Businesses and Global Averages, PWC Global Economic Crime Survey, 2005–06 (per cent)

Type of economic crime[a]	All Hong Kong businesses N = 100	Hong Kong businesses with activities in the mainland N = 46[b]	Global average N = 5428[c]
Total economic crime	26	29	43
Asset misappropriation	19	14	30
Accounting fraud	8	10	12
Corruption and bribery	9	14	13
Money laundering	4	2	4
IP infringement	7	21	15

Sources: PWC (2007a, 2007b).

Notes: [a] The Global Economic Crime Survey was conducted in 2007 and refers to victimisation in the previous two years; [b] sub-sample of Hong Kong respondents who had business activities in China and were asked to report victimisation that occurred in their mainland business; [c] total number of business respondents interviewed in 40 countries and victimised anywhere.

The ICAC 2006 *Annual Survey* reported that 2.8 per cent of about 1500 citizens contacted had been the victims of corruption by government or business representatives (ICAC 2006).[4] The survey also indicated low tolerance of corruption, with 66 per cent of respondents saying that it was totally unacceptable. Nearly one-quarter of respondents, however, believed that corruption might increase in the future because of the growing volume of commercial exchange with mainland China, where corruption is more prevalent. Similar concerns were raised following the 1997 hand-over of Hong Kong to China. For example, Chan (2001) questioned whether increasing social and economic integration with the mainland would provide further opportunities for corruption and negatively affect the business culture in Hong Kong. Official data from the ICAC do not support this hypothesis. Immediately following ICAC's inception, the rate of reported corruption cases was at its highest (71 per 100 000 population), but quickly fell to 35 per 100 000 in the early 1980s (Figure 2.1, top graph). It peaked in 2000, following the hand-over and the Asian financial downturn, but dropped back to 55 per 100 000 in 2004 and kept falling, to 48 per 100 000 in 2010. Looking at Figure 2.1, we must keep in mind that the numbers of corruption cases reported to ICAC reflect the public's willingness to report and ICAC's proactive policies as much, if not more, as actual levels of corrupt practices. ICAC is rated highly by the Hong Kong population, with 99 per cent of respondents stating in 2004 that ICAC deserved their support (ICAC 2006).

During ICAC's early years, the bulk of cases related to corruption in government departments (83.5 per cent in 1975). Over time, the relative proportion of

---

4   No respondent to the 2006 UNICVS in Hong Kong reported any incident of corruption by officials (Broadhurst et al. 2010).

cases relating to the government sector decreased, and, in 1988, the balance shifted, with the majority of cases originating in the private sector (Figure 2.1, bottom graph). The proportion of reports relating to public bodies (for example, hospitals) has remained small—from 3.7 per cent in 1975 to 6.5 per cent in 2010. These trends, again, reflect ICAC's policies more than the actual extent of corruption and bribery. The initial focus of ICAC was to control the extensive corruption in the public and government sectors; once this was achieved, ICAC officers turned to corruption in the private sector and uncovered many cases. The rise in the number of cases originating in the private sector does not mean that corruption was not present before, but rather was less subject to control (Lo 1993, 2003).

Figure 2.1 Cases of Corruption Reported to Hong Kong ICAC, 1975–2010: Rate per year (top) and types of case (bottom)

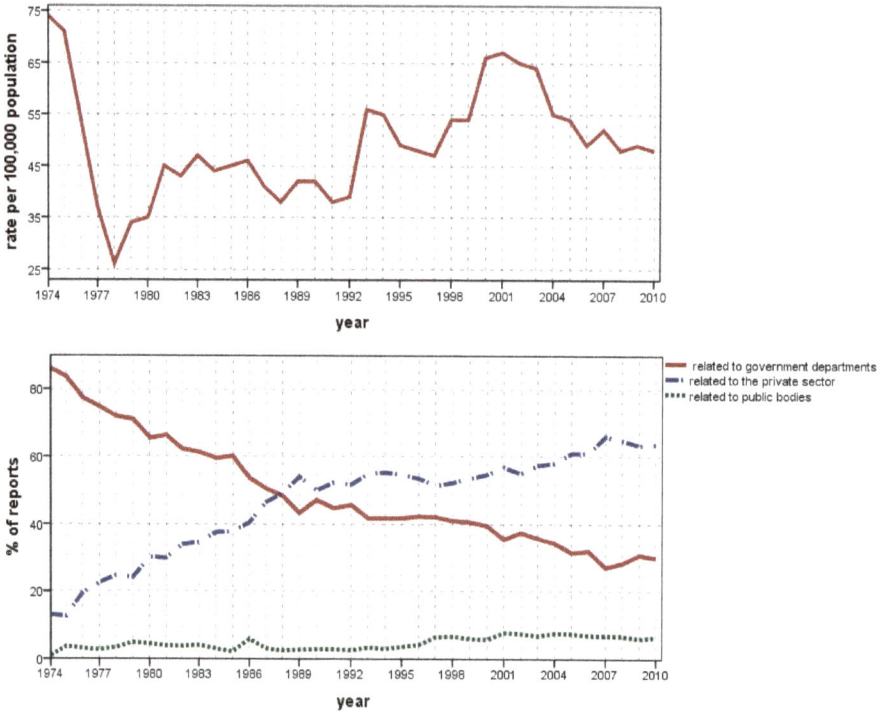

Sources: Hong Kong Independent Commission Against Corruption (<www.icac.org.hk>). Rates (top graph) calculated using population data from <www.databank.worldbank.org>

Another threat to business comes from organised crime, particularly the infamous Hong Kong triads or 'black' societies. Typical triad-related activities include blackmail, extortion, price fixing and protection rackets involving local shops, small businesses, restaurants, construction sites, wholesale and retail markets, and places of public entertainment. Smuggling, counterfeiting, money laundering and credit-card fraud constitute other important sources of illicit profit that harm legitimate businesses. In the early 2000s, triads started to counterfeit CDs and DVDs, as technology made it easier to mass-produce them. In 2003, an officer from the Hong Kong Organised Crime and Triad Bureau successfully infiltrated the Woh Sing Woh triad, whose members were involved in the manufacturing and distribution of pirated video compact discs (VCDs). Gang members were selling the VCDs through about 20 street stalls and were able to earn up to HK$50 000 a day in profit. About 40 people were arrested (*The Standard* 2003). On occasion, triads have teamed up with legitimate businesses to monopolise newly developing markets, such as home decoration companies, waste disposal, non-franchised public transport routes and elements of the film industry (Broadhurst and Lee 2009; Chu 2005).

Despite periodic alarm over their influence, triad involvement in recorded crime has remained static at between 3 and 4 per cent of all recorded crime in Hong Kong over the past 20 years (Broadhurst and Lee 2009). In 2004, official statistics estimated the rate of triad-related offences was 37 per 100 000—down from 44 per 100 000 in 1999. During the pre-ICAC period, the climate of rampant corruption, particularly within the police, provided fertile ground for triad-related activities, but the suppression of corruption and bribery among police and other government agencies, along with police reforms, has somewhat limited the growth of the triads. In the past decade, however, Hong Kong triad members have increased their activities in China, particularly in Guangdong Province and Shenzhen, where elements of the emerging market economy were unprotected by law, creating opportunities for protection and corruption (Broadhurst and Lee 2009).

Policing and Crime Control in Hong Kong

Hong Kong's low crime rate might reflect the relative effectiveness of law enforcement with a comparatively high incarceration rate, large police force and significant public resources allocated to crime control and security. Hong Kong has its own police force, independent of that of the mainland, and has retained its criminal justice system based on English common law since reunification. In 2004, 10.5 per cent of Hong Kong's total budget was allocated to security (<www.budget.gov.hk/2004/>), with the police force totalling 32 254 sworn officers including auxiliaries, or a rate of 469 per 100 000 population (Hong Kong Police Force 2009b). This is larger than other Asian and most Western jurisdictions. In addition, Hong Kong supports a relatively large private policing and security sector.[5] The death penalty was abolished in 1991,[6] but Hong Kong

---

5   In 1999, there were 722 registered security and guarding companies in Hong Kong, employing approximately 160 000 registered personnel (Personal communication, Security and Guarding Services Industry Authority HK SAR). In comparison, according to Nalla and Hoffman (1996), there were about 200 security companies in Singapore, which employed between 15 000 and 20 000 private police—a ratio of about two private police to every public police officer, while Hong Kong's ratio is closer to five.
6   No execution had taken place since 1966.

has a moderately high rate of incarceration per 100 000 persons. According to Hong Kong Correctional Services Department's figures, the average daily prison population in 2004 was 13 138, or a rate of 193 per 100 000 population; however, the rate is inflated by the significant number (up to one-third) of mainland Chinese who are incarcerated for immigration offences that include short mandatory imprisonment.[7]

Hong Kong's use of imprisonment seems to be supported by the population. The 2006 UNICVS asked respondents what sentence they thought a twenty-one-year-old recidivist burglar should receive for stealing a colour television. Nearly 60 per cent of Hong Kong respondents opted for a prison sentence, followed by 28 per cent who favoured community service. The proportion of respondents who chose imprisonment was much higher than the international average of 38 per cent (Broadhurst et al. 2010).[8]

Conscious efforts have been made to increase the legitimacy of the Hong Kong Police, and the successful transition from a once suppressive colonial quasi-military police force into the current professional and modern police service with its client-oriented consensus policing style has contributed to increasing reporting rates and effective crime prevention. Corruption—once endemic—has been successfully controlled and the Hong Kong Police have generally received the support of the citizens. The 2006 UNICVS found that 96 per cent of respondents thought that police in their area had done a 'fairly good job' or a 'very good job' at controlling crime and 94 per cent either fully agreed or tended to agree with the statement that police do everything they can to help. Of victims of crime who reported the incident to the police, 67 per cent were satisfied with the police response (Broadhurst et al. 2010).

Hong Kong residents are aware that their city is safe. In the UNICVS, few respondents (5.6 per cent) indicated that they felt 'a bit' or 'very unsafe' in Hong Kong streets after dark. Of all the cities surveyed, Hong Kong recorded the lowest level of concern about street crime, followed by the Scandinavian countries. Similar results were found for crime against households: nearly three-quarters of respondents (71.8 per cent) felt that it was unlikely that their home would be burgled in the coming year; only 1 per cent thought a burglary was 'very likely', and 27.2 per cent perceived it was 'likely'. People aged fifty-five and over were less concerned about their household being victimised than younger people aged twenty-five to thirty-four years. Compared with the other industrialised cities that participated in the UNICVS, Hong Kong residents were

---

7   This figure includes inmates in prisons, detention centres, rehabilitation centres, training centres and drug-addiction treatment centres (Hong Kong Correctional Services Department: <www.csd.gov.hk/english/ins/ins_stat/files/chartdata2009_htm>).

8   The proportion of respondents who opted for a prison sentence was generally higher in common-law countries (for example, England and Wales, 51 per cent) than in civil-law countries (van Dijk et al. 2007).

far less likely to have alarms or special security doors installed in their house; however, nearly half the respondents said they were taking part in formal and informal systems of neighbourhood watch (Broadhurst et al. 2010:Ch. 7).

State action, however, only partly accounts for the low levels of crime and fear of crime experienced in Hong Kong. Broadhurst et al. (2008) argue that this is the result of a complex mixture of cultural traditions, proactive crime prevention and the increasingly professionalised police service. Family oriented Confucianist values, a large police force that focuses on a client-services approach, strict firearms laws, high levels of formal and informal surveillance, effective control of cross-border crime, an ageing population, ethnic homogeneity, proactive efforts to suppress organised crime and corruption, and severe punishment for the convicted all serve to reduce opportunities for crime.

Crime and Policing in Mainland China

Crime Trends and Common Crime

Until 1986, when, for the first time, China submitted its national crime statistics to Interpol, crime statistics were classified as state secrets (Zhong 2009a). In 1987, the first issue of the *China Law Yearbook* reported national crime statistics. Along with a variety of other indices, official crime statistics are reported yearly by the National Bureau of Statistics of China (<www.stats.gov.cn/english/statisticaldata/yearlydata/>), but are not disaggregated by province or city. Depending on their seriousness and the harm caused, offences are classified as criminal (more serious) or public security (less serious) cases. In this section, we focus only on criminal cases. Unlike federal countries such as the United States and Australia, which administer criminal law at each state's level, mainland China has a national criminal law and criminal procedural law. Local police departments are supposed to follow a standardised procedure to record crimes, and statistics are compiled at the provincial and national levels.

Drawing from official and other sources, Zhong (2009a) cites an overall rate of recorded criminal cases of 59 per 100 000 population in 1951, falling to 44 per 100 000 in 1960 and 30 per 100 000 in 1965, before creeping back up to 56 per 100 000 in 1978. In 1981, which was described as 'the year of the crime wave' (Bakken 2005:64), the overall crime rate reached 89 per 100 000. The next seven years saw a general decline, with rates per 100 000 of 52 in 1985 and 75 in 1988. In 1989, the rate of recorded crimes more than doubled to 182 per 100 000, and with some fluctuations kept going up to reach 363 per 100 000 in 2004, the year preceding the ICBS. The clearance rate for criminal cases in China is surprisingly high compared with Western standards: from 77.5 per cent of recorded crimes solved in 1951, to about 90 per cent in the late 1950s.[9] From then to the year 2000, clearance rates oscillated between 55 and 80 per cent, but fell to 40–45 per cent from 2000 to 2004 (Zhong 2009a:100). While the volume of crime has increased in China in the recent period of rapid modernisation, the increase has not been uniform across all crime types. Liu (2005) used annual time-series data on major crimes in China from 1978 to 1999 to analyse the level of change by type of crime. He found that economically motivated crimes, such as larceny, fraud and robbery, increased at a faster rate than others. Grand larceny—defined as theft to a value of CNY3000 (US$370) and more—increased the most (9042 per cent over 21 years), then robbery (2722 per cent), followed by fraud (692 per cent). In contrast, homicide and rape increased at the slower rates of 253 per cent and 131 per cent respectively.

In 2005, the overall crime rate across mainland China was relatively low at 356 per 100 000 population (see Table 2.5). This figure, however, includes only the most serious cases—that is, those categorised as criminal rather than public security offences. Thefts represented the bulk of all recorded crimes (242 per 100 000), and the official rate of homicide stood at 1.6 per 100 000.

As in the rest of the world, in China, official crime statistics do not provide an accurate picture because only a small proportion of all crimes comes to the attention of the police: victims' reporting behaviour varies over time; crime definitions change;[10] and recording standards might not be consistent (see He and Marshall 1997). In China, seemingly more so than in industrial countries, crime has been chronically under-recorded by police (Yu and Zhang 1999). Bakken (2005) argues that under-recording and fluctuations in rates of police recording of crime in the 1980s and mid-1990s were, in part, due to the differential emphasis over time on 'case-cracking' bonuses: during periods when bonuses were indexed to clearance rates, police officers tended not to record hard-to-solve cases, such as rape cases, so they could show high clearance rates. When less importance was given to clearance rates, crime rates started to increase as police recorded a broader range of cases, but, at the same time, clearance rates declined. In the late 1990s, it became evident that bonuses did not boost police effectiveness, and the practice was reduced or stopped.

Yu and Zhang (1999) discussed the findings of the large-scale National Study of the Crime Problem in Modern China, conducted across mainland China in

9   Zhong (2009a) notes that during the three years 1958–60, crime rates were low and clearance rates extremely high. She suggests that these were the early years of the Great Leap Forward, and generally inflated figures were published on all types of topics.

10   For example, in China, offences are classified as criminal offences or public security offences depending on their seriousness. Until 1992, the monetary threshold that differentiated theft as a public security offence from theft as a criminal offence in urban areas was CNY80, but, in 1992, it was raised to CNY500. In the few years post 1992, overall crime rates fell significantly, but this was because a large proportion of thefts was no longer being recorded as criminal offences but as public security offences (Zhong 2009a).

the late 1980s, which examined police crime-recording patterns. They found that under-recording of crime occurred at the local, provincial and national levels. The authors suggest that between 1985 and 1988, only about one-third of all crime incidents reported to the police were counted in the official crime statistics. Homicide had the highest recording rate (88 per cent) and theft, the lowest. Taking into account the under-recording and other factors related to offence classification, the overall crime rate in China in 1990 was estimated to be 800 per 100 000 population, rather than the official published rate of 200 per 100 000 (Yu and Zhang 1999:256). Yu and Zhang suggest that under-recording was probably not as high in the pre-reform period, but economic reforms and social change in the 1980s have led to an increase in crime and in the police workload, without a comparable increase in material and human resources. Based on the findings of the National Study, the Chinese Government has made changes to police procedures and recording rates have increased, suggesting that official rates in the past decades are becoming more accurate.[11]

Although two completed victimisation surveys have been conducted in Beijing, in 1994, and in Tianjin, in 2004, it is difficult to compare their results with official statistics because different offences are included and victim surveys count all types of victimisation regardless of their seriousness or official classification. The 1994 UNICVS Beijing sample of 2000 people over the age of sixteen was interviewed face-to-face, and 12.6 per cent reported at least one victimisation in the past 12 months of any of the standard UNICVS household and personal crimes; the majority of victims had experienced the theft of a bicycle (10.9 per cent) (Zhu et al. 1995).[12] Ten years later, in Tianjin, one of the largest cities in mainland China, Messner et al. (2007b) found that in the past year (2003) 11.5 per cent of respondents had been victims of personal theft, 2 per cent of robbery and another 2 per cent of assault. This study considered only incidents that occurred in public places.[13]

---

11   Although homicide seems to be the most accurately recorded crime, there are large differences between the officially publicised rate and the 'internal' rate, circulated among officials. Internal figures for homicide for the period 2000–03, obtained by Bakken (Personal communication, 17 November 2010), produce rates per 100 000 of 3 in 2000, 3.7 in 2001, 4.1 in 2002, and 3.8 in 2003. In contrast, official rates of homicide were: 2.2 in 2000 and 2001, 2.1 in 2002, and 1.9 in 2003.

12   A repeat of the Beijing UNICVS was conducted in 1996 by the UNODC and the Institute of Crime Prevention (Ministry of Justice, PRC), but the results were not published.

13   The Tianjin study primarily examined the relationship between lifestyle/routine activities and victimisation, and did not use the standard UNICVS questionnaire, although crimes were similar (personal theft, robbery, and assault and threats) but limited to those that occurred in a public place. The sample consisted of about 2500 respondents aged eighteen years and over, who were asked about victimisation within the past five years (1999–2003) and the past year (2003). The unusual administration of the questionnaire might have influenced the willingness of respondents to report crime victimisation (see Messner et al. 2007b for details).

Crimes against Business, Non-Conventional and Organised Crime

The Global Retail Theft Barometer is the only survey we found that had been conducted in mainland China and focused on crimes against business—in this case, retail. Forty-six large retailers were interviewed in Beijing, Guangdong and Shanghai about their losses due to theft. The survey estimated that losses totalled US$1.089 billion or 1.1 per cent of total retail sales. In China, 18 per cent of shrinkage was due to various pricing and accounting practices, while the remaining 82 per cent was attributed to theft by customers (48 per cent) and employees (24 per cent) and fraud by suppliers (6 per cent). Errors and fraud by suppliers accounted for a smaller proportion of loss in China than in Hong Kong (18 per cent versus 25 per cent and 6 per cent versus 9 per cent respectively); theft by employees was slightly more frequent in China (24 per cent compared with 19 per cent in Hong Kong) (Bamfield 2009).

Another survey, the PWC Global Economic Crime Survey (PWC 2007a), gives us some indication of the risk of victimisation from the perspective of foreign investors. Globally, 21 per cent of companies reported that they had been victims of corruption/bribery by a perpetrator located overseas, and 17 per cent of these perpetrators were from China. The highest risk, however, was for IP infringement—that is, the illegal reproduction of products protected by copyright, trademarks or patents: 41 per cent of companies surveyed suffered from IP infringements; of these, 44 per cent of perpetrators originated in China. Across the 40 countries and 5400 companies that participated in the survey, about 500 respondents had business interests in mainland China. More than one-quarter of them (26 per cent) worried about corruption and bribery, and 23 per cent about IP infringement occurring in China. While their perception of the risk of IP infringement in mainland China was notably higher than for other regions (Europe, 16 per cent, and North America, 19 per cent), they also perceived the risk of corruption and bribery was substantially higher in China compared with Europe (18 per cent) and North America (12 per cent).

China has never been free of corruption, but its frequency and costs are increasing. According to a study by the Chinese Academy of Sciences and Qinghua University (cited in Yu 2008), no cases before 1992 reached CNY100 000 (US$13 000). Post 1992, 73 per cent of cases exceeded this amount, 32 per cent involved more than CNY1 million (US$130 000) and 11 per cent were in excess of CNY10 million (US$1.3 million). Organisational bribery—that is, bribery financed by companies to get market advantages—is also on the rise. Targets of bribery are no longer limited to state officials but include employees and executives of rival companies and specialised government branches. In the mainland, corruption in the public sector is already a major source of domestic discontent. Yu (2008) linked a number of popular protests nationwide to evictions and land acquisitions by corrupt local government officials in collusion with property developers. Since there were few responsive official channels for people's grievances, with petitions least effective, public protests were often the only recourse.

Apart from the police, three government agencies deal with cases of corruption: the Central Commission for Discipline Inspection (the Chinese Communist Party's disciplinary apparatus), the Ministry of Supervision, which oversees the behaviour of government agencies, and the Supreme People's Procuratorate (including the General Bureau of Anti-Corruption), a branch of the judiciary. Neither the judiciary nor any other anti-corruption mechanism is, however, independent of the Communist Party. Corruption statistics are available only on an irregular basis, making the study of trends impossible. Wedeman (2006) and Yu (2008) remark that many reports of corruption are not acted upon and only a relatively small proportion of all reported cases are prosecuted; most are ignored or dealt with administratively. Yet, the Chinese Government has shown concern at the extent of corrupt practices both in the public and in the private sectors, and every three to four years, campaign-style actions are launched to fight corruption. While these might reduce petty corruption, they do little to stamp out grand corruption. Cases that are prosecuted are often harshly punished, sometimes through the death penalty, although public figures tend to receive more lenient sentences (Fan and Cha 2008).

Policing and Crime Control

Social control in China is achieved through a mixture of formal and informal mechanisms. Klein and Gatz (1989:169) remark that 'social control is formally invested in less formal structures…formal agencies make informal groups the locus of social control'. The policing system consists of a network of social-control institutions, which apart from the public security organs per se includes the neighbourhood committees, the work units, the household registration system and, more recently, an emerging private security industry. Among other responsibilities, the neighbourhood committees and the work units operate closely with the Public Security Bureau (PSB or People's Police) to manage social order at the grassroots level. The household registration system (*hukou*) is under the jurisdiction of the local police and aims at maintaining social stability by controlling people's movement and place of residence.[14] In China, crime is a morally charged behaviour, which brings shame not only to the perpetrators but also to their family and the social organisations to which they belong.

---

14   The purpose of the *hukou* system goes beyond population control. The *hukou* system forms the basis of the allocation of state services and benefits. There are two types of *hukou*: for rural and urban dwellers. Citizens with agricultural *hukou* are not entitled to state benefits, apart from the right to farm, while those with

Therefore, private, social and state entities are expected to mobilise to control crime, in a process in which 'the formal mixes with the informal and the private blurs with the public' (Zhong 2009a:110). The traditional policing functions of law enforcement, order maintenance and public service are mostly performed by the People's Police under the Ministry of Public Security and the People's Armed Police (PAP), a paramilitary force deployed to ensure domestic safety and public order that is controlled by the Central Military Commission and the State Council. Both have equivalent powers such as the power to arrest and question suspicious persons, and to search and seize property. The difference between the two police forces is difficult to describe. Sun and Wu (2009) suggest that the People's Police tend to handle public security or criminal cases while the PAP focuses on cases that potentially threaten the stability of the state, such as large-scale disorder (and riots), organised crime and terrorism, but this might further evolve with the new *People's Armed Police Act* promulgated in 2009.

Unlike in Hong Kong, in the mainland, low crime rates cannot be directly correlated with the strength of the police force as China has a rather low police–public ratio. In 1997, data provided to the United Nations by Chinese authorities indicated that the rate of police officers per 100 000 population was 96, but it appears this figure relates only to the People's Police. From numbers provided by Zhong and Grabosky (2009), we estimate that in the period 2003–07, and including both People's Police and PAP, the ratio was 181 per 100 000 persons.[15] This figure is comparable with that of Japan, but lower than Western countries and 2.5 times lower than Hong Kong. An important evolution of the policing system in China, however, is the emergence of private security in the 1980s and its spectacular growth since then. Two major factors, relating to China's economic transformation, account for the introduction of the private security industry. First, the police lacked the resources to deal with rapidly climbing rates of crime in the 1980s. Second, foreign investors were reluctant to accept the Chinese police's direct involvement in their company's internal security, and preferred using private security services. Modelled on Hong Kong's guarding and security agencies, the first mainland security services company started operating in 1985 in the Shenzhen SEZ, and within a few years all major cities had permitted their use. By December 2005, it was estimated that there were four million security guards nationwide (Zhong 2009b). Unlike the regulation of such services in the West, private security companies in China are under the

---

non-agricultural *hukou* receive various privileges and benefits. It is difficult to transfer from an agricultural to a non-agricultural *hukou*, which makes it difficult for rural workers to migrate to cities in search of work. For more detail on these institutions of social control in China, see Zhong (2009a).

15   Zhong and Grabosky (2009:439) report that the number of public security police personnel in 2003 was 1.7 million, and the number of People's Armed Police personnel in 2007 was 660 000. Based on a total population of 1.3 billion, these figures result in a rate of 181 per 100 000.

direct control of the police, and it appears they carry out up to one-third of all police work including catching suspects (Dutton 2005; Zhong and Grabosky 2009).

China's incarceration rate—118 per 100 000 population in 2003—is roughly in line with international averages (Walmsey 2005). On the other hand, China, in addition to imprisonment, applies the death penalty on a large scale, although the exact number of executions is unknown. Trevaskes (2010b; see also Johnson and Zimring 2009) estimates that each year more people are executed in China than in the rest of the world combined. In 2005, nearly 70 crimes attracted the death penalty, including economic crime and corruption, but it seems there is little consistency in its application and few checks and balances. The recent introduction of the mandatory review of death sentences by the People's Supreme Court appears to have had a check on the use of the death penalty.[16] It is estimated that about 8000 people are executed each year with probably a greater number during 'strike-hard' campaigns (Fan and Cha 2008; Wang 2007). In China, as in Hong Kong, the population seems to support harsh punishment. The 1994 Beijing ICVS found that 84 per cent of Chinese respondents chose imprisonment as a suitable sentence for the twenty-one-year-old recidivist burglar, which was the highest rate among the 58 nations surveyed (Bakken 2004).

Faced with rising crime rates in the post-reform period, the Chinese Government launched several national 'strike-hard' campaigns, in 1983–86, 1996–97 and 2001–02. Tanner (2005:171) describes this campaign-style policing as 'concentrated, fixed-term, special targeting of particular categories of crime for arrest and severe punishment'. Through mass rallies and public parading of offenders, the Government endeavoured to convince large numbers of citizens to get involved in the campaigns, but Tanner argues that such mass involvement is on the decline. Moreover, these 'strike-hard' campaigns have been criticised because of their excessive punishment, particularly the extensive use of the death penalty, and the lack of any long-term effectiveness or deterrence value. As mobilising the masses to fight crime became increasingly difficult, the police forces needed to reform to keep pace with the rapidly changing social and economic environments. In an effort towards modernisation and professionalisation, the Chinese police became less concerned with political matters and more focused on order maintenance, crime control and law enforcement. Wong (2002) describes the many changes that took place throughout

---

16   Although reforms in respect to the death penalty are in process and the number of offences that attract the death penalty has declined (to about 50), the absence of reliable data makes it difficult to assess the impact of these important changes. It is likely that if the number of death sentences decreases, replaced with a greater use of the suspended death penalty, the rate of incarceration will increase (Personal communication, 27 October 2010, Professor Lu Jianping, Beijing Normal University, and Professor Liang Genlin, Peking University).

the public security organisations from the late 1980s: changes in values, culture and management philosophy; the reorganisation and standardisation of the police forces' structure and practices; the introduction of personal rewards; increased professionalisation through the development of police academies; and perhaps most importantly, the adoption in 1995 of the Law on People's Police of the PRC, which institutionalised and regulated the structure, operations and powers of the People's Police. New proactive rather than reactive policing practices were implemented. For example, starting in Shanghai in 1993 and soon spreading to all cities, conventional beat policing (foot patrols) was introduced as a mechanism to help police react to problems quickly, prevent crime and improve citizen–police relations. Another innovation was the establishment in 1996 of a national telephone emergency hotline to report crime, seek help and register complaints. (For a detailed review of police reforms in China, see Dutton 2005; Wong 2002, 2004, 2011.) Wong (2004) suggests that police reforms have also been prompted by the Chinese police's perceived lack of legitimacy and the deteriorating relationship between the police and the public. For example, in 2003, police had been accused of engaging in illegal behaviour, receiving bribes, abusing their power and brutalising suspects.[17] In the next section, we explore in more depth the attitudes of the Chinese population to crime and a variety of social issues and their perception of the police and other institutions.

Public Attitudes to Crime and Public Security

The extent that crime generates fear and concern and the level of public confidence in police are routine questions in household victimisation surveys and are of interest to businesses, especially those sensitive to changes in discretionary consumer behaviour. Public opinion can be influential in focusing government attention on neglected issues; however, surveys of attitudes to crime in China are scarce. Although perceptions about crime might not always reflect actual risks of crime, they often give an indication of unease over change. Both the pace of social change and the perceived effectiveness of police (among other agencies) in maintaining law and order are most likely to impact on perceptions of crime. Confidence in police, as one of the most visible symbols of the state, will thus act as a litmus test of the legitimacy of governance, and the extent of crime (and corruption) becomes a proxy measure of government performance. In an authoritarian state, this conflation of cause and effect creates ambiguity over what crime signifies, and statistics about crime are highly sensitive facts. Therefore, not surprisingly, we have limited data on the fear of crime in China but we can draw on two earlier studies produced by the Ministry of Public

---

17   Wong (2004), for example, reports the case of Sun Zhigang, who was beaten to death in Guangzhou in 2003, and of Li Siyi, a three-year old girl who died of starvation after the police arrested her mother but did not allow her to organise for the care of her daughter.

Security (MPS) and the UNICVS in the late 1980s and early 1990s respectively and two later studies conducted in 2003 by the Chinese National Bureau of Statistics and a commercial marketer.

The Sense of Public Security survey reported the responses of a national survey by the MPS of 12 652 respondents over the age of eighteen (84.3 per cent response rate to 15 000 distributed questionnaires) undertaken in December 1988 (Chang 1990). This survey asked five basic questions.

1. What is your evaluation of the contemporary situation of public security?

2. What is your personal perception of the current state of social order?

3. Are you afraid to go out alone at night?

4. Are you afraid of a stranger visiting you when you are home alone?

5. Does a woman need a companion in order to go to work safely on a night shift?

The author provided little detail, merely stating: 'on all these five questions, respondents split approximately 50-50' (Chang 1990:125). Almost half (49.1 per cent) the respondents feared going out alone at night—noted by the author as unexpected and much higher than reported by Beijing residents five years later. The 1994 Beijing UNICVS reported that only 19.5 per cent felt unsafe walking alone after dark (Zhu et al. 1995:Table 7, p. 210).

'Crime in violation of the laws' was identified as the biggest problem in the area of social order by 35.4 per cent of the respondents, and 19.3 per cent cited 'confused social order'. In response to a question about 'crime cases that might be a threat to you', most feared property crime, followed by violent crime and 'hooligan' assault. Only 18.9 per cent of the respondents reported they would seek the help of police officers if their personal safety or that of their property were in danger. Chang concluded that the sense of security is lower than it was previously and he noted that among social issues (for example, social mobility, education, social order), which respondents were asked to rank, 44 per cent ranked 'salary and prices' and 28 per cent ranked 'public order' first. Among respondents, 17.7 per cent stated that they or members of their family had been illegally assaulted, and the author concluded that the sense of security thus arose from indirect experiences, concluding that 'too much attention to crime in the media will not be acceptable because it might create a climate of terror' (Chang 1990:127). This argument and its ancillary about the harm of publishing crime statistics have been frequently put to the first author by PSB officers and might partly account for the secrecy around crime and local criminal statistics.[18]

---

18   Although police approaches to attitude and victimisation surveys might be changing.

Gauging the salience of the crime problem compared with other problems is relevant to our understanding of the impact of crime. We ask business about how crime is perceived and the extent that crime and security and corruption are seen as obstacles to business activity compared with other issues such as consultation, tax and regulatory demands on business. As we report in Chapter 8, both these issues are indeed ranked by many businesses as problems and obstacles, but in this respect are business concerns any different from those of the public in general? Two relatively recent surveys are discussed here as a guide to the salience of crime: the Chinese Mainland Marketing Research Company (N = 10 716) face-to-face survey of attitudes to migrants, perceptions of current public security, corruption, government effectiveness/efficiency and community involvement in 32 cities in China in September 2003 (Nielsen and Smyth 2005) and an official annual national survey that began in 2003 on the public sense of security.

The Nielsen and Smyth (2005, 2009)[19] analysis of this survey was concerned to show the relationship between perceptions of public safety and the rapid changes in Chinese urban life, especially the influx of 'unruly' migrants from the countryside. They reported that 37.1 per cent of the sample was satisfied with the current level of public security, 27.8 per cent was not and the remaining substantial proportion (35.1 per cent) indicated neutrality. Their path analysis of these data suggested that the respondents' perceptions of security could be accounted for by routine activity theory. From this perspective, the influx of internal migrants to the cities was the equivalent of an increase in the numbers of motivated offenders while confidence in police and informal (guardians) was in decline. Respondents who felt that officials neglected their duties and were inefficient and corrupt were also more likely to perceive their risks of victimisation as higher. In other words, there was little confidence in formal guardians such as the police, and informal guardianship (community involvement) played a minor role in satisfaction with public security. They observed that urban residents (in particular older and more wealthy respondents) who felt uncomfortable with the floating migrant populations were also more likely to be less satisfied with public security.

The National Public Sense of Security Survey (NBS 2007) aims to gauge the feelings of the masses about public security and their evaluation of local social security and public order, the presence of guard posts and security patrols, intensity of crackdowns ('strike hard') on illegal and criminal activity, and what concerns the masses. The survey has been conducted since 2003, however, at the time of writing, the latest survey reported was for 2007. The survey reports are briefly described and provide no analysis of demographic variations or details

---

19   This survey is based on interviews in urban shopping malls and yielded 8152 useable responses from respondents aged fourteen to eighty-eight (see Nielsen and Smyth 2005).

of definitions of all the questions. The item on the public's sense of overall safety in the 2007 sweep reported continued improvement in perceptions of public safety, with the majority of respondents (93.3 per cent) reporting feeling 'very safe' (20.8 per cent), 'safe' (42.8 per cent) or 'basically safe' (29.7 per cent), while the remainder felt 'less safe' (5.2 per cent) or 'unsafe' (1.5 per cent). As noted above, the Beijing UNICVS reported that in 1994 nearly one in five stated they felt a 'bit' or 'very unsafe' and a small minority (5.6 per cent) of Hong Kong respondents in 2006 reported being 'a bit' or 'very unsafe'. In neither survey was there an option for being 'basically safe', whatever that might imply, and its inclusion frustrates any comparisons.

The National Public Sense of Security Survey has in each sweep asked respondents to nominate the issue of most concern to them. The initial list of nine topics was expanded in 2006 to 13 topics. Thus, prior to 2006, medical care, food hygiene, product safety and 'others' were not among topics to choose from; however, of interest to us is that 'corruption' has been one of the topics from the onset. The topics relating to medical care, food hygiene and product safety were added to the list at a time when such issues were gaining attention in media and government circles. As Table 2.3 shows, corruption has been ranked third (15.9 per cent of the sample), fifth (12.6–14.3 per cent) and sixth (7.6–9.1 per cent) among all the topics, showing a consistent level of salience among Chinese. Until the addition of 'medical care' to the list of topics, 'social issues'—perhaps better captured by the idea of social values—was the most frequently nominated issue of concern. 'Social issues' also captures the notion of social behaviour, manners, adherence to rules and the like and so is a measure of concern over social change. The report provides no further breakdown of the responses (for example, by age, sex or place) and therefore provides only a limited perspective of the salience of one type of crime (that is, corruption). Since multiple responses were not allowed to this question, the relative salience of different issues of concern among respondents is unknown. Table 2.3 shows the persistent concern over corruption and social issues or values among Chinese. Since definitions of these topics are not provided, it is worth noting that perceptions of corruption are likely to be based on the more general idea of official misconduct rather than only the very serious offence of acceptance of bribes, so take into account relatively less serious conduct such as dereliction of duty, drunkenness and bullying by officials (Wedeman 2008).

Table 2.3 The Salience of Social Concerns in China, 2003–07 (percentage ranking each topic first)

Ranking	2003	2004	2005	2006	2007
1	Social issues 20.2	Social issues 19.0	Social issues 18.5	Social issues 15.0	Medical care 15.3
2	Unemployment 17.3	Social security 17.1	Social security 17.5	Medical care 14.9	Social issues 14.3
3	Corruption 15.9	Unemployment 16.8	Education 16.0	Social security 14.9	Social security 13.2
4	Social security 15.6	Education 14.5	Unemployment 15.4	Education 12.8	Education 12.6
5	Education 13.7	Corruption 14.3	Corruption 12.6	Unemployment 10.7	Unemployment 10.3
6	Wages 6.9	Wages 8.4	Wages 7.5	Corruption 9.1	Corruption 7.6
7	Environmental protection 4.3	Environmental protection 4.7	Environmental protection 5.8	Wages 6.0	Wages 7.0
8	Housing 4.00	Housing 3.37	Housing 4.4	Environmental protection 4.1	Environmental protection 4.7
9	Land requisition & relocation 2.1	Land requisition & relocation 2.0	Land requisition & relocation 2.3	Food hygiene 3.4	Housing 4.7
10	Not asked	Not asked	Not asked	Housing 3.3	Food hygiene 4.2
11	Not asked	Not asked	Not asked	Safety of product 2.1	Safety of product 2.1
12	Not asked	Not asked	Not asked	Land requisition & relocation 1.9	Others 2.0
13	Not asked	Not asked	Not asked	Others 1.8	Land requisition & relocation 2.0

Sources: NBS (2003, 2004, 2005c, 2006b, 2007).

Note: Percentages rounded to nearest decimal point.

Turning to the perceptions of the Chinese population about their policing institutions, 83 per cent of respondents in the 1994 Beijing UNICVS thought that the police were doing a good job at controlling crime. But, the majority (57.5 per cent) of the crime victims who had reported the incident to the police were dissatisfied with the police response, mainly because the police failed to recover their property or find and apprehend the offender (Zvekic and Alvazzi del Frate 1995). Survey data collected in 2003 in eight Chinese cities (including Shanghai and Xi'an) indicated that nearly three-quarters of respondents trusted the police (17 per cent said they trusted police a lot and 55 per cent, to a degree).[20] Support was not uniform, as younger Chinese reported lower levels of trust in police than older ones, and respondents who perceived they had some political power and influence were more likely to trust police than those without such perceived power (Wu and Sun 2009).

The *Communiqué on the National Public Sense of Security Survey* shows the results of the 2007 attitude survey of respondents' satisfaction with law-enforcement agencies (NBS 2007). The survey as described by the National Bureau of Statistics is an annual (since 2003) nationwide, multi-stage, stratified, proportional probability sample of 101 029 randomly selected households from which one member over the age of sixteen completes the questionnaire.[21] Even allowing for the awkward translation provided in the official English version, the format of the questions is unconventional, as Table 2.4 illustrates: the majority of respondents reported being 'satisfied' or 'basically satisfied' with the performance of public security agencies. The surveys presented above indicate a high level of support for the police force, but we must keep in mind that citizens might be reluctant to express negative opinions of these institutions and the attitudes expressed are unrelated to actual experiences of crime victimisation.

Table 2.4 Attitudes of the Masses to Public Security Agencies in 2007 (per cent)

Agency	Satisfied	Basically satisfied	Not satisfied
Public Security Bureau	46.5	45.2	8.3
People's Court	48.1	46.8	5.1
People's Prosecutorate	51.6	44.2	4.2
Judicial administrative agencies	49.0	46.3	4.7
Social security governance office	50.6	44.2	5.2

Source: NBS: <www.stats.gov.cn:82/tjsj/qtsj/shtjnj/2007/t20081208_402524098.htm> (in Chinese).

Note: This question appears only in the 2007 survey and no trends are available.

---

20   Results are presented in Wu and Sun (2009). The survey was conducted through face-to-face interviews by the Chinese Academy of Social Science Research Centre in Beijing, Chongqing, Dalian, Guangzhou, Nanjing, Qingdao, Shanghai and Xi'an. The sample was selected randomly, but included only 800 respondents, and we might wonder about the representativeness of such a small sample relative to the size of the Chinese population. In addition, the respondents' city was not recorded; therefore, any examination of potential city effects is impossible.

21   The National Bureau of Statistics, however, does not provide further details on the means of administration, although we understand that it is by way of self-administered questionnaire delivered and retrieved by the bureau or its delegates.

Crime and Policing in Shanghai, Shenzhen and Xi'an

Unfortunately, only the *Shanghai Statistical Yearbook* (Shanghai Municipal Statistics Bureau 2006) provides detailed crime statistics; official data for the two other cities are sparse (Table 2.5). We gathered further information on crime and policing in the three mainland cities from a review of Chinese and English-language media reports (Appendix C). We present a brief chronological discussion of the crime problems and trends in each city.

Table 2.5 Mainland China: Police-recorded crime (including attempts) overall and by city, 2005 (rate per 100 000 population)

	Mainland	Shanghai	Shenzhen	Xi'an
All crime[a]	356	719	949	292
Homicide (completed)	1.6	1.4	4.5[b]	-
Aggravated assault	12	12	-	-
Robbery	26	14	465[c]	-
Fraud	16	56	-	-
All theft[d]	242	542	-	-
Grand larceny[e]	86	-	-	-

Sources: Government of Xi'an (2006); NBS (2006a); Shanghai Municipal Statistics Bureau (2006); Zhong (2009a).

Notes: [a] Except for homicide, rates per 100 000 have been rounded to the closest whole number; [b] rate for 1995, cited in Tan and Xue (1997); [c] rate for 2003, estimated from Chow (2004); [d] includes all thefts of value of more than CNY500 (US$60); [e] grand larceny consists of theft with a value of more than CNY3000 (US$400).

Shanghai

The media suggested a rise in reported crime in the mid-1990s; however, a major problem appeared to be an increasing number of economic crimes, particularly stock exchange fraud. The number of securities-related fraud jumped from two in 1991 to 240 in 1993. Stockbrokers blamed the lack of regulations for the growing rate of economic crime because, although the Shanghai Stock Exchange started operating in 1990, by 1995 there were still no national regulations as well as a lack of personnel to enforce local regulations. Corruption was also a concern, and, in 1994, the police set up task forces to deal with economic crime, particularly in government departments. For homicide, we estimate that, in 1995, the rate was about 0.7 per 100 000 population—that is, about half that of 2005. In 1998, citizens complained that Shanghai was no longer a low-crime city and that robbery, theft and burglary were on the rise. Yet, the police estimated that 30 000 to 40 000 criminal offences were reported in 1997—that is, a crime rate of about 350 per 100 000. The perceived increase in crime was attributed to a growing income gap, unemployment and the influx of migrant workers living in poor conditions. The courts reported that in 1998 the number of criminal trials had decreased compared with 1997, but cases of economic crime had increased by 12 per cent. In 1999, another task force was established to deal with economic crime. In June 1999, the Shanghai Police Municipal Investigative Team Against Economic Crime successfully prosecuted its first case of fraud-related crime. Weng Changzhong was arrested on charges of defrauding CNY290 million from 17 Shanghai banks over a four-year period. By claiming his registered company owned multiple assets, Weng was able to obtain loans, but disappeared each time repayments were due.

In 1996, Shanghai took part in the national strike-hard anti-crime campaign and deployed 20 000 public security and police officers along with civilian security personnel to patrol the streets. In 2000, patrolling was extended to cover night-time and focus on 24-hour convenience stores and financial institutions. In the early 2000s, the media mentioned fluctuations in the rate of crime with an increase in 2003. The police still blamed migrant workers for a large proportion of the crimes committed in Shanghai, but reported that the proportion of crimes committed by migrants had decreased from 80 per cent in 1998 to 45 per cent in 2002. The police chief complained of a lack of police and planned to increase the size of the force from 260 officers per 100 000 population in 2004 to 300 in 2009. Compared with the average for China (181 per 100 000), Shanghai seems to have a rather large police force, which is complemented by a sizeable private security industry. Dutton (2005:215) estimated that in 1998 there were 27 000 private security officers in Shanghai—that is, nearly half the number of police officers.

In 2005 the overall official crime rate in Shanghai was about twice the national rate. The homicide rate was on par with the national average, rates of assault and robbery were relatively lower, but rates of fraud and theft were much higher. This is consistent with the media reports that emphasised the rise in economic crime in the past 15 years. Economic crime might partly account for the doubling in the overall crime rate between 1997 and 2005, although it seems that street crime had also risen.

Shenzhen

The increase in crime started earlier in Shenzhen and has been more dramatic than in Shanghai. Shenzhen's crime trends illustrate the way in which social disorder often accompanies rapid modernisation and economic growth. Economic development in the Shenzhen SEZ attracted millions of rural migrants from all over China, many of whom were unemployed. The city was unable to quickly establish a reliable system of dispute settlement or create the circumstances for effective public order. It is estimated that the rate of serious crime increased by 67 per cent from 1993 to 1994. Tan and Xue (1997) reported a very rapid rise in homicide, from 1.38 per 100 000 in 1990 to 4.49 in 1995. Following complaints by business people and visitors about the absence of police officers in the SEZ, in 1993, Shenzhen Municipality introduced police patrols (Wong 2002:307). As in Shanghai, here, the economic boom led to an increase in fraud and corruption, although some perpetrators were punished harshly. In July 1994, Liu Jianyi was executed by firing squad for defrauding his employer, Shenzhen Eastern Development Company, of more than US$20 000. Liu used his connections to secure contracts for the sale of pharmaceuticals. After he was paid for the products he kept the money, but when deliveries were not made, the fraud was discovered. When asked how he felt about Liu's execution, the director of Shenzhen Eastern Development said, 'Happy! Yes, very happy.'

The security problem was also aggravated by an inflow of triad-related gangs (Wang et al. 2003). By 1992, every district of Shenzhen had fallen to triad activities (mostly from Hong Kong but also Taiwan and Macau) and, in 2000, more than one million 'black society' members were estimated to be active in China (Broadhurst and Lee 2009). Incidents of extortion by triad-related groups became more frequent and continue to occur. For example, in January 2006, two bombs exploded at a supermarket owned by French retail giant Carrefour following cash demands made through an anonymous phone call. One customer was injured. Three other stores reported similar phone calls and were evacuated. Police arrested three people following the explosion.

With crime still rising, the police cooperated with customs in 2001 to crack down on smuggling, and with financial, taxation and industrial administrations in 2002 in an effort to reduce commercial and economic crime. A year later, police launched a 'storm operation' targeting serious crimes such as homicide, robbery and kidnapping. The aim was not only to improve social order, but also to protect the safety of Hong Kong people doing business and shopping in Shenzhen, because about that time as many as 30 Hong Kong people per month were kidnapped by Shenzhen criminals. In 2003, however, the PRC abolished the border permits controlling access to Shenzhen and abandoned the custody and repatriation system long used to expel beggars and indigents. The inadequacy of the local procurator's office, the shortage of police and corruption among them made Shenzhen more vulnerable to crime: overall crime surged, with more than 100 000 offences recorded in 2003 (or a rate of about 1300 per 100 000 population). In a single year murder and assault increased by one-third and kidnapping by 73 per cent. The Shenzhen police and courts were overwhelmed (Broadhurst and Lee 2009). Some business owners started to deal with the crime problem themselves. In October 2003, a middle-aged woman was caught stealing four fish and containers of yoghurt in a supermarket. The head of security forced the woman to stand outside the shop holding a sign reading 'I am shameless. I'm a thief'. Although the store manager had no right to punish shoplifters using public humiliation, most local retailers agreed with the punishment. A small shopkeeper said, 'I don't see anything wrong with the woman wearing the sign. She deserves it.' Retailers agreed that police did not treat shoplifters seriously enough.

High-level corruption and gang-related attacks did little to boost citizens' confidence. In 2003, Shenzhen's former Deputy Mayor was sentenced to 20 years' jail for abusing his authority for personal gain, and accepting bribes from businesspeople. The same year, local gangsters tried to bomb a police car in a war of intimidation. Some police were involved in providing protection to triads who operated vice premises. Crime in Shenzhen became so serious that a senior police official was forced to apologise over the city's crime problem, and called in the Army to assist with foot patrols. Additional officers were employed, bringing the total police force to an estimated 16 000 officers, or a rate of 188 per 100 000 population, in 2005. While this is on par with the national average (181 in 2007), it is lower than Shanghai (260 in 2004), and much lower than Hong Kong (496 in 2004). Crime rates peaked in 2003–04 and thereafter declined in line with a surge in the apprehension and detention of offenders (Zhong 2009a:Ch. 7).

Xi'an

We found little information on crime and policing in Xi'an from official sources or newspapers. In 2005, the overall rate of officially recorded crime was 292 per 100 000, which was lower than the national average as well as crime rates in Shanghai and Shenzhen. The *Xi'an Yearbook* reported that the 2005 rate was down 17 per cent on 2004, and that the clearance rate had increased by 10 per cent. Theft by employees, however, was mentioned as a growing problem in Xi'an, with more than 900 cases discovered between 2003 and 2008. A large proportion of these cases had been targeting state-owned companies. In one case, theft by employees, combined with bribery and corruption, led to the loss of nearly US$1 million. A Xi'an prosecutor indicated that the Xi'an Government was taking the loss of government-owned assets very seriously. For example, in August 2010, the Xi'an Intermediate People's Court convicted Zheng Shaodong, a former assistant to the Minister of Public Security, of abusing his position to benefit others in return for more than US$12 million in bribes between 2001 and 2007. Zheng was sentenced to death, but the sentence was suspended because he confessed his crimes and returned most of the illegally obtained money.

Anecdotal evidence suggests that homicide numbers had increased, which prompted the Xi'an Public Security Bureau to implement a new anti-homicide policy in 2001, in which the Director and Deputy Director of the PSB were directly responsible for dealing with all homicide cases. This strategy aimed for 'two decreases and one increase': a decrease in the number of homicide cases and the number of offenders, and an increase in the clearance rate of homicide cases.

In 2004, the Xi'an Government took some innovative action to control crime. Because of a shortage of police personnel, the Government started outsourcing some public security work to contractors in some villages. Contractors are responsible for preventing fire, robbery and vandalism. They do not have similar powers to police, such as arresting people or investigating crime, but when they discover problems they report to and seek help from police. In mid-2004, 16 villages were using contractors.

In 2005, the Chinese Central Government declared Xi'an 'the best city for public security governance'. In 2006, informal interviews with 20 Xi'an citizens, including teachers and government officers, revealed that 80 per cent of the interviewees believed that Xi'an was a safe place to live; however, they also said that burglary and thefts were the biggest problems.

It is difficult to compare rates of crime in Hong Kong and the mainland because of differences in crime classification, particularly for less serious offences. The rate of homicide, however—one of the most serious crimes—was lowest in Hong Kong and highest in Shenzhen in 2004–05. Hong Kong and Shanghai recorded similar rates of theft and fraud, which were higher than the overall Chinese average. Both cities are important financial and commercial centres, and this might explain their higher rates of fraud and economic crime. The next section compares a range of crime and criminal justice indicators in China, Hong Kong and some Asian and Western countries, using standardised data.

Comparing China and the World

So far we have examined crime and policing in Hong Kong and the mainland, drawing mainly from national figures, but it is also important to consider how the situation in China compares with other industrialised countries and developing economies. Many obstacles, such as different definitions and counting rules, make it difficult to compare national statistics from various countries. In this section, we use data on crime, police strength and levels of incarceration gathered mostly by the United Nations and somewhat standardised to enable international comparability.[22]

---

22   We have tried to use the available data closest in time to the years of the China ICBS. Figures in this section might vary slightly from those already reported because of revision, standardisation and different collection methods; however, these figures are consistent between countries.

Homicide data are often used for comparative purposes because homicide is much less subject to the vagaries of reporting, recording and definitional changes than less serious crimes, which are also less likely to be reported. Figure 2.2 presents rates of police-recorded homicide and robbery, drawing on various sweeps of the UN Surveys of Crime Trends and Operations of Criminal Justice Systems (CTS),[23] for Hong Kong, mainland China and selected countries in Asia, Europe and America.

Looking at homicide, we see that Hong Kong has one of the lowest rates among Asian countries and in the world. At 0.6 per 100 000 population, it is comparable with Japan (0.5) and lower than Singapore (0.9), Australia (1.6), England and Wales (1.6) and mainland China (2.1). The rate of homicide in the mainland is higher than in the industrialised countries included in the comparison except the United States (4.6),[24] but much lower than Eastern European countries (particularly Russia, with a rate of 19.8 per 100 000) and developing countries in Asia (for example, Thailand, 8.5, and the Philippines, 7.6). For robbery, we see an opposite pattern to homicide, with higher rates of robbery in Western countries. These might be the result of higher reporting rates by victims compared with developing countries and the availability of more attractive targets[25] (see, for example, van Dijk et al. 2007). Hong Kong's rate of robbery is about one-third that of England and Wales and the United States, half that of Macau, but about twice that of mainland China. The rate of robbery for the mainland is among the lowest in the chart, but higher than Singapore (11.5 per 100 000) and Japan (4.1 per 100 000).

---

23   The survey is conducted annually by the UN Office on Drugs and Crime via a questionnaire sent to each member state. The questionnaire consists of a series of questions asking for data on the main components of the criminal justice system. Member states provide as much or as little data as is practicable for them, therefore, data are not consistently provided. For less serious crimes, the official rates are more of an image of the effectiveness of police than a record of crime because reporting rates might be low and the police ability to record crimes might be limited, particularly in developing countries.

24   If we consider the 'internal' rate of homicide reported in Footnote 11 (this chapter), we see that the unofficial rate of homicide in China might be comparable with that of the United States.

25   In developing countries, robberies might also be more often lethal—hence counted as homicides—than in developed countries.

Figure 2.2 Homicide and Robbery Recorded by Police: Hong Kong, mainland China and selected countries (rate per 100 000 population)

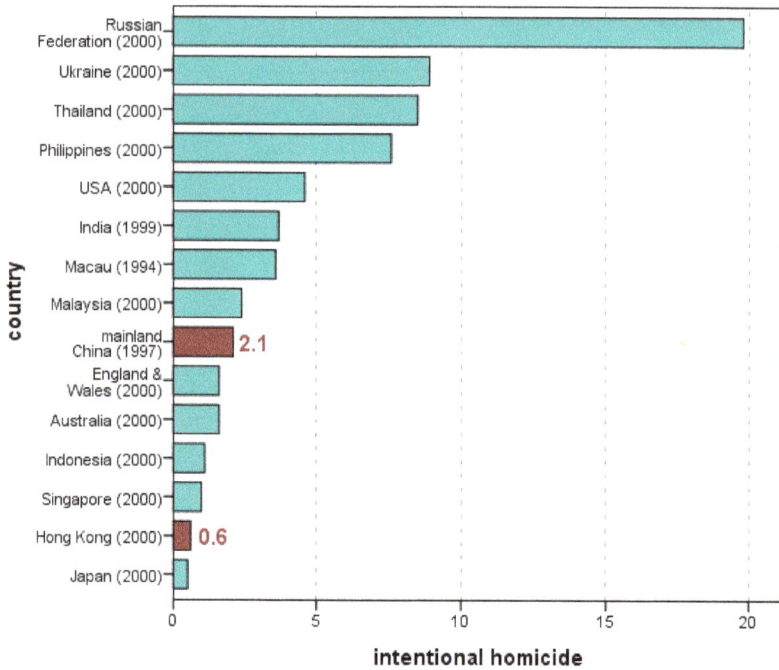

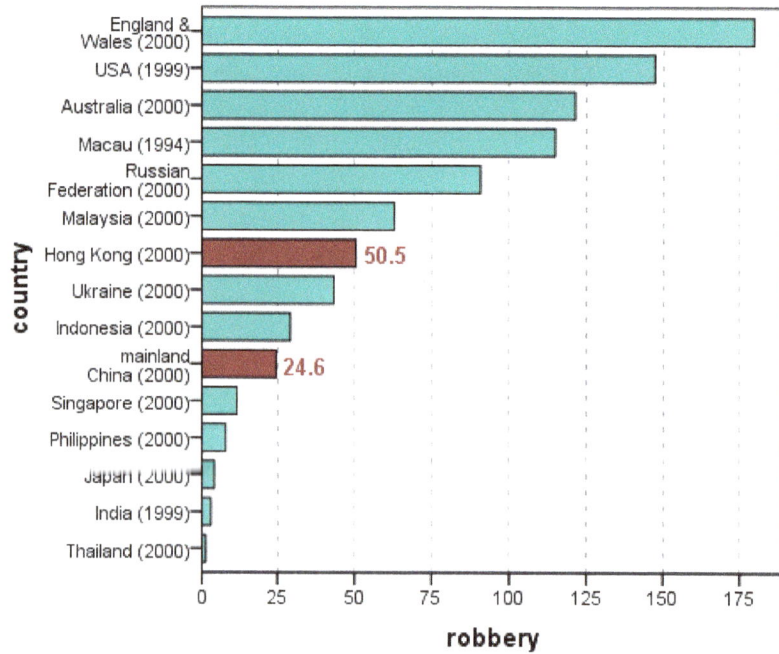

Source: UNODC (2004).

Victimisation surveys are one way to avoid some of the pitfalls attached to official crime data. Unfortunately, as noted earlier, mainland China participated in only one of the sweeps of the UNICVS—in 1994—and it is likely that, in more than 10 years, the level of victimisation has changed. Hong Kong did not take part in the 1992–94 UNICVS, but the Hong Kong Government ran its own Crime Victim Survey (CVS) in 1994 (Census and Statistics Department, Hong Kong 1999), using broadly comparable questions to the UNICVS (see Broadhurst et al. 2010 for a detailed comparison of the UNICVS and Hong Kong CVS).[26] Beijing recorded a higher overall five-year victimisation rate than three other Asian cities (52.2 per cent compared with 43.8 per cent for Jakarta, 43.7 per cent for Mumbai and 40.1 per cent for Manila), but was lower than most European nations (ranging from 52.6 per cent for Albania and Macedonia to 77 per cent for Bulgaria and the Netherlands) (van Dijk 2000). Beijing's higher rate was, however, due only to higher rates of bicycle theft, because for all other crimes, Beijing had a similar or lower likelihood of victimisation than these three Asian cities (Figure 2.3). Beijing and Manila recorded rates of bicycle theft more than five times those of Mumbai and Jakarta (10.9 per cent and 9.5 per cent). Apart from this unusually high figure, Beijing's rates of burglary (1.5 per cent), robbery (0.5 per cent) and assault and threats (1.5 per cent) were in line with or lower than rates in Mumbai (1.3 per cent, 0.6 per cent and 1.6 per cent respectively for each type of crime), Jakarta (3 per cent, 1.4 per cent and 1.6 per cent), and Manila (2.9 per cent, 2.7 per cent and 1.6 per cent). With 2.2 per cent of burglary, Hong Kong rated higher than Beijing and Mumbai, but lower than Manila and Jakarta. Hong Kong's rates were the lowest for robbery (0.4 per cent) and assault (0.2 per cent).

Turning to the strength of the police forces, the seventh CTS shows that in 2000 Hong Kong had one of the largest police forces per capita, with 496 police per 100 000 persons (Figure 2.4). Only a few countries, such as Italy (560), Portugal (485) and Ukraine (470), were comparable with Hong Kong,[27] and most Asian jurisdictions had proportionally smaller police forces. Hong Kong's large police force also exceeded that of most industrialised nations such as the United States (244), Australia (219) and England and Wales (210). In contrast, mainland China had a rather low police–public ratio, as noted above. The 1997 data provided to the United Nations by Chinese authorities indicated a rate of police officers per 100 000 population of 96, but it appears to count only the People's Police. The rate doubles to 181 per 100 000 persons when we consider the estimate from Zhong and Grabosky (2009) that includes both People's Police and People's Armed Police, and is comparable with that of Japan—lower than Western countries and 2.5 times lower than Hong Kong.

---

26   The CVS does not provide an overall rate of victimisation because different units of measurement are used for personal crime (individuals) and household crime (households).

27   Data for the Russian Federation were provided only for 1994, and the rate was a very high 1222 police per 100 000.

Figure 2.3 One-Year Victimisation Rates by Selected Crimes in Five Asian Cities, 1994 (per cent)

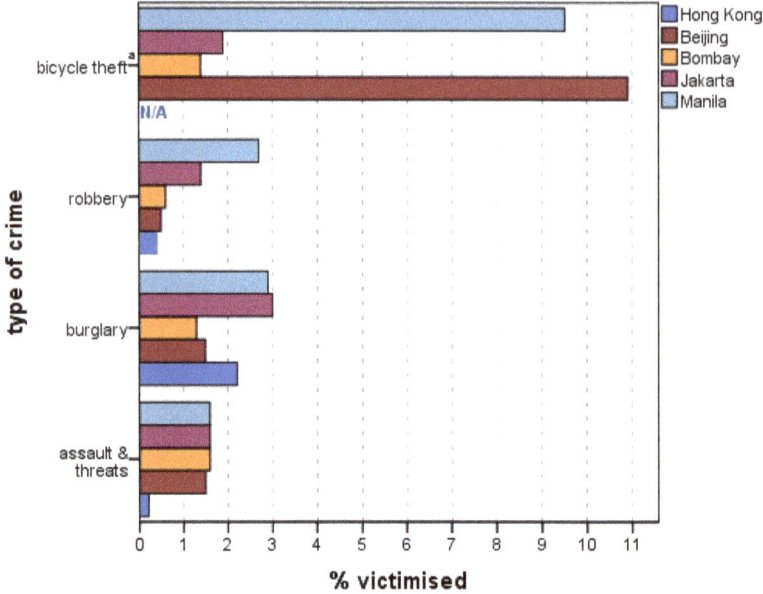

Sources: Census and Statistics Department, Hong Kong (1999:118); data are not available for bicycle theft. Other cities: Zvekic and Alvazzi del Frate (1995:19).

Note: [a] Bicycle theft rates are based on owners, not the whole population.

Figure 2.4 Rates of Police Officers in Hong Kong, Mainland China and Selected Countries (per 100 000 population)

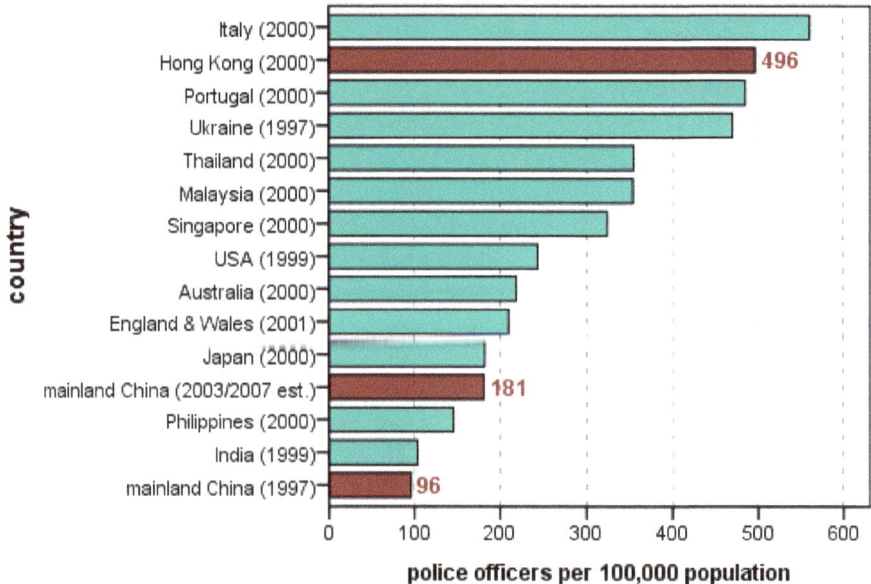

Sources: UNODC (2004); China (2003–07) estimated from Zhong and Grabosky (2009).

Figure 2.5 presents incarceration rates in a number of countries between 2003 and 2005. At 189 per 100 000, Hong Kong's rate was on par with Macau (197), higher than England and Wales (141), Australia (117) and Japan (58), but lower than Thailand (264) and Singapore (392). The rate in the mainland (118) was lower than in Hong Kong,[28] as well as Macau, Singapore and Thailand. Both the mainland and Hong Kong, however, had notably lower rates than the United States (726—the highest in the world) (Walmsey 2005, 2006).

Figure 2.5 Rates of Incarceration in Hong Kong, Mainland China and Selected Countries (per 100 000 population)

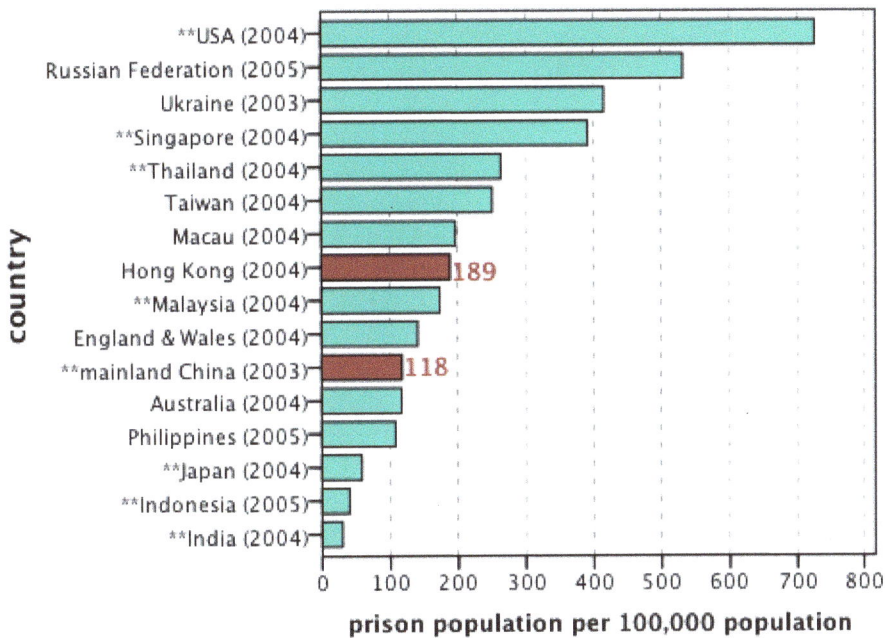

Sources: Walmsey (2005, 2006).

Note: The countries marked with asterisks are those where the use of capital punishment is still legal.

To conclude this comparative section, we examine Transparency International's corruption index, which does not directly measure the prevalence of corrupt practices, but provides a reliable indication of the extent of corruption using the experiences and perceptions of a range of experts. The most frequently used global indices of corruption are the Corruption Perception Index (CPI) and the Bribe Payers Index (BPI).[29] CPI scores relate to perceptions of the degree of

---

28   Seymour (2005) argues that official rates are under-reported and estimates the rate of imprisonment in 2003 to be 160 per 100 000, which puts mainland China closer to Hong Kong.

29   The CPI has been published since 1995 and the BPI since 1999. The 2005 CPI was constructed using 16 sources originating from 10 independent institutions, and ranked 159 countries. For the full list of countries' index and information on how it is constructed, see: <www.transparency.org/policy_research/surveys_

corruption in the public and political sectors as seen by businesspeople and country analysts. The BPI examines the 'supply side' of corruption by ranking leading exporting countries in terms of the likelihood that their companies will pay bribes to public officials in key emerging markets. Both CPI and BPI scores range between 0 (highly corrupt) and 10 (totally 'clean'). Figure 2.6 presents the 2005 CPI and 2006 BPI for selected countries. The countries perceived as the least corrupt (that is, highest-ranking) were: Iceland (9.7), Finland (9.6), New Zealand (9.6) and Denmark (9.5), followed by Singapore (9.4). Hong Kong (8.3) was ranked fifteenth, but mainland China received a much lower score—of 3.2—ranking it seventy-eighth out of 159 countries. While China's score was lower than Singapore's and Hong Kong's, it was similar to or higher than other Asian nations, such as India (2.9), the Philippines (2.5) and Indonesia (2.2). China also ranked ahead of Ukraine (2.6) and the Russian Federation (2.4).

In terms of the propensity of companies to offer bribes overseas, the country perceived as the least likely to do so was Switzerland (7.8). Japan ranked eleventh with a score of 7.1, followed by Singapore (6.8). Hong Kong ranked eighteenth with a score of 6, ahead of Taiwan (twenty-sixth, score of 5.4). While Hong Kong was assessed as a country where officials were relatively unlikely to accept bribes, this did not, however, translate into transparent business practices. Mainland China ranked second-last (4.9), just below Russia (5.2) and ahead of India (4.6). On both indices, mainland China scored low, suggesting that practices of both accepting and offering bribes are widespread. Official records of bribery and corruption cases are sparse. More than other types of crime, corruption is difficult to measure because of its clandestine and diffuse nature, and petty corruption is more likely to be exposed than grand corruption involving elites.

---

indices/cpi/2005> The BPI was published in 2002 and 2006. We use the 2006 ranking, which is closest to the years when the ICBS was conducted. The 2006 BPI drew from a sample of 11 000 businesspeople in 125 countries, and ranked 30 leading exporting countries. For details, see: <www.transparency.org/policy_research/surveys_indices/bpi/bpi_2006>

Figure 2.6 Corruption Perception Index, 2005, and Bribe Payers Index, 2006, Hong Kong, Mainland China and Selected Countries

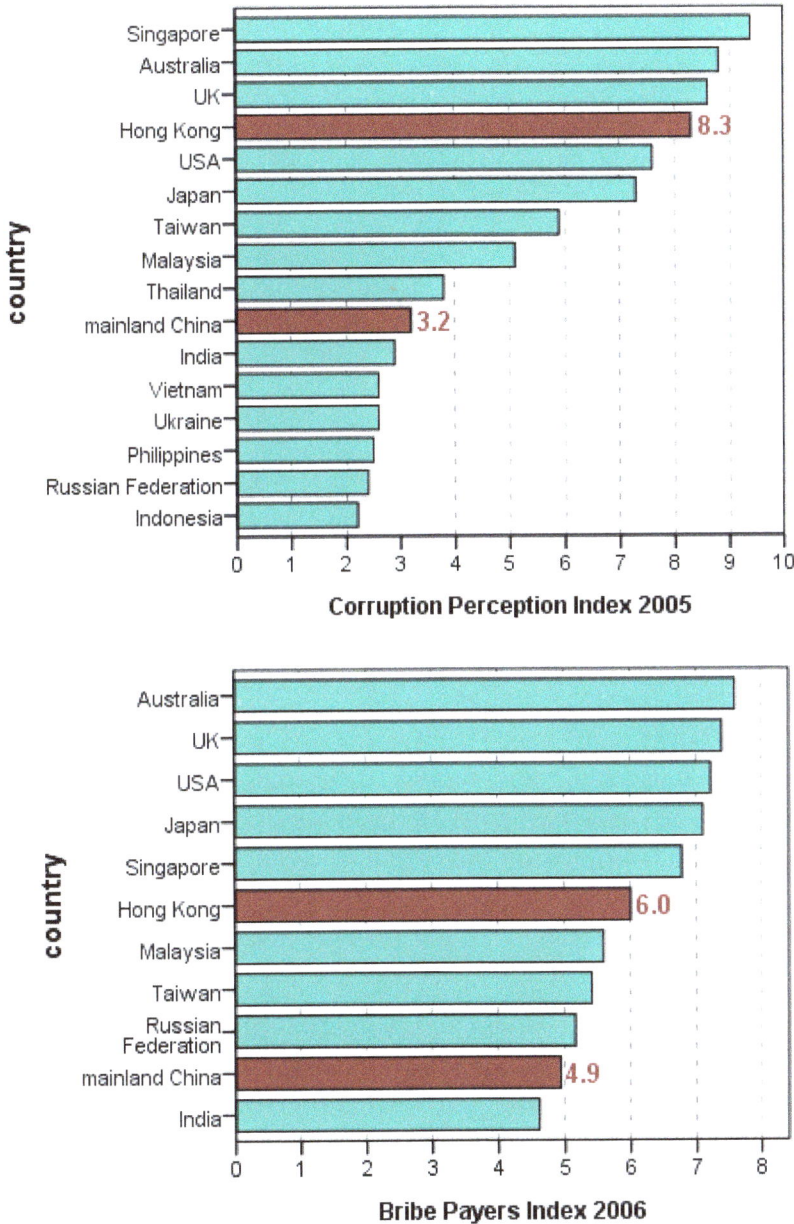

Source: Transparency International.

Note: CPI scores relate to perceptions of the degree of corruption as seen by businesspeople and country analysts; BPI scores rank leading exporting countries in terms of the likelihood that their companies will pay bribes to public officials in emerging markets; both indices range between 10 (totally clean) and 0 (highly corrupt).

Modernisation and Crime

The figures we have reviewed above are consistent with the broader literature on crime in China, and confirm that, regardless of the measures we use, crime rates in mainland China and Hong Kong are relatively low compared with many industrial and developing countries, particularly post-communist and transitional societies (Messner et al. 2007a). Hong Kong has long had a reputation as both a thriving and a safe city. In contrast, for 30 years following the establishment of the People's Republic of China in 1949, China's economy stagnated, despite efforts to increase industrial and agricultural production through economic planning led by the Central Government. After Mao's death in 1976, rapid economic reforms and modernisation processes were implemented. The path to a 'socialist market economy' was rewarding, with a consistent annual growth in GDP of 9–10 per cent since 1990 and an almost sevenfold increase in average incomes between 1985 and 2006 (Yu 2008). Increasing economic prosperity, however, was accompanied by a rise in crime—described in a Chinese metaphor as 'flies and mosquitoes coming through the window of reform' (Zhong 2009a:99).

Liu (2004, 2005, 2006) argues that the Chinese transition from planned command economy to a market economy required a fundamental ideological and institutional turnaround. In the pre-reform period, egalitarianism was a tenet of Chinese communism and government policy and ideology discouraged the pursuit of individual economic interests. Under the new post-reform economic orientation, however, the values of the market—such as entrepreneurial motivation, individual economic ambition and personal success—started to be seen as essential to achieve economic growth. Numerous opportunities for private businesses have emerged and, according to Liu (2006:128), 'getting rich by any means has become a national spirit'. Liu suggests that traditional modernisation theory—which attributes the rise in crime in developing countries to the breakdown of traditional society, social disorganisation, anomie and weakened social control—only partly applies in the Chinese context. He links the predominant increase in economically motivated crime compared with other forms of crime to the intense economic focus fostered by the Government and the market institutions.

While economic motivation can account for the significant rise in property crimes and the less spectacular rise in violent crime, it does not explain why, despite profound social and economic transformations, Chinese society maintained comparatively low rates of crime. Messner et al. (2007a) suggest that the combination of a set of 'master forces' and 'pathway forces' can help explain this apparent contradiction. Master forces are those that accompany modernisation and have been linked to rises in crime, such as urbanisation, growing inequality, large-scale migration of labour and weakened social controls. These master forces exist in modern China as in other rapidly industrialising and modernising nations, and have expanded opportunities for crime. On the other hand, and unlike in Eastern European post-communist societies, in China, the transition to a market economy has been managed by a strong central government, which has retained control over organisational structures and successfully maintained an effective framework for both formal and informal social controls (the pathway forces). For example, the migration of workers towards cities such as Shenzhen has not resulted in the spread of shanty towns or the large-scale disorganisation often seen in cities in developing countries, although it has been accompanied by a notable increase in both violent and property crimes. In summary, while the process of industrialisation and economic development in China, as in other new economies, has been accompanied by rising crime rates, a strong central government has succeeded in mitigating the negative consequences of modernisation in a society where collective informal social-control mechanisms remain important.

The crime situation in mainland China, however, is paradoxical. On the one hand, the active role of a strong state has mitigated the criminogenic processes associated with modernisation; on the other hand, the tight control by the state over the economy has created ample opportunities for crime by government and business elites. Wedeman (2005) and others (for example, Brody and Luo 2009; Messner et al. 2007a; Pei 2007; Yu 2008) argue that the rise of corruption is due to structural opportunities brought about by the interface of both a command and market economy and the implementation of selective market mechanisms within a government-planned economy, where the Chinese Government has retained significant control over the economy and the business world. The coexistence of state and privately owned businesses creates opportunities for local officials to use their power for monetary advantages. The perception of the risks of getting caught is low, putting little restraint on behaviour. Strong state control seems to have inhibited the development of strong independent legal institutions, able to settle disputes fairly and control elite crime.[30] Following the Wuhan Court scandal, the Chinese Government initiated reforms to try to stamp out corruption in the justice system and other parts of government.[31] Corruption remains an issue of widespread concern, however, especially the role of officials (in the vernacular known as 'umbrellas') in protecting the emerging phenomena of 'black societies' or organised crime groups (see Qiu 2008; Tan and

---

30 Legal institutions are not exempt from corruption. The biggest judicial corruption scandal in recent years occurred in the Wuhan Court (Hubei Province) and involved nearly 100 judges and court officials. The case, tried in 2004, revealed an ingrained network of corrupt officials at all levels of the Wuhan court system and exposed an organised system of bribe extraction that included taking bribes from both plaintiffs and defendants, manufacturing court cases, abusing the power of judges to suspend business operations or confiscate property, and receiving bribes for delivering beneficial judgments (Human Rights in China 2005).
31 For detail of anti-corruption mechanisms and reforms in China, see Guo (2006).

Yang 2009). Corruption undermines the goal of market reforms by substituting market forces with corrupt distribution of opportunities, and increases income disparities. Henderson (2007) argues that civil society needs to play a leading role because an impartial and independent judicial system, including anti-corruption agencies, is crucial to maintain stability and encourage investment. Pei (2007) warns that endemic corruption might ultimately threaten China's economic growth in a way similar to Indonesia and Japan, where widespread corruption has led, in part, to political upheaval and economic stagnation.

The UNICBS, like the omnibus crime victim surveys that address household and personal crime victimisation, provides an independent measure of the crime risks faced by Chinese businesses. In the context of China, where crime statistics—despite recent concessions to the need for evidence-based sources—have long been regarded as state secrets, alternative measures of the prevalence and nature of crime are an essential means of estimating the impact of crime. Such surveys help assess the likely scale and scope of risks of crime and are most valuable when repeated. In the next chapter, we outline the methods and limitations of the UNICBS snapshot of crimes against business in China.

3. ICBS Instrument, Methodology and Sample

Development of the China ICBS Questionnaire

The China ICBS questionnaire was adapted from the 2000 UN Interregional Crime Research Institute (UNICRI) version of the ICBS that was used in Central Eastern Europe. In order to examine new areas of crime but keep the questionnaire to a reasonable length, questions about violence at work were removed, and the section dealing with protection money was combined with the section on intimidation/extortion. New sections were included on computer-related crime and infringement of intellectual property (IP). Overall, the questionnaire included 120 pre-coded questions, available in English, Cantonese and Mandarin. The Chinese versions were translated from the original English version with the assistance and advice of the Crime Prevention Institute of the PRC's Ministry of Justice.

The UNICBS questionnaire first asked respondents about their company characteristics—for example, business sector, main activities, number of employees and annual turnover. The next section measured the respondents' perceptions of institutional obstacles to doing good business, such as the ease of dealing with various types of business regulations, crime, and bribery and corruption.[1] The main section then inquired about the prevalence, during the past 12 months, of nine common crimes against businesses (burglary, vandalism, theft of and from vehicles, theft by employees, theft by customers, theft by outsiders, robbery, assault, and IP infringement); crimes that are more likely to specifically target businesses (fraud by employees and outsiders, bribery, and intimidation, extortion or request for protection money); and finally, computer-related crimes, such as hacking and Internet fraud. When bribery and/or intimidation/extortion were mentioned, respondents were asked about the perpetrator and some details of the incident.

For each type of crime, respondents who reported victimisation incidents were asked whether the company reported the incident to the police. In-depth questions about responses to victimisation were included for the most serious of the 10 common crimes and the business-related crimes. If the incident was

---

1 Fourteen questions were adapted from the World Bank's Private Sector Survey (Brunetti et al. 1997) and included in the UNICBS in 2000. The questions about obstacles to doing business were asked early in the survey in order to avoid respondents' answers being tainted by their recollection of victimisation; however, we will discuss perceived obstacles to doing business after the prevalence of victimisation.

reported to the police, respondents were asked why the company decided to report the crime, whether it was satisfied with the police response, and, if not, the reason(s) for dissatisfaction. If the incident was not reported, respondents were asked the reason(s) why.

The instrument concluded with general questions about crime prevention and the company's involvement in crime-prevention practices, and the respondent's opinion of the police and its effectiveness in addressing crimes against business. Most questions were close-ended and allowed a single answer. Standard answers were presented for open-ended questions, such as those asking about reason(s) for reporting or not reporting victimisation, and multiple answers were usually allowed. Responses additional to the interviewer's prompts were recorded on a separate sheet. Interviewers often reminded the respondents to exclude incidents mentioned previously.

Two pilot studies were conducted to test the length, logic, likely response rate, Chinese wording and format of the questionnaire: the Cantonese version of the ICBS China questionnaire was piloted in Hong Kong in 2003 (N = 612) and Shenzhen (N = 112) and the Mandarin version in Shanghai in 2005 (N = 30). Data from the pilot studies were not counted as part of the final survey, but were useful to develop the questionnaire, test the Chinese translations and improve the instructions given to interviewers.

Hong Kong Pilot Survey, 2003

The work on the pilot survey was funded by a seed grant from Hong Kong University (2002–03) in conjunction with the UNICRI and the UN Office on Drugs and Crime (UNODC) to extend both the methodology (telephone interview strategies versus face-to-face methods) and scope (new crimes) of the UNICBS.

Development of the Questionnaire and Implementation

The standard UNICBS questionnaire was translated in Cantonese. Because of the additional questions on IP infringement and computer-related crime, and to reduce respondents' burden, the following sections of the original questionnaire were reduced or excluded.

- Obstacles to doing business: items relating to foreign exchange regulations, price control, investment policies, starting up a business, and political instability were removed from the list of potential obstacles, reducing the number of questions from 14 to eight.

- Insurance: the number of questions relating to insurance was reduced to a single question: 'do you have insurance?'
- Violence at work: the whole section (10 questions) was omitted from the Hong Kong pilot.
- Losses due to crime: one question on the amount of monetary loss was included, but probing questions to estimate amounts lost through crime and asked of respondents who did not know the specific amount were omitted.
- Bribery: prevalence questions were retained, but most of the questions on the perception of the frequency and modus operandi were omitted.
- Corruption and protection money: the section on corruption was combined with the section on bribery, and the section on protection money was combined with that on extortion.

New questions included

- one about IP infringement, which was added to the list of common crime; IP infringement was defined as 'illegal reproduction of products and counterfeiting, when patents/trademarks/copyrights/designs owned by your company have been used by others without your permission'
- one in the section on fraud by employees regarding corporate payment or credit-card fraud committed by an employee.

At the end of the victimisation component of the survey instrument, a section on computer-related crime comprising 17 questions was included. Questions on cyber crime were adapted from the Hong Kong UNICVS (Broadhurst et al. 2010). Three questions assessed the extent and the ways in which businesses used computers and the type of protection (for example, antivirus or firewall software) installed on their computers. Questions about computer-related victimisation included: Internet fraud; attacks through malicious software such as viruses, malware and spyware; threats of harm online or through email; unrequested lewd communication; and software copyright violation. Respondents who mentioned incidents of computer-related victimisation were asked whether they reported to the police or other organisations, and how satisfied they were with the response.

The pilot survey was based on a sample of telephone numbers randomly selected from the Yellow Pages (business phone) directory and used a computer-aided telephone interview (CATI) system. It was implemented in Hong Kong in July 2003 and referred to victimisation that occurred from 1 January to 31 December 2002. The response rate was 28 per cent, producing a sample of 612 businesses. Appendix D presents the results of the Hong Kong ICBS Pilot Survey.

What Was Learned from the Hong Kong Pilot?

Various sampling procedures were tested for the pilot survey and the approach, based on random dialling from the Yellow Pages business directory, yielded a satisfactory distribution of business activity when compared with Hong Kong Census and Statistics Department estimates of business sectors and industry/commercial business registries (see Census and Statistics Department, Hong Kong 2006). Based on a victimisation rate of 17 per cent (the highest rate in the pilot for fraud by outsiders), we calculated that a sample of about 1500 businesses would produce at least 250 companies that had experienced some type of victimisation in each city. This figure was adequate to perform reliable basic statistical analyses.

Following the Hong Kong pilot, the survey instrument was further reduced to encourage a higher response rate and minimise respondent burden. Some general questions about the business were removed (for example, when did you start your business, any foreign investment, are you involved in import/export). Overall, the pilot survey indicated that the Chinese version of the UNICBS was culturally appropriate and conducting the survey using CATI was feasible.

Some findings from the pilot were unexpected. There was a higher level of concern about corruption and crime than about conventional 'impediments' to business such as tax regimes, import/export controls, and labour, safety and environmental regulations. This was somewhat inconsistent with Hong Kong's well-regarded and efficient anti-corruption and enforcement capabilities and overall reputation for clean government (as noted in the data reported by Transparency International in the previous chapter). We also found surprising that a similar proportion was concerned by a lack of consultation with business, and that smaller but not negligible groups of respondents complained about changes in law and tax regulations. Tax and regulatory controls in Hong Kong are relatively simple and easy to deal with compared with other jurisdictions. These findings could suggest higher levels of unreported crime against business, particularly corruption; however, since many Hong Kong companies have business interests in the mainland, we suspected that respondents might have conflated their perception of doing business in Hong Kong with their experiences or perception of the mainland, where widespread corruption and complex regulatory practices have been noted.

In order to test this hypothesis, we decided to include an additional item about the location of the company's premises (only in Hong Kong, only in mainland China, or both in Hong Kong and in the mainland), and to ask Hong Kong respondents two sets of questions about their perception of potential obstacles to doing good business: one set about doing business within Hong Kong, and one set about doing business in the mainland. With these additional questions, we could test whether respondents with business activities in both Hong Kong and the mainland had similar views on the business environment in both jurisdictions, and whether respondents with business activities only in Hong Kong had different perceptions. As a consequence of this distinction, a larger sample for Hong Kong than for other cities was thought necessary. As it turns out, a significant number of businesses in mainland China also had businesses in Hong Kong and the survey failed to fully capture the likely effect of this on their crime experience.

To ensure reliability and statistical power, we aimed for a larger sample of about 1800 business respondents in Hong Kong and between 1000 and 1200 respondents in the other cities. Assuming a similar response rate of 28 per cent across the four cities in the final survey, we set up the research team with a sufficient number of interviewers with the aim of contacting about 20 000 businesses overall. Appendix E outlines the content of the final survey instrument, and Appendix F provides a copy of the instrument used in the China ICBS.[2]

Survey Mode and Sample Selection

The ICBS China was conducted in two phases: in Hong Kong, between November 2005 and mid-January 2006, referring to victimisation that occurred in 2004; in Shanghai, Shenzhen and Xi'an, in mid-2006, referring to victimisation that occurred in 2005. All interviews were conducted using computer-assisted telephone interviewing (CATI)—that is, interviewers read the instructions and the questions from a computer screen; answers were entered directly into the computer system and used to select the next question. This process effectively reduces the potential for routing errors by interviewers. All interviews were conducted from the Hong Kong University Social Sciences Research Centre, as the cost of calling long distance from Hong Kong to the mainland cities was comparable with that of employing mainland research agencies and ensured closer quality control. Calling from Hong Kong also avoided the process of obtaining official approval from each city for the questionnaire in the mainland. All interviewers spoke fluent Cantonese, Mandarin and English, and received appropriate training in applying the survey protocol, including two days of intensive practice and preparation. Quality checks were carried out at each stage of the process to ensure satisfactory standards of performance. A validation assessment was conducted on the day following the survey, through a telephone call-back to randomly selected respondents.

---

2   The standard ICBS questionnaire is available online at <www.crime.hku.hk/victims.htm>

Sampling

Slightly different sample frames were used in Hong Kong and in mainland China. In Hong Kong, businesses were selected randomly from the business section of the White Pages telephone directory published by PCCW, Hong Kong's leading telecommunication provider. The advantage of PCCW's White Pages is that virtually all businesses, except perhaps some home businesses, are listed in the directory. They are listed by name, however, not by business sector. Therefore, the validity of information provided by respondents could be checked only through call-backs to the business.

In mainland China, we used the Yellow Pages directory published by China Telecom as the sampling frame. The directory includes all phone numbers registered for business purposes with China Telecom, the largest state-owned landline service in 21 provinces including Shanghai Municipality, Guangdong Province (Shenzhen) and Shaanxi Province (Xi'an). Using China Telecom Yellow Pages guaranteed an extensive coverage of businesses. Companies are categorised by business sector, thus ensuring the accuracy of information on each company surveyed. The representativeness of the Yellow Pages directory, however, is unknown, and inquiries made to China Telecom over the directory's percentage coverage of businesses did not yield any results. It is likely that businesses in rural areas and small businesses, such as convenience stores, are under-represented in the UNICBS China.

In all cities, business numbers were randomly drawn from the directories and five attempts were made to call these numbers. Upon successful contact, the person who answered the phone was asked to refer the call to the manager of the company or other persons who understood the operation of the company well if they themselves did not. These respondents were invited to participate in the survey; if they refused, they were not replaced, and the next business on the list was called. The process continued until the desired number of completed interviews was reached.

Response Rate

The research team made approximately 18 300 phone calls to businesses. In total, 5117 business respondents completed the survey: 1817 businesses in Hong Kong; 1110 in Shanghai; 1112 in Shenzhen; and 1078 in Xi'an. The completion rate across the four cities was 28 per cent. An additional 12 per cent of respondents started the survey, but did not complete it, reflecting the demanding nature of the questionnaire. Response rates varied substantially between cities. It was particularly low in Hong Kong (18 per cent) compared with the average for the three mainland China cities (41 per cent). Shenzhen had the highest response rate (54 per cent), followed by Xi'an (39 per cent) and Shanghai (34 per cent). Response rates might also reflect, to some degree, the salience of concerns about crime, and this can play a role in the willingness of respondents to participate in a survey. Response rates to business surveys are generally lower than for household surveys (KPMG Forensic 2004; Taylor 2002) particularly when seeking interviews with management, who often perceive that surveys are time consuming.[3] This was found to be a recurring problem in Hong Kong, where company managers and others who had enough company knowledge to complete the survey were often too busy to do so upon initial contact. Based on this experience, the method of contact was modified in 2006 in the mainland cities. Rather than requesting to complete the interview at the time of initial contact, appointments were made to arrange a convenient time to conduct the interview. This method boosted the success rate in mainland cities. Interviewers also found that some businesses in the mainland were convinced to participate because the University of Hong Kong—cited as the UNICBS China host in the questionnaire introduction—is a well-known university and has a high reputation in China.

Limitations of the UNICBS

The general limitations that exist within telephone surveys also apply to the UNICBS China. These include: possibilities of sampling error, under-reporting, telescoping, erroneous responses, systematic mistakes and improper coding and processing of data—although in respect to the last two problems CATI helps mitigate coding errors. Crime surveys are prone to a number of response errors. First, participants might not recall trivial incidents that occurred during the survey period. They might recall only incidents that were serious but occurred outside the survey period. Some respondents might fail to realise that an incident is relevant, or they might be unwilling to report certain incidents. Therefore, the UNICBS measures only crimes that respondents were prepared to reveal to interviewers.

Despite the assistance of CATI, interviewers might commit errors during data collection, such as misinterpreting answers or mistakenly entering the wrong code. Together, these factors might affect the reliability of the data obtained.

---

3   For example, the response rate via telephone interview for the Hong Kong UNICVS in 2006 was 49 per cent, but the KPMG Forensic (2004) survey of crime against business conducted by mail in 2004 yielded a success rate of only 22 per cent. Generally, response rates of about 25 per cent are considered good in commercial surveys. The Central Eastern Europe ICBS had a surprisingly high average response rate of 65 per cent (ranging between 30 per cent in Moscow and 99 per cent in Tirana). In many of the cities (but not Moscow) the survey was, however, conducted face-to-face, and this method usually yields higher response rates than telephone surveys.

Every effort, however, was made during the administration, data coding and analysis stages to minimise these problems. A small number of cases were excluded due to data inconsistencies or partial completion of the questionnaire.

No weighting was applied to the data regarding business sectors and business size because we lacked accurate information about the overall distribution of business by sector and the numbers employed in businesses, particularly for the mainland. As noted below, however, for Hong Kong, information about the population of businesses was available and this enabled us to compare our sample with official census data. The proportion of businesses in each sector of economic activity in the sample differs from official statistics of contribution to GDP by sector of activity, which suggests the China ICBS sample might not be representative of the population of businesses at least in terms of sector of activity.

In Chapter 9, we will discuss the limitations of the survey in more depth and suggest ways of improving its instrument and methodology. In the next section, we describe the sample of businesses in the China ICBS; then, we proceed to describe victimisation by common crime in Chapter 4, followed by fraud, bribery and extortion victimisation in Chapter 5.

Characteristics of the China UNICBS Sample

This section describes the characteristics of the sample of businesses that were surveyed in the 2005–06 UNICBS in terms of business activities, size of workforce and locations of premises in each city. These characteristics are described only for those premises that were surveyed. Depending on the size of the companies and whether or not they had branches in other locations, the figures reported might or might not reflect the whole of each surveyed business's activities and features. The sample consisted of a total of 5117 businesses selected at random in Hong Kong (35.5 per cent), Shanghai (21.7 per cent), Shenzhen (21.7 per cent) and Xi'an (21.7 per cent).

Business Sector

Across the four cities, the four leading sectors of business activity were manufacturing (33.7 per cent), wholesale and distribution (25.2 per cent), non-food retail (24.3 per cent) and professional services (21.5 per cent) (Table 3.1). Food retailing, unspecified trading and financial services each represented less than 10 per cent of the sample. A relatively large proportion of businesses (17.5

per cent) were also engaged in other types of business activity. Some respondents described their company as a 'headquarters' (16.4 per cent) or 'branch/chain shop' (10.6 per cent), but did not provide further information on their activity.

Table 3.1 Business Sector by City and Overall, 2005–06 China UNICBS Sample (per cent)

Business sector[a]	Hong Kong N = 1817	Shanghai N = 1110	Shenzhen N = 1112	Xi'an N = 1078	All businesses N = 5117
Manufacturing	23.5	44.2	43.4	30.1	33.7
Wholesale/distribution	18.1	26.8	23.9	36.7	25.2
Retail—non-food	20.9	22.3	22.7	33.8	24.3
Professional services	20.9	23.3	19.8	22.5	21.5
Retail—food	10.5	4.5	3.1	7.2	6.9
Trade (unspecified)	4.8	1.5	1.3	0.6	2.4
Financial services	2.5	1.6	1.2	1.1	1.7
Other sectors	24.9	12.3	14.7	13.5	17.5
Head office	6.5	23.3	24.9	17.2	16.4
Branch/chain shop	3.4	17.2	12.9	13.4	10.6

Note: [a] Multiple answers were allowed, so percentages add up to more than 100 per cent.

Respondents were asked to nominate all their company's activities at the premises surveyed, which could crossover two or more sectors. Just over half (55 per cent) the respondents indicated that their business was involved in only one sector of activity, 33 per cent in two sectors, and 12 per cent in three or more sectors. There were differences between cities: a larger proportion of Hong Kong businesses (67.2 per cent) cited a single sector compared with 48.6 per cent of mainland businesses, and 29.8 per cent of Hong Kong businesses but 34 per cent of mainland businesses mentioned two sectors of activity. This suggests that mainland businesses had more diversified lines of business and explains why there was a higher proportion of mainland businesses represented in each sector of activity. To be able to conduct statistical analyses on the factors linked to the likelihood and type of victimisation, we needed to recode each business's sector of activity into a single variable made up of mutually exclusive categories. The following decisions were applied.

- First, the sectors were combined into five categories: manufacturing, retail (including food and non-food retail), wholesale/distribution and unspecified trade, financial and professional services, and other sectors; the last category includes those who described their activity as headquarters and branch/chain (coded as administration and management).

- Businesses with a single sector of activity and those with two sectors of activities that had been combined were coded according to the above categories.

- When two or more sectors had been mentioned and one of them was 'headquarters/branch', this answer was eliminated and the case was coded according to the actual sector. A similar process was applied when respondents had mentioned 'other sector' along with other responses.

For about 20 per cent of businesses, no single sector of activity could be identified from the responses given. We were able to refine our coding scheme by using the answers given to two other survey questions: location of premises (for example industrial estate, shopping precinct, serviced building), and does your premises belong to a chain of shops? The answer to these questions permitted us to assess the most likely sector of activity when several were mentioned. For example, if respondents said they were involved in retail and wholesale, and their premises was located in a shopping precinct, we coded the main sector of activity as 'retail'; if respondents mentioned manufacturing and retail, and their premises was located in an industrial estate, their business was coded as 'manufacturing'. Table 3.2 presents the main sector of activity of the surveyed businesses in each city and overall, and Figure 3.1 (top) compares businesses in Hong Kong and the mainland.

Table 3.2 Main Sector of Business Activity by City and Overall (per cent)

Main business sector	Hong Kong N = 1817	Shanghai N = 1110	Shenzhen N = 1112	Xi'an N = 1078	All businesses N = 5117
Manufacturing	23.5	44.2	43.4	30.1	33.7
Retail	27.4	13.1	14.2	25.2	21.0
Financial & professional services	22.8	20.8	16.9	20.4	20.6
Wholesale/distribution/ trade	18.6	14.6	11.4	20.9	16.7
Administration/ management and other sectors	7.7	7.3	14.0[a]	3.3	8.1

Note: [a] A relatively large proportion of Shenzhen's businesses described their activities as headquarters or branches, without specifying a sector of activity.

There were significant differences in business activities between Hong Kong and the mainland and some differences between the three mainland cities. Significantly more companies were engaged in manufacturing in the mainland than in Hong Kong (34.9 per cent and 23.5 per cent respectively), while businesses in Hong Kong were more likely to be involved in retail (27.4 per cent compared with 17.4 per cent in the mainland). Similar proportions of businesses were engaged in the other sectors of activity in Hong Kong and the mainland.

The distribution of businesses by sector of activity was comparable in Shanghai and Shenzhen: manufacturing was the largest sector (43–44 per cent of businesses), followed by financial and professional services (17–21 per cent), and retail and wholesale/distribution (11–15 per cent). Reflecting variant development and government policies, Xi'an had a different pattern of business activity, with only 30 per cent of businesses involved in manufacturing but 25 per cent in retail. A similar proportion of businesses (20 per cent) were active in the wholesale/distribution and financial and professional services sectors. About one-quarter of companies in Shanghai and Shenzhen were headquarters, with a lesser proportion in Xi'an (16.4 per cent) and only 6.5 per cent in Hong Kong.

Figure 3.1 Main Business Sector and Size of Workforce, Hong Kong and Mainland China

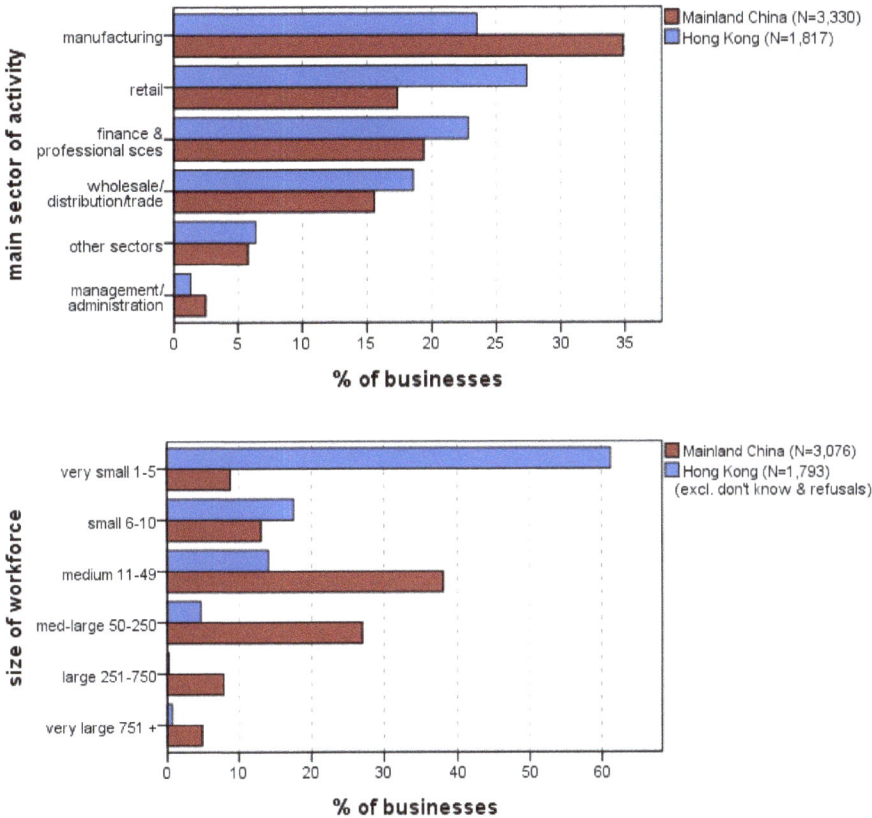

A record of the total number of registered companies in Hong Kong and their sector of economic activity is available from the Census and Statistics Department (2006) and we are able to assess the representativeness of the Hong Kong sample of businesses. Such data are not available, however, for the mainland.[4] Our Hong Kong sample of 1817 businesses represented 0.61 per cent of the population of registered companies (in 2005). Of these 296 249 companies, 61 per cent were engaged in the wholesale and retail sector, 22 per cent in financial and professional services, 5 per cent in manufacturing and 12 per cent in other various sectors of activity. Therefore, we see from Table 3.2 that the manufacturing sector (23.5 per cent) is over-represented in the Hong Kong ICBS sample (by a factor of about four), while the combined wholesale and retail sectors (46 per cent of the sample) are under-represented. The share of businesses in the financial and professional services sector and various other sectors is on par with the population.

For mainland businesses, we can perform only a gross approximation of the sample representativeness using contribution to GDP (see the economic characteristics of the four cities presented above). Economic sectors' contribution to GDP is not an adequate way to estimate representativeness because it does not take into account the size of the companies—for example, a small number of very large factories will contribute more to GDP than a great number of small workshops. Given the limited amount of information we could gather on businesses activities in the mainland, we present below this crude estimation of the representativeness of the mainland sample. The Shanghai sample seems representative of the economic activities of the city, since the secondary sector contributed 48 per cent of GDP in 2005, and, in our sample, 44.2 per cent of businesses are manufacturers; however, manufacturing seems under-represented in the Shenzhen and Xi'an samples: while the secondary sector contributed 61 per cent to Shenzhen's GDP and 44 per cent to Xi'an's GDP, 43.4 per cent of the Shenzhen sample and 30.1 per cent of the Xi'an sample were involved in manufacturing.

Annual Turnover and Workforce

The majority of data on the companies' annual turnover are missing, with only 30.5 per cent of valid answers. Interviewers frequently noticed a certain reluctance from respondents to reveal financial data and were instructed not to probe or press for an answer given the apparent sensitivity, particularly among mainland respondents. There were more valid answers in Hong Kong (42 per cent) than Shanghai (28 per cent), Shenzhen (20 per cent) or Xi'an (24 per cent). Based on the figures available, there were no major differences in mean annual turnover between Hong Kong and the mainland, or between the four cities.

---

4   We did find a record of the total number of mainland companies earning more than CNY5 million and similar data for Shanghai (NBS 2007; Shanghai Municipal Statistics Bureau 2006, 2010). Unfortunately, as described in the next section, the majority of data on our businesses' turnover was missing, which made it impossible to compare our sample of mainland businesses with the population.

With so much missing information, however, this variable is not useful, and we use the number of employees at the premises surveyed (full-time, part-time and casual) as a proxy to estimate the size of the businesses.

More than 40 per cent of all businesses were small, with 10 or less employees; more than one-quarter (27.9 per cent) had 11 to 49 employees, and about 18 per cent had between 50 and 250 employees. Nearly two-thirds of Hong Kong businesses were very small (one to five employees) and nearly 80 per cent had 10 or less employees—in contrast with the mainland where only 21.9 per cent of the businesses surveyed employed 10 or less people (Figure 3.1, bottom). In the three mainland cities, the majority of the businesses surveyed were medium to medium-large (50 to 250 employees), although companies in Xi'an tended to be smaller than those in Shanghai and Shenzhen (Table 3.3).

Table 3.3 Size of Workforce, 2005–06 China UNICBS Sample (per cent)

Workforce (N full and part-time employees)	Hong Kong N = 1817	Shanghai N = 1110	Shenzhen N = 1112	Xi'an N = 1078	All businesses N = 5117
Very small: 1–5	61.2	5.0	5.2	14.7	27.1
Small: 6–10	17.6	11.9	10.0	14.9	14.1
Medium: 11–49	14.1	37.1	33.5	36.1	27.9
Medium-large: 50–250	4.7	27.7	29.5	18.2	17.9
Large: 251–750	0.3	7.2	9.9	4.9	4.9
Very large: 751 +	0.7	4.3	5.5	3.9	3.2
Don't know/refusals	1.4	6.8	6.4	7.3	4.9

The size of businesses varied by sector of activity (Table 3.4). Three sectors—manufacturing, administration/management, and financial and professional services—tended to have larger workforces (more than half of these businesses had workforces totalling between 11 and 250 workers). The majority of retail businesses were small: 63.3 per cent employed 10 or less people, and only 4.1 per cent had more than 250 employees. The size of the workforce is consistent with the repartition of businesses by city and sector; a larger proportion of manufacturing businesses were located in the mainland and they tended to have a larger workforce, but a majority of retail businesses were located in Hong Kong and they tended to have a smaller workforce. With fewer manufacturing companies than Shanghai and Shenzhen, Xi'an had a larger proportion of small businesses although still far less than Hong Kong.

Location of Businesses

Respondents were asked two questions about the location of their premises. First, whether their premises was located in a town or city centre, in a built-up area outside a city centre, in the countryside or somewhere else. The second question was more precise and included seven response options: an industrial estate or business park, an indoor shopping precinct, an outdoor shopping precinct, a main shopping street, an out-of-town commercial area, a serviced building for small businesses or another location. This question is important to assess whether some business locations are more prone to victimisation than others and provides information on the types of crime-prevention initiatives more likely to be effective in certain locations.[5] On the last question, respondents could pick several answers. The variable was simplified by combining several categories. When businesses mentioned several locations that could not be combined, a single location was selected based on the type of business, its size and whether it was located in the city centre or out of town. For example, if a business's main sector of activity consisted of financial or professional services, and the respondent said the premises was located in a main shopping street and a serviced building, we coded the location as serviced building, because we assumed the serviced building was located in a shopping street. The four main locations were: industrial or business area, which included industrial estates, business parks and out-of-town commercial areas; shopping area, which included indoor and outdoor shopping precincts and main shopping streets; serviced building for small businesses; and other locations.

Table 3.4 Size of Workforce by Main Business Sector (per cent)

Size of workforce (N employees)[a]	Manufacturing N = 1634	Retail N = 1035	Wholesale/ trade N = 808	Financial & professional services N = 1008	Other sectors N = 382	All sectors N = 4867
1–10	28.2	63.3	53.1	42.7	34.6	43.3
11–49	28.1	23.6	32.7	32.2	36.1	29.4
50–250	29.6	9.1	11.4	17.3	19.4	18.8
251+	14.1	4.1	2.8	7.8	9.9	8.5

Note: [a] Excluding 'don't know' and refusals.

Not surprisingly, the location of business premises was related to the type and size of the business. Businesses involved in manufacturing were more likely to be located in industrial or business areas, retail businesses were most often located in shopping areas, and financial and professional services, as well as smaller wholesale and trading businesses, in serviced buildings. Across the four cities, more than one-third of businesses (35.6 per cent) were located in industrial or business areas (Table 3.5). In Shenzhen, half the businesses were located in such areas; in Shanghai, 43.3 per cent; and this relates to the predominance of the

---

5   For example, the notion of 'crime prevention through environmental design' was first formulated by criminologist Ray Jeffery (1971) and developed by others (for example, Newman 1972).

manufacturing sector and larger businesses in these two cities. More premises in Hong Kong and Xi'an were in shopping areas because of the larger proportion of food and non-food retailers in these two cities.

Table 3.5 Location of Business Premises by City (per cent)

Location	Hong Kong N = 1817	Shanghai N = 1110	Shenzhen N = 1112	Xi'an N = 1078	All businesses N = 5117
Industrial and business area	23.9	43.3	50.0	32.6	35.6
Shopping area	34.2	19.8	21.9	33.0	28.2
Serviced building	26.7	20.5	22.1	15.4	22.0
Other locations	15.1	9.7	12.7	19.0	14.2

Although the questionnaire referred only to victimisation at the premises surveyed, respondents were asked whether their company had other premises, and where these premises were located. We were particularly interested in the opinion of Hong Kong respondents who also ran businesses in the mainland. A significantly larger proportion of mainland companies had multiple premises compared with Hong Kong (40.9 per cent and 28.8 per cent respectively), and this is consistent with their generally larger size. The majority of the businesses surveyed (84.9 per cent) were located in a single jurisdiction (56.5 per cent in mainland China and 28.5 per cent in Hong Kong), although they could have several premises within this jurisdiction. A slightly higher proportion of Hong Kong businesses also had premises in mainland China (19.9 per cent) compared to mainland businesses with other premises in Hong Kong (12.5 per cent). Table 3.6 shows that businesses with premises in both Hong Kong and the mainland were generally larger. For example, just more than 10 per cent of Hong Kong businesses with premises in the mainland had between 50 and 250 employees, compared with only 3.4 per cent of single-premises companies. Among the three mainland cities, Shenzhen companies were the most likely to have premises in Hong Kong as well (21.7 per cent, compared with 11.7 per cent for Shanghai and 5.2 per cent for Xi'an). This is not surprising since Hong Kong and Shenzhen are adjacent to each other and have strong commercial and financial links.

Table 3.6 Size of Workforce by Location of all Premises (per cent)

Size of workforce[a]	All N = 1793	HONG KONG No premises in mainland N = 1435	Premises in mainland N = 358	All N = 3074	MAINLAND No premises in HK N = 2686	Premises in HK N = 388
1–10	79.9	83.6	65.4	22.0	23.3	12.8
11–49	14.3	12.6	20.9	38.1	39.1	31.4
50–250	4.7	3.4	10.1	27.1	26.8	28.8
251 +	1.1	0.4	3.6	12.8	10.8	27.0

Note: [a] Defined as N full and part-time employees and based on N = 4867 businesses, excluding 'don't know' and refusals; missing values on location of premises were coded as Hong Kong only or mainland only.

Interviewees

We hoped to be able to interview people in managerial positions as often as possible, because they should have the most knowledge about the business, in terms of both company background and potential victimisation. Across the four cities, 47.6 per cent of respondents occupied managerial positions: 22.8 per cent were the owners, managing directors or chief executives; 17.1 per cent were the managers of the premises surveyed; and 12.6 per cent occupied various executive positions such as financial director, production manager or company secretary (including 4 per cent of respondents who were responsible for the company's security). Other interviewees (52.4 per cent) included clerks, sales assistants and other non-executives.

Although the proportions varied between the mainland cities, overall, we interviewed significantly more executives in Hong Kong than in the mainland (65.5 per cent and 45.2 per cent respectively). In Xi'an, 50.5 per cent of the respondents were executives; in Shanghai, 47.7 per cent; and in Shenzhen, 37.7 per cent. The interviewee's position was related to the size of the company: more managers completed the survey in small to medium businesses than in larger companies, where predominantly employees were interviewed. This explains why more managers were interviewed in Hong Kong, since the majority of the businesses surveyed were small or medium-sized. One drawback is that while executives and managers have more knowledge about the business and its victimisation, they are also very busy people and, therefore, are more likely to refuse being interviewed or are unable to complete the survey. It is probable that the low response rate in Hong Kong is partly due to this problem. On the other hand, non-executive employees, as expected, knew less about the business. For example, while many respondents refused to reveal the annual turnover of the company, between 34 and 47 per cent of managers provided an answer compared with less than 20 per cent of employees. We found a consistent pattern where non-executive respondents were more likely than managers to answer 'don't know' on many of the survey questions: less than 2 per cent of managers could not answer questions about victimisation compared with 4–5 per cent of non-managerial staff; on the crime-prevention questions, up to 15 per cent of non-executive respondents responded that they did not know. This has of course implications for the accuracy of the information we received, as employees might also have answered questions for which they did not have complete or accurate knowledge. It also suggests that future surveys of this nature need to reconsider how best they might boost the involvement of senior staff and managers. We now turn to the prevalence and type of victimisation against business, which we describe in the next two chapters.

4. Common Crimes against Business

We refer to 'common' crime when talking about conventional crime or 'street' crime, such as burglary, robbery or theft, which is perpetrated against both individuals and businesses. The next chapter examines crime that is more likely to specifically target businesses or commercial enterprises, such as fraud, bribery and corruption, and computer-related crime. Here, we focus on nine common crimes: burglary, vandalism, vehicle theft, theft from a vehicle, theft by customers, theft by employees, theft by outsiders, robbery, assault, and an 'unspecified offences' category. First, we report rates of victimisation by city. Then, we consider whether victimisation varies by business sector and by business size, and examine interactions between these characteristics. Finally, we compare the rates found in the China ICBS with those of other victimisation surveys. Unless otherwise specified, percentages are based on the total numbers of respondents (that is, the 'N' value), including 'don't know' and refusals, which is the standard way of reporting crime victimisation in UN surveys (see van Dijk et al. 2007).

Rates of Victimisation by City

Table 4.1 presents rates of victimisation overall and by city for each of the common crimes. This is a simple measure of the prevalence of victimisation—that is, the percentage of businesses which reported having been the victim of at least one incident during the survey period (2004 for Hong Kong and 2005 for the mainland cities). Overall, in the 12-month reference period of the China UNICBS, 6.7 per cent of businesses across the four cities reported at least one incident of victimisation by common crime. Hong Kong businesses reported the highest rate (8.3 per cent), followed by those in Shenzhen (7.4 per cent), Shanghai (5 per cent) and Xi'an (4.9 per cent). Rates in Hong Kong and Shenzhen were comparable, but significantly higher than those in Shanghai and Xi'an. The crimes most likely to affect the businesses across the four cities were burglary (3.7 per cent) and theft by outsiders (3.1 per cent). The prevalence of other types of crime was less than 2 per cent, ranging from 0.6 per cent for vehicle theft to 1.8 per cent for vandalism and theft by employees.

Considering only the combined rate for all crime types is misleading. In Figure 4.1, we group the mainland cities and compare the prevalence of common crime with Hong Kong. As the figure shows, the higher overall rate of victimisation in Hong Kong compared with the mainland cities was driven by the high prevalence of theft by customers (3.1 per cent and 1 per cent respectively, $p < 0.001$). Hong Kong's rates of theft by outsiders, robbery and vehicle theft were, however, significantly lower than those of the mainland cities combined, and for the other offences, they were comparable. Shenzhen, on the other hand, recorded consistently higher rates of victimisation across a number of crimes: vandalism (2.6 per cent versus 1.6 per cent for the three other cities combined), vehicle theft (1.1 per cent versus 0.5 per cent), theft by employees (3 per cent versus 1.5 per cent), theft by outsiders (4.3 per cent versus 2.8 per cent), robbery (2.4 per cent versus 0.4 per cent—nearly three times that of Xi'an and 10 times that of Hong Kong), and assault (1.2 per cent versus 0.5 per cent) (Table 4.1). Among the three mainland cities, Shenzhen had the highest rates of victimisation for all crime types, except theft by customers. Shanghai and Xi'an showed a comparable rate of overall victimisation (5 per cent and 4.9 per cent respectively).

Table 4.1 Victimisation by Common Crime: One-year prevalence rates by city and overall (per cent)

Type of crime victimisation[a]	Hong Kong N = 1817	Shanghai N = 1110	Shenzhen N = 1112	Xi'an N = 1078	Total N = 5117
All common crimes	8.3***	5.0	7.4**	4.9	6.7
Burglary	3.1	3.5	4.6	3.7	3.7
Theft by outsiders	2.4†	2.6	4.3**	3.6	3.1
Vandalism	1.4	1.4	2.6*	2.1	1.8
Theft by employees	1.7	1.5	3.0*	1.1	1.8
Theft by customers	3.1***	1.1	0.6††	1.3	1.7
Robbery	0.3††	0.2††	2.4***	0.9	0.9
Theft from vehicle	0.6	1.0	1.0	0.9	0.8
Vehicle theft	0.3†	0.5	1.1*	0.8	0.6
Assault	0.7	0.1	1.2*	0.6	0.6
Other offences	1.5**	0.5	0.9	0.6	1.0

* $p < 0.05$ ** $p < 0.01$ *** $p < 0.001$, rate is significantly higher

† $p < 0.05$ †† $p < 0.01$, rate is significantly lower

Note: [a] Rates refer to the 12-month period from 1 January to 31 December 2004 for Hong Kong, and 1 January to 31 December 2005 for Shanghai, Shenzhen and Xi'an.

Figure 4.1 One-Year Prevalence of Common Crime, Hong Kong (2004) and Mainland (2005)

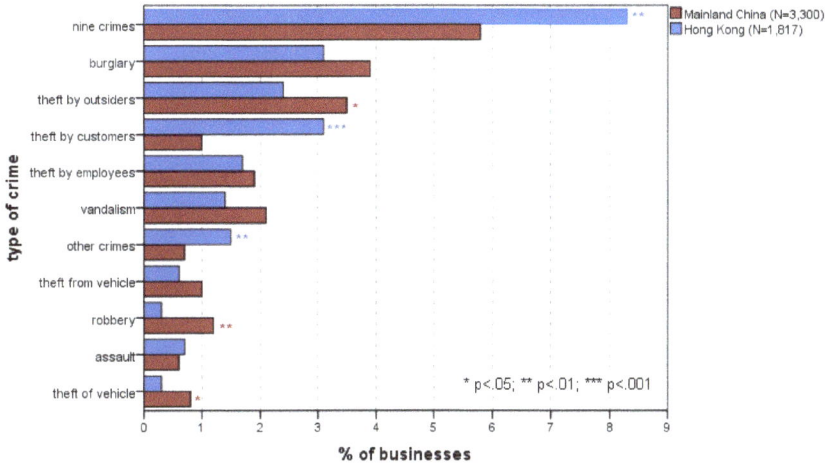

Victimisation by Business Sector and Business Size

While we see a greater prevalence of crimes against business in Shenzhen, differences between cities are only one representation of victimisation patterns. Victimisation can also vary according to sectors of activity, location and business size. It is likely that some types of crime occur more frequently in some business sectors—for example, we can expect theft by customers (shoplifting) to be more prevalent in the retail sector than in other sectors of activity. Victimisation risks might also be related to the size of the business. Because of the large amount of missing data on annual turnover, we do not examine this factor in relation to victimisation risks.

Victimisation by Business Sector

For all common crimes combined, businesses involved in retail were significantly more likely to be victimised than those in other sectors of activity (Table 4.2). Just more than 9 per cent of retailers reported some victimisation, compared with 4.2–6.8 per cent (average 6 per cent) in other sectors. As expected, retailers were particularly prone to theft by customers (5.2 per cent), but also by outsiders (4 per cent). Manufacturing businesses, on the other hand, had the lowest prevalence of theft by customers (0.8 per cent), but were significantly more at risk of theft by employees (2.3 per cent) than other sectors. Wholesalers and traders were least likely to be victimised by any type of common crime (4.2 per cent overall).[1]

Table 4.2 One-Year Prevalence of Common Crime by Main Sector of Activity across Four Cities (per cent)

Type of crime victimisation	Manufacturing N = 1726	Retail N = 1073	Wholesale/ trade N = 852	Finance & professional services N = 1053	Other sectors N = 413
All common crimes	6.4	9.1**	4.2††	6.8	5.6
Burglary	4.2	4.2	2.0††	4.2	1.9
Theft by outsiders	3.2	4.0*	1.6†	3.7	1.7
Vandalism	1.9	2.1	1.3	2.1	1.2
Theft by employees	2.3*	2.1	0.6††	1.8	1.7
Theft by customers	0.8	5.2***	0.4	1.3	0.7
Robbery	1.0	0.4	0.6	0.9	1.7
Theft from vehicle	0.9	0.7	0.4	1.1	1.0
Vehicle theft	0.6	0.5	0.2	0.9	1.0
Assault	0.8	0.6	0.5	0.7	0.5
Other offences	1.0	1.0	0.8	1.0	1.2

$*\ p < 0.05$ $**\ p < 0.01$ $***\ p < 0.001$, rate is significantly higher

$†\ p < 0.05$ $††\ p < 0.01$, rate is significantly lower

The manufacturing sector had the highest rate of theft by employees. In both Shanghai and Shenzhen, more than 40 per cent of businesses were engaged in manufacturing (Table 3.2), yet Shenzhen recorded a significantly higher rate of such thefts than Shanghai. Shenzhen also had a higher share of large and very large companies than Shanghai, which can account for the difference in rate of theft by employees. The relationship between the risk of victimisation and the size of the business also explains some of the variation in rates of victimisation between the cities: Hong Kong tended to have smaller businesses than the mainland and less victimisation, except in the case of shoplifting, for which very small businesses were more at risk.

Victimisation by Business Size

In these analyses, we again use the number of employees as a proxy for estimating business size. From Table 4.3, we see that, except for theft by customers, the likelihood of victimisation generally increases with the size of the business.

---

1 The subgroup of traders in unspecified goods (N = 122) had a particularly low victimisation rate of 1.6 per cent.

For all common crimes combined, large businesses (those with more than 250 employees) were victimised at nearly twice the rate of small and medium businesses (fewer than 50 employees). Medium-large and large businesses (50 or more employees) were statistically significantly more likely to be the victims of burglary, vandalism, theft by employees, theft by outsiders, robbery and assault than smaller businesses. For other types of crime, differences are not statistically significant, but victimisation rates are higher for larger businesses, apart from theft by customers. While small businesses—that is, those with 10 or less employees—seemed to be protected from many common crimes, they were most prone to theft by customers (2.7 per cent, $p < 0.01$). These businesses are likely to be small retail shops, which might have lacked resources to implement surveillance systems. The rate of theft by employees in small businesses was significantly lower than in larger ones, perhaps because they were often owned and run by family members.

Table 4.3 One-Year Prevalence of Common Crime by Size of Workforce across Four Cities (per cent)

Size of workforce[a] Type of victimisation	Small N = 2107	Medium N = 1430	Medium-large N = 917	Large N = 413	Total N = 4867
All common crimes	6.6	5.8	8.0	10.4**	6.9
Burglary	2.9†	3.5	5.1**	5.8*	3.8
Theft by outsiders	2.6	3.1	4.1*	5.3***	3.2
Vandalism	1.4†	1.6	3.1**	2.7	2.7
Theft by employees	0.9†	1.6	3.4***	4.4***	1.9
Theft by customers	2.7***	1.1	0.9	2.2	1.8
Robbery	0.4†	0.8	1.9***	1.7*	0.9
Theft from vehicle	0.5†	0.8	1.2	1.7*	0.8
Vehicle theft	0.3†	0.8	0.9	1.0	0.6
Assault	0.5	0.6	0.8	1.7**	0.7
Other offences	1.1	0.5	1.1	2.2	1.0

* $p < 0.05$ ** $p < 0.01$ *** $p < 0.001$, rate is significantly higher

† $p < 0.05$, rate is significantly lower

Note: [a] Number of employees (part and full-time, excluding 'don't know'/refusal)—small, 1–10; medium, 11–49; medium-large, 50–250; large, more than 250.

Interaction Between City, Business Sector and Business Size

Analyses conducted so far suggest that for most types of crime, rates of business victimisation were higher in Shenzhen than in other cities, but theft by customers was more prevalent in Hong Kong. Two sectors of business activities were more prone to victimisation, but this depended on the type of victimisation: the retail sector was at heightened risk of theft by customers and outsiders, and companies in the manufacturing sector were more likely to be victims of theft by employees. Apart from theft by customers, which was most prevalent against small businesses, risks of victimisation generally increased with the size of the business. We now examine whether correlations between business sector and size are present across the four cities. Details of victimisation rates by city and sector, and by city and business size, are presented in Appendix G, Tables G.1 and G.2.

Table G.1 confirms that retailers were significantly more likely to be victims of theft by customers and outsiders than other businesses, but only in Hong Kong and Shanghai. Since the Hong Kong sample consisted of about one-quarter of retailers, it is not surprising to find a high rate of shoplifting there. Shanghai retailers also had a higher risk of victimisation by shoplifting, but only about one-third that of Hong Kong (3.4 per cent compared with 9.2 per cent), probably because retail businesses accounted for only 13 per cent of the Shanghai sample. In Shenzhen, businesses that provide financial and professional services were particularly at risk of vandalism (5.3 per cent, $p < 0.05$) and theft by outsiders (7.4 per cent, $p < 0.05$). Across the four cities, the wholesale/trade sector tended to report lower rates of victimisation, but this was not significant.

While we find few sector effects, Appendix Table G.2 shows a strong and consistent effect of business size, with on the whole greater levels of victimisation against medium-large/large businesses. Hong Kong and Shanghai recorded similar levels of theft by customers in small businesses (3.1 per cent and 3.2 per cent respectively). In Shanghai, shoplifting was significantly more prevalent in small businesses (one–10 employees) than in larger ones, but in Hong Kong, the relationship was not significant because the highest rate of shoplifting occurred in the largest businesses (10.5 per cent for companies with more than 250 employees). This suggests that compared with Shenzhen and Xi'an, retailers in Hong Kong were generally prone to experiencing shoplifting, with the few larger companies most at risk. In part this might also reflect the nature of retail trading in Hong Kong where larger retail outlets dominate shopping zones (for example, Kowloon and Causeway Bay) and are designed to attract overseas visitors as well as local shoppers. As a consequence, these retailers can attract gangs of thieves, often from the mainland or further abroad.

Victimisation by Location of Premises

Respondents only reported victimisation that occurred on the premises surveyed, but were asked whether the company had other premises and their location (that is, Hong Kong or mainland). Looking at all common crimes combined, Hong Kong businesses with other premises in the mainland were significantly more likely to be victimised than their counterparts without premises in the mainland, and mainland businesses with premises in Hong Kong also had a higher rate of victimisation than mainland businesses with no premises in Hong Kong, but the difference was not statistically significant (Table 4.4). For nearly all types of common crime, businesses with premises in both the mainland and Hong Kong tended to have a higher risk of victimisation, with statistically significant differences in rates of victimisation for theft by employees. Theft by customers again was the exception and Hong Kong businesses with premises only in Hong Kong showed a rate double that of Hong Kong businesses with additional premises in the mainland.

Table 4.4 One-Year Victimisation Rates for Businesses with Premises in Hong Kong or Mainland Only, or Hong Kong and Mainland (per cent)

	Hong Kong (2004)		Mainland (2005)	
Type of victimisation	No premises in mainland N = 1456	Premises in mainland N = 361	No premises in HK N = 2889	Premises in HK N = 411
All common crimes	7.8	10.0**	5.4	8.0
Burglary	3.0	3.9	3.8	4.6
Theft by outsiders	2.2	3.0	3.4	4.1
Vandalism	1.4	1.4	2.0	2.7
Theft by employees	1.1	4.2***	1.7	3.4***
Theft by customers	3.4***	1.7	1.1	0.5
Robbery	0.1	0.8*	1.1	1.7
Theft from vehicle	0.5	0.8	1.0	0.7
Vehicle theft	0.2	0.6	0.8	0.7
Assault	0.6	1.1	0.5	1.5
Other offences	1.5	1.7	0.5	1.7**

* $p < 0.05$ ** $p < 0.01$ *** $p < 0.001$

The differential risk of victimisation between the two groups of businesses, however, is related to the size of businesses rather than the location of their premises. We ran the same analyses based only on the number of premises but not considering the location of the other premises. For burglary, theft by employees, theft by outsiders and other unspecified crimes, large differences in victimisation emerged and companies with multiple premises had a significantly higher risk of victimisation than those with single premises. This pattern occurred because businesses with multiple premises, regardless of where they were located, were generally larger, and, as reported above, larger business size was associated with higher risk of victimisation. But again, the exception was theft by customers, with no differences in victimisation rates between single and multiple-premises companies.

In Hong Kong, the prevalence of theft by customers was lower for businesses with multiple premises than those with single premises, which appears to contradict the general pattern of victimisation just described. Theft by customers was, however, the only type of crime that was most prevalent in smaller retail businesses, and in Hong Kong, the majority of retailers (80 per cent) operated small businesses. Therefore, it is not surprising that single-premises companies—most likely retail shops—experienced more theft by customers than larger, non-retail, multiple-premises companies.

Considering now the specific location of the premises surveyed, Table 4.5 reveals a pattern consistent with other analyses: businesses located in shopping areas were significantly more likely to be victimised than those in other locations, but this was due only to high rates of theft by customers and by outsiders. This is not surprising since retail shops were those most often located in shopping areas and they were particularly prone to theft by customers and outsiders. A more interesting finding is that companies operating from serviced buildings reported a significantly lower rate of theft by employees than others. Companies located in serviced buildings tended to be smaller than in other locations, which goes some way in accounting for their lower victimisation rates. It is likely, however, that the level of security typically available in serviced buildings also helped reduce the likelihood of criminal victimisation.

Table 4.5 One-Year Prevalence of Common Crime by Location of Premises across Four Cities (per cent)

Type of victimisation	Industrial/ commercial area[a] N = 1823	Shopping area N = 1441	Serviced building N = 1125	Other locations N = 728
All common crime	5.8	9.1***	5.4	5.8
Burglary	3.7	4.0	3.1	3.8
Vandalism	1.8	1.7	1.6	2.6
Vehicle–related crime[b]	1.3	1.2	0.7	1.2
Theft by employees	2.1	2.2	0.8†	1.9
Theft by customers	0.7	4.2***	0.6	1.1
Theft by outsiders	2.9	4.2*	2.3	2.6
Violent crime[c]	1.4	1.1	0.8	1.2
Other offences	0.6	1.3	1.2	1.0

$* p < 0.05$ $*** p < 0.001$, rate is significantly higher

$† p < 0.05$, rate is significantly lower

Notes: [a] Includes industrial estates, business parks and commercial areas; [b] includes theft of vehicle and theft from vehicle; [c] includes robbery and assault.

Monetary Loss Due to Common Crime

Respondents who mentioned one or several instances of victimisation were asked to estimate the amount of monetary loss that resulted from the most serious incident. Of the 328 businesses that were victimised and provided details about the most serious incident of common crime, 10.6 per cent reported no monetary loss; however, nearly one-quarter of respondents (22.6 per cent) did not know whether the incident incurred losses for the business or refused to answer this question. On Figure 4.2, we see that there are no major differences in the amount lost between the cities. All businesses reported some monetary losses in Xi'an, but nearly one-third (31.5 per cent) suffered relatively small losses (less than US$250) from the crime. One in five victimised businesses in Shanghai had losses in excess of US$5000—a slightly higher proportion than in the other cities.

Figure 4.2 Monetary Loss in Most Serious Incident of Victimisation by Common Crime

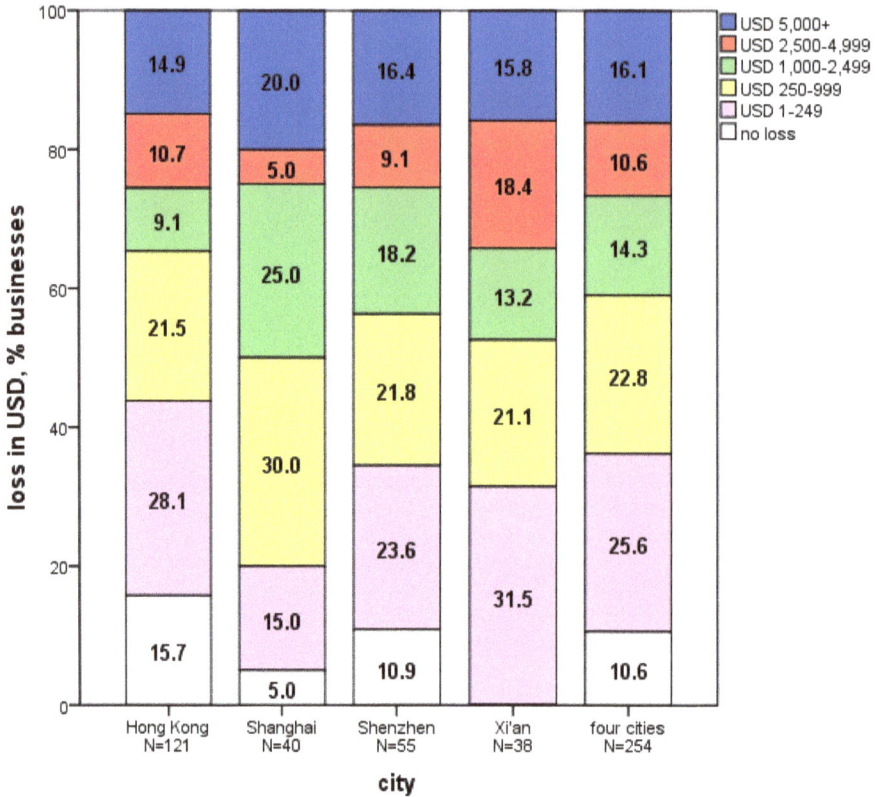

Across the four cities and excluding businesses that reported no monetary losses, the average loss due to the most serious criminal incident was US$5680; the median, however, was much lower at US$640 (Table 4.6). We use median losses for comparative purposes, as the median is less sensitive to extreme values than the mean. The median loss was lowest in Hong Kong (US$576) and highest in Shanghai (US$1230).

Table 4.6 Monetary Loss Due to Common Crime: Mean, median and estimated total loss by city

Average loss	Hong Kong N = 102	Shanghai N = 38	Shenzhen N = 49	Xi'an N = 38	Total N = 227[a]
Mean, most serious incident, US$	7,002	5,329	4,867	3,528	5,680
Median, most serious incident, US$	576	1,230	861	769	640
Total loss, most serious incident, US$1000	856	268	345	183	1,652
Total loss, all incidents, US$1000[b]	1,528	812	919	479	3,738

Notes: [a] Based on respondents who reported a loss—that is, excluding N = 74 who did not know or refused to answer, and N = 27 who reported no monetary loss; [b] this estimate includes losses due to multiple victimisations—that is, by different offence types, but not losses due to repeat victimisation (that is, several incidents of the same offence type).

Based on the losses that respondents reported for the most serious incident of common crime, we estimated that together the businesses we surveyed had lost a total of US$1.65 million from the most serious incident of common crime (Table 4.6). If we combine the monetary losses from *all* the incidents of common crime—that is, counting losses due to victimisation by different offences for businesses that had been victimised more than once—our estimate more than doubles, to US$3738. (Note that this figure is underestimated as it does not include losses due to repeat victimisation by the same offence.) The largest amount was lost in Hong Kong (US$1.5 million), followed by Shenzhen (less than US$1 million).

Not surprisingly, the cost of the criminal incident varied depending on the type of crime (Table 4.7). In terms of median losses from the most serious incident (middle column), we see that unspecified offences were the most costly (median US$1845), followed by assault and theft by employees (US$1538). Theft by outsiders and theft by customers incurred the lowest median amounts of loss— US$246 and $256 respectively. Theft by customers was most likely to happen in small retail shops where customers would be able to steal only small, relatively inexpensive items. If, however, we consider the total amounts lost to each type of common crime (right-hand column), theft by employees incurred by far the largest loss, of more than US$1.3 million—double the total cost of theft of a vehicle (US$680 000). Monetary losses due to customer theft totalled a relatively modest amount (US$33 000) because, as indicated by the mean and median, each incident incurred only small losses.

Table 4.7 Monetary Loss Due to Common Crime: Mean, median and estimated total loss by type of crime

Type of victimisation	Most serious incident only[a]		All incidents
	Mean loss US$	Median loss US$	Estimated total loss, US$1000
Theft by employees	18 554	1538	1371
Vehicle theft	17 700	1230	680
Burglary	3354	1230	559
Theft by outsiders	2096	246	357
Theft from vehicle	8680	861	290
Other offences	6400	1845	272
Robbery	2764	923	115
Vandalism	455	369	40
Theft by customers	400	256	33
Assault	1538	1538	21
All offences	5680	640	3738

Notes: [a] Based on respondents who reported a loss—that is, excluding N = 74 who did not know or refused to answer, and N = 27 who reported no monetary loss; [b] estimates do not include losses due to repeat victimisation—that is, businesses victimised in several incidents by the same offence type.

Across the four cities, 38.4 per cent of the surveyed businesses were insured against damages and loss caused by crime. Perhaps reflecting their knowledge of the higher crime risk in their city, Shenzhen businesses were more likely to take out insurance than those in other cities: 45.6 per cent were insured compared with 38.8 per cent in Shanghai, 36 per cent in Hong Kong and 34.6 per cent in Xi'an (the difference was statistically significant). These figures are consistent with worldwide rates reported by PriceWaterhouseCoopers (PWC 2007b), which found that globally an average of 39 per cent of companies had taken out insurance to cover economic crime losses (the figure for Hong Kong was 38 per cent). The likelihood of being insured increased with the size of the business: less than one-third of businesses with five or fewer employees were insured, but 47 per cent of those with 50–250 employees and half those with more than 250 employees ($p < 0.001$). Small food retailers were the least likely to have insurance. Of the 328 businesses that were victimised by common crimes, just less than half were insured in Shenzhen (43.4 per cent), with smaller proportions in the other cities: 37.9 per cent in Hong Kong, 36.5 per cent in Xi'an and 29.1 per cent in Shanghai.

Comparison with Other Victimisation Surveys

Several surveys of crime against business using a comparable instrument to the ICBS have been conducted in Europe and Africa, which gives us an opportunity to compare the level of victimisation reported in China with that of other countries. We focus on three surveys: the Western Europe ICBS conducted in 1993–94 in six Western European countries and Australia (van Dijk and Terlouw 1996); the Central Eastern Europe ICBS conducted in 1999 in nine countries (Alvazzi del Frate 2004); and the Crime and Corruption Business Survey (CCBS) conducted in 2006 in Nigeria (Nigerian NBS 2009, 2010). In 2006, the University of Hong Kong also conducted the UNICVS for the first time in Hong Kong (Broadhurst et al. 2010). The UNICVS was concerned with the victimisation of individuals but allows us to compare the prevalence of victimisation against business with that of victimisation against individuals for conventional crimes. We use the results from Hong Kong and international averages from the fifth sweep of the UNICVS 2004–05 (van Dijk et al. 2007) to compare individual risks of crime with those of businesses.

Although no overall figure of the prevalence of common crime was reported in the Western Europe ICBS, the rate for a single crime—theft by customers, outsiders and employees—reported in the Western Europe ICBS (60 per cent) was nearly nine times higher than the overall rate of common crime in the China ICBS (6.7 per cent). Rates of victimisation by type of crime were higher in Western Europe than in China, ranging between 3.6 times higher for robbery (3.3 per cent and 0.6 per cent respectively) to 16 times higher for theft from a vehicle (13 per cent and 0.8 per cent respectively) (Figure 4.3). Large differences were present for theft by customers, outsiders and employees (combined) and burglary. The Western Europe survey found that 60 per cent of companies had been the victims of theft by any person compared with about 5 per cent in China; and that nearly 29 per cent had been burgled compared with 4 per cent in China. The Western Europe ICBS sample comprised nearly 70 per cent of retail businesses, which would inflate the rate of theft by customers. Violent crime was also more prevalent in Western Europe: 8.5 per cent of respondents mentioned an assault and 3.3 per cent a robbery, whereas less than 1 per cent of Chinese respondents had been victimised by either of these crimes.

Figure 4.3 One-Year Prevalence of Common Crime, China ICBS (2004–05) and Western Europe ICBS (1993–94)

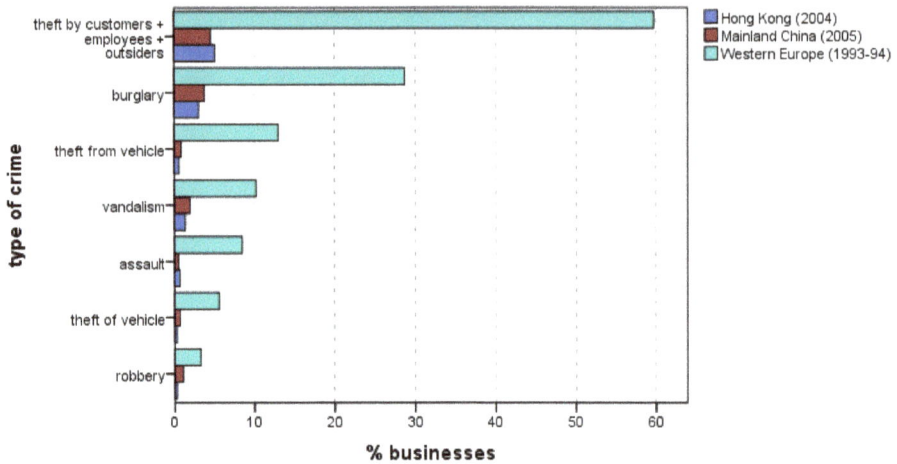

The Western Europe ICBS examined factors linked to victimisation only in relation to retail and found little differences in victimisation between businesses trading in various goods. Businesses with a larger floor surface were more at risk of theft by customers than those with a smaller floor surface. Western European companies were often victimised repeatedly by the same offence, particularly theft. In addition, businesses were much more likely than households to be the victims of burglary and theft of a vehicle.

Rates of overall victimisation by common crime were also much lower in China than in Eastern Europe. The Eastern Europe ICBS found that on average 27 per cent of businesses were the victims of at least one of nine conventional crimes[2]—that is, four times the rate reported in Chinese cities (6.2 per cent; Figure 4.4). There were, however, variations by city: the lowest rate of 7 per cent—which is close to that of the China ICBS at 6.1 per cent—was observed in Zagreb; the highest, 42 per cent, was in Vilnius and Budapest. Looking at individual types of crime, every city in the Eastern Europe ICBS consistently recorded higher rates than the Chinese cities, ranging from more than twice the rate of assault to eight times the rate of theft from a vehicle. Across the cities surveyed in the Eastern Europe ICBS, larger businesses also reported higher rates of victimisation for all types of crime than smaller businesses.

2   The nine crimes include: burglary, vandalism, theft of a vehicle, theft from vehicle, theft by customers, theft by employees, theft by outsiders, robbery and assault. The category 'other unspecified offences' is not included in the count.

Figure 4.4 One-Year Prevalence of Common Crime, China ICBS (2004–05) and Central Eastern Europe ICBS (1999)

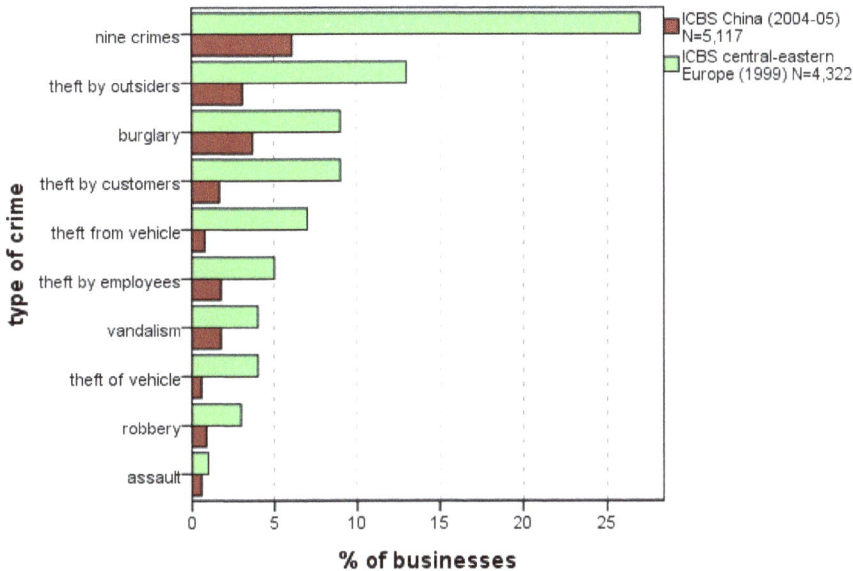

It is more difficult to compare the overall rate of victimisation in the China ICBS with the Nigerian CCBS because questions on theft by employees and theft by outsiders also included fraud. For the types of crime that are comparable, the Nigerian CCBS found rates of victimisation ranging from 1.5 times higher than the ICBS for theft of vehicles (7 per cent in the Nigerian CCBS versus 4 per cent in the China ICBS) to 14 times higher for assault and threats (14 per cent in the CCBS versus 1 per cent in the ICBS).

Some types of common crimes are directly comparable with the Hong Kong UNICVS (Table 4.8). In Hong Kong, businesses were at much greater risk of burglary than households (3.1 per cent and 0.6 per cent respectively), but less likely to be the victims of assault (0.7 per cent versus 1.3 per cent). While no car theft was reported in the Hong Kong UNICVS in 2005, 0.2 per cent of business respondents mentioned the theft of a vehicle. Car ownership rates are low in Hong Kong, but companies would be more likely to use vehicles for business than individuals, which can explain the higher rate of vehicle theft in the ICBS. The Eastern Europe ICBS found that burglary and theft of a vehicle were more likely to target business premises than households. Rates of theft from a vehicle and robbery were comparable in the Hong Kong UNICVS and the ICBS.

For the five crimes considered here—burglary, theft of, and from a vehicle, robbery, and assault—average ICBS rates for mainland cities were higher than those reported in the 2005 Hong Kong UNICVS. The prevalence of business victimisation in mainland cities, however, was lower than the international average for household and personal victimisation, apart from burglary, which was similar.

Table 4.8 One-Year Prevalence of Selected Common Crimes, Hong Kong UNICVS and China ICBS (per cent)

Type of crime victimisation	UNICVS		ICBS	
	Average main cities one year[a]	Hong Kong 2005	Hong Kong 2004	Average mainland cities 2005
Burglary	3.2	0.6	3.1	3.9
Theft of vehicle	1.3	0.0	0.2	0.8
Theft from vehicle	4.4	0.5	0.6	1.0
Robbery	2.4	0.4	0.3	1.2
Assault	4.0	1.3	0.7	0.6

Sources: International UNICVS (van Dijk et al. 2007:Appendix 9, Table 2); Hong Kong UNICVS (Broadhurst et al. 2010).

Note: [a] Surveys were conducted in 33 capital cities from developed and developing countries in 2004–05.

This chapter examined the prevalence of common crimes against business in Hong Kong and China. At least one common crime was reported by 343 businesses (6.7 per cent) in our sample and most of them were victims of more than one crime. Apart from theft by customers, which was more prevalent in Hong Kong than in the other cities, Shenzhen recorded higher rates of common crime, particularly robbery, vandalism and theft by outsiders and employees. Hong Kong and mainland companies with cross-border operations were at higher risk of victimisation, but this was in part mediated by the size of the business, since larger businesses were more likely to be victimised and they were also those more likely to operate across borders.

Comparisons with the Western Europe and Eastern Europe ICBSs indicated that rates of common crime against business in China (both Hong Kong and the mainland) were lower than in a number of other industrialised and transitional countries; the overall rate of common crime was four times lower than the rate found in the Eastern Europe ICBS, and nine times lower than that found in the Western Europe ICBS. Comparison with the UNICVS, however, indicates that, as in most other countries, in China, businesses were more at risk of burglary than households. In the next chapter, we focus on less-conventional crimes including bribery and extortion, and again compare results in China with those from other surveys.

5. Fraud, Bribery, Extortion and Other Crimes against Business

We use the term 'non-conventional' to denote crimes that are more likely to be directed primarily at businesses because of their size, resources and the types of activity they perform. The ICBS examined fraud by employees and outsiders, Internet fraud, bribery, extortion and intimidation, infringements of intellectual property (IP) (counterfeiting) and computer-related victimisation. A single question was asked in relation to bribery and corruption: 'did anyone try to bribe you, other managers, your employees, or obtain bribes from the company in relation to its activities?' That is, the question referred to bribes received by employees presumably at the expense of the business as well as times when members of the company were asked to pay bribes to an outsider to receive services. Responses to the follow-up questions on bribery suggest that respondents reported incidents only when bribes were requested from the company. Extortion refers to incidents of intimidation and requests for protection money, and included: 'for example, extorting money from your company, threatening and intimidating managers and/or employees, threatening product contamination, etc.' Infringement of IP was defined as *the use by others without your permission of patents, trademarks, copyrights, designs owned by your company*, and included software copyright violation.[1] Computer-related victimisation consists of a broad range of incidents such as attacks by a virus or malicious software, unsolicited emails and communication, and email threats. Because some of these are extremely common—for example, virus attacks or unsolicited emails—we focus mainly on Internet-related fraud when purchasing items or banking.

Rates of Victimisation by City

Fraud was the most frequently reported type of non-conventional crime victimisation (13.4 per cent)[2] (Table 5.1). Eight per cent of businesses had been defrauded by outsiders, such as clients, suppliers or other businesses. Just over 4 per cent (4.6 per cent) of businesses were victims of fraud while purchasing goods or doing banking online, and 3.7 per cent were defrauded by employees.

---

1   The survey asked two separate questions: one on IP infringement and one on software copyright violation. These two items cover acts such as the counterfeiting of goods and products including software as well as the distribution of illegal copies, and belong to a similar domain; therefore, we combine the results of the two questions under the heading 'IP and software copyright violation'.
2   This could reflect the fact that three questions were asked about fraud, but only one question about the other types of crime.

Incidents of bribery were mentioned by about 6 per cent of respondents, and the same proportion reported incidents of IP and software copyright infringement. Extortion and intimidation occurred less frequently (2.3 per cent).

Different victimisation patterns were apparent in Hong Kong and the mainland (Figure 5.1). While overall levels of fraud were similar, Hong Kong companies were more prone to fraud by outsiders than their mainland counterparts (9.9 per cent versus 6.9 per cent, $p < 0.001$), and mainland businesses appeared more at risk of Internet fraud (5.3 per cent) than Hong Kong businesses (2.3 per cent, $p < 0.001$). Fraud by employees was the least frequent type of fraud, with similar prevalence reported in Hong Kong and the mainland (3.6–3.8 per cent). Looking at bribery and extortion, we see a reverse pattern between Hong Kong and the mainland. The rate of bribery was about three times higher in the mainland (8 per cent) than in Hong Kong (2.7 per cent, $p < 0.001$). On the other hand, extortion and intimidation were much more prevalent in Hong Kong (3.1 per cent) than in the mainland (1.8 per cent, $p < 0.01$).

Table 5.1 One-Year Prevalence of Victimisation by Non-Conventional Crime by City (per cent)

Type of crime victimisation[a]	Hong Kong N = 1817	Shanghai N = 1110	Shenzhen N = 1112	Xi'an N = 1078	Total N = 5117
All fraud[b]	13.5	10.5††	15.4*	14.1	13.4
Fraud by outsiders	9.9***	4.9†††	8.2	7.7	8.0
Bribery	2.7	6.5	8.5***	9.0***	6.1
IP and software copyright violation	3.5	5.9	9.1***	7.6*	6.1
Internet-related fraud[c]	2.3†††	4.3	6.3**	6.4**	4.6
Fraud by employees	3.8	3.1	4.2	3.4	3.7
Extortion/intimidation	3.1**	0.9††	3.1**	1.3	2.3

* $p < 0.05$ ** $p < 0.01$ *** $p < 0.001$, rate is significantly higher

†† $p < 0.01$ ††† $p < 0.001$, rate is significantly lower

Notes: [a] Rates refer to the 12-month period from 1 January to 31 December 2004 for Hong Kong, and 1 January to 31 December 2005 for Shanghai, Shenzhen and Xi'an; [b] includes fraud by employees, outsiders and Internet-related fraud; [c] includes fraud while purchasing or banking online; percentages are based on N = 3818 respondents who used the Internet for business purposes: Hong Kong, N = 1102, Shanghai, N = 954, Shenzhen, N = 959, Xi'an, N = 803.

Figure 5.1 Prevalence of Non-Conventional Crime, Hong Kong (2004) and Mainland (2005)

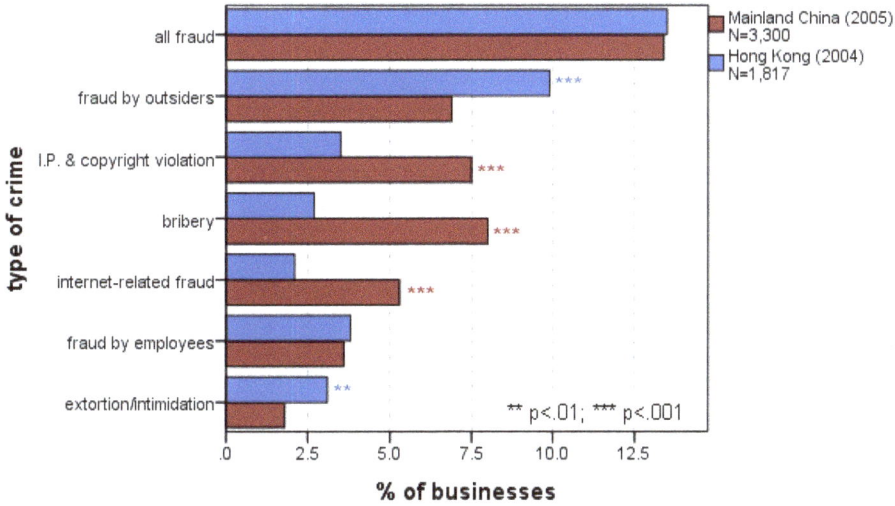

For all non-conventional crimes, Shanghai businesses reported lower victimisation rates than those in Shenzhen or Xi'an. Shanghai's overall rate of fraud was the lowest of the four cities (10.5 per cent versus 13.5–15.4 per cent, $p < 0.01$), as was the rate of fraud by outsiders (4.9 per cent versus 7.7–9.9 per cent, $p < 0.001$). Internet-related fraud was more frequent in Shanghai than in Hong Kong, but not as prevalent as in Shenzhen or Xi'an. Unlike the other cities, Shenzhen had high levels of both bribery and extortion/intimidation (8.5 per cent and 3.1 per cent respectively). Shenzhen businesses experienced incidents of extortion/intimidation at a rate similar to Hong Kong businesses, but about three times that of Shanghai (0.9 per cent) and Xi'an (1.3 per cent). For all other types of crime, Shenzhen and Xi'an recorded comparable rates of victimisation.

Fraud against Business

Three types of fraud were examined in the ICBS: fraud by employees, fraud by outsiders and Internet-related fraud. First, we look at the likelihood of victimisation by business sector, then depending on the size of the business and the location. Finally, we discuss the monetary losses that were associated with the fraud.

Rates of Fraud by Business Sector

The wholesaling and trading sector reported a significantly higher overall level of fraud than other sectors, but this was due only to the higher prevalence of fraud by outsiders (10.2 per cent) in this sector (Table 5.2). Retailers also reported a higher rate of fraud by outsiders (9.3 per cent) than the manufacturing and the financial and professional services sectors. The retail sector reported a slightly lower rate of Internet-related fraud (3.7 per cent) than other sectors (4.3–5.4 per cent).

Table 5.2 Fraud by Business Sector across Four Cities, 2004–05 (per cent)

Type of crime victimisation	Manufacturing N = 1726	Retail N = 1073	Wholesale/trade N = 852	Financial & professional services N = 1053	Other sectors N = 413	Total N = 5117
All fraud[a]	13.9	13.4	16.0*	11.5	11.1	13.4
Fraud by outsiders	7.6	9.3*	10.2**	6.4	5.3	8.0
Internet-related fraud[b]	5.4	3.7	4.6	4.3	4.3	4.6
Fraud by employees	3.8	3.6	3.6	3.6	3.4	3.7

* $p < 0.05$ ** $p < 0.01$

Notes: [a] Includes fraud by employees, by outsiders and Internet-related; [b] includes fraud while purchasing or banking online; percentages are based on N = 3818 respondents who used the Internet for business purposes.

Appendix H (Table H.1) presents the overall rates of fraud by city and business sector. We saw above that across all four cities fraud was more prevalent in the wholesale and trading sector than in other sectors. This was particularly strong in Xi'an and, to a lesser extent, in Shenzhen, but not in Hong Kong, where levels of fraud were similar across the manufacturing, retail and wholesale sectors, or in Shanghai, where fraud was less prevalent in the wholesale sector. In Xi'an, nearly 21 per cent of respondents in the wholesale and trading sector said their company had been the victim of fraud (compared with 8.2–16 per cent in the other sectors, $p < 0.01$), and this was related to a very high prevalence of fraud by outsiders in the wholesaling sector (13.8 per cent compared with 2.8–7.4 per cent in the other sectors, $p < 0.001$). In Shenzhen, the difference between sectors was not statistically significant, although the prevalence of fraud was higher in the wholesaling and trading sector (19.7 per cent versus 12–15.5 per cent).

Rates of Fraud by Business Size

The overall level of fraud was comparable across businesses regardless of size (13.2–14.3 per cent), but the size of the company was relevant for specific types of fraud (Table 5.3). Small businesses of 10 or less employees were significantly more prone to fraud by outsiders than larger companies (9.6 per cent compared with 7.6 per cent for medium and 6.8 per cent for medium-large firms); however, the largest businesses, with more than 250 employees, seemed to be somewhat protected from fraud by outsiders (4.4 per cent were victimised). While fraud by outsiders was prevalent against small businesses, fraud by employees was far less frequent against small businesses of 10 or less employees than larger ones (2.7 per cent versus 4.1–5.1 per cent). This is consistent with the lower rate of theft by employees recorded in small businesses and again could be associated with the likelihood that these small businesses are often run by family members. The largest businesses were also most at risk of Internet-related fraud (7.7 per cent versus 3.1 per cent for small companies). One explanation is that large companies often have networks of interconnected computers, which increases the risk of cyber victimisation.

Table 5.3 Fraud by Business Size across Four Cities, 2004–05 (per cent)

Type of crime victimisation	Small[a] N = 2107	Medium[a] N = 1430	Medium-large[a] N = 917	Large[a] N = 413	Total N = 4867
All fraud[b]	13.2	14.3	13.2	14.3	13.6
Fraud by outsiders	9.6***	7.6	6.8	4.4††	8.1
Internet-related fraud[c]	3.1	5.3	4.7	7.7**	4.6
Fraud by employees	2.7††	4.7	4.1	5.1	3.8

** $p < 0.01$ *** $p < 0.001$, rate is significantly higher

†† $p < 0.01$, rate is significantly lower

Notes: [a] Number of employees (part and full-time): small, 1–10, medium, 11–49, medium-large, 50–250, large, 251 or more; [b] includes fraud by employees, outsiders and Internet-related; [c] includes fraud while purchasing and banking online; percentages are based on N = 3635 respondents who used the Internet for business purposes.

Although the overall prevalence of fraud in Hong Kong (13.5 per cent) was comparable with that of the mainland cities (13.4 per cent), including for fraud by employees (3.8 per cent versus 3.6 per cent), there was a large difference in rates of fraud depending on the size of the company. In Hong Kong, rates of fraud ranged between 10.6 and 14 per cent in businesses with up to 250 employees; however, in large businesses (more than 250 employees), the rate of fraud jumped to 31.6 per cent (Appendix H, Table H.2). This figure is significantly higher than for both smaller companies within Hong Kong and companies of similar size in the mainland and is due to the much higher rate of fraud by employees in large Hong Kong businesses (21.1 per cent compared with an average of 3.6 per cent for businesses with fewer than 250 employees). Businesses with more than 250 employees in the mainland also recorded much lower rates of fraud by employees than those in Hong Kong (5.5 per cent in Shanghai, 4.7 per cent in Shenzhen, and 2.1 per cent in Xi'an).

Rates of Fraud by Location of Premises

Table 5.4 presents rates of fraud victimisation depending on the number and location of business premises. For businesses located in Hong Kong, whether they had premises in the mainland or not made little difference to their likelihood of fraud victimisation; however, mainland businesses with additional premises in Hong Kong had significantly higher rates of all types of fraud combined (18.2 per cent), as well as Internet-related fraud (8.3 per cent) and fraud by employees (6.3 per cent), than their mainland counterparts. Interestingly, Hong Kong businesses without premises in the mainland had a higher rate of fraud by outsiders (10.1 per cent) than those with premises in the mainland (8.9 per cent) but this was not statistically significant. This is related to the fact that smaller businesses were more at risk of fraud by outsiders, unlike other kinds of fraud; there were more small businesses in Hong Kong, and smaller businesses were also less likely to have additional premises.

Again, the differential risk of victimisation is not due to the location of the premises *per se*, but to the size of the business. Regardless of the location of additional premises, businesses that operated from multiple premises tended to be larger and were at greater risk of fraud victimisation: multiple-premises companies, regardless of location, were significantly more likely to be victimised by fraud (16.4 per cent) than single-premises businesses (11.7 per cent, $p <$ 0.001). For fraud by employees, differences in rates of victimisation are also explained by the size of the business: the larger the business, particularly in manufacturing and retail, the greater the risk of employee fraud. General and specific locations of premises had little impact; this is an offence committed 'from inside'.

Table 5.4 Fraud by Location of Business Premises, 2004–05 (per cent)

| | Location of surveyed premises | | | |
| | Hong Kong (2004) | | Mainland (2005) | |
Type ofvictimisation	No premises in mainland N = 1456	Premises in mainland N = 361	No premises in HK N = 2889	Premises in HK N = 411
All fraud[a]	13.5	13.6	12.7	18.2*
Fraud by outsiders	10.1	8.9	6.7	8.3
Internet-related fraud[b]	2.3	2.3	5.2	8.3***
Fraud by employees	3.7	4.2	3.2	6.3*

$^* p < 0.05$ $^{***} p < 0.001$

Notes: [a] Includes fraud by employees, outsiders and Internet-related; [b] includes fraud while purchasing or banking online; percentages are based on N = 3818 respondents who used the Internet for business purposes.

Incidence and Monetary Loss Due to Fraud

The overwhelming majority of businesses that were victims of fraud by employees reported less than five incidents by different perpetrators in the past year (Table 5.5). Although the number of incidents of fraud by outsiders was slightly larger than fraud by employees, across the four cities about 90 per cent of respondents said they were victims of fewer than five incidents during 2005.

Overall, our sample lost an estimated US$15.07 million to fraud. The mean monetary loss due to all incidents of fraud by employees varied greatly between the cities, but the median loss was comparable (about US$1100–1300). In all cities except Shenzhen, about 30 per cent of victimised businesses suffered a loss of more than US$5000, with a smaller proportion in Shenzhen (20 per cent). Overall, incidents of fraud by employees cost our respondents more than US$7.5 million, and nearly 80 per cent of that amount was lost in Hong Kong.

The monetary loss resulting from outsider fraud was highest in Shanghai, where half the businesses victimised reported a loss of more than US$5000. The median loss in Shenzhen was US$3690, but in Hong Kong and Xi'an, it was comparable with the loss caused by employee fraud (US$1280 and $1230 respectively). The total loss due to fraud by outsiders (US$7.5 million) was comparable with that lost through employee fraud, but losses were more equally spread across the four cities. The largest total loss occurred in Shanghai (US$2.5 million) and the smallest in Xi'an (US$1.2 million).

Lesser amounts of money were lost due to Internet-related fraud than to other types of fraud, and the majority of victimised businesses (77.8 per cent) did not actually lose any money. For those who did, losses were relatively minor, with the median loss ranging from US$37 in Xi'an to US$123 in Shanghai. Compared with the two other types of fraud, Internet-related fraud incurred relatively smaller losses, particularly in Hong Kong, where we estimated businesses lost a total of less than US$400. Most of the money stolen through Internet fraud was in Shenzhen, where companies lost nearly US$45 000.

Table 5.5 Fraud: Number of incidents and monetary loss

	Hong Kong	Shanghai	Shenzhen	Xi'an	Total
FRAUD BY EMPLOYEES	N = 69	N = 34	N = 47	N = 37	N = 187
N incidents					
Less than 5 (%)	97.0	100.0	95.0	98.0	97.0
Monetary loss[a, b]					
Mean in US$	85 673	10 733	20 872	8192	42 828
Median in US$	1280	1230	1107	1230	1230
Percentage loss more than US$5000	31.0	29.6	20.0	29.2	27.9
Estimated total loss US$1000[c]	5912	365	981	303	7561
FRAUD BY OUTSIDERS	N = 179	N = 54	N = 91	N = 83	N = 407
N incidents					
Less than 5 (%)	89.0	89.6	96.3	88.5	90.5
Monetary loss[a, d]					
Mean in US$	11 520	46 293	18 559	14 518	17 917
Median in US$	1280	5535	3690	1230	1280
Percentage loss more than US$5000	28.2	50.0	42.3	26.9	33.3
Estimated total loss, US$1000[c]	2062	2500	1689	1205	7456
INTERNET FRAUD	N = 25	N = 41	N = 60	N = 51	N = 177
Monetary loss[a]					
No monetary loss (%)	80.0	68.3	83.0	78.4	77.8
Of those with a loss (N = 39)					
Mean in US$	77	254	4407	273	1301
Median in US$	64	123	89	37	64
Percentage loss more than US$5000	0.0	0.0	20.0	0.0	5.0
Estimated total loss, US$1000[c]	0.4	3	45	3	51
Estimated total loss for all types of fraud, US$1000[c]	**7974**	**2868**	**2715**	**1511**	**15 068**

Notes: [a] Loss amounts are for all incidents that occurred during the reference year; [b] mean and median are based on N = 136 respondents—that is, excluding N = 51 who did not know or refused to answer; [c] estimates are for the whole sample and were calculated by substituting the mean loss by offence for 'don't know' and refusals; [d] mean and median are based on N = 327 respondents—that is, excluding N = 80 who did not know or refused to answer.

Bribery and Extortion

Characteristics of Bribery and Corruption Incidents

Across the four cities, 6.1 per cent of respondents reported one or more incidents of bribery. Bribery was most prevalent in the manufacturing sector (7.8 per cent, $p < 0.001$) and the 'other unspecified sectors'category, but rarest in the retail sector (3.5 per cent) (Table 5.6). Incidents of bribery were increasingly prevalent as businesses became larger—for example, 3.6 per cent of small businesses (that is, with 10 or fewer employees) reported incidents of bribery compared with 10.9 per cent of those with more than 250 employees.

The rate of bribery for Hong Kong businesses with additional premises in the mainland was more than twice the rate of those without such premises (4.7 per cent and 2.2 per cent respectively, $p < 0.01$). A similar pattern emerged for mainland businesses: those with additional premises in Hong Kong experienced a significantly higher rate of bribery (11.4 per cent) than those without premises in Hong Kong (7.5 per cent) (Table 5.6). While rates of bribery were higher in the mainland than in Hong Kong, it was not their location but their size that made these businesses more vulnerable to bribery. Larger businesses were more prone to being asked for bribes, and businesses with multiple premises were generally larger than single-premises companies. The data also suggest that business activities involving engagement outside the home jurisdiction increase the risk of bribery and larger businesses might also offer more attractive targets than smaller businesses.

In Hong Kong and Xi'an, there were significant differences in the rates of bribery between the manufacturing sector and the other sectors. In Hong Kong, 5.2 per cent of manufacturers reported incidents of bribery compared with an average of 1.9 per cent in the other sectors combined; in Xi'an, 12.6 per cent of manufacturers had been victims of bribery, compared with an average of 7.4 per cent in other sectors. In Shanghai and Shenzhen, the prevalence of bribery was comparable across the sectors (Appendix H, Table H.1).

Table 5.6 Prevalence of Bribery and Extortion by: a) Business sector, b) Business size, and c) Number of premises, across four cities 2004–05 (per cent)

	A) Business sector				
Type of crime victimisation	Manufacturing N = 1726	Retail N = 1073	Wholesale/ trade N = 852	Finance & professional services N = 1053	Other sectors N = 413
Bribery/corruption	7.8***	3.5	5.0	6.3	7.3
Extortion/ intimidation	2.0	3.2**	0.7	2.8	2.9
	B) Business size[a]				
	Small N = 2107	Medium N = 1430	Medium-large N = 917	Large N = 413	
Bribery/corruption	3.6	7.6**	7.9**	10.9***	
Extortion/ intimidation	2.2	2.0	2.3	4.1**	
	C) Business premises				
	Surveyed premises in Hong Kong		Surveyed premises in mainland		
	No premises in mainland N = 1456	Premises in mainland N = 361	No premises in HK N = 2889	Premises in HK N = 411	
Bribery/corruption	2.2	4.7**	7.5	11.4**	
Extortion/ intimidation	3.3	2.8	1.7	2.9	

** $p < 0.01$ *** $p < 0.001$

Note: [a] Number of employees (part and full-time): small, 1–10, medium, 11–49, medium-large, 50–250, large, 251 or more; based on N = 4867 businesses—that is, excluding respondents who did not know the size of the workforce or refused to answer.

In Hong Kong, Shanghai and Shenzhen, the perpetrators of bribery were significantly more likely to be managers or employees from other companies than any other person (Table 5.7). Managers or employees of other firms were involved in 79.2 per cent of bribery cases in Hong Kong, 77.5 per cent of cases in Shanghai, and 62.6 per cent in Shenzhen. Bribery by officials (Legislative Council members, government, tax or court officials, and police or custom officers) was rare in Hong Kong (4.2 per cent)[3] compared with the mainland. In Xi'an, however, more than half the incidents of bribery were due to various types of officials, and 44.8 per cent to managers and employees from other companies. In all cities, members of the Legislative Council or National People's

---

3   We note, however, the higher rate in Hong Kong of respondents who did not know who the perpetrator was or refused to answer (16.6 per cent compared with rates of less than 10 per cent in the mainland).

Congress were the least frequent requestors of bribes, followed by police or custom officers, then by government, taxation or court officials. The incidence of bribery (how many times it happened in 2005) was the highest among those businesses victimised in Shenzhen (on average, just more than four times [mean 4.2 times]).

Table 5.7 Bribery and Corruption: Number of incidents and perpetrators by city (per cent)

	Hong Kong N = 49	Shanghai N = 72	Shenzhen N = 94	Xi'an N = 97	Total N = 312
N incidents					
Less than 5	94.2	90.0	89.3	100.0	93.0
5 or more	5.8	10.0	10.7	0.0	7.0
Mean N incidents[a]	2.9	3.2	4.2	3.4	3.5
Perpetrator					
Managers/employees from other companies	79.2	77.5	62.6	44.8	63.1
Government officials[b]	2.1	14.1	15.4	30.2	17.6
Police or customs officers	2.1	2.8	9.9	14.6	8.5
Legislative Council member (HK)/deputy to NPC (mainland)[c]	0.0	0.0	2.2	3.1	1.6
Don't know/refusal	16.6	5.6	9.9	7.3	9.2

Notes: [a] In 2004 for Hong Kong and 2005 for the mainland cities; [b] includes government, taxation and court officials; [c] NPC = National People's Congress.

Characteristics of Extortion and Intimidation Incidents

Extortion and intimidation were less prevalent than bribery, with 2.3 per cent of respondents mentioning one or more incidents. The retail sector recorded the highest level of victimisation (3.2 per cent, $p < 0.01$; Table 5.6). Extortion and intimidation were also relatively more frequent in the finance and professional services (2.8 per cent), and other unspecified sectors (2.9 per cent), but this was not significant. The number and location of premises other than those surveyed did not significantly impact the likelihood of extortion and intimidation, but the size of the business did, with large businesses more likely to be the victims.

Extortion and intimidation were significantly more frequent in Hong Kong and Shenzhen, where 3.1 per cent of businesses were victimised compared with 1.3 per cent in Xi'an and 0.9 per cent in Shanghai (Table 5.1). In Shenzhen, there were no statistically significant differences in rates of extortion/intimidation depending on the sector of economic activity, but in Hong Kong retailers had a higher rate of victimisation (4.8 per cent) than respondents in other sectors (2.5 per cent average). In both Hong Kong and Shenzhen, larger companies (250+ employees) were significantly more likely to become the victims of extortion and intimidation than smaller ones (10.5 per cent versus 3.1 per cent respectively in Hong Kong and 5.8 per cent versus 2.7 per cent in Shenzhen) (Appendix H, Table H.2).

In Shanghai and Shenzhen, about 10 per cent of victimised businesses experienced more than five incidents (Table 5.8). The mean number of incidents was lowest in Xi'an (2) and highest in Shenzhen (2.9). In all cities except Shenzhen, extorting money from the company was the most prevalent type of attack, ranging from 60 per cent in Shanghai to 66.7 per cent in Hong Kong, but only 31.4 per cent in Shenzhen. In contrast, in Shenzhen, threatening and intimidating managers or employees were the most frequent kinds of attack (62.9 per cent of incidents, compared with 30–36 per cent in the other cities). The higher rate of assault that was reported by Shenzhen businesses might be linked to such incidents. Across all cities, threats of product contamination were rare; nevertheless, respondents mentioned seven cases.

The modus operandi for incidents of extortion was more likely to involve walking into the premises and/or phone calls than face-to-face contact in other locations or written communication. In Hong Kong, walking into the premises was mentioned far more often than phone calls, but in Shenzhen and Xi'an phone calls were the method used the most frequently. This might be related— at least when we compare Shenzhen and Hong Kong—to the higher prevalence of intimidation in Shenzhen and of extortion of money in Hong Kong. Weapons (knives mainly) were used in only 5 per cent of these cases, and more often in Shenzhen and Xi'an than in Hong Kong (never reported by Shanghai respondents).

Table 5.8 Extortion and Intimidation: Characteristics of incidents by city (per cent)

	Hong Kong N = 57	Shanghai N = 35	Shenzhen N = 10	Xi'an N = 14	Total N = 116
N incidents					
Less than 5	94.2	90.0	89.3	100.0	93.0
5 or more	5.8	10.0	10.7	0.0	7.0
Mean N incidents[a]	2.6	2.6	2.9	2.0	2.6
What happened?[b]					
Extorting money	66.7	60.0	31.4**	64.3	55.2
Threatening people	35.1	30.0	62.9*	35.7	43.1
Threatening contamination	5.2	10.0	5.7	14.3	6.9
Modus operandi[b]					
Walk-in to premises	64.9	50.0	34.3	21.4	49.1
Telephone calls	28.1	40.0	45.7	50.0	37.1
Face-to-face in another location	12.3	0.0	20.0	28.6	15.5
Written communication	7.0	20.0	2.9	7.1	6.5
Perpetrator[b]					
Local organised crime group	49.1	30.0	40.0	28.6	42.2
Rival business	3.5	20.0	2.9	28.6	7.8
International organised crime group	1.8	0.0	2.9	0.0	1.7
Others	47.4	60.0	60.0	57.1	53.4

* $p < 0.05$ ** $p < 0.01$

Notes: [a] In 2004 for Hong Kong and 2005 for the mainland cities; [b] multiple answers were possible, total might add up to more than 100 per cent.

Local organised crime groups were blamed for the incidents by just under half of Hong Kong respondents, 40 per cent of respondents in Shenzhen and about 30 per cent in Shanghai and Xi'an. Rival businesses were blamed in 28.6 per cent of cases in Xi'an and 20 per cent in Shanghai. International organised crime groups were rarely or not at all mentioned across the four cities. We speculate that the higher prevalence of extortion in Hong Kong and intimidation in Shenzhen is linked to the involvement of triad or 'black' societies. The relatively high proportion of respondents in the two cities who blamed local organised crime confirms this hypothesis, and the direct 'walk-in' approach is a method common to triad-related gangs. The large proportion of respondents who mentioned 'others' (respondents were often uncertain about how to identify the source of threats) as perpetrators makes it difficult to analyse the responses in any greater detail.

Other Crimes against Business

Intellectual Property and Software Copyright Violation

Overall across the four cities 6.1 per cent of respondents reported IP and copyright violations (Table 5.1). Such violations were significantly more frequent in the mainland (7.5 per cent) than in Hong Kong (3.5 per cent). Shenzhen, with 9.1 per cent, and Xi'an, with 7.6 per cent, recorded particularly high rates. The retail sector had the lowest rate of IP and copyright violations (3.3 per cent) and the finance and professional services sector had the highest (8 per cent, $p < 0.01$). The strongest indicator of the likelihood of victimisation through IP and copyright violation was the size of the business, with risks increasing along with the size of the business. Only 3.9 per cent of small companies (up to 10 employees) mentioned IP violations, but 7.6 per cent of medium (11–49 employees), 8 per cent of medium-large (50–250 employees) and 9.4 per cent of large (251 or more employees) companies did. It is likely that the high rate of such violations in the finance and professional services sector is due in part to the number of designers and software creators in this category.

Monetary losses due to IP and copyright violations were not negligible, at least in Hong Kong. Overall, we estimated that our respondents lost US$1.53 million; however, most of that monetary loss occurred in Hong Kong (US$1.4 million), with much smaller amounts lost in Shenzhen (US$121 000), Xi'an (US$3500) and Shanghai (US$1900). The average amount of loss in each incident of IP and copyright violation varied greatly between the cities. In Hong Kong, each incident of IP theft cost the company about US$22 000 and in Shenzhen, US$1200. In Shanghai and Xi'an, average losses were relatively minor (US$29 and $42 respectively).

Computer-Related Victimisation

Apart from fraud through the Internet, respondents were asked about a variety of other Internet-related victimisation, including attacks on computers through malicious software, and unwanted communication. Of the 3818 business respondents who used the Internet in their business, only 6.4 per cent did not have some form of protective software (for example, firewall or anti-virus program) or did not know. Across the four cities, nearly two-thirds of respondents (63.4 per cent) reported some type of attack on their computer through malicious software such as viruses, malware or spyware, or hacking, but this was more frequent in the mainland (69.3 per cent) than in Hong Kong (48.8 per cent). In addition, 37.7 per cent had received lewd or obscene unwanted communication via emails or while online, with comparable proportions in Hong Kong and the mainland. Fewer, however, reported receiving threats of harm or physical attacks via email (2.6 per cent overall). The questions on cyber victimisation had many limitations when applied to the business context and we discuss these further in our general conclusion. Suffice to note that in 2005–06 Web 2.0 applications, especially social networking and related software and robust versions of web-interface applications (for example, Internet Explorer 7.0), were relatively novel.

Comparison with Other Business Victimisation Surveys

Few surveys are available that can be directly compared with the China ICBS. Apart from the Western Europe and Central Eastern Europe ICBSs, which used the same instrument as the China ICBS, other surveys of business victimisation have focused on different types of crime and/or have used different questionnaires. While this is a frequent problem in comparative criminology, it is not insurmountable and, in this section, we attempt to draw comparisons for at least some types of victimisation against business that have been studied in the developed and developing worlds. First, we look at the Western and Central Eastern Europe ICBSs, the surveys closest to the China ICBS; then we turn to the Nigerian CCBS, which surveyed the same types of crime as the ICBS but recorded incidents of victimisation in different ways. Finally, we draw from PriceWaterhouseCooper's Global Economic Crime Survey to assess whether mainland China, as an emerging market, differs from other emerging markets in terms of crime and corruption.

Western and Central Eastern Europe ICBSs

Again, looking only at Australia and six countries in Western Europe, we find that the rate of fraud by employees in our Chinese cities (3.7 per cent) was higher than the average in Western countries (2.1 per cent); there were variations between countries, which ranged from a low of 1.3 per cent in France and Switzerland to 3.1 per cent in Germany. Fraud by outsiders, however, seemed much less frequent in China (8 per cent) than in Europe, where, on average, 23.1 per cent of companies reported at least one incident of victimisation. The Netherlands recorded the lowest rate, of 12.6 per cent, and France the highest, with 42.3 per cent (van Dijk and Terlouw 1996).

The Western Europe ICBS had a single measure—called corruption—which combined bribery and extortion. Using the same measure in the China ICBS, we see from Figure 5.2 that corruption, as defined in the Western Europe ICBS, was more frequent in mainland cities (8.4 per cent) than in Western Europe (2.6 per cent and ranging between 1.5 per cent in Italy and 4.8 per cent in France). The way in which data were presented precludes a more detailed comparison; however, we suspect that the prevalence of bribery in Western Europe was comparable with that of Hong Kong (2.7 per cent) but that extortion was more frequent in Hong Kong than in Western Europe.

Figure 5.2 One-Year Prevalence of Fraud and Corruption: China ICBS (2004–05) and Western Europe ICBS (1993–94)

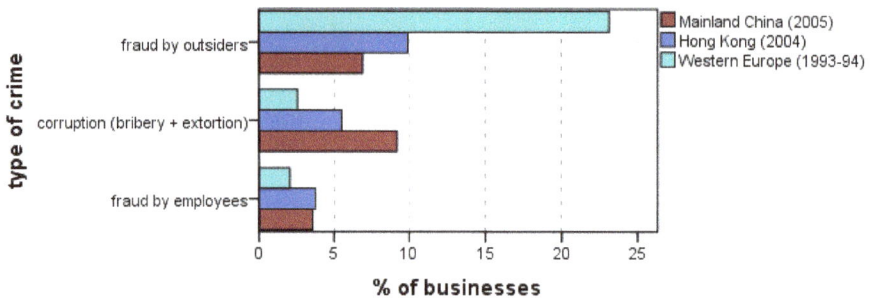

On average, rates of fraud by outsiders, fraud by employees and bribery were three times higher in the 1999 Central Eastern Europe ICBS than in the China ICBS, and the rate of extortion was four times higher. Zagreb reported the lowest prevalence of fraud by employees (4 per cent)—similar to that of China (3.7 per cent). Of all the Eastern European cities, Tirana had the lowest prevalence of fraud by outsiders (16 per cent), which was nevertheless double that of China (8 per cent). Considering only the mainland, we see that all rates on Figure 5.3 were lower in the mainland than in Eastern Europe. Across the Eastern European cities that were surveyed, fraud victimisation was highest in the wholesale sector—a finding consistent with the China ICBS. It is difficult to compare the prevalence of bribery in Eastern European cities with that of China because the Eastern Europe ICBS included two questions (one dealing with personal experience of being offered a bribe, and one dealing with requests or demands for bribes from the company) while the China ICBS included only one general question. Nine per cent of Eastern European respondents mentioned having been offered bribes, ranging from 5 per cent in Sofia and Vilnius to 17 per cent in Minsk. Larger proportions of respondents said that someone had tried to obtain bribes from the company (19 per cent on average, ranging from 4 per cent in Tirana to 46 per cent in Minsk). Hong Kong businesses reported lower rates of bribery in the ICBS (2.7 per cent) than any Eastern European city, and the average level of bribery reported in the mainland was half that reported in the Eastern Europe ICBS. The rate of extortion was higher in Hong Kong than in the mainland, but it was only one-third of the average across Eastern European cities.

Figure 5.3 One-Year Prevalence of Fraud, Bribery and Extortion: China ICBS (2004–05) and Central Eastern Europe ICBS (1999)

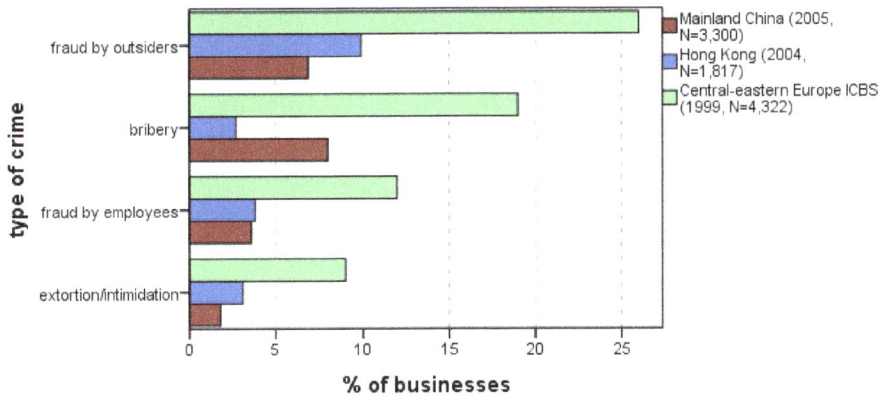

Nigerian Crime and Corruption Business Survey

Crimes were counted in slightly different ways in the Nigerian Crime and Corruption Business Survey (CCBS) and the China ICBS. It is, however, still possible to conduct meaningful comparisons between the two surveys by recalculating victimisation rates in the ICBS in a way that matches more closely that of the Nigerian CCBS. To compare rates of theft and fraud in the two surveys, we combined the ICBS theft and fraud by employees, and theft and fraud by outsiders.[4] Nigerian businesses reported both types of crime more frequently than Chinese businesses (Figure 5.4). The prevalence of theft and fraud by employees was particularly high in Nigeria—about four times that of China (21.6 per cent versus 5 per cent).

---

4   We include in the combined rate all businesses that have been the victims of *at least one* incident of theft or fraud. When businesses have been victims of both theft and fraud, we count this as one incident of victimisation.

For bribery and corruption, the Nigerian CCBS examined only requests for bribes by public officials and government employees, while the China ICBS included those by managers or employees of other businesses. The CCBS recorded as bribery the number of times a bribe was actually paid by a business in order to get a service, not, like in the ICBS, the number of times that a bribe was requested but not necessarily paid. Therefore, in the comparison between the two surveys, it is likely that the level of corruption in Nigeria is underestimated compared with China. The prevalence of bribery in Shenzhen and Xi'an (8.5 per cent and 9 per cent respectively) as counted in the ICBS was similar to that recorded in the Nigerian CCBS (9.4 per cent), but lower in Shanghai (6.5 per cent) and of course Hong Kong (2.7 per cent). We saw, however, in Table 5.7 that across the four Chinese cities about 63 per cent of incidents of bribery involved members of other businesses rather than officials. Counting, therefore, only requests for bribes made by government officials, including legislators, police and customs officers, we find that the level of bribery reduces to 2.2 per cent overall: 0.6 per cent in Hong Kong and 3.1 per cent in the mainland—1.4 per cent in Shanghai, 3.1 per cent in Shenzhen, and 4.9 per cent in Xi'an; that is, an average in the mainland less than half that of Nigeria.

Figure 5.4 One-Year Prevalence of Theft/Fraud, Bribery and Extortion: China ICBS (2004–05) and Nigeria CCBS (2006)

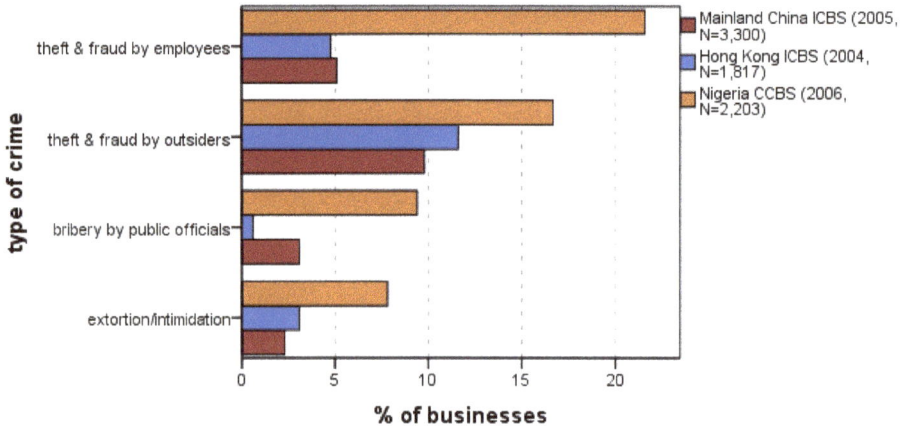

Unlike in China, in Nigeria, payments of bribes were more likely to be made by small (fewer than 50 employees) rather than large businesses, and the main reason a bribe was paid was to receive better treatment. Many businesses said they had to pay bribes more than once, to different public officials—for example, 63 per cent of bribes were paid to police officers, the most frequently cited public officials to receive bribes; 26 per cent were paid to customs officers, and 15 per cent to various elected officials. In China, the pattern of corruption was different: of the 113 incidents of bribe requests by public officials, nearly half were made by various government officials (47.8 per cent), 29.2 per cent by elected officers (most of them in the mainland), and 23 per cent by police or customs officers. In the Nigerian survey, a large proportion of the bribes were paid in relation to traffic offences and to speed up or alter the results of police investigations, which accounts for the large proportion of bribes paid to police officers. The ICBS did not ask the purpose of bribes, but the results suggest different purposes: procurement of services to the Government and possibly political advantage.

In Nigeria, 7.8 per cent of respondents mentioned that their company had been the victim of extortion or intimidation—a rate more than double that of the ICBS in Hong Kong (3.1 per cent) or Shenzhen (3.1 per cent), the cities with the highest rates. The modus operandi was similar in both countries, but weapons— mainly guns rather than knives—were used more often in Nigeria than in China (in 20 per cent and 5 per cent of incidents respectively).[5]

PriceWaterhouseCoopers' Global Economic Crime Survey

Three economic crimes included in the PriceWaterhouseCoopers (PWC) survey can be compared with the ICBS, although definitions do not cover exactly the same criminal acts: asset misappropriation, corruption and bribery (including extortion), and IP infringement. As we have seen before, PWC's study defined asset misappropriation as 'the theft of company assets (including monetary assets/cash or supplies and equipment) by company directors, others in fiduciary positions or an employee for their own benefit', which also included embezzlement and deception by employees. The definition clearly includes theft and fraud/deception by employees. Although the definition did not explicitly include outsiders to the company, we understood that 'others in fiduciary positions' related to persons within or outside the company such as accountants and bankers, and, by extension, others who had a contractual relation with the company, such as suppliers, and who could exploit that relationship to their benefit. Therefore we combined the ICBS rates of theft by employees, fraud by employees and fraud by outsiders to create a variable comparable with PWC's asset misappropriation. With regards to bribery and corruption, PWC defines bribery as 'typically, the unlawful use of an official position to gain an advantage in contravention of duty. This can involve the promise of an economic benefit or other favour, the use of intimidation or blackmail. It can also refer to the

---

5   Weapons were also used often in incidents of common crime in Nigeria, ranging from 56 per cent during theft from a vehicle to 87 per cent during robbery. The ICBS did not ask about the use of weapons in the commission of common crimes.

acceptance of such inducements.' The PWC survey included racketeering and extortion in its definition of corruption and bribery. In the comparison below, we have combined the ICBS rates of bribery and extortion.

PriceWaterhouseCoopers in its 2007 report of the Global Economic Crime Survey highlights the increasing concern about crime, and particularly corruption, in emerging markets such as Brazil, India, Russia and mainland China. While the PWC survey did not interview business respondents in mainland China, we have the opportunity to examine rates of crime against business in these emerging markets as well as mainland China. Figure 5.5 presents rates of victimisation for three types of crime as reported in the Global Economic Crime Survey and the ICBS in the mainland.

Figure 5.5 One-Year Prevalence of Theft/Fraud, Bribery and Extortion and IP Infringement: Mainland China ICBS (2004–05) and PWC Global Economic Crime Survey (2007–09)

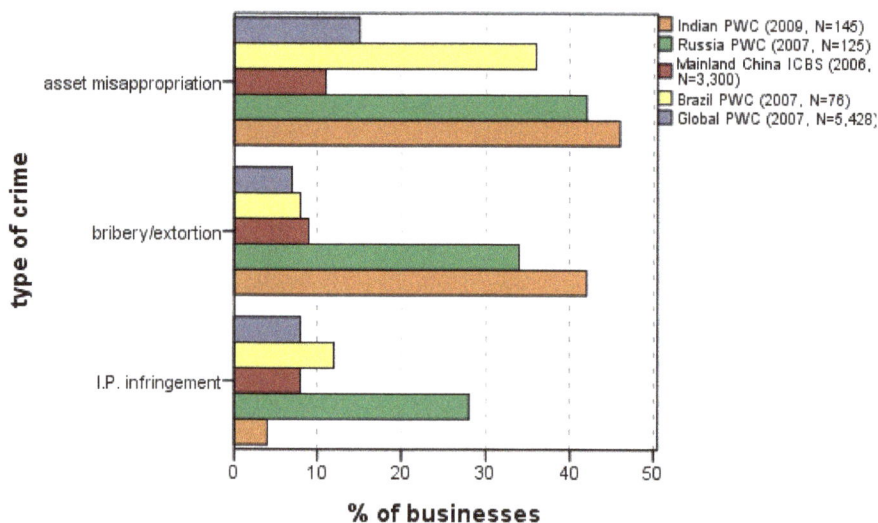

Sources: PriceWaterhouseCoopers (2007a, 2009, 2010a, 2010b).

Overall, rates of crime against business in mainland China were close to the average across all 40 countries and lower than those in other emerging markets. The prevalence of asset misappropriation was similar in Brazil, India and Russia, ranging from 36 to 46 per cent. Globally, it stood at 15 per cent—slightly higher than in mainland China (11 per cent). Bribery and extortion were most common in India, where 42 per cent of businesses said they had been victimised. In Russia, about one-third of respondents mentioned incidents of bribery/extortion against their company, but only 8 per cent in Brazil, which was close to the average global rate of 7 per cent. In China, one in 10 companies reported one or several incidents of bribery or extortion, which was higher than the global average but again lower than in Russia and India. Theft of IP is increasingly becoming a global concern and while rates of IP infringement were much higher in mainland China than in Hong Kong as well as the rate recorded in India by PWC (4 per cent), they were on par with the global PWC average (8 per cent) and just below Brazil (12 per cent). In contrast, more than one-quarter of Russian companies said they had been victims of IP infringement. While the perception was that IP infringement and corruption were high in the international business community (PWC 2007a), the prevalence of actual victimisation in China was not as high as in other emerging markets. We must remember, however, that the ICBS surveyed the experiences of companies located in China. Companies located elsewhere in the world that trade with China might have different experiences when dealing with Chinese businesses, and this was predominantly the focus of the PWC survey (2007a).

Other Crimes against Business Surveys

We only found one business victimisation survey that examined cyber victimisation: the Crime Against Business Survey conducted by the British Chambers of Commerce (2004). Of the 2788 businesses that took part in the survey, just over half (52 per cent) had been subject to virus infection and nearly three-quarters (73 per cent) said that they had received unwanted spam emails. Hacking in the business's computer system, which is potentially more damaging to business, was much less frequent and mentioned by only 6 per cent of respondents. The high rate of attacks by malicious software and unwanted email communication recorded in the ICBS is not specific to China but seems to be a global phenomenon for both businesses and individuals.

This chapter focused on business victimisation by non-conventional crime and found that various types of fraud were the most frequently mentioned and involved 13.4 per cent of businesses across the four cities. Shenzhen was significantly more at risk (15.4 per cent) of fraud than other cities, and Shanghai was the least likely to suffer although it was still reported by 10.5 per cent of its businesses. The size of companies played a less important role in varying the risks of fraud victimisation, but nevertheless larger businesses were more at risk of fraud by outsiders and Internet-related fraud. IP and copyright infringements were significantly more of a problem in Shenzhen (9.1 per cent) and Xi'an (7.6 per cent) than in Shanghai (6.5 per cent) and Hong Kong (2.7 per cent).

About 6 per cent of businesses reported at least one incident involving bribery, with Shenzhen and Xi'an reporting significantly higher risks (8.5 per cent and 9 per cent respectively) and Hong Kong the lowest (2.7 per cent). In Xi'an, officials and members of other firms were as likely to be involved in bribery, but in Hong Kong, employees of other companies were involved in four out of five reports. Incidents of extortion were more frequent in Hong Kong and Shenzhen (3.1 per cent) than in the other cities, which can be attributed to the long-established activities of triad-related groups (Hong Kong or Taiwan based) who capitalised protection on the opening up of the special economic zone in Shenzhen. Comparisons with the available data from the Western and Eastern Europea ICBSs and Nigerian CCBS showed that, as with common crime, risks were much lower in China for all of the non-conventional crimes. In addition, the emerging economies of Brazil, India and Russia had a higher prevalence of non-conventional crimes than mainland China. This chapter and the previous one have begun to examine which factors, such as economic sector and business size, are associated with the likelihood of becoming a victim of crime. In order to design and implement effective crime-prevention measures, it is important to understand the correlates of victimisation and how these work together. The next chapter attempts to answer this question.

6. Predictors of Business Victimisation

The descriptive analyses performed so far suggest that business size was a major predictor of victimisation, but that, for some crime types, business sector and city also had some effect. Because the proportions of businesses of different sizes involved in various sectors of activity differ across the four cities, it is necessary to control for sector and size effects in order to present a valid picture of city effects, if any exist. In this chapter, we try to disentangle the relative impact of four factors—business size, sector of activity, location of premises, and city—on business victimisation by conducting a series of logistic regressions. We describe first how we constructed a business size scale that takes into account the number of employees, but also other indicators. Then, we examine the most likely predictors for each type of victimisation. Finally, we summarise what the ICBS revealed about risks of victimisation against business in China.

Business Size Scale

Three of the ICBS measures were used to construct a business size scale: 1) size of workforce, 2) number of sectors of activity in which each business was operating, and 3) single versus multiple premises. Each item forming the scale was coded and scores were added up to form a business size scale that could range from three (very small) to 13 (very large). Since the three indicators used to construct the scale have been described in Chapter 3, we summarise only the coding scheme below and present details in Table 6.1.

- Size of workforce: the number of full and part-time employees was available for 95.2 per cent of the sample (N = 4867 businesses). Six categories were created—from very small to very large business.

- Number of sectors of business activity: 10 sectors of activity were recorded in the dataset—manufacturing, non-food retail, food retail, wholesale, distribution, financial services, professional services, sub-branch, head office, and other unspecified sectors. At least one main sector of activity was available for all businesses. In addition, some indicated that the company operated across several sectors (up to four) and these were recorded.

- Number of premises: data were available for 98.7 per cent of the sample. Three categories were created.

The three measures were positively and significantly correlated (Table 6.2). Missing values on the variables of size of workforce and number of premises were replaced with the means calculated by city and sector. We tried to include some measure of turnover in the business size scale, but with more than two-thirds of data missing, it was not possible to create a meaningful measure. The computed business size scale ranged from three to 13 (mean = 5.7, median = 6). Confirming previous results, the average size of businesses in Hong Kong was significantly smaller on the scale (4.35) than business size in Shanghai (6.65), Shenzhen (6.73) or Xi'an (6.11).

Table 6.1 Three Business Size Measures

	Code	N employees	Size of business	%
Size of workforce	1	1 to 5	Very small	27.0
	2	6 to 10	Small	14.8
	3	11 to 49	Medium	29.8
	4	50 to 250	Medium-large	20.3
	5	251 to 750	Large	4.9
	6	751 and more	Very large	3.2
	Code	**N sectors of activity**	**Size of business**	**%**
Sectors of activity	1	1	Small	55.3
	2	2	Medium	32.5
	3	3	Medium-large	8.6
	4	4 or more	Large	3.6
	Code	**N premises**	**Size of business**	**%**
Number of premises	1	One premise at the surveyed location	Small	63.8
	2	Other premises in HK *or* the mainland	Medium	28.9
	3	Other premises in *both* HK and mainland	Large	7.3

Table 6.2 Correlations Between Three Business Size Measures

(N = 5117)	**N sectors**	**N premises**
N employees	0.177***	0.293***
N sectors		0.157***

*** $p < 0.001$

Business Size and Victimisation

Using the business size scale, we ran a series of t-tests to examine whether there were significant differences between the average size of businesses that had been victimised and those that had not (Table 6.3). Although differences are not large, the overall pattern confirms previous analyses that for most common and non-conventional types of crime the risk of victimisation increases with the size of the business. For example, the average score on the business size scale for companies that had been victims of any common crime was 6.03, compared with 5.71 for non-victimised companies ($p < 0.001$). The largest differences were found for theft by employees (score of 6.95 for victimised versus score of 5.71 for non-victimised companies, $p < 0.001$) and Internet-related fraud (score of 6.9 for victimised versus score of 5.69 for non-victimised companies, $p < 0.001$).

Table 6.3 Business Size and Victimisation Prevalence: t-tests on business size scale by type of victimisation

	Victimised?	N	Mean size on scale	Mean difference	t-test
Any common crime	Yes	328	6.03	0.31	2.80**
	No	4789	5.71		
Burglary	Yes	186	6.34	0.63	4.31***
	No	4931	5.71		
Vandalism	Yes	94	6.35	0.63	3.06**
	No	5023	5.72		
Vehicle-related crime	Yes	57	6.51	0.79	3.02**
	No	5060	5.72		
Theft by employees	Yes	93	6.95	1.24	6.07***
	No	5024	5.71		
Theft by customers	Yes	89	5.23	-0.52	2.46*
	No	5028	5.74		
Theft by outsiders	Yes	159	6.39	0.68	4.30***
	No	4958	5.71		
Violent crime	Yes	59	6.58	0.86	3.34**
	No	5058	5.72		
Other common crimes	Yes	50	6.13	0.40	1.44
	No	5067	5.73		
All fraud	Yes	687	6.01	0.32	3.97***
	No	4430	5.69		
Fraud by employees	Yes	187	6.34	0.63	4.31***
	No	4930	5.71		
Fraud by outsiders	Yes	407	5.57	-0.18	1.80
	No	4710	5.75		
Internet-related fraud	Yes	177	6.90	1.20	8.07***
	No	4940	5.69		
Bribery	Yes	312	6.57	0.89	7.85***
	No	4805	5.68		
Extortion	Yes	116	5.88	0.15	0.81
	No	5001	5.73		
IP and copyright violation	Yes	312	6.62	0.94	8.26***
	No	4805	5.68		

$^* p < 0.05$ $^{**} p < 0.01$ $^{***} p < 0.001$

Theft by customers, however, was a notable exception to the general model. For this type of crime, the pattern is reversed and smaller businesses were more likely to be victims (score of 5.23 for victimised versus score of 5.74 for non-victimised companies, $p < 0.05$). Small and non-significant differences in average business size were found for fraud by outsiders and extortion, suggesting that small and large businesses were equally likely to be targeted.

Predictors of Business Victimisation

The previous analysis confirmed that, for many of the crimes surveyed, business size was a major predictor of victimisation; however, we saw previously that business sector, city and, to some extent, the location of the business premises also had some effects. To estimate the relative impact of these four factors in each type of crime, we conducted binary logistic regressions—a statistical technique appropriate for dichotomous dependent variables, such as the incidence of victimisation. Variables were introduced by block-wise entry in the following order: 1) business size, using the scale as a continuous variable; 2) main sector of business activity; 3) location of premises; and 4) city. To assess the impact of each of the four factors, we examine the Nagelkerke R-squared at each step (or block) of the regression analysis.[1] Table 6.4 presents the amount of variance explained by each predictor for each type of victimisation.

Although the overall model is significant for the majority of the types of crime considered (apart from vandalism and vehicle-related crime), the four predictors together do not explain a great amount of variance. The highest amount is 14.9 per cent for theft by customers and the lowest is 2.1 per cent for fraud by outsiders. In the majority of the regression analyses, size and sector account for more variance than city or location of premises, although there are some exceptions. We review below the summary diagnostics for each type of victimisation.

Predictors of Victimisation by Type of Crime

Burglary

About half of the variance explained (1.3 per cent) is accounted for by the size of the business, and another third by a small sector effect, with wholesaling and trading businesses less likely to be burgled than those in other sectors.

---

1 Nagelkerke R^2 is a pseudo-R^2, which attempts to quantify the proportion of explained variance in the logistic regression model in a way similar to the R^2 in linear regression, although the variation in a logistic regression model must be defined differently.

Vandalism

There is a small effect of business size (1 per cent of the variance explained). It is likely the effect is not strong because, as we have seen before, businesses of medium to large size were the ones most at risk of vandalism, not the very large ones.

Theft of and from Vehicle

Nearly half of the total 2.7 per cent variance explained is due to the effect of business size, with other factors contributing negligible amounts. It is probable that larger businesses owned a larger fleet of vehicles than smaller ones, and therefore were more at risk of theft of and from vehicles.

Theft by Employees

Compared with other types of crime, here, a higher amount of variance is explained by the four factors combined (7.9 per cent). Half of that variance (3.9 per cent) is due to the size of the business, with larger businesses at greater risk of theft by employees. Another 1.8 per cent and 1.1 per cent are explained by the city and the location of the premises, respectively. Businesses in Hong Kong and Shenzhen were at more risk compared with those in Shanghai and Xi'an; however, companies located in serviced buildings that provided for small business tended to be relatively better protected from theft by employees.

Theft by Customers

Nearly 15 per cent of variance (the highest proportion among all crime types) is explained by the four factors. In contrast with most of the other crimes, for theft by customers, the size of the business did not have a significant effect (0.8 per cent of variance explained, n.s.), and this is because both the smallest and the largest businesses were more likely to be targeted. Not surprisingly, more than half the variance (9 per cent) is explained by the sector of activity, with retail shops significantly more likely to become victims of theft by customers. The location of the premises adds another 2.9 per cent of variance explained, and, consistent with the previous finding, businesses located in indoor and outdoor shopping areas were more prone to theft by customers. Finally, there was a small city effect (2.2 per cent of variance explained), with Hong Kong businesses more at risk of theft by customers.

Theft by Outsiders

Business size and sector each explain 1.4 and 1.3 per cent of variance respectively; larger businesses were significantly more at risk of theft by outsiders, but wholesalers and traders were least likely to be targeted. There are no significant location or city effects, each accounting for less than 1 per cent of variance.

Robbery and Assault

For these two violent crimes, the city effect is the strongest, with 4 per cent of variance explained. The city effect accounts for more than half the total variance explained (6.6 per cent). Violent crime, particularly robbery, was significantly more prevalent in Shenzhen, but rare in Shanghai. It was also more likely to target larger businesses (1.7 per cent of variance is explained by business size).

Fraud by Employees

Less than 3 per cent of variance is explained by the four factors combined, and nearly half (1.3 per cent) by the effect of business size. Like many of the other types of crime, the risk of fraud by employees increased with the size of the business. It is likely that larger businesses offer more opportunities for fraud and reduced chances of detection among a large workforce. It is to be expected that the location of the premises does not explain much variance, because this is an offence committed 'from the inside', regardless of location.

Fraud by Outsiders

Most of the variance explained (only 2.1 per cent overall) is accounted for by two factors: city and sector. Fraud by outsiders was significantly lower in Shanghai. While wholesalers and traders were relatively protected from theft by outsiders, they were, however, particularly prone to fraud by outsiders, although sector explains only 0.7 per cent of variance. It is not surprising that traders were prone to being defrauded, since their activity is based on a large number of transactions.

Internet-Related Fraud

Again, business size (risks increasing with business size) is the main predictor of Internet fraud and accounts for 1.1 per cent of variance explained. In addition, there are some city effects, with a higher prevalence in Shenzhen and Xi'an, but a significantly lower prevalence in Hong Kong.

Bribery

More than half the variance is accounted for by business size (3 per cent of 5.8 per cent total variance explained) and another 1.8 per cent by the city, with bribery particularly prevalent in Xi'an. Retailers were the least likely to be asked for a bribe, although the effect is small (0.7 per cent of variance explained).

Extortion and Intimidation

Overall, 5.8 per cent of variance is explained by the four factors, but city (3.2 per cent) and sector (2 per cent) are the main predictors. Businesses in Hong Kong and Shenzhen were most at risk of extortion. Again, wholesalers and traders seemed somewhat protected. Size had a negligible (0.1 per cent) effect.

IP and Software Copyright Infringement

The size of the business is the strongest predictor of victimisation, accounting for 3.3 per cent of variance explained, with the larger companies more at risk. There is also a sector effect (1.4 per cent of variance explained) and a city effect (0.9 per cent of variance). Retailers had a significantly lower risk of victimisation than other sectors, particularly manufacturing and financial and professional services. Unlike manufacturers and designers, who own patents and trademarks, retailers rarely own IP rights over the products they sell. The prevalence of IP and copyright violation was lowest in Hong Kong and Shanghai. Hong Kong generally has stronger laws and enforcement mechanisms against this type of crime than the mainland.

Table 6.4 Stepwise Logistic Regression with Four Predictors of Business Victimisation: Variance explained at each step and overall

Predictor of victimisation[a]	STEP 1 Size[b]	STEP 2 Economic sector[c]		STEP 3 Location of premises[c]		STEP 4 City[c]		OVERALL MODEL	H-L (df), p[d]
Type of victimisation									
Any common crime[e]	0.4***	1.2*	Retail (+)	0.6*	All shopping areas (+)	1.7***	HK/Shenzhen (+)	3.9***	8.45 (8), p=0.39
Burglary	1.3***	1.0*	Wholesaling (-)	0.1		0.1		2.5***	6.33 (8), p=0.61
Vandalism	1.0**	0.5		0.4		0.5		2.4*	8.10 (8), p=0.42
Theft of and from vehicle	1.5*	0.5		0.5		0.2		2.7	20.10 (8), p=0.01
Theft by employees	1.9***	1.1		1.1*	Serviced buildings (-)	1.8**	HK/Shenzhen (+)	7.9***	10.90 (8), p=0.21
Theft by customers	0.8	9.0***	Retail (+)	2.9***	All shopping areas (+)	2.2**	HK (+)	14.9***	16.42 (8), p=0.04
Theft by outsiders	1.4***	1.3*	Wholesaling (-)	0.5		0.5		3.7***	6.00 (8), p=0.68
Robbery & assault	1.7**	0.6		0.3		4.0**	Shenzhen (+) Shanghai (-)	6.6***	5.87 (8), p=0.66
Other common crimes	0.4**	0.1		1.0		3.3***	HK (+)	4.8**	8.01 (8), p=0.43
Fraud by employees	1.3***	0.1		0.0		0.8*	HK (+)	2.2**	6.39 (8), p=0.60
Fraud by outsiders	0.2	0.7**	Retail/ Wholesaling (+)	0.2		1.0***	HK (+) Shanghai (-)	2.1***	14.05 (8), p=0.08
Internet-related fraud	4.4***	0.4		0.3		1.3***	HK (-)	6.4***	5.99 (8), p=0.65
Bribery	0***	0.7*	Retail (-)	0.3		1.8***	Xi'an (+)	5.8***	8.99 (8), p=0.34
Extortion	1**	2.0*	Wholesaling (-)	0.5		3.2***	HK/Shenzhen (+)	5.8***	5.46 (8), p=0.71
IP and SW copyright violation	3.3***	1.4***	Retail (-)	0.5**	Serviced buildings (-)	0.9**	HK/Shanghai (-)	6.1***	7.95 (8), p=0.44

* $p < 0.05$ ** $p < 0.01$ *** $p < 0.001$

Notes: [a] Each column indicates the amount of variance explained by the single variable entered at that step; the amount of variance explained is estimated using the Nagelkerke R^2; [b] size based on the business scale as a continuous variable; for business size, all statistically significant relationships indicate that business size and risks of victimisation are positively associated; [c] (+) indicates higher risks of victimisation; (-) lower risks of victimisation; a statistically non-significant (that is, $p \geq 0.05$) H-L test suggests that the model fits the data well; [d] the Homer–Lemeshow (H-L) statistic is a goodness-of-fit test, which assesses the fit of a logistic model against the actual outcomes; [e] includes burglary, vandalism, theft of and from vehicle, theft by employees, customers and outsiders, robbery, assault and threats, and other common crimes.

Summary of Predictors of Victimisation

One of the main findings of the China ICBS is that the size of a business is the strongest predictor of victimisation for most types of common and non-conventional crimes, apart from theft by customers, which was more prevalent in small retail businesses. Two sectors of activity were associated with the risk of victimisation: the retail sector was particularly prone to theft by customers, and the wholesaling sector was somewhat protected from crime apart from fraud by outsiders, which was more prevalent in that sector. Finally, some city effects were present: overall, victimisation was higher in Shenzhen, particularly for violent crime, but not for theft by customers. The latter was most frequent in Hong Kong, probably because of the high proportion of retailers in this city.

The general pattern between business size and victimisation suggests that targets that provided more opportunity for gain were more likely to be victimised. This pattern fits well with the principles of opportunity/situational theories: a suitable attractive target and the absence of capable guardians are parts of the alchemy of victimisation. Situational theories might have better explanatory power when approached from a victimisation rather than an offending perspective. This is because the situational crime-prevention approach merely postulates the presence of a motivated offender and does not attempt to determine the offender's specific motivation or what causes motivation to commit crime (Clarke 1997). An examination of some of the sector/victimisation prevalence patterns (Table 6.4) further supports an opportunity-theory interpretation of the data. For instance, customer theft was more prevalent against retailers than any other type of business; and it was also more prevalent against small businesses, which were less likely to have implemented anti-shoplifting measures. Theft by customers was rare in the manufacturing sector where customers were more likely to be other manufacturers, wholesalers or retailers. On the other hand, manufacturers were more likely to be the victims of burglary. They stock large amounts of goods and materials, and their premises were generally located in industrial zones away from the 'public eye' of more populated residential areas, which made them more attractive targets for burglars.

The wholesaling and trading sector was particularly at risk of fraud by outsiders, but not theft by outsiders. This pattern is also consistent with a situational theory of victimisation: wholesale and trading companies, although they were not particularly large businesses, were likely to perform a large number of business transactions, some of them complex, but rarely involving cash payments. They offer an attractive target for fraud by a third party. The businesses' sector of activity, however, only partly explains victimisation, as Shanghai had a similar proportion of wholesale businesses to the other mainland cities, yet its rate of fraud was lower. Situational factors can also account for the low rate of fraud by employees in very small businesses (up to five employees).

Businesses run by family members probably constituted a large proportion of such small businesses. Also a small business with fewer employees allows for a degree of intimacy that could offer some protection against fraud by insiders because working in close contact in such businesses would make it difficult to defraud the business without being noticed.

An interesting pattern of victimisation emerges when looking at bribery/corruption and extortion/intimidation. Broadly, the mainland cities reported a higher prevalence of bribery than Hong Kong, but businesses in Hong Kong and Shenzhen were more prone to extortion. Shenzhen presented high rates of both bribery and extortion. Bribery tended to target larger businesses predominantly in the manufacturing sector, and these were more likely to be located in mainland China, particularly Shenzhen. Bribery was also common in Xi'an, but unlike in Shanghai and Shenzhen, where people from other businesses were the ones soliciting bribes, the majority of perpetrators in Xi'an were government and public officials. This is likely linked to the characteristics of Xi'an: an inland, relatively isolated city, dominated by state-owned enterprises and where the traditional values of the Communist Party have retained more influence than in Shanghai or Shenzhen. The lower level of bribery/corruption in Hong Kong, on the other hand, is the result of the Government's anti-corruption efforts, particularly the proactive Independent Commission Against Corruption (ICAC), which has focused on both government and corporate acts of corruption. This result is consistent with the results from the 2005 Hong Kong UNICVS, in which respondents reported no incidents of corruption.

The size of the business was not significantly correlated to the prevalence of extortion/intimidation, but the sector was, with retailers and, to some extent, financial services more at risk. A sector effect is not sufficient to explain that pattern, as Shanghai had a comparable proportion of retail businesses to Hong Kong, yet, extortion was infrequent in Shanghai. The two cities of Shenzhen and Hong Kong are located close to each other. The border between Hong Kong SAR and the PRC is fairly porous, and we know the Hong Kong triads have expanded their activities in southern China. Therefore, we speculate that the higher prevalence of extortion/intimidation among Hong Kong and Shenzhen businesses is linked to the involvement of organised crime and triad societies.

7. Reporting Crime Victimisation and Satisfaction with Police Response

The willingness of crime victims (whether a business or an individual) to report crime to police or other law-enforcement agencies, such as an anti-corruption body, is in part a reflection of their confidence in these agencies. Omnibus crime victim surveys, such as the UNICVS, which measure the prevalence of crimes against households and individuals, find large variations in the willingness of victims to report a crime. Reporting 'rates' have been found to vary according to the nature and severity of the offence as well as the age and gender of the victim, and, in relevant offences, the degree of intimacy with the offender(s). The role of insurers in requiring victims to report crime before processing claims for typical offences such as vehicle theft and household burglary helps generate higher levels of reporting to police. Vehicle theft is a useful marker of the role that mandatory vehicle insurance (as in Hong Kong and China) plays and it is usually the case that more than 90 per cent of victims report having contacted police in the case of vehicle theft. Fundamental differences in the willingness to report to police are also related to the degree to which the victim feels that the matter is private and the extent that harm or injury has occurred. Businesses are often just as reluctant to report offences, especially fraud, as individuals, as this might have an impact on the reputation of the business, and they often prefer to deal with insider theft or fraud privately (Shover and Hochstetler 2006; Shury et al. 2005).

This chapter first examines the level of official reporting to police (and other agencies) for all types of business victimisation and how reporting rates vary across offence types and businesses. Then, we analyse the reason(s) why some businesses chose to report the crime incidents and others opted not to. Focusing on businesses who did report to the police, we examine how these respondents felt about the ways in which police dealt with the complaint; were they satisfied with the police response, and, if not, why. Since the analysis is based only on victims of crime (and in the case of reasons further reduced to only the most serious incident), the number of cases is often too small for a very detailed analysis in some categories. The results from these analyses are compared with similar victimisation surveys from other parts of the world. Finally, the last section looks at what respondents thought of the overall police performance in relation to business and crime prevention.

Reporting Crime Victimisation to Police

Victims of all types of common crime were asked about the most recent incident 'did you or anyone else from the company report the incident to the police?'. Victims of fraud, bribery and extortion, and computer-related crime were asked whether all, most or just some of the incidents were reported to the police. For bribery/corruption, reporting agencies included specialised anti-corruption agencies, and for computer-related crime, they included Internet service providers and system managers. First, we examine rates of reporting for all crimes and compare reporting rates in Hong Kong and the mainland, then analyse the reason(s) businesses gave for reporting or not reporting the incident.

Rates of Reporting for Crimes against Business

Common crimes committed by outsiders such as burglary, vandalism, theft of or from vehicles, theft by outsiders, robbery and assault were well reported, ranging, across the cities, between 71.7 per cent for theft by outsiders and 96.4 per cent for vehicle theft (Table 7.1).[1] In the four cities, victimised businesses appeared more reluctant to report theft by customers and employees (38.2 per cent and 52.7 per cent respectively) than other crimes, particularly in Hong Kong. Reporting rates were generally higher in mainland cities than in Hong Kong. Apart from car theft, which was virtually universally reported, and assault (75 per cent and 80 per cent of cases reported in Hong Kong and the mainland respectively), Hong Kong's rates of reporting were significantly lower (between 10 per cent and 30 per cent) than those from the mainland. Overall, reporting rates were comparable in the three mainland cities. There were two exceptions: vandalism was reported at a lower rate in Shanghai (68.8 per cent) than in Shenzhen (89.7 per cent) or Xi'an (82.6 per cent), and theft by employees was more often reported in Shenzhen (63.6 per cent) than in Shanghai (47.1 per cent) or Xi'an (33.3 per cent).

Across the four cities, non-conventional crimes were less often reported to police than conventional ones, ranging between 6.4 per cent for bribery and 32.1 per cent for fraud by employees. The level of reporting of internet-related fraud (23.2 per cent) was lower than that of other types of fraud (averaging 30 per cent). The reporting rate for bribery was particularly low irrespective of location, but

---

1   The high level of reporting to police of vehicle theft is reassuring (as to reliability) since it conforms to expectations given mandatory reporting associated with compulsory third-party insurance. Such insurance has been compulsory in mainland China since May 2004 and has greatly increased the rate of comprehensive insurance, especially for commercial vehicles; see Article 17 of the Law of the People's Republic of China on Road Traffic Safety (Order of the President No. 8), adopted at the Fifth Meeting of the Standing Committee of the Tenth National People's Congress of the People's Republic of China on 28 October 2003, <english.gov.cn/laws/2005-09/07/content_29966.htm>

it was the only crime with a slightly higher reporting rate in Hong Kong (8.1 per cent) than in the mainland (6.1 per cent). For other non-conventional crimes, Hong Kong's reporting rates were lower than the mainland's. For the most part, rates of reporting were comparable between the three mainland cities, but there were two exceptions. Half the incidents of extortion were reported in Shanghai compared with only about one-third in Shenzhen and Xi'an. In Shenzhen, 9.1 per cent of intellectual property (IP) infringements were reported compared with half in Shanghai and one-quarter in Xi'an.

Table 7.1 Reporting to Police, All Types of Crime, Hong Kong and Mainland (per cent)

Type of crime victimisation	Hong Kong	Mainland	Total
Common crime			
Theft of vehicle (N = 31)	100.0	96.2	96.4
Theft from vehicle (N = 42)	60.0	90.6*	82.9
Burglary (N = 187)	70.2	83.1	79.1
Vandalism (N = 94)	65.4	83.8*	78.5
Assault (N = 32)	75.0	80.0	78.1
Robbery (N = 44)	60.0	79.5	77.3
Theft by outsiders (N = 159)	51.2	79.3***	71.7
Theft by employees (N = 93)	41.9	58.1	52.7
Theft by customers (N = 89)	26.8	57.6**	38.2
Other offences (N = 50)	57.1	90.9*	72.0
Non-conventional crime			
Fraud by employees (N = 187)	23.1	37.2*	32.1
Extortion (N = 122)	22.9	37.3	30.2
Fraud by outsiders (N = 407)	21.8	36.0**	29.7
IP and copyright violation (N = 312)	6.3	18.5*	16.0
Internet-related fraud (N = 177)[a]	12.0	25.0	23.2
Bribery (N = 315)[b]	8.1	6.1	6.4

$^* p < 0.05$ $^{**} p < 0.01$ $^{***} p < 0.001$

Notes: [a] Refers only to incidents that were reported to law-enforcement agencies; [b] refers to incidents that were reported to the police and/or anti-corruption agencies.

The lower level of reporting criminal incidents in Hong Kong compared with the mainland is consistent with the results of the Hong Kong UNICVS, which found that for most crimes, and particularly the less serious offences, reporting rates in Hong Kong were lower than the international average (Broadhurst et al. 2010). As noted, vehicle and some other forms of theft had higher reporting rates than other offences, as insurance services typically require that a crime be reported to the police before processing a claim. No differences, however, were found in rates of reporting between businesses with and without insurance. Third-party vehicle insurance is compulsory and Article 98 of the Law of the People's Republic of China on Road Traffic Safety provides for severe penalties for a failure to insure;[2] however, the extent of insurance coverage for theft and other crimes against business is unknown.

Reporting to Police by Characteristics of Businesses

We were interested to examine whether there were any differences between businesses that reported incidents of victimisation against them and those that did not. We have seen above that businesses located in the mainland were significantly more likely to report some types of offence to the police than Hong Kong businesses. Other factors of interest were size of businesses, sector of activity, single or multiple premises, amount of monetary loss due to victimisation, and whether businesses were insured. We found that the only factor consistently differentiating businesses that reported to the police and those that did not was the size of the company.

Using the business size scale described in Chapter 6, we ran a series of t-tests to analyse whether there were significant differences between the average size of victimised businesses that did report their victimisation to the police and those that did not (Table 7.2). Although differences are not large, the overall pattern is that larger businesses were significantly more likely to contact police than smaller ones. For example, the average score on the business size scale of companies that had reported the most serious incident of victimisation by common crime was 6.4, compared with 5.1 for companies that did not report ($p < 0.001$). The largest differences were found for theft by outsiders (score of 6.83 for reporting versus score of 5.29 for non-reporting companies, $p < 0.001$), vandalism (score of 6.66 for reporting versus score of 5.2 for non-reporting companies, $p < 0.001$), theft by customers (score of 6.12 for reporting versus score of 4.67 for non-reporting companies, $p < 0.01$), fraud by employees (score of 7.23 for reporting versus score of 5.92 for non-reporting companies, $p < 0.01$) and theft by employees (score of 7.56 for reporting versus score of 6.27 for non-reporting companies, $p < 0.01$). For some types of crime—mostly non-conventional ones—differences in the size of the reporting and non-reporting businesses were not statistically significant. The lack of statistical power is likely related to the small proportions of these offences that were reported in the survey.

---

2   In June 2010, additional requirements for commercial vehicles were imposed by the PRC Ministry of Commerce: 'Circular of China Insurance Regulatory Commission Concerning Regulating the Administration on Premium Rates in the Insurance Clauses of Commercial Motor Vehicles', <english.mofcom.gov.cn/aarticle/policyrelease/announcement/200712/20071205275856.html>

Table 7.2 Business Size and Reporting to Police: *t*-tests on business size scale by type of victimisation

Type of victimisation[a]	Reported to police?	N	Mean size on scale	Mean difference	*t*-test
Most serious common crime[b]	Yes	234	6.40	1.30	5.15***
	No	94	5.10		
Burglary	Yes	148	6.56	1.00	2.74**
	No	38	5.56		
Vandalism	Yes	74	6.66	1.46	2.96**
	No	20	5.20		
Theft from vehicle	Yes	35	6.69	0.26	0.02
	No	7	6.43		
Theft by employees	Yes	49	7.56	1.29	3.08**
	No	44	6.27		
Theft by customers	Yes	34	6.12	1.45	3.18**
	No	55	4.67		
Theft by outsiders	Yes	114	6.83	1.54	4.40***
	No	45	5.29		
Violent crime[c]	Yes	47	6.73	0.73	1.74
	No	12	6.00		
Fraud by employees	Yes	60	7.23	1.31	4.33***
	No	127	5.92		
Fraud by outsiders	Yes	121	6.29	1.03	4.99***
	No	286	5.26		
Internet-related fraud[d]	Yes	41	6.96	0.08	0.24
	No	136	6.88		
Bribery[e]	Yes	20	6.80	0.24	0.54
	No	292	6.56		
Extortion	Yes	35	6.22	0.49	1.212
	No	81	5.73		
IP and copyright violation	Yes	50	6.78	0.19	0.74
	No	262	6.59		

* $p < 0.05$ ** $p < 0.01$ *** $p < 0.001$

Notes: [a] Theft of vehicle is not included because virtually all victims reported to the police; [b] includes burglary, vandalism, theft of and from vehicle, theft by employees, customers and outsiders, robbery, assault, and other unspecified crimes; [c] includes assault and robbery; [d] refers only to incidents that were reported to law-enforcement agencies; [e] refers to incidents that were reported to the police and/or anti-corruption agencies.

There was no correlation between sector of activity and the likelihood of reporting victimisation to the police.[3] For a number of crimes, we found that Hong Kong businesses with additional premises in the mainland reported their victimisation at a higher rate than businesses with single premises in Hong Kong, but this was related to the size of the businesses, as companies with multiple premises were larger than those with single premises. Monetary losses due to crime were generally higher for businesses that reported, but that relationship was not statistically significant. For example, the average monetary loss due to the most serious common crime against reporting businesses amounted to US$6801 compared with US$2943 for non-reporting businesses.

Although there was no direct correlation between the likelihood of reporting the crime to the police and whether or not businesses had insurance, we found that larger businesses—that is, those with the highest reporting rates—were more likely to have insurance.[4] This suggests that requirements by insurance companies to report criminal victimisation in order to process claims are related to the likelihood of reporting, but that other factors are also at play. Large businesses might have a policy of systematically reporting criminal victimisation. They might also be in a better position to do so than smaller companies because of specialised security personnel who have the time, expertise and resources to deal with criminal incidents.

Reasons for Reporting Crime to the Police

Respondents who indicated that their business had been victimised by one or several common crimes were asked to select the incident they regarded as the most serious. If that most serious incident was reported, they were asked the reasons the company reported this crime; if the incident was not reported, they were asked the reasons it was not. For each question, a list of reasons was provided, from which respondents could select several. They could also specify their own reasons. A similar set of questions was asked for each type of fraud, bribery, extortion and computer-related victimisation. The reasons for reporting or not reporting the crime to police were thus restricted to the crime incident identified by the respondent as the most serious. Many of the businesses were victims of more than one crime but we do not explore the reporting behaviour of all the crime incidents mentioned in the survey.

---

3   The only significant relationships between sector and reporting were that businesses in manufacturing were more likely to report vandalism than businesses in other sectors, and retailers were significantly less likely to report theft by outsiders than businesses in other sectors of activity.
4   Insured businesses had a mean score of 6.10 and uninsured businesses a mean score of 5.5 on the business size scale ($p < 0.001$).

Reasons for Reporting Common Crime

Of the 328 businesses that mentioned at least one incident of victimisation by common crime, one-third regarded burglary as the most serious incident, and about 11–12 per cent selected theft by customers, employees or outsiders (Table 7.3). For the other crimes, responses varied between 1.2 per cent for assault and 6.1 per cent for robbery, with about 12 per cent selecting other unspecified crimes. Overall, 71.3 per cent of the most serious incidents had been reported to the police: all assaults and vehicle thefts, about 80 per cent of burglaries and robberies, half the thefts from vehicles, and lesser proportions for the other crimes. Questions about reasons for or against reporting were asked only about these 'most serious' crimes.

Table 7.3 Most Serious Common Crime and Reporting to Police

Most serious crime	N	Percentage of all crimes	Reported to police %
Burglary	115	35.1	80.9
Theft by customers	41	12.5	36.6
Theft by employees	39	11.9	46.2
Theft by outsiders	37	11.3	70.3
Robbery	20	6.1	80.0
Vehicle theft	15	4.6	100.0
Vandalism	10	3.0	70.0
Theft from vehicle	6	1.8	50.0
Assault	4	1.2	100.0
Other crimes	41	12.5	90.2
Total	328	100.0	71.3

Reasons given by respondents for reporting crime are presented in Table 7.4. Overall, over one-third of those who reported to the police did so because they believed that crimes are serious events that should be reported, and an equal proportion did so to recover property. About one in five respondents wanted the offender to be caught and punished, and 17.1 per cent hoped it would prevent crime from happening again. Less than 5 per cent of respondents mentioned getting compensation or insurance purposes as reasons for reporting the crime to police.

There were differences in the reasons invoked by businesses in the four cities. The duty to report crime was more often invoked in Shenzhen (43.5 reporting) and Hong Kong (40.9 reporting) than Shanghai (26.1 reporting) and Xi'an (21.1 reporting). In contrast, Shanghai and Xi'an respondents were significantly more likely to mention recovering property (50 reporting) than those in Shenzhen (32.3 reporting) and Hong Kong (23.9 reporting). More than half the businesses in Xi'an were motivated by incapacitation and punishment (55.3 reporting), and this is significantly higher than for those in Shenzhen (22.6 reporting), Shanghai (15.2 reporting) and particularly Hong Kong (8 reporting). Finally, more than one-quarter of Shenzhen respondents invoked preventative reasons (to stop it happening again) compared with 17.4 per cent in Shanghai, 12.5 per cent in Hong Kong and 10.5 per cent in Xi'an. Once again, the fact that Shenzhen businesses felt more duty-bound to report crime and more motivated to stop it from reoccurring than businesses from other cities might reflect their greater risk of victimisation.

Table 7.4 Reasons for Reporting Most Serious Common Crime to Police by City and Overall (reporting)

Reasons for reporting[a]	Hong Kong N = 88	Shanghai N = 46	Shenzhen N = 62	Xi'an N = 38	Total N = 234
Crimes should be reported/ serious events	40.9	26.1	43.5	21.1*	35.5
To recover property	23.9	50.0**	32.3	50.0**	35.5
Wanted offender to be caught/punished	8.0	15.2	22.6	55.3***	20.9
To stop it happening again	12.5	17.4	27.4	10.5	17.1
To get compensation from the offender	1.1	6.5	9.7	2.6	4.7
For insurance purposes	5.7*	0.0	0.0	0.0	2.1
Other reasons	25.3	15.2	11.3	7.9	16.7

$* p < 0.05$ $** p < 0.01$ $*** p < 0.001$

Note: [a] Multiple answers were possible; total might add up to more than 100 per cent.

There are also some relationships between the types of crime and the motivations for reporting them. Vehicle theft, robbery, burglary and theft by employees were more likely to be reported to recover property, but theft by outsiders or customers, assault and vandalism because they were seen as serious events that should be reported. As mentioned above, few businesses said they reported the crime because they had to for insurance purposes.

Reasons for Reporting Fraud, Bribery, Extortion and Other Crimes

For less-conventional crimes, reporting rates were relatively low and it is not possible to perform meaningful statistical analyses with such a small number of cases. Therefore, Table 7.5 presents the reasons for reporting to police given by respondents for five types of crime, and we highlight in the text any large and/ or significant differences between cities.

Fraud by Employees

Across the four cities, the reasons most frequently cited for reporting fraud by employees were the duty to report crime (36.7 per cent) and to recover the stolen property (31.7 per cent). About one in five victims (21.7 per cent) mentioned crime prevention (to stop it happening again), and one in 10 hoped to have the offender caught and punished. The motivation to recover property was highest in Shanghai (53.3 per cent) compared with other cities (approaching statistical significance, $p = 0.07$). In Hong Kong, more respondents invoked the duty to report crime (62.5 per cent compared with 20–33.3 per cent in other cities).

Table 7.5 Reasons for Reporting Non-Conventional Crimes against Business (per cent)

Reasons for reporting[a]	Fraud by employees N = 60	Fraud by outsiders N = 121	Internet-related fraud N = 177	Bribery N = 20	Extortion N = 35
To recover property	31.7	40.5	12.2	15.0	11.4
Crimes should be reported/ serious events	36.7	18.2	31.7	25.0	34.3
Wanted offender to be caught/punished	10.0	18.2	7.3	25.0	8.6
To stop it happening again	21.7	11.6	29.3	10.0	31.4
To get compensation from the offender	6.7	9.1	4.9	0.0	2.9
For insurance purposes	0.0	3.3	0.0	0.0	2.9
Other reasons	10.0	13.2	29.3	25.0	28.6

Note: [a] Multiple answers were possible; total might add up to more than 100 per cent.

Fraud by Outsiders

Overall, recovering property was the dominant reason for businesses to report fraud by outsiders (40.5 per cent compared with 3.3–18.2 per cent for the other reasons). The duty to report crime and the desire to punish the offender came second, with 18.2 per cent of victims mentioning them. Prevention, compensation and insurance purposes were cited by relatively few businesses, but 13.2 per cent invoked other reasons. A different pattern of motivations emerged in Hong Kong. There, the major reason for reporting was the duty to report crime (35.9 per cent), followed by the desire to recover stolen property (20.5 per cent), and these differences between Hong Kong and mainland cities were statistically significant. In Xi'an and Shanghai, recovering property was the first reason provided by half the businesses, but punishment was a stronger motivation to report than in Hong Kong and Shenzhen; getting the offender punished was cited by 35.3 per cent of victims in Xi'an and 27.8 per cent in Shanghai compared with about 7 per cent in the two other cities ($p < 0.01$).

Internet-Related Fraud

Incidents of fraud on the Internet were reported to the police but also to other agencies such as Internet service providers and system managers. The leading reasons for reporting online fraud were the duty to report crime (31.7 per cent) and crime prevention (29.3 per cent). Duty to report crime was most frequently cited in Hong Kong (66.7 per cent), but less often in the other cities (17–33 per cent). Stopping the crime from happening again was a major reason in Shenzhen (46.7 per cent) and Xi'an (29.4 per cent), but was not mentioned in Hong Kong and Shanghai.

Bribery

A small proportion of businesses that were victims of bribery reported the incident to the authorities. One-quarter of respondents each invoked the duty to report crime, a desire to see the offender punished and other unspecified reasons. Fifteen per cent of respondents hoped to recover property and 10 per cent wanted to stop it from happening again. Duty to report was the most frequently cited reason in Hong Kong (50 per cent), and getting the offender caught and punished was most frequently cited in Shenzhen (60 per cent).

Extortion and Intimidation

The duty to report crime (34.3 per cent) and the desire to stop it from happening again (31.4 per cent) were the two most frequently invoked reasons for reporting extortion and intimidation. But while crime prevention was a major motivation across the four cities (ranging between 20 and 40 per cent of respondents), the duty to report crime was prominent only in Hong Kong (46.2 per cent) and Shenzhen (41.7 per cent), less so in Shanghai (20 per cent), and not at all mentioned in Xi'an. The desire to recover property was mentioned only in Shenzhen and Xi'an (25 per cent and 20 per cent respectively). Nearly 30 per cent of respondents cited other unspecified reasons for reporting.

Reasons for Not Reporting Crime to the Police

Reasons for Not Reporting Common Crime

The reason most often invoked for not reporting crime across the four cities (Table 7.6) was that the incident was not serious enough (38.3 per cent), followed by other unspecified reasons (30.9 per cent). About 15–16 per cent of respondents mentioned lack of time/too much trouble or the slight chance of success as reasons for not reporting to the police, and nearly one in 10 cited a lack of evidence. Between 1 and 6 per cent cited each one of the other reasons (not company policy, no insurance claim involved, police not interested, and internal matter), but no-one said it was because of fear of reprisals or fear of negative publicity. The reason that the incident was not serious enough to warrant reporting was mentioned least often in Hong Kong (35.1 per cent) and Shenzhen (35.7 per cent) and most often in Shanghai (55.6 per cent). Shanghai businesses provided only two reasons for not reporting: lack of seriousness, which was invoked by more than half the respondents, and the fact that involving police was not appropriate because the incident was an internal matter, which was invoked by one-third—and significantly more often than in the other cities. In Xi'an, 28.6 per cent of respondents thought police would not be able to do anything and 14.3 per cent that the police would not be interested in the matter. The police's potential lack of interest in the complaint was mentioned only in Xi'an. Lack of time was cited more often in Hong Kong (19.3 per cent) and Shenzhen (14.3 per cent) than in Xi'an (7.1 per cent) and Shanghai (0 per cent).

Table 7.6 Reasons for Not Reporting Common Crime to Police by City and Overall

Reasons for not reporting[a]	Hong Kong N = 57	Shanghai N = 9	Shenzhen N = 14	Xi'an N = 14	Total N = 94
Not worth reporting/not serious enough	35.1	55.6	35.7	42.9	38.3
Police wouldn't have been able to do anything/slight chance of success	17.5	0.0	7.1	28.6	16.0
Lack of time/too much trouble	19.3	0.0	14.3	7.1	14.9
Lack of proof/evidence/ witnesses	14.0	0.0	0.0	7.1	9.6
Involving police not appropriate/internal matter	1.8	33.3**	7.1	0.0	5.3
Police wouldn't have done anything/not interested	0.0	0.0	0.0	14.3*	2.1
No insurance claim was involved	1.8	0.0	0.0	0.0	1.1
Not company policy	1.8	0.0	0.0	0.0	1.1
Fear of reprisals/negative publicity	0.0	0.0	0.0	0.0	0.0
Other reasons	33.3	22.2	28.6	28.6	30.9

* $p < 0.05$ ** $p < 0.01$

Note: [a] Multiple answers were possible; total might add up to more than 100 per cent.

Overall, similar reasons for not reporting were given across the various types of crime, but there was one exception: that the incident was an internal matter not appropriate for police was mentioned significantly more often in cases of theft by employees (25 per cent).

Reasons for Not Reporting Non-Conventional Crime

The reasons that businesses gave for not reporting non-conventional crime against them are presented in Table 7.7. Across the four cities and the five types of crime, the reason most frequently invoked for not reporting the crime was that it was not serious enough. Other reasons varied by type of crime.

Table 7.7 Reasons for Not Reporting Non-Conventional Crimes to Police by Type of Crime

Reasons for not reporting[a]	Fraud by employees N = 127	Fraud by outsiders N = 286	Internet-related fraud N = 136	Bribery N = 292	Extortion N = 81
Not worth reporting/not serious enough	33.1	32.2	36.0	28.1	37.0
Lack of time/too much trouble	14.2	10.1	13.2	4.1	9.9
Police wouldn't have been able to do anything/slight chance of success	5.5	15.4	2.9	2.1	6.2
Lack of proof/evidence/witnesses	8.7	8.0	2.2	5.1	13.6
Involving police not appropriate/internal matter	12.6	4.2	2.9	9.2	11.1
Police wouldn't have done anything/not interested	1.6	5.6	1.5	1.7	1.2
No insurance claim was involved	1.6	1.7	2.2	0.3	1.2
Not company policy	2.4	0.0	3.7	8.2	2.5
Fear of reprisals	0.0	0.0	0.0	3.8	4.9
Fear of negative publicity	0.0	0.0	0.0	0.7	0.0
Other reasons	32.3	35.3	45.6	37.3	22.2

Note: [a] Multiple answers were possible; total might add up to more than 100 per cent.

Fraud by Employees

About one-third of victims did not report because they did not regard the incident as serious enough, and an equal proportion gave other unspecified reasons for not reporting. About 14 per cent did not have time or thought reporting was too much trouble. More than 12 per cent of respondents regarded the incidents of fraud by employees as internal matters, inappropriate for police action. This is a lower proportion than for theft by employees (25 per cent), but slightly higher than for the other crimes. Less than 10 per cent of respondents mentioned the other reasons, but none cited fear of reprisals or fear of negative publicity as a deterrent from reporting.

Fraud by Outsiders

Following from lack of seriousness (32.2 per cent) and unspecified reasons (35.3 per cent), the second most frequently cited reasons for not reporting fraud by outsiders were the small chance of success (15.4 per cent) and lack of time (10.1 per cent). In Hong Kong, the slight chance of success (22.1 per cent) was cited significantly more often than in the mainland cities (2.8–13.1 per cent, $p < 0.01$).

Internet-Related Fraud

Nearly half the respondents cited other unspecified reasons for not reporting the fraud (45.6 per cent), followed by lack of seriousness (36 per cent) and lack of time (13.2 per cent). Two to three per cent of victims mentioned the other reasons. Across the four cities, similar proportions of businesses mentioned each reason for not reporting.

Bribery

The relatively high proportion of bribery victims who cited other unspecified reasons for not reporting (37.3 per cent) might indicate some reluctance in explaining their decision not to report. Second in the list of reasons for not reporting was that the incident was not serious enough (28.1 per cent), then that it was an internal matter inappropriate for police action (9.2 per cent) or that reporting was not company policy (8.2 per cent). In Hong Kong, victims were more likely to nominate procedural issues and pessimism (lack of proof/ evidence/slight chance of success: 24.5 per cent) than in mainland cities (4–6 per cent), but less likely to nominate internal matter/company policy than in mainland cities (17–22 per cent). Nearly 4 per cent of respondents mentioned fear of reprisals as a deterrent for reporting. Although this is a small proportion, fear of reprisals was mentioned solely in relation to bribery and extortion. It was also mentioned significantly more often in Xi'an (9.5 per cent), where officials were more often the perpetrators, than in Hong Kong (2.2 per cent), Shanghai (1.6 per cent) or Shenzhen, where it was not cited at all.

Extortion and Intimidation

Lack of seriousness was the most frequently cited reason for not reporting extortion (37 per cent), followed by unspecified reasons (22.2 per cent). More than 13 per cent invoked lack of evidence as justification, and a similar proportion (11.1 per cent) said that the incident was an internal matter. Nearly 5 per cent cited fear of reprisals as a deterrent for reporting. To a lesser extent than in the case of bribery, Hong Kong victims were more prone than their mainland counterparts to cite procedural reasons, but less likely to mention company policy or the fact the incident was an internal matter to explain why they did not report the offence.

Satisfaction with Police Response

Common Crimes

Across the four cities, about half the businesses that reported victimisation by conventional crime were satisfied with the police response (Table 7.8). There were no striking differences between the four cities, although a slightly lower proportion of Xi'an victims expressed satisfaction (44.7 per cent) than others (50–55 per cent).

The reasons most often given for dissatisfaction with the police response were that police did not do enough (40.7 per cent) or that they were not interested (28.6 per cent). Similar proportions were dissatisfied because police did not find or apprehend the offender (19.8 per cent) or did not recover the stolen property (15.4 per cent). Less than 10 per cent of dissatisfied respondents mentioned the other reasons (police did not keep them informed, were slow to arrive or were impolite), but nearly 30 per cent cited other reasons but no further details about the substance of these 'reasons' were recorded.

Reasons for dissatisfaction varied by city, but because numbers are small, the differences did not reach statistical significance. Respondents in Hong Kong were less likely to say that police did not do enough (33.3 per cent) than in mainland cities (42.1–47.1 per cent) or were not interested (14.8 per cent versus 23.5–39.3 per cent among mainland cities). Greater proportions of Hong Kong respondents, however, were dissatisfied because the police did not keep them informed (22.2 per cent) or did not treat them politely (14.8 per cent); by comparison, lack of information was not mentioned at all in Shanghai and by only 3.6 per cent of respondents in Shenzhen and 10.5 per cent, in Xi'an. No respondent from Shenzhen thought that police were impolite and less than 6 per cent in Shanghai and Xi'an. But we note that more than half of Shanghai respondents invoked other unspecified reasons, with lesser proportions in Shenzhen and Xi'an. Two reasons for dissatisfaction cited more frequently in Xi'an than in the other mainland cities were that police did not recover the stolen property (26.3 per cent compared to 11.8–14.3 per cent) and that they did not apprehend the offender (26.3 per cent compared to 11.8–21.4 per cent). This might be related to Xi'an businesses' greater interest in incapacitation and punishment and recovery of property as motivations to report victimisation to police. There might be both economic (Xi'an is the poorest city of the four surveyed) and cultural reasons for the emphasis on recovery of property and punishment in Xi'an.

Table 7.8 Satisfaction with Police Response to Common Crime and Reasons for Dissatisfaction, by City and Overall

	Hong Kong N = 88	Shanghai N = 46	Shenzhen N = 62	Xi'an N = 38	Total N = 234
Satisfied with police response	55.7	54.3	50.0	44.7	52.1

Of those dissatisfied, reasons for dissatisfaction[a]

Police...	Hong Kong N = 27	Shanghai N = 17	Shenzhen N = 28	Xi'an N = 19	Total N = 91[b]
Did not do enough	33.3	47.1	42.9	42.1	40.7
Were not interested	14.8	23.5	39.3	36.8	28.6
Didn't find or apprehend the offender	18.5	11.8	21.4	26.3	19.8
Didn't recover property or goods	11.1	11.8	14.3	26.3	15.4
Didn't keep us properly informed	22.2	0.0	3.6	10.5	9.9
Were slow to arrive	3.7	11.8	14.3	0.0	7.7
Didn't treat us correctly/ were impolite	14.8	5.9	0.0	5.3	6.6
Other reasons	22.2	52.9	28.6	21.1	29.7

Notes: [a] Multiple answers were possible, so total might add up to more than 100 per cent; [b] the number of businesses that were dissatisfied with the police response (N = 91) and that of businesses that were satisfied (N = 122) do not add up to the total number of businesses who reported to police (N = 234) because 21 respondents did not know or refused to answer questions on satisfaction with police.

Fraud and Other Crimes against Business

Overall, the level of satisfaction with the police response to non-conventional crimes is comparable with that of conventional crime. About half the victimised businesses that reported the crime were satisfied with the response of the police or other agencies (for bribery and cyber fraud), ranging from 46.7 per cent for fraud by employees to 55 per cent for bribery (Table 7.9). We examine whether differences were found between the four cities, and the reasons for dissatisfaction that businesses provided. Again, because of the small number of businesses that reported non-conventional crimes, relatively large differences between cities might not reach statistical significance.

Fraud by Employees

Across the four cities, 46.7 per cent of respondents were satisfied with the police treatment of their complaint of fraud by employees, but there were large disparities between the cities. In Hong Kong, the highest proportion of respondents (68.8 per cent) indicated they were satisfied with the police response, followed by Shanghai (53.3 per cent). Levels of satisfaction, however, were lower in Shenzhen (35.3 per cent) and particularly Xi'an, where just one-quarter of businesses expressed satisfaction.

The main reasons for dissatisfaction overall were that police were not interested in the complaint (45.5 per cent) or did not do enough (41 per cent) to solve it. That police were not interested was the dominant reason in Xi'an (71.4 per cent), followed by the concern that police did not do enough (42.8 per cent). Half of Shenzhen respondents believed that police were not interested, but only one-quarter believed that police did not do enough. Lack of police action was the leading cause of dissatisfaction for Shanghai businesses (60 per cent).

Fraud by Outsiders

Overall, 48.8 per cent of businesses were satisfied with how the police handled their complaint of fraud by outsiders. The highest level of satisfaction was found in Shanghai (61 per cent) but those in Shenzhen (43.3 per cent) and Xi'an (41.2 per cent) were less satisfied. Many dissatisfied victims (44.4 per cent) invoked unspecified reasons, and comparable proportions of respondents (about one in five) mentioned that police did not do enough, did not apprehend the offender, did not recover the property and were not interested as sources of dissatisfaction. None of the Hong Kong respondents complained that police did not find the offender.

Table 7.9 Satisfaction with Police Response to Non-Conventional Crime and Reasons for Dissatisfaction, by Type of Crime

	Fraud by employees N = 60	Fraud by outsiders N = 121	Internet fraud[a] N = 41	Bribery[a] N = 20	Extortion N = 35
Satisfied with police (and others') response	46.7	48.8	51.2	55.0	51.4

Of those dissatisfied, reasons for dissatisfaction[b]

Police...	Fraud by employees N = 22	Fraud by outsiders N = 54	Internet fraud N = 14	Bribery N = 6	Extortion N = 16
Did not do enough	41.0	20.4	35.7	0.0	43.8
Were not interested	45.5	16.7	35.7	16.7	31.3
Didn't find or apprehend the offender	0.0	22.2	7.1	0.0	12.5
Didn't recover property or goods	9.1	18.5	14.3	0.0	6.3
Didn't keep us properly informed	4.5	1.9	7.1	16.7	0.0
Were slow to arrive	18.2	5.6	14.3	0.0	0.0
Didn't treat us correctly/ were impolite	4.5	1.9	0.0	0.0	0.0
Other reasons	31.8	44.4	35.7	33.4	31.3

Notes: [a] Reporting authorities include: for bribery, police and anti-corruption agencies; for Internet fraud, police, Internet service providers and web/system managers; [b] multiple answers were possible, so total might add up to more than 100 per cent; for each type of crime, the number of businesses that were dissatisfied with police response and that of businesses that were satisfied do not add up to the total number of businesses who reported to police because various numbers of respondents did not know or refused to answer questions on satisfaction with police.

Internet-Related Fraud

The businesses most satisfied with the responses to Internet-related fraud were those in Shanghai (83.3 per cent), with the other cities ranging between 33.3 and 52.9 per cent satisfaction. The two leading reasons for dissatisfaction—each cited by 35.7 per cent of respondents—were that police (or other agencies) did not do enough or were not interested. A lack of police action was mentioned by one-third of Hong Kong respondents, and a lack of interest by police by 20 per cent of Xi'an businesses.

Bribery

More than half the reporting victims (55 per cent) were satisfied with police or anti-corruption agencies' response to their complaint. Hong Kong businesses expressed the highest level of satisfaction (75 per cent) and Shenzhen businesses the lowest (40 per cent). Only three respondents provided specific reasons for dissatisfaction.

Extortion and Intimidation

Just more than half (51.4 per cent) the businesses that reported incidents of extortion or intimidation were satisfied with the action of the police. Again, satisfaction was highest in Hong Kong (69.2 per cent). It was lower in Xi'an (40 per cent) and particularly Shanghai (20 per cent). The main reasons for dissatisfaction were that police did not do enough (43.8 per cent) and were not interested (31.3 per cent). No businesses in Hong Kong mentioned the police's lack of interest, but this was the leading cause of dissatisfaction in Shenzhen.

Incidentally—but perhaps somewhat revealing about the demands on business and apparent limits to civic action—was that in Hong Kong and Shenzhen about one-fifth of those who did not report common crime indicated that this was because of a 'lack of time' and/or that it was 'too much trouble to report'. This reason also featured (albeit less frequently) for fraud-related offences but not bribery. The notion that 'time pressure' might override other considerations in the decision to report or not is unusual but has been noted in the Hong Kong ICVS as a factor cited by individuals who were victims of either trivial or non-trivial crimes (Broadhurst et al. 2010).

In general, the survey respondents in Hong Kong had a more positive assessment of the police response. This was notable in respect to serious offences such as bribery and fraud by employees. Apart from Xi'an, however, where respondents tended to be more pessimistic about fraud, differences between the cities were small and statistical tests of significance were unreliable given the small number of subjects. This more positive attitude of Hong Kong business to policing is reinforced in respect to general attitudes to police performance in dealing with crime problems where the findings show less dissatisfaction than in other cities. In the next section, we compare the reporting behaviour of our sample with similar studies and conclude this chapter by exploring further the attitudes of business to police as well as their knowledge of and response to collective efforts to prevent crime.

Comparison with Other Victimisation Surveys

We are not able to compare patterns of reporting in China with those of Western Europe because few details were available in van Dijk and Terlouw (1996), except that burglary and theft of vehicle were reported by more than 90 per cent of the victims, but crimes committed by employees were reported by only one-third of the victims. To still be able to compare rates of reporting to police between China and Western countries, we use the results of the British Commercial Victimisation Survey, conducted in 2002 in England and Wales, but which focused on only two sectors: retail and manufacturing (Shury et al. 2005). First, we turn to the results of the Central Eastern Europe ICBS (Alvazzi del Frate 2004).

Central Eastern Europe ICBS

Figure 7.1 compares the rates of reporting common crime and non-conventional crime to police in mainland China, Hong Kong and Central Eastern Europe. Although rates by crime are different for each country, a similar pattern of reporting is present in all locations: theft of vehicle, burglary, robbery and assault are most likely to be reported to the police, with decreasing rates for the other types of crime and particularly the non-conventional crimes. For all types of crime, apart from bribery, we find the highest levels of reporting to police in mainland China. For many common crimes, Hong Kong's level of reporting was not as low as that of Eastern Europe, but closer to it than the mainland's—for example, 83 per cent of burglary victims said they reported the crime to the police in the mainland, but only 70 per cent and 67 per cent did in Hong Kong and Eastern Europe, respectively. One exception is theft of a vehicle, which was reported by all Hong Kong victims and 96 per cent of mainland victims, but by 61 per cent of victims in the Eastern Europe ICBS. This is likely to be related, as noted above, to the requirement by insurance companies to report vehicle theft, and vehicle insurance was compulsory in both Hong Kong and the mainland at the time of the survey.

While the level of reporting to police was consistently higher in China than in Central Eastern Europe for common crimes, differences were not as sharp for non-conventional crimes such as extortion and fraud. For example, fraud by outsiders was reported by 34 per cent of businesses in Eastern Europe and 36 per cent in the mainland (but only 22 per cent in Hong Kong). In all locations, bribery had the lowest level of reporting of all crimes (ranging from 2 to 8 per cent). Given the context of widespread corruption of public officers in Central Eastern Europe and the mainland, this result is not unexpected, but it is somewhat surprising that only 8 per cent of businesses that were victims of bribery in Hong Kong reported the incident, given the highly regarded and proactive ICAC.

Figure 7.1 Reporting to Police: China ICBS, Hong Kong (2004) and mainland (2005), and Central Eastern Europe ICBS (1999)

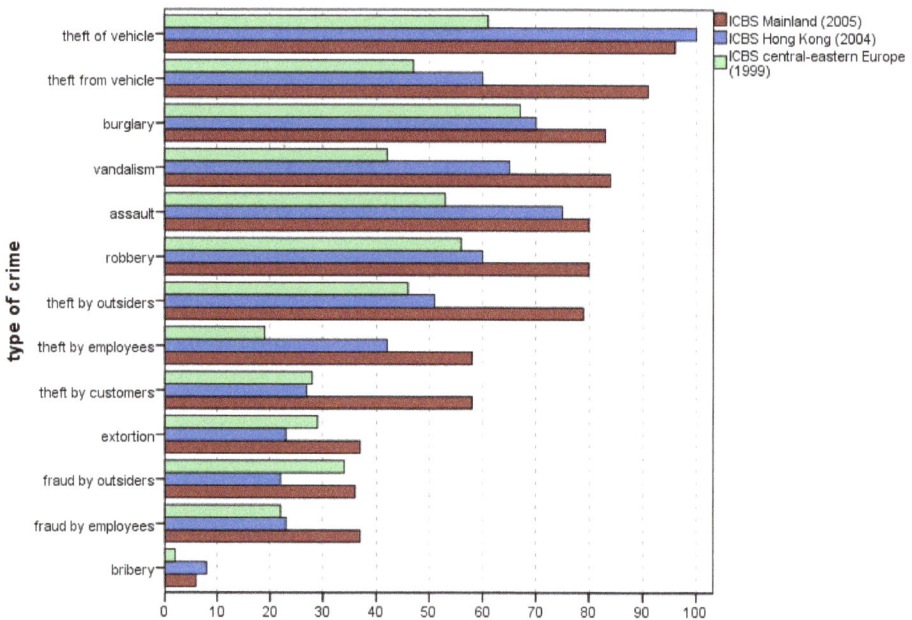

Less than half the respondents who had reported a common crime to the police in the Eastern Europe ICBS were satisfied with the police response (42 per cent). The main reasons for dissatisfaction were that police did not do enough, did not recover the stolen property and were not interested in the complaint. The level of satisfaction with the police response is only slightly lower than in the China ICBS and the reasons for dissatisfaction are similar.

British Commercial Victimisation Survey

For most of the common and non-conventional crimes, reporting levels in the British Commercial Victimisation Survey (ComVS)[5] and the China ICBS were comparable (Figure 7.2). The reporting of assaults in both the manufacturing

---

5   The British Commercial Victimisation Survey was conducted by telephone and based on a sample of 4000 retailers and 2500 manufacturers. Across the two sectors, the overall rate of common crime was 66 per cent.

and the retail sectors was much lower in the United Kingdom than in China, but this is probably due to the broader scope of the assault category in the ComVS, which included threats and intimidation as well as actual physical violence. Businesses would be less likely to report threats of assault but more likely to report actual violence. In the manufacturing sector, theft by employees was reported more often in China (55 per cent) than in Britain (32 per cent), with an opposite pattern for fraud by employees in the retail sector (46 per cent reported in Britain versus 28 per cent in China). It is difficult to explain this result, but some confusion in the definition of fraud and theft might play a role.

Figure 7.2 Reporting to Police: China ICBS (2004–05) and British ComVS (2002) by type of crime

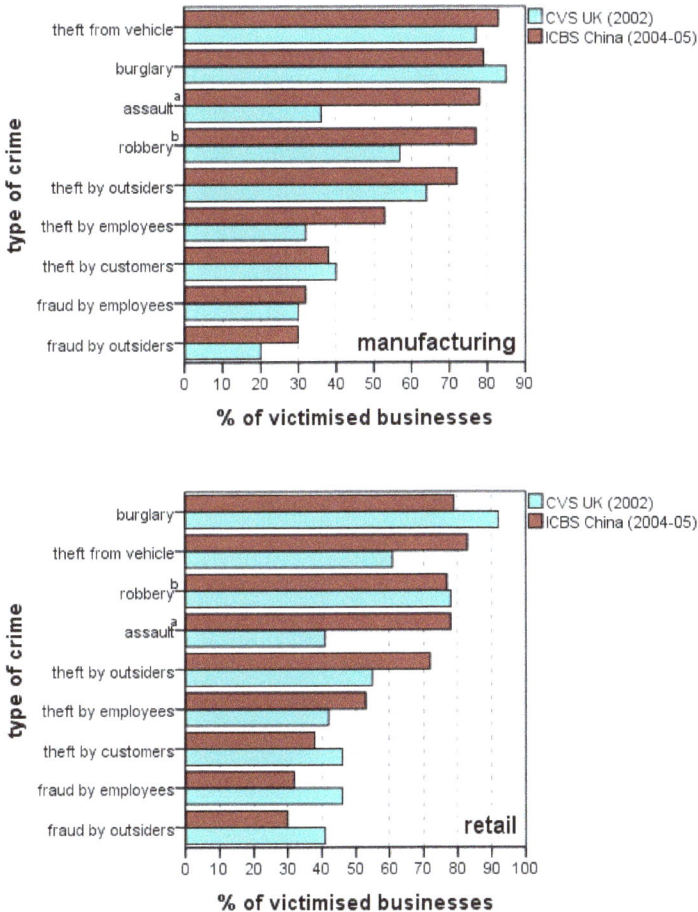

Notes: [a] The ComVS includes actual assaults as well as threats of assault, which are less likely to be reported to the police; [b] the ComVS includes robberies and attempted robberies.

Among retailers, 4 per cent were the victims of fraud by employees and 18 per cent of fraud by outsiders. Among manufacturers, 2 per cent were the victims of fraud by employees and 8 per cent of fraud by outsiders (Shury et al. 2005).

The British ComVS indicates that business respondents' satisfaction with the police response was only slightly higher than in the China ICBS (59 per cent). In Britain, however, the main reason for dissatisfaction was that police were too slow to react to a call, followed by lack of interest in the complaint.

International and Hong Kong UNICVS

Table 7.10 presents the rates of reporting to the police for five common crimes in the Hong Kong UNICVS—a survey of the general population—and the China ICBS. Looking first at Hong Kong, we see that rates of reporting are similar for vehicle theft and burglary, but much lower for the other three crimes in the UNICVS than in the ICBS—that is, businesses were more likely than individuals to report theft from a vehicle, robbery and assault. Although the surveys provide only limited information, we can hypothesise that insurance requirements to report criminal incidents in order to process claims are part of the explanation. For both individuals and businesses, compulsory vehicle insurance would make it mandatory to report vehicle thefts, and it is probable that a large proportion of individuals and businesses would have insured their home and their premises against burglary.[6]

For the other three crimes, the UNICVS found that individuals tended to report only the most serious incidents (for example, those resulting in injuries or with a large monetary loss). Businesses might tend to report thefts from a vehicle because: a) they have insurance against such theft; and/or b) the loss of stock due to such theft is likely to be important. Businesses are likely to report violent crimes—assault and robbery—if they targeted their staff, and particularly if a staff member was injured.

On average, a larger proportion of UNICVS victims who had reported their victimisation to the police were satisfied with that response (66.6 per cent) compared with the businesses in Hong Kong (52.7 per cent satisfied), but reasons for dissatisfaction were similar. It could be that police provided a better service to individual victims of personal crime, or that business respondents had higher expectations.

---

6   We note, however, that only a small proportion of participants explicitly indicated that they reported the incident for insurance purposes; the duty to report such serious events was the leading reason for contacting police.

Table 7.10 Reporting to Police, Hong Kong UNICVS and ICBS China

Type of crime victimisation	UNICVS			ICBS
	Average main cities five years[a]	Hong Kong 2001–05	Hong Kong 2004	Average mainland cities 2005
Burglary	68	77	70	83
Theft of vehicle	89	91	100	96
Theft from vehicle	53	29	60	91
Robbery	49	42	60	80
Assault	31	35	75	80

Sources: International UNICVS (van Dijk et al. 2007:Table 12, pp. 267–8); Hong Kong UNICVS (Broadhurst et al. 2010).

Note: [a] Surveys were conducted in 33 capital cities of developed and developing countries in 2004–05.

Satisfaction with Police and Crime Prevention

In the preceding section, businesses that had been victimised by conventional or non-conventional crime and who reported the crime were asked how satisfied they were with the way in which police dealt with that particular incident. Here we examine business respondents' opinion about the overall police performance. The first question measured how satisfied all respondents were with the way in which police handled crime problems: 'in general, how satisfied or dissatisfied are you with the way the police deal with the crime problems facing business in this area?' Possible answers were: 'very satisfied', 'fairly satisfied', 'neither satisfied nor dissatisfied', 'fairly dissatisfied', and 'very dissatisfied'. The second question probed reasons for dissatisfaction, and was asked only to respondents who had indicated they were fairly or very dissatisfied, and those who were neutral. Nine standard answers were possible but respondents were invited to give their own reasons.

Satisfaction with the Way Police Deal with Crime Problems

Overall, about half the respondents (49.5 per cent) were satisfied with law-enforcement agencies; only 7.5 per cent clearly expressed that they were dissatisfied (Table 7.11). A large proportion of respondents, however, did not express an opinion: 21.7 per cent said they were neither satisfied nor dissatisfied (neutral), and 21.3 per cent said they did not know or refused to answer. The level of satisfaction with the way police dealt with crime problems was significantly lower in Shenzhen compared with the other cities ($p < 0.01$).

Shanghai had the largest proportion of respondents who expressed satisfaction (53.4 per cent), followed by Xi'an (50.8 per cent) then Hong Kong (48.9 per cent). The proportion of respondents who were dissatisfied with the police was significantly lower in Hong Kong (2.7 per cent) than in the other cities, and largest in Shenzhen and Xi'an (12.7 and 12.1 per cent respectively).

An experience of victimisation tainted respondents' perception of police performance in the mainland, but not in Hong Kong. Comparing the response of the victims of any crime (common and non-conventional) with those of non-victims, we find that in Hong Kong, 47 per cent of victims and 49.4 per cent of non-victims were fairly or very satisfied with the performance of their police. In contrast, in the mainland, only 37.3 per cent of victims were fairly or very satisfied, compared with 52.4 per cent of non-victims ($p < 0.001$), with similar patterns in each mainland city.

Table 7.11 Satisfaction with Police Performance by City and Overall (per cent)

	Hong Kong N = 1817	Shanghai N = 1110	Shenzhen N = 1112	Xi'an N = 1078	Total N = 5117
Very/fairly satisfied	48.9	53.4	45.2**	50.8	49.5
Neutral	20.7	22.3	25.9	18.4	21.7
Very/fairly dissatisfied	2.7**	5.5	12.7	12.1	7.5
Don't know/refusal	27.7	18.8	16.2	18.7	21.3

** $p < 0.01$

Reason for Dissatisfaction with the Way Police Deal with Crime Problems

Respondents who were neutral, fairly and very dissatisfied with the performance of the police (N = 1492) were asked the reasons for their dissatisfaction; multiple answers were allowed (Table 7.12). Unfortunately, a large proportion of respondents (37.7 per cent)[7] answered 'other reasons' but did not specify what those reasons were. The reason cited by the largest proportion of dissatisfied respondents (17.3 per cent) was that law-enforcement agencies took too long to react to incidents. The second reason, mentioned by comparable groups, was that police were not interested in reported crime (13.5 per cent) and that respondents had no day-to-day contact with police (12.3 per cent). Smaller numbers of respondents cited each of the other reasons.

---

7   Of those who cited 'other reasons' for dissatisfaction (N = 562), only a minority (12.2 per cent) mentioned one or more of the standard reasons, as well as 'other reasons'. One-third of respondents cited only 'other reasons', but did not elaborate.

Table 7.12 Reasons for Dissatisfaction with Police Performance by City and Overall (per cent)

Reasons for dissatisfaction[a]	Hong Kong N = 427	Shanghai N = 308	Shenzhen N = 429	Xi'an N = 328	Total N = 1492
Police take too long to react to incidents	4.7***	15.9	25.2	24.7	17.3
Police not interested in reported crimes	3.5***	14.6	21.4	15.2	13.5
No day-to-day contact with police	37.2***	2.3	2.1	2.7	12.3
Police do not react to alarms going off	3.0***	7.1	9.1	10.4	7.2
Police do not catch or prosecute offenders	0.9**	4.9	3.3	5.5	3.4
Police involved in corruption	0.2***	1.9	3.7	6.4***	2.9
Police not seen in this area	4.0	2.6	1.9	2.4	2.7
Police give little information on crime reported	1.6	1.6	2.1	1.5	1.7
Too much hassle to report	0.9	2.6	0.9	2.1	1.5
Other reasons	26.2	41.7	48.1	37.5	37.7

** $p < 0.01$ *** $p < 0.001$

Note: [a] Multiple answers were possible, so total might add up to more than 100 per cent.

Looking at Table 7.12, we see some important differences in perceptions of the police between the cities. In Hong Kong, the main reason for dissatisfaction was the absence of day-to-day contact between businesses and police (37.2 per cent), but in mainland cities this reason was mentioned by only 2–3 per cent of respondents and did not seem very important. In the mainland, dissatisfaction was significantly more likely than in Hong Kong to be associated with perceptions of ineffective and neglectful law-enforcement practices such as taking too long to react to incidents (Shenzhen and Xi'an, about 25 per cent; Shanghai, 15.9 per cent versus Hong Kong, 4.7 per cent), and not being interested in reported crime (Shanghai and Xi'an, about 15 per cent; Shenzhen, 21.4 per cent versus Hong Kong, 3.5 per cent). Although differences are smaller, similar patterns are present between Hong Kong and the mainland for the failure of police to react to alarms and to catch or prosecute offenders. As could be expected from the rates of victimisation, dissatisfaction because of the perception that law enforcers were involved in corruption was mentioned more often in the mainland, particularly in Xi'an, than in Hong Kong (Xi'an, 6.4 per cent; Shenzhen, 3.7 per cent; Shanghai, 1.9 per cent; versus Hong Kong, 0.2 per cent).

Crime Prevention

Two questions were asked about contact between businesses and the local government (for example, council) and the police regarding crime problems and crime prevention (apart from reporting crime): 'did your business have any contact with the local council/local police about crime or corruption problems, or crime prevention in 2004?' Another question concerned crime-prevention initiatives by businesses themselves: 'to your knowledge, have businesses in this area taken any kind of cooperative action against crime and corruption or extortion, such as sharing security patrols, setting up a business watch or ring, phone alarm system', and so on, and whether they would be interested in participating in such initiatives.

Overall, 15 per cent of the businesses surveyed had contact with the local council or the police about crime problems or crime prevention (Table 7.13). These contacts were significantly more likely to happen in the mainland cities than in Hong Kong (16–23 per cent compared with 5.1 per cent respectively). For the majority of businesses, such contact involved the police rather than the council. This is likely to be a function of the Hong Kong Fight Crime Committee structure, which includes local or district Fight Crime Committees who play a role in prevention and awareness of crime. Given the relatively greater concern about crime in Shenzhen compared with the other cities, businesses there were also more interested in taking cooperative action and more aware of such activity, while Hong Kong businesses were least likely to seek involvement.

Table 7.13 Contact with Council or Police about Crime Prevention by City

	Hong Kong N = 1817	Shanghai N = 1110	Shenzhen N = 1112	Xi'an N = 1078	Total N = 5117
Aware of cooperative action on crime prevention by local businesses	8.3***	15.6	20.2	18.5	14.6
Interested in participating in cooperative action on crime prevention by local businesses	20.7***	25.7	34.9	30.1	26.9
Had contact with local council and/or police about crime and crime prevention	5.1***	16.3	22.9	22.3	15.0
Of those who had contact with local council or police					
	N = 92	N = 255	N = 181	N = 240	N = 768
Council only	19.6	6.6	5.5	8.8	8.5
Police only	66.3	76.3	72.2	75.0	73.3
Both council and police	14.1	17.1	22.3	16.2	18.2

*** $p < 0.001$

Respondents whose business had been the victim of a common or non-conventional crime were not more likely to be aware of local crime-prevention initiatives, but they were more interested in participating in cooperative action to promote crime prevention (Table 7.14). They were also more likely to have taken the initiative to discuss crime-prevention strategies by contacting the local council or the police. The experience of victimisation prompted these respondents to try to prevent further victimisation. Yet, only about one-third of victimised respondents indicated that they had an interest in crime prevention (compared with about one-quarter of those who had not been victimised).

Table 7.14 Contact with Council or Police about Crime Prevention by Victimisation

	Victimised by common crime		Victimised by non-conventional crime	
	Yes N = 328	No N = 4789	Yes N = 1155	No N = 3962
Aware of cooperative action on crime prevention by local businesses	14.6	14.6	16.0	14.4
Interested in participating in cooperative action on crime prevention by local businesses	35.7***	26.2	33.2***	25.4
Contact with local council and/or police about crime and crime prevention	34.1***	13.7	22.5***	13.4

*** $p < 0.001$

In this chapter, we found that businesses were more willing to report common crimes than non-conventional crimes to the police, and that businesses in the mainland were significantly more likely to report common and non-conventional crimes than those in Hong Kong. Bribery was least likely to be reported (only 6.4 per cent of all incidents were) and vehicle theft was the most likely (96.4 per cent). Only about one in five businesses in Hong Kong and just more than one in three in mainland cities reported fraud to the police. Reporting behaviour did not vary significantly by business sector, whether the business was insured or not, or in respect to the size of the loss; however, once again, the larger the business, the more likely it was to report crimes to police, which could be because large companies have a wider exposure to risk and often have specialised security staff and policies mandating the reporting of crime to police. When we compared the reporting behaviour of Chinese business with comparable surveys such as the Central Eastern Europe survey and the British Commercial Victimisation Survey, we found similar patterns of reporting behaviour, but Chinese—especially mainland—businesses were much more likely to report to police than Central Eastern European businesses.

The main reason for not reporting crime to the police was that the incident was not serious enough and this was mentioned by nearly 40 per cent of victims in relation to common crime and by 30 per cent in relation to non-conventional crime. Lesser proportions of respondents believed that the police would not be able to do anything, that they did not have enough evidence, or that it took too much time or was too much trouble. About half of businesses were satisfied with the response of police when they did report a crime and there was little difference between the cities, albeit those in Xi'an expressed the least satisfaction. Most dissatisfaction was due to the view that police had not done enough or lacked interest, followed by failure to catch the offender or recover property.

About half of businesses were satisfied with the way in which the police dealt with the general crime problems facing business, although Shenzhen businesses expressed higher levels of dissatisfaction than other cities, perhaps because the experience of victimisation negatively tainted views of police. There is room to develop partnerships with police and local authorities in crime prevention since only about one in six businesses had contact with police and were aware of cooperative action against crime. About one in four was interested in participating in cooperative activities and those that had been victimised were more interested in but not necessarily more aware of crime-prevention activities. Hong Kong businesses were the least interested in cooperative action while Shenzhen businesses were the most interested (that is, 34.9 per cent compared with 20.7 per cent in Hong Kong)—perhaps not surprising, given the relative risks of crime in both cities.

8. Perceptions of Business Environment and Crime Trends

All respondents were asked their opinion about several potential obstacles, including regulatory controls, to doing good business in the mainland. Hong Kong respondents were also asked about obstacles to doing good business within Hong Kong. While mainland businesses based their answer on their own experience, only the 20 per cent of Hong Kong businesses with additional premises in the mainland could talk from experience; others expressed their perception of what doing business in the mainland was like. Although a number of mainland businesses also had premises in Hong Kong (12.6 per cent), they were not directly asked about potential obstacles in Hong Kong. Eight potential obstacles were surveyed: export/import regulations, labour regulations, tax regulations, safety and environmental regulations, changes in law and regulations, lack of consultation with the business sector, crime and insecurity, and corruption. Respondents ranked each potential obstacle on a three-point scale: 'no obstacle', 'moderate obstacle' and 'very strong obstacle'. Items about potential obstacles were asked early in the questionnaire and before respondents were prompted to recall whether their business had been victimised by crime. Thus, the effect of victimisation on perception should not be due to a 'response set' or item order effect—that is, because they had thought about their victimisation they were prompted to be more negative when answering questions about obstacles.

Respondents were also queried about their overall perception of the crime problem: first, whether they believed that the general level of crime had gone up, had remained the same, or had decreased in the past two or three years; then two questions focused on bribery and corruption, and extortion and intimidation and how common these practices were in the respondent's sector of activity.

Obstacles to Doing Good Business in Hong Kong

The series of questions on obstacles to business in Hong Kong was posed only to business respondents in Hong Kong. Their responses are presented in Table 8.1. Lack of consultation with the business sector was seen as a moderate to very strong obstacle by the largest proportion of businesses (42.7 per cent). This was followed by crime and insecurity (36.4 per cent), changes in law (34.8 per cent) and corruption (34.3 per cent). With the relatively low level of crime in Hong Kong, it was somewhat surprising to see that crime and insecurity as well as corruption were considered obstacles by more than one-third of respondents. Given the much lower prevalence of bribery and corruption in Hong Kong compared with the mainland and the presence of strong anti-corruption agencies, we hypothesised that corruption would not be seen as such a major obstacle to doing business in Hong Kong. We were surprised that more than one-third of Hong Kong businesses were concerned by corruption. A larger proportion of businesses with additional premises in the mainland rated corruption as an obstacle to doing business in Hong Kong (41.3 per cent) than those without premises in the mainland (32.6 per cent).

Table 8.1 Obstacles to Doing Business in Hong Kong: Hong Kong respondents who answered moderate to very strong obstacle (per cent)

Obstacle	Premises in mainland N = 361	No premises in mainland N = 1456	All Hong Kong respondents N = 1817
Lack of consultation with business sector	46.3	41.8	42.7
Crime and insecurity	37.7	36.1	36.4
Changes in laws	40.2*	33.4	34.8
Corruption	41.3**	32.6	34.3
Labour regulations	30.2	33.0	32.4
Tax regulations	36.8*	29.7	31.1
Safety/environmental regulations	31.0	30.6	30.7
Export/import regulations	41.0***	23.6	27.0

$* p < 0.05$ $** p < 0.01$ $*** p < 0.001$

About twice as many Hong Kong respondents with premises in the mainland cited export/import regulations as obstacles as those with premises only in Hong Kong (41 per cent and 23.6 per cent respectively). It could be that those businesses which export and import goods between Hong Kong and the mainland experience difficulties doing so. The fact that changes in laws and regulations were cited as an obstacle by 40.2 per cent of Hong Kong businesses with premises in the mainland compared with 33.4 per cent of businesses without premises in the mainland might also relate to similar problems. Businesses with operations in the mainland were also significantly more likely to see tax regimes as an obstacle. This might arise because of the many different forms of tax levied (26 types of tax, including value added tax [VAT], business turnover and employee levies), the prevalence of local/provincial taxes and the complications of the tax receipt/credit system adopted on the mainland. Yet, nearly 30 per cent of Hong Kong businesses without mainland premises also saw tax regulations as a problem, and, in the context of the relatively simple, fixed low-tax regime prevailing in Hong Kong, this was unexpected. According to the 2009 'Forbes

Magazine Tax Misery & Reform Index' survey, China has the highest-cost tax regime in the Asia-Pacific while Hong Kong offers the least expensive and most administratively simple system (Anderson 2009).[1]

Impact of Victimisation on Respondents' Perception

The experience of crime victimisation altered Hong Kong respondents' perception of potential obstacles to business. Respondents whose company had been victimised tended to perceive greater obstacles to business than those who had not been victimised (Table 8.2). This varied, however, according to the type of victimisation, with victimisation by non-conventional crime affecting respondents' views more strongly than by common crime.

All potential obstacles to business were mentioned by larger proportions of victims than non-victims of common crime, but the largest difference and the only statistically significant one was found between those who cited crime and insecurity as an obstacle (50 per cent of victims compared with 35.2 per cent of non-victims). Other factors and possible interactions between them might not yield statistically significant results because the statistical analyses lack power due to the small numbers of victims. The impact of victimisation on respondents' perception was comparable regardless of whether or not they operated business premises in the mainland.

Differences in perception of obstacles to doing business in Hong Kong were larger for respondents who had been victimised by non-conventional crime. They consistently cited more obstacles to doing business than non-victimised respondents, and the differences were statistically significant for all proposed obstacles, apart from export/import regulations. While the proportions of respondents who mentioned specific obstacles were different for those with or without premises on the mainland, the pattern of responses (that is, those who had been victimised tended to mention more obstacles) was similar between the two groups of businesses.

---

1   According to the *Forbes* Magazine Survey, China's tax on corporate income is 25 per cent, 45 per cent on personal income, 49 per cent for employers' social security, 23 per cent for employees' social security and a 17 per cent tax on goods and services. Hong Kong's tax regime is ranked the least expensive in the Asia-Pacific, with corporate tax standing at 16.5 per cent, personal income tax at 15 per cent and employer and employee social security levies both 5 per cent.

Table 8.2 Obstacles to Doing Business in Hong Kong and Victimisation: Hong Kong respondents who answered moderate to very strong obstacle (per cent)

Respondents	Victim of any common crime		Victim of any non-conventional crime	
Obstacle	Yes N = 150	No N = 1667	Yes N = 313	No N = 1504
Lack of consultation with business sector	49.3	42.1	53.0***	40.6
Crime and insecurity	50.0***	35.2	46.3***	34.3
Changes in laws	43.3*	34.0	43.1***	33.0
Corruption	39.3	33.9	45.7***	32.0
Labour regulations	36.7	32.0	38.7**	31.1
Tax regulations	36.7	30.6	36.4*	30.0
Safety/environmental regulations	38.3*	30.0	40.3***	28.7
Export/import regulations	26.7	27.1	28.1	26.8

$* p < 0.05$ $** p < 0.01$ $*** p < 0.001$

It is not surprising that business respondents who have directly experienced criminal incidents would rate crime and insecurity as obstacles to doing business. What is more surprising is that their experience seemed to colour their perception of all aspects of doing business. Perhaps the victimisation had made it harder to run a profitable business and thus all aspects of business appeared more difficult.

Obstacles to Doing Good Business in the Mainland

Perception of Hong Kong and Mainland Businesses

Table 8.3 presents respondents' perception of obstacles to doing good business in the mainland, for all businesses and according to the location of their premises. Overall, corruption, and crime and insecurity were regarded as moderate to very strong obstacles by about half the businesses surveyed, followed by lack of consultation with the business sector (42.2 per cent). The other potential obstacles were seen as problematic by lesser proportions of respondents (from 36.3 per cent for changes in law down to 26 per cent for labour regulations).

Although the proportions of respondents who ranked each potential obstacle as moderate or very strong varied between mainland and Hong Kong businesses, the ranking order was broadly similar. Hong Kong businesses with or without premises in the mainland were consistently more negative than mainland businesses. For all groups of businesses, corruption, and crime and insecurity were ranked the highest, but Hong Kong respondents with premises on the mainland were the most negative, with about 78 per cent regarding corruption, and crime and insecurity as obstacles to business. Hong Kong businesses without premises in the mainland—that is, expressing their perception rather than their actual experience—were less negative (59.8 per cent and 58.1 per cent rated crime and insecurity, and corruption respectively as obstacles), but significantly more so than mainland businesses (who rated crime and insecurity, and corruption at 41.2 per cent and 46.5 per cent respectively). Hong Kong businesses with premises in the mainland tended to rank export/import regulations as more problematic than those with no premises in the mainland and mainland businesses. This probably reflects their experience of exporting and importing goods between Hong Kong and the mainland, and on to world markets. Overall, labour regulations were ranked as the least problematic (although still high at 61.2 per cent for Hong Kong businesses with premises in the mainland, 40.6 per cent for Hong Kong businesses without premises in the mainland, and 15.7 per cent for mainland businesses). Generally, Hong Kong businesses operating in the mainland reported regulatory and crime/corruption issues as substantially more of a problem than mainland companies or Hong Kong businesses that did not operate in the mainland.

Table 8.3 Obstacles to Doing Business in the Mainland by Location of Premises: Respondents who answered moderate and very strong obstacle (per cent)

| | MAINLAND | HONG KONG | | |
| | | Premises in | No premises | |
Obstacle	All respondents N = 3300	mainland N = 361	in mainland N = 1456	TOTAL N = 5117
Corruption	46.5	77.9***	58.1***	52.0
Crime and insecurity	41.2	78.1***	59.8***	49.1
Lack of consultation with business sector	36.8	67.6***	48.1***	42.2
Changes in laws	26.8	71.5***	49.1***	36.3
Tax regulations	28.5	67.6***	44.5***	35.8
Safety/environmental regulations	17.4	67.9***	49.0***	30.0
Export/import regulations	17.8	72.0***	45.8***	29.6
Labour regulations	15.7	61.2***	40.6***	26.0

*** $p < 0.001$

Perception of Mainland Businesses by City

Looking at how businesses in each mainland city ranked the obstacles to doing business in the mainland (Table 8.4), we see a different pattern in each city. Corruption was rated as a moderate to very strong obstacle by the largest proportion of businesses in Shanghai and Xi'an (41.5 and 47.1 per cent respectively), but not in Shenzhen, where crime and insecurity came first (57 per cent), followed by corruption (51 per cent). The differences of opinion about crime and insecurity and corruption between the mainland cities reflect the pattern of victimisation between these cities: Shenzhen businesses tended to have a higher risk of victimisation than the two other cities, but the prevalence of bribery and corruption was similar.

Comparable proportions of respondents in the three cities rated lack of consultation with the business sector, tax regulations and changes in laws as obstacles. The lower level of concern about export/import regulations in Xi'an (13.9 per cent versus 19–20.3 per cent in Shanghai and Shenzhen) is probably related to the lower proportion of manufacturers who were likely to engage in this activity. Labour regulations were a low concern in Shanghai (rated as an obstacle by only 4 per cent of respondents) compared with Shenzhen (23 per cent) and Xi'an (20.3 per cent), and this finding is difficult to interpret, especially given that controversial changes to labour regulation (China Contract Law)[2] designed to protect blue-collar workers were widely discussed by local and foreign business groups throughout 2006–07 before being introduced at the beginning of 2008. It is, however, likely that the 2001 reforms to labour laws, especially labour contracts promulgated by the Shanghai Municipality, helped reduce the burden on employers and introduced a degree of flexibility not found in other cities (Chen 2009; Zhu et al. 2002).

---

2   See The Labor Contract Law of the People's Republic of China, adopted at the Twenty-Eighth Session of the Standing Committee of the Tenth National People's Congress of the People's Republic of China on 29 June 2007, effective on 1 January 2008: <www.fdi.gov.cn/.../FDI.../Laws/GeneralLawsandRegulations/BasicLaws/P020070831601380007924.pdf>

Table 8.4 Obstacles to Doing Business in the Mainland: Mainland respondents who answered moderate to very strong obstacle by city (per cent)

Obstacle	Shanghai N = 1110	Shenzhen N = 1112	Xi'an N = 1078	All mainland respondents N = 3300
Corruption	41.5	51.0***	47.1	46.5
Crime and insecurity	27.2	57.0***	39.4	41.2
Lack of consultation with business sector	33.2	39.2*	38.0	36.8
Tax regulations	27.7	28.8	29.1	28.5
Changes in laws	27.7	28.2	24.5	26.8
Export/import regulations	19.0	20.3**	13.9	17.8
Safety/environmental regulations	15.1	20.1**	17.0	17.4
Labour regulations	4.0	23.0***	20.3***	15.7

$^* p < 0.05$ $^{**} p < 0.01$ $^{***} p < 0.001$

Impact of Victimisation on Respondents' Perception

As Table 8.5 shows, there was a general tendency by respondents who had been victimised to perceive greater obstacles to doing good business in the mainland. This perception was not restricted to crime and insecurity, and corruption, but extended to all types of obstacles, particularly for mainland respondents. It seems that their victimisation experience, whether it occurred on the mainland or in Hong Kong, gave these businesses a more negative view of the business environment in the mainland.

Significantly larger proportions of mainland respondents victimised by common or non-conventional crime reported obstacles to doing business in the mainland than non-victims. As in Hong Kong, here, variations between victims and non-victims were larger for victimisation by non-conventional crime. The most marked differences were found for crime and insecurity, cited by 62.1 per cent of victims of common crime compared with 40 per cent of non-victims, and corruption, cited by 67.3 per cent of victims of non-conventional crime compared with 41.5 per cent of non-victims.[3]

---

3 For both obstacles to doing business in Hong Kong and the mainland, we examined the impact of specific types of crime (for example, fraud versus bribery) on respondents' perception. We found no differences between the crimes and, therefore, used the combined variable (any common or non-conventional crime victimisation), which increased the number of cases, hence the statistical power of analyses.

Table 8.5 Obstacles to Doing Business in the Mainland and Victimisation: Hong Kong and mainland respondents who answered moderate to very strong obstacle (per cent)

Respondents	MAINLAND		HONG KONG		MAINLAND		HONG KONG	
	Victim of any common crime		Victim of any common crime		Victim of any non-conventional crime		Victim of any non-conventional crime	
Obstacle	Yes N = 190	No N = 3110	Yes N = 150	No N = 1667	Yes N = 648	No N = 2652	Yes N = 313	No N = 1504
Corruption	63.7***	45.5	69.3*	61.4	67.3***	41.5	69.3**	60.5
Crime and insecurity	62.1***	40.0	68.7	63.0	56.8***	37.4	71.6**	61.8
Lack of consultation with business sector	44.2*	36.4	56.7	51.6	52.2***	33.1	59.7**	50.4
Tax regulations	35.8*	28.1	53.3	48.7	41.0***	25.5	57.5**	47.3
Changes in laws	35.8**	26.3	60.0	52.9	37.3***	24.3	60.7**	52.0
Export/import regulations	28.9***	17.1	52.7	50.9	28.4***	15.2	57.2*	49.8
Safety/environmental regulations	26.8**	16.8	60.0*	52.1	23.6***	15.9	59.7**	51.3
Labour regulations	25.3***	15.1	49.3	44.3	23.6***	13.8	55.0***	42.6

$* p < 0.05$ $** p < 0.01$ $*** p < 0.001$

Hong Kong respondents' perception of the business situation in the mainland was affected in a slightly different way. While there were no major differences of opinion between those with premises in the mainland and those without such premises, respondents who experienced non-conventional crime were consistently and significantly more negative about the business environment in the mainland than non-victims. Table 8.5 shows a similar pattern, however, between victims and non-victims of common crime, with victims expressing more negative perceptions, with differences in proportions of the same magnitude as for non-conventional crime. We suspect that the analyses lack statistical power because of the small number of Hong Kong victims.

Comparing Perceptions in Hong Kong and the Mainland

Looking at how businesses in each mainland city ranked the obstacles to doing business in their own jurisdiction, both Shenzhen and X'ian ranked corruption, and crime and insecurity as the main obstacles (Table 8.4). Although the proportion of respondents who rated each of the eight potential obstacles as moderate to very strong varied between Hong Kong businesses rating obstacles in Hong Kong and mainland businesses rating obstacles in the mainland, all ranked corruption, crime and insecurity, and lack of consultation with the business sector higher than other obstacles. Mainland businesses referring to the mainland, however, placed corruption first, next crime and insecurity, and then lack of consultation, while Hong Kong businesses referring to Hong Kong put lack of consultation first, next crime and insecurity (on par with changes in laws and regulations), and then corruption.

Apart from corruption, and crime and insecurity, which higher proportions of mainland respondents regarded as obstacles in the mainland (46.5 per cent and 41.2 per cent respectively) compared with Hong Kong respondents within Hong Kong (34.3 per cent and 36.4 per cent respectively), all other types of obstacles were mentioned by higher proportions of Hong Kong businesses referring to Hong Kong than by mainland businesses referring to the mainland (Figure 8.1).

Figure 8.1 Obstacles to Doing Business in the Mainland by Mainland Respondents and in Hong Kong by Hong Kong Respondents

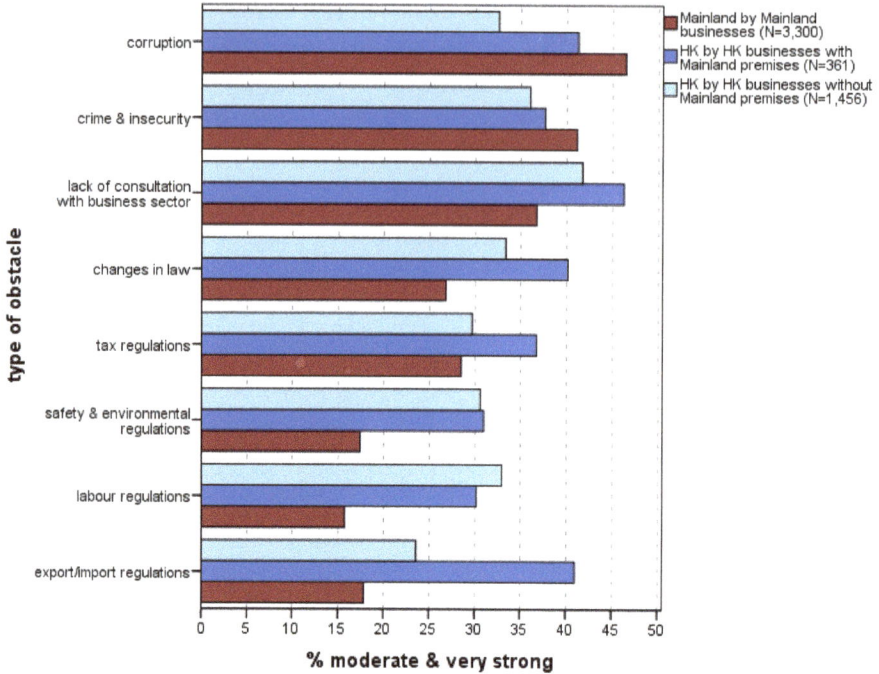

Interestingly, all Hong Kong respondents generally rated the situation in the mainland worse than the situation in Hong Kong, whether they had premises in the mainland or not, but those who did have premises on the mainland were the most negative. A surprising result, however, is that Hong Kong respondents with premises in the mainland tended to also rate the situation in Hong Kong worse than their counterparts without premises in the mainland. A possible explanation is that Hong Kong businesses with premises in the mainland also had higher rates of victimisation. The main reason for this effect, however, is that these businesses were generally larger, and, as reported previously, larger business size was associated with higher risk of victimisation and also a greater likelihood of reporting the matter to police.

Obstacles to Doing Good Business by Sector

In this section, we examine whether respondents operating in different business sectors had similar perceptions about potential obstacles to business. Table 8.6 presents the obstacles to business in Hong Kong that were ranked highest by Hong Kong's respondents, and the obstacles to business in the mainland that were ranked highest by mainland respondents, by sector of activity (based on the percentage of respondents in each sector who perceived the various obstacles as moderate to very strong).

Regardless of their main sector of activity, mainland businesses ranked obstacles to business in similar ways. Although percentages varied, across all sectors corruption was cited as an obstacle by the largest proportion of respondents (45.4–52.6 per cent). Crime and insecurity were ranked equal first with corruption or second (38.7–49.4 per cent). Lack of consultation with the business sector came equal second or third (35.8–43.6 per cent). These were followed by changes in law and tax regulations, mentioned by 31–36 per cent of respondents across all sectors.

In Hong Kong, the relevance of potential obstacles differed according to the economic sector. Lack of consultation with the business sector was perceived as an obstacle by the largest proportion of respondents across all business sectors (37.2–52.1 per cent), but in the financial/professional services sector, changes in law were also perceived as an obstacle by a similar proportion of respondents (44.7 per cent).

Respondents in the manufacturing and wholesale/trading sectors ranked corruption, export/import regulations and changes in law as equal second most important obstacles. These are the two sectors most likely to engage in export/import activities and, therefore, to feel the impact and potential limitations of the regulations as well as of frequent changes to these regulations. Manufacturers were most likely to be the victims of bribery and corruption and therefore to perceive these practices as obstacles. For retailers, the second most important obstacles to business were crime and insecurity (36.9 per cent). This correlates with the high rate of theft as well as extortion and intimidation reported in the retail sector. In contrast, only 9.1 per cent of retailers perceived corruption as an obstacle, which accords with the relatively lower rate of this practice in their sectors. Other sectors were also concerned with crime and insecurity, but ranked them third. Changes in law, tax and labour regulations were ranked second or third by most respondents.

We conclude this section by noting that Hong Kong respondents were generally more negative than mainland respondents, particularly those with premises in the mainland. Although the perception of what constituted obstacles to business in Hong Kong varied depending on sectors of activity, lack of consultation with business was ranked as the main obstacle. For mainland businesses, corruption was the main obstacle, with crime and insecurity, and lack of consultation featuring as either second or third depending on sector. Much higher proportions of Shenzhen respondents ranked crime and insecurity, and corruption as major obstacles, which again is consistent with their experiences of victimisation. The experience of victimisation appeared to engender a more negative view of all obstacles, not just crime and insecurity, although the effect was stronger for non-conventional crime than for common crime in Hong Kong.

Table 8.6 Ranking of Obstacles to Doing Good Business in Hong Kong and the Mainland (per cent)

	Manufacturing	Retail	Wholesale/trade	Finance & professional services	Other sectors
Obstacles to doing business in mainland by mainland respondents (N = 3300)[a]					
	N = 1299	N = 575	N = 514	N = 639	N = 273
Ranked 1	Corruption, 47.8*	Corruption, 45.4; Crime & insecurity, 44.7	Corruption, 48.3	Corruption, 52.6*	Corruption, 51.2; Crime & insecurity, 49.4
Ranked 2	Crime & insecurity, 40.1	Lack of consultation, 35.8	Lack of consultation, 40.7; Crime & insecurity, 38.7	Lack of consultation, 43.6**; Crime & insecurity, 41.1	Lack of consultation, 41.3
Ranked 3[b]	Lack of consultation, 37.2	Tax regulations, 31.5	Changes in law, 31.6	Changes in law, 34.8***; Tax regulations, 33.9*	Changes in law, 35.9**; Tax regulations, 32.5
Obstacles to doing business in Hong Kong by Hong Kong respondents (N = 1817)[a]					
	N = 427	N = 498	N = 338	N = 414	N = 140
Ranked 1	Lack of consultation, 52.1**	Lack of consultation, 40.6	Lack of consultation, 45.0	Lack of consultation, 47.6; Changes in law, 44.7**	Lack of consultation, 37.2
Ranked 2	Changes in law, 39.9; Export/import regs, 38.8***; Corruption, 38.6	Crime & insecurity, 36.9	Corruption, 37.1; Export/import regs, 36.3***; Changes in law, 36.0	Corruption, 42.9***	Labour regs, 34.6; Changes in law, 33.3
Ranked 3	Crime & insecurity, 36.8	Labour regs, 32.2; Changes in law, 31.8	Crime & insecurity, 32.6	Crime & insecurity, 37.6; Tax regulations, 36.5*; Safety regulations, 35.6*	Crime & insecurity, 31.2; Corruption, 27.5

$* p < 0.05$ $** p < 0.01$ $*** p < 0.001$

Notes: [a] Percentages refer to the proportion of respondents who ranked an obstacle as moderate to very strong; significance (indicated by *) refers to statistically significant differences for each obstacle across sectors of activity; [b] significantly greater proportions of mainland businesses in the manufacturing sector mentioned export/import regulations (22.6 per cent) and safety and environmental regulations (19.6 per cent) as moderate to strong obstacles compared with other sectors (16.8 per cent and 16.7 per cent respectively). but these did not rank high compared with other obstacles.

Perception of Crime Trends

So far we have focused on our respondents' specific victimisation experiences and broad perceptions about selected issues that might impact on their business. In this section, we turn our attention to their broader views on the extent of and trends in crime in their respective city with the question: 'In general, have crime problems for your company increased, decreased or remained the same over the last two to three years?' Two further questions probed more specifically how common they believed practices of bribery and extortion were: 'Do you believe such practices (bribery/extortion) are common in your line of business? Are they extremely common, fairly common, not very common or not common at all?' We assume that it is likely that respondents who believed that bribery occurred frequently in their line of business would see it as an obstacle more than those who did not. Likewise, those who thought that crime problems had increased would be more prone to perceive crime as an obstacle than those who did not think crime was on the rise.

Trends in Crime

Across the four cities, nearly three-quarters of respondents felt that for their company, crime problems had been stable in the past two or three years and only 8 per cent felt that crime problems had increased (Table 8.7). In Hong Kong, the majority (more than 90 per cent) of respondents said that crime had remained stable, with about 5 per cent thinking that crime had increased or decreased respectively. The last two categories were more likely to be food retailers. In the mainland, a greater proportion of respondents than in Hong Kong felt crime problems had decreased (overall 29.5 per cent and 33.6 per cent in Shenzhen) and 9.6 per cent felt they had increased. So, while Shenzhen stands out as the city where businesses were most at risk of victimisation, it was also the place where a greater proportion of respondents felt that the situation had improved.

Table 8.7 Perception of Crime Trends by City and Overall (per cent)

Perception that	Hong Kong N = 1817	Shanghai N = 1110	Shenzhen N = 1112	Xi'an N = 1078	Total N = 5117
Crime has remained the same or not sure	90.3***	68.5	55.2	58.9	71.4
Crime has decreased	4.6†††	23.8	33.6	31.1	20.6
Crime has increased	5.1	7.7	11.2	10.0	8.0
Bribery is very/fairly common	6.5†††	13.2	14.5	13.7	11.2
Extortion is very/fairly common	4.6***	1.7	2.4	1.4	2.8

*** $p < 0.001$, significantly higher than other cities

††† $p < 0.001$, significantly lower than other cities

Not surprisingly, in both Hong Kong and the mainland, business respondents who had been victimised were more likely to say that crime had increased. Table 8.8 presents the overall pattern, but a similar pattern was replicated in each city. Respondents' perception seemed to be particularly affected by the experience of common crime: those who had been the victims of common crime were about four times more likely to say that crime had increased than those who had not been victimised. Victims of non-conventional crime were just more than twice as likely as non-victims to say that crime had increased.

Looking at sectors of activity, we see in Table 8.9 that manufacturers were most likely to state that crime problems had increased. This view is not consistent with actual risks of victimisation by common crime because it was the retail rather than the manufacturing sector that was most prone to common crime victimisation, but this did not seem to affect retailers' views on the prevalence of crime. Larger businesses were more likely than smaller ones to perceive that crime problems had increased: the mean score on the business size scale of those who perceived an increase in crime was 6 compared with 5.71 for others ($p < 0.01$), which matches their higher rate of victimisation. This size effect is likely to be related to the manufacturers' perception of increased crime problems since businesses in that sector tended to be the largest.

Table 8.8 Perception that Crime had Increased and Victimisation (per cent)

Type of victimisation	Victimised	Not victimised
Common crime	27.7***	6.7
Non-conventional crime	14.4***	6.2
Any type of crime	15.4***	5.4

*** $p < 0.001$

Table 8.9 Perception that Crime had Increased and Actual Victimisation by Sector (per cent)

	Manufacturing N = 1726	Retail N = 1073	Wholesale/trade N = 852	Financial & professional services N = 1053	Other sectors N = 413
Perception that crime has increased	9.3*	7.6	6.6	7.2	8.7
Percentage of businesses victimised by:					
Common crime	6.0	8.9**	4.1	6.6	5.8
Non-conventional crime	23.0	20.9	23.6	22.3	23.7
Any type of crime	26.1	26.7	25.9	26.1	26.4

* $p < 0.05$ ** $p < 0.01$

We also found a consistent relationship between respondents' perception that crime had increased or remained stable and their judgment of the business environment. Across the four cities, respondents who thought that crime had increased were significantly more likely to rate not only crime and insecurity as an obstacle to doing business, but also most of the other obstacles. Again, this suggests respondents do not differentiate between the types of difficulties they experience in running their business, but give a global judgment of their business situation.

Commonness of Bribery and Extortion

Across all the cities, more than 10 per cent of respondents (11.2 per cent) felt that bribery and corruption were fairly or very common in their line of business (Table 8.7). Rates in mainland cities were about twice as high as the rate in Hong Kong, which parallels the prevalence of bribery victimisation found in the survey. There were no differences between the mainland cities. For both bribery and extortion, business respondents who had been the victims of these crimes were more likely to say that these practices were common. Of the 312 respondents whose company had been the victim of bribery, 42.9 per cent believed that the practice was widespread, but only 9.1 per cent of those who were not victims ($p < 0.001$). Similarly, of the 116 victims of extortion, 19.8 per cent perceived the practice was common compared with 11 per cent of non-victims ($p < 0.01$).

From Table 8.10, we see that businesses engaged in manufacturing were more likely than others to say that bribery was fairly and very common (13.8 per cent, $p < 0.01$). Large businesses were also more prone to believe that bribery was common (the mean score on the business size scale of those who perceived bribery to be common was 6.27 compared with 5.66 for others, $p < 0.001$), which again mirrors their higher rate of victimisation. Respondents who perceived that bribery and corruption were common in their line of business were more likely than other respondents to rate corruption as an obstacle to doing good business, as well as most of the other obstacles, in both Hong Kong and the mainland.

Table 8.10 Perception that Bribery and Extortion Were Common and Actual Victimisation by Sector (per cent)

	Manufacturing N = 1726	Retail N = 1073	Wholesale/trade N = 852	Financial & professional services N = 1053	Other sectors N = 413
Perception that bribery was very/fairly common	13.8**	9.1	11.6	9.0	10.7
Percentage victim of bribery	7.8***	3.5	5.0	6.3	6.2
Perception that extortion was very/fairly common	2.3	4.7**	1.9	2.8	2.0
Percentage victim of extortion	2.0	3.2**	0.7	2.8	2.6

$^{**} p < 0.01$ $^{***} p < 0.001$

The pattern of perceptions regarding the commonness of extortion was the reverse of that for bribery. Hong Kong respondents were significantly more likely to say that extortion and intimidation were fairly or very common than mainland respondents (4.6 per cent and 1.8 per cent respectively), and this reflected their greater risk of victimisation, although Shenzhen respondents tended to find extortion more common than in Shanghai and Xi'an. Retailers were most likely to find extortion common in their sector, which is consistent with the higher prevalence of extortion in that sector (Table 8.10). Surprisingly, smaller businesses were more likely to perceive that extortion was a common practice than larger ones, although larger businesses had higher risks of victimisation (the mean score on the business size scale of those who perceived extortion to be common was 5.38 compared with 5.74 for those who did not, $p < 0.05$). Although not all relations were statistically significant, respondents who thought that extortion was common were overall more negative about the general business environment, and mentioned more obstacles to doing business than the other respondents.

The broad perceptions of the extent of crime, bribery and extortion reported above confirm that crime has a significant overall impact on business confidence as well as confidence in the police (and perhaps by implication the state). The experience of crime victimisation undermines not only confidence but generates a sense that unfavourable conditions are encountered in respect to security and also in respect to the general regulatory demands of the state. In mainland cities, a (perceived) decline in crime was observed for between 23.8 and 33.6 per cent of businesses, while Hong Kong businesses noted little change; this mirrors the significant fluctuations in crime that occurred in the mainland (and Shenzhen in particular) against the relative stability of the low crime rates observed in Hong Kong over the past decade.

Bribery rather than extortion was seen as very or fairly common in the mainland—again reflecting the relative risks for business and the notoriety of this crime in China. Extortion, on the other hand, was noted in Hong Kong and Shenzhen, which points to a concern with the role of triad-related crime groups. It is notable that for the most part, perceptions about crime and the actual experience of victimisation are closely related; those who had avoided crime victimisation perceived that the risks of crime were lower than victims and they also believed that general conditions were less negative.

In summary, when considering the potential obstacles they faced in running their business, respondents ranked crime and corruption as important issues and often ahead of problems such as labour and taxes. Corruption was perceived as either a moderate or a serious obstacle by more than half of businesses (52 per cent), followed by crime and insecurity (49 per cent) and lack of consultation (42 per cent). Respondents in Shenzhen were the most likely to see crime and insecurity as the most serious obstacle (57 per cent) and those in Shanghai (27 per cent) were the least likely—a result consistent with Shenzhen's higher risk of crime. Hong Kong respondents ranked lack of government consultation with business as the most serious obstacle. Those operating in the mainland as well as Hong Kong, however, ranked corruption, and changes in laws and export/import regulations more highly than businesses operating only in Hong Kong. Among mainland businesses, corruption was ranked first, followed by crime and insecurity, and lack of consultation with business. Generally, Hong Kong businesses were more negative than mainland businesses about most issues, and for all respondents, the impact of crime victimisation tended to taint perceptions negatively not only in relation to crime and insecurity but also across all the potential obstacles.

In relation to crime trends over time, businesses that had been victimised were significantly more likely to perceive that crime had increased, although, overall, the majority of businesses (71.4 per cent) thought crime had remained about the same. Hong Kong respondents were the most likely (90.3 per cent) and those in Shenzhen the least likely to see crime as remaining stable (55.2 per cent); however, despite their higher victimisation rate, in Shenzhen, respondents (33.6 per cent) were more likely to perceive that crime had decreased over the past two to three years. Hong Kong respondents did not perceive that bribery was common (6.5 per cent did compared with 14.5 per cent of Shenzhen businesses), but they were significantly more likely than mainland businesses to see extortion as commonplace, albeit by a small percentage (that is, 4.6 per cent compared with 1.7 per cent of Shanghai businesses).

9. Summary, Implications and Future Directions

In this final chapter, we briefly summarise the main results of the China ICBS, with the prevalence of common and non-conventional crimes illustrated in Figures 9.1 and 9.2. The overall direct costs of crime incurred by our sample of businesses are estimated and extrapolated to the wider business community. We review the findings in respect to willingness to report to police and satisfaction with the police response, as well as general attitudes to crime trends and crime prevention. Where possible, we compare the results of this survey with those of a similar nature conducted in other parts of the world. Next, we return to the theories of crime and modernisation that we outlined in the introduction and discuss how well the findings of the ICBS and comparisons with other surveys fit these theories. From the comparisons, we are able to offer some general conclusions about the relative success or otherwise of managing the presumed crime risks associated with the transition from command-and-control economies to market-oriented economies as in the case of China, Eastern Europe and Russia.

In China, where detailed criminal statistics still seem to be regarded as state secrets and, for the most part, are available only at the aggregated national level, reliance on such official measures as guidance on trends in crime is even more problematic than usual. Even when such official data are available, they might be defined or collected in ways that make them only marginally useful to the interests of business. Consequently, the data provided by the ICBS can serve as an alternative or proxy measure of the level and nature of crime experienced by businesses in China. Such surveys provide valuable independent primary sources about crime and capture experiences and relationships otherwise neglected by police records. They are not, however, without limitations, which we discuss in detail below along with the possible remedies for some of the problems encountered in this prevalence study.

Summary of Results

Prevalence of Victimisation

Among the 5117 Chinese businesses surveyed by the ICBS, more than one-quarter (26.2 per cent) reported at least one incident of common or non-conventional crime over the past year. In Shenzhen, nearly 31 per cent of businesses had been victimised, which was significantly higher than in the other cities (22.2 per cent in Shanghai, 24.5 per cent in Hong Kong and 28.3 per cent in Xi'an). Businesses were at much higher risks of victimisation by non-conventional crimes (that is, fraud, bribery, extortion and IP infringement) than victimisation by common crime: across the four cities, the rate of non-conventional crime (22.6 per cent) was 3.4 times that of common crime (6.7 per cent). There were differences between the cities: in Hong Kong, respondents reported 2.3 times more non-conventional crime than common crime, but in Xi'an, it was five times more. Figure 9.1 summarises prevalence rates for common crime and Figure 9.2, for non-conventional crime in each of the cities.

Across the sample, 343 respondents (6.7 per cent) mentioned one or several incidents of common crime (of nine canvassed such as burglary, theft, robbery or assault) and most were the victims of more than one of these offences. Hong Kong's overall victimisation rate by common crime was higher than that of the mainland cities combined (8.3 per cent compared with 5.8 per cent). This higher rate, however, was largely due to a single crime—theft by customers—which was significantly more frequent in Hong Kong (3.1 per cent) than in the other cities (1 per cent) and was linked to Hong Kong's higher proportion of retailers. If we exclude theft by customers, Shenzhen stands out as the city with the highest rates of common crime (about 8 per cent)—particularly robbery, vandalism and theft by employees and outsiders—while both Shanghai and Xi'an recorded lower levels (about 5 per cent).

Figure 9.1 Prevalence of Common Crime in Four Chinese Cities

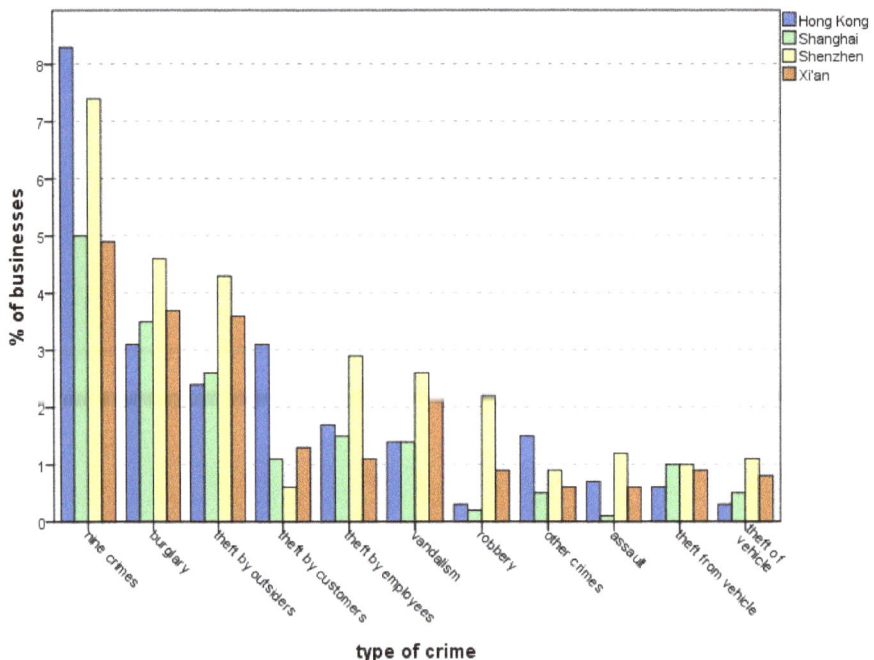

Businesses in Shenzhen were also at much higher risk of non-conventional crime (27.9 per cent) than those in Xi'an (25.3 per cent) and Hong Kong and Shanghai (19.5 per cent). Fraud was the most frequent type of economic crime reported by 13.4 per cent of businesses, with a significantly higher proportion in Shenzhen (15.4 per cent) (Figure 9.2). Just over 6 per cent of respondents mentioned one or several incidents of bribery, but there was a large difference between Hong Kong (2.7 per cent) and the mainland (8 per cent). In Xi'an, bribery was just as likely to involve officials as members of other companies, but officials were least likely to be involved in Hong Kong where bribes were sought by managers and employees of other companies in four out of five incidents. Although Shenzhen businesses also reported a high level of bribery, this was less likely to involve officials than in Xi'an. We speculate that the higher level of bribery reported by Xi'an businesses arises from the dominance of state-owned enterprises (SOEs) and the more recent commercialisation of its industry compared with Shanghai and Shenzhen. Extortion and intimidation were most common in Hong Kong and Shenzhen, and we attribute the relatively higher levels of such activities in both cities to the long-established activities of triad-related groups who capitalised upon the market for (illicit) protection on the opening up of the special economic zone in Shenzhen.

Intellectual property and copyright theft were reported by about 6 per cent of businesses, but this was significantly more of a problem in Shenzhen (9.1 per cent) and Xi'an (7.6 per cent) than in Shanghai (5.9 per cent) and particularly Hong Kong (3.5 per cent). The lack of follow-up questions on IP theft limited our ability to explore this offence, which is likely to have become more prevalent since 2004–05. In the absence of questions about foreign ownership or partnerships, it is not possible to assess whether foreign companies are at greater risk than local companies in respect to IP theft. The lower rate of IP theft in Hong Kong is, however, likely to reflect the stricter laws,[1] as well as concerted efforts by customs and police to crack down on these offences. Combined with a well-funded private and public education program that employed popular film and music entertainers who stressed the impact of such theft on creative industries, the criminalisation of IP in Hong Kong has advanced more than in mainland China.

---

1   See Hong Kong Copyright Ordinance (Cap 528) 1997 and subsequent amendments in 2007 that promoted corporate responsibility by holding directors liable.

Figure 9.2 Prevalence of Non-Conventional Crime in Four Chinese Cities

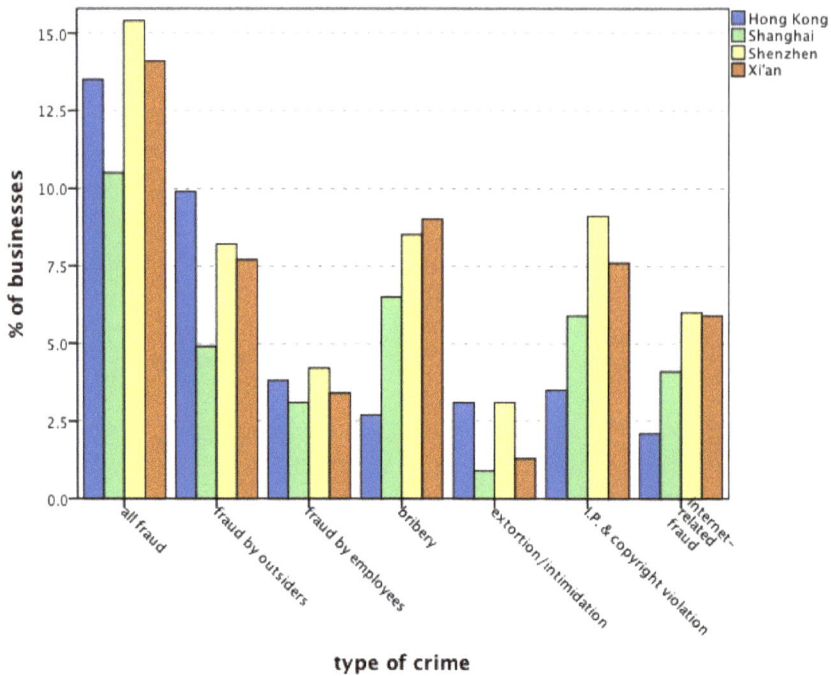

type of crime

For the majority of the crimes we surveyed, the size of the company was the strongest predictor of victimisation. The prevalence of common crime was positively correlated with the size of companies, with the exception of theft by customers, which was significantly more likely to target small (retail) businesses. Larger businesses were also at higher risk of victimisation by non-conventional crime; however, the size of the business did not affect the likelihood of extortion, and smaller businesses had a higher prevalence of fraud by outsiders.

Costs of Crime

For our businesses, the amount of direct monetary loss due to crime was significant.[2] All offences of common crime cost US$3.74 million (in Hong Kong, US$1.53 million).[3] In both Hong Kong and the mainland, the greatest amount of 'shrinkage' due to common crime came from theft by employees, which totalled US$1.37 million or nearly 38 per cent of the total monetary loss. On top of these losses to common crime, the various types of fraud and IP infringement incurred

---

2 Indirect costs from lost productivity and the administrative consequences of the crime (for example, reporting to police, filing insurance claims, and so on) are not included in any of our estimates.

3 This is a conservative estimate because the calculation is based on different offences of common crime, but not multiple incidents of the same offence (the survey did not ask respondents about the frequency of victimisation by common crimes). In contrast, losses due to *all* incidents of fraud that occurred during the reference years are counted in the estimates.

losses about four times larger than common crime and reached US$16.61 million. Again, this estimate is conservative because no data were collected with respect to monetary losses caused by bribery and extortion. Combining losses due to common crime and those due to non-conventional crime, we estimate that for our sample of 5117 Chinese businesses, monetary losses reached US$20.35 million in one year. Bearing in mind the difference in per capita income and pay levels for workers between Hong Kong and mainland cities, the impact of such losses is significantly greater for mainland businesses.[4]

We know from the census that 296 249 companies were registered in Hong Kong in 2004 and can, therefore, extrapolate our estimates to the population of businesses (Census and Statistics Department, Hong Kong 2006). Our sample of 1817 businesses represents approximately 0.61 per cent of all businesses in Hong Kong, but it includes more manufacturing and fewer retail businesses than indicated in the census. After weighting for these differences, we estimate that in 2004 Hong Kong businesses lost US$169.27 million to all offences of common crime. Using a similar procedure, we estimate that for the entire population of Hong Kong businesses, annual losses to non-conventional crime reached US$1.35 billion. Therefore, a conservative estimate of the cost of common and non-conventional crime to the Hong Kong business community was US$1.52 billion in 2004. To place these losses in context, we can roughly compare them with a UK study of the impact of fraud conducted under the auspices of the Association of Chief Police Officers (ACPO). This study estimated that in 2005 the direct cost of fraud (which included IP crime) for the whole of the United Kingdom was approximately £12.98 billion (US$23.2 billion). When broken down by sector, about £3.76 billion (US$6.73 billion) in losses came from the business sector, £2.75 billion (US$4.92 billion) from individuals, and £6.47 billion (US$11.6 billion) from the public sector (Levi et al. 2007).[5]

The direct cost of crime for our sample of 3300 mainland businesses was about US$2.21 million for common crime and US$7.22 million for non-conventional crime. We cannot extrapolate these figures to the population of companies in Shanghai, Shenzhen and Xi'an because we do not have census data or estimates of the number of distinct businesses in these cities, as we have for Hong Kong. The 2006 *China Statistical Yearbook* states that across all sectors there were

---

4   Although on a converging trend at about 2 per cent a year since the post-reform period (Lei and Yao 2008), the income gap (either per capita or purchasing power parity) between Hong Kong and China remains substantial. Based on Table 1.1, the ratio of average annual income for employees varied from 12.5:1 for Hong Kong compared with Xi'an, through to 3.85:1 compared with Shanghai and 3.4:1 compared with Shenzhen. The purchasing power parity (PPP) ratio for Hong Kong to China as a whole is, however, nearly 6.5 to 1 (World Bank n.d.).

5   The conversion of British pounds to US dollars as of 30 June 2005 was US$1.79 per £1. Levi and Burrows (2008) also note a number of caveats and difficulties in making such estimates and have erred on the conservative side.

582 977 businesses[6] throughout China with income of CNY5 million or above. The Shanghai Municipal Statistical Bureau (2006) reported that 31 370 businesses with income of CNY5 million or more operated in the municipality (manufacturing, construction, wholesale and retail),[7] but the number of businesses in the finance sector was not reported for 2005. In our survey, respondents were generally reluctant to report company income or annual turnover so we cannot estimate what proportion of our sample represents businesses with incomes above the threshold for inclusion in official statistics. According to recent sources, 90 per cent of approximately 43 million companies that operate in China are private and the number of private registered businesses grew at 30 per cent per annum between 2000 and 2009 (*The Economist*, 10 March 2011:13).[8]

It is unlikely that our mainland sample reflects the distribution of business by sector, income or workforce size in mainland China. In the absence of a known denominator for distinct businesses in our three mainland cities, we cannot extrapolate losses with great confidence. Based on the State Council's National Economic Census (NBS 2005a) undertaken by the National Bureau of Statistics, we can, however, approximate the probable universe of secondary and tertiary enterprises in the three mainland cities. The scale of the census is indicative of the vast number of different kinds of non-agricultural enterprises that make up commercial business in China. The census contacted some five million legal units, seven million establishments and about 40 million self-employed individuals or privately owned enterprises and deployed three questionnaires depending on the kind of unit contacted: corporate, establishment/industry and self-employed (Li 2006). We combine the number of corporate, industrial entities and private or self-employed businesses to estimate the population of business in our surveyed cities; however, our results must be treated with caution because we find contradictions in the available summaries and insufficient explanation in the available tables to determine precisely the counting and categorisation

---

6　The 2006 *China Statistical Yearbook* describes the 2005 population of mainland companies as follows: manufacturing, 219 463; construction, 58 750; wholesale and retail, 177 629; food and hotel, 35 689; finance, 82 453; and travel, 8993 (NBS 2006a).

7　The Shanghai data reported 14 769 manufacturing businesses, 2422 in construction, 4371 in wholesale and 9788 in retail. The share of businesses that reached the income threshold had also grown by about 40 per cent across all sectors in the period 2005–09.

8　*The Economist* cites Zheng Yumin, Secretary of the Commerce Department of Zhejiang, in relation to data possibly reflecting the 2009 census. The same report also estimates that private companies now contribute about 70 per cent of GDP and that the role of state-owned-enterprises, which once accounted for almost all business, has steadily declined since the 1980s.

rules.[9] With these caveats in mind, we proceed to 'guesstimate' the proportion of the population of reported businesses (legal entities, establishments and privately owned) that our sample for each city represents.[10]

We calculate two estimates of the population of businesses in Shanghai, Shenzhen and Xi'an. The first likely overestimates the number of businesses; the second is more conservative. In the first estimate, we combine the number of businesses in the three categories—legal entities, establishments and privately owned—which results in what we call the 'maximum' population (see Table 9.1 for the summary of the calculations). We suspect, however, that there is an overlap between legal entities and establishments and a number of businesses might be counted twice. Therefore, in the second estimate, we exclude legal entities and combine only establishments and privately owned businesses to obtain a population of businesses, which we call the 'minimum' population. Based on these maximum and minimum figures, our samples represent the following proportions of the total business population in each city: Shanghai, 0.102 to 0.151 per cent; Shenzhen, 0.267 to 0.313 per cent; Xi'an, 0.337 to 0.380 per cent. From these approximations, we estimate the range of the monetary loss to the business community in each of the mainland cities. Across the three cities, we suggest that losses due to all crime totalled between US$4.17 and $5.61 billion and that about one-quarter of these losses were the result of common crime (that is, US$0.96–1.28 billion). Losses for Shanghai were the largest, ranging between US$2.45 and $3.61 billion, followed by Shenzhen, between US$1.20 and $1.41 billion, and Xi'an, between US$0.52 and $0.59 billion. In short, our 'guesstimate' puts the overall annual business losses to crime in the three mainland cities altogether at a midpoint of about US$4.9 billion.

---

9   For example, the government press releases report different numbers for the entities in scope, so that contrary to Li (2006), 30 million rather than 40 million self-employed enterprises are noted. See Government of People's Republic of China (2005).
10   For sources all retrieved on 18 May 2011, see for Shanghai: NBS (2005a); for Xi'an: NBS (2005d); for Shenzhen: NBS (2005b).

Table 9.1 Estimates of Monetary Loss Due to Crime in Three Mainland Cities, 2005

	Shanghai		Shenzhen		Xi'an	
N business in ICBS sample	1112		1110		1078	
Total monetary loss in ICBS sample, US$ million	3.682		3.755		1.993	
	Minimum	Maximum	Minimum	Maximum	Minimum	Maximum
Population of businesses[a]	742 000	1 086 000	355 000	415 500	283 363	319 766
ICBS sample as a proportion of the population of businesses	0.151%	0.102%	0.313%	0.267%	0.380%	0.337%
Monetary loss for population of businesses, US$ billion	2.45	3.61	1.20	1.41	0.52	0.59
Average total monetary loss, US$ billion	3.03		1.30		0.56	

Notes: [a] Based on First National Economic Census (NBS 2005a) of secondary and tertiary enterprises; minimum number includes establishments and self-employed or privately owned enterprises; maximum number includes legal entities, establishments and self-employed or privately owned enterprises.

These estimates show that losses due to crime were not negligible. How much of these losses was reported to the police, perhaps in the hope of recovering at least part of the money or having the perpetrator punished?

Reporting Crime and Satisfaction with Police

There was more willingness by business to report common crimes than non-conventional crimes, and mainland businesses were significantly more likely than those in Hong Kong to report both common and non-conventional crimes. In Hong Kong, of all incidents of common crime, 53.5 per cent were reported to the police compared with 79 per cent in the mainland. Across the cities, less than one-quarter of all incidents of non-conventional crime were reported: 19.1 per cent in Hong Kong and 23.2 per cent in the mainland. Once again, large businesses were more likely to report crimes to police than small businesses. A possible explanation is that large companies have a wider exposure to risk and often have specialised security staff and policies mandating the reporting of crime to police. For the majority of respondents who did not report the crime to the police, it was because the incident was not serious enough or, for crime by staff, because it was dealt with internally. Of those who did report, about half were satisfied with the police response and no significant differences were observed between the cities, but Xi'an businesses expressed the least satisfaction. Dissatisfaction was mostly due to the view that police did not do enough or lacked interest, followed by failure to catch the offender or recover property. In general, Hong Kong respondents were more positive about the police response than their mainland counterparts, especially in respect to bribery and theft by employees, but since they reported less often than in the mainland, they might have reported more serious incidents.

When asked about their general judgment about police efficacy in relation to the crime problems facing business in their area, about half the businesses were satisfied; however, experiences of victimisation negatively affected the perception of police effectiveness. As a result, Shenzhen respondents, who had higher risks of victimisation, had a significantly more negative view of police action in general.

Crime Prevention

Our survey shows that there is room for Chinese business to develop partnerships with police and local authorities in crime prevention since only about one in six companies had contact with police, local councils or government and were aware of cooperative action against crime (for example, joint security patrols, business watch groups, alarms/CCTV, and so on), and one in four was interested in participating in such cooperative activities. Victimised businesses were more interested in being involved in collective action, but were not necessarily more aware of crime-prevention activities. Hong Kong businesses were the least interested in cooperative action (20.7 per cent were) and Shenzhen businesses were the most interested (34.9 per cent). This is probably associated with the relative risks of crime in both cities. Larger companies were more aware of crime-prevention initiatives and more interested in participating than smaller ones. They were also more likely to have had contact with police or local government about crime prevention, which is again probably due to their generally higher rate of victimisation. Given their economic weight, larger companies might be able to exert greater influence over crime-prevention policy and the deployment of police.

Perception of Crime Trends and Obstacles to Doing Good Business

Across the four cities, the majority of respondents (71.4 per cent) thought that crime levels had remained stable over the past two or three years, but, as would be expected, those who had been victimised were more likely to say that crime had increased. Yet, despite their higher rate of victimisation, one-third of respondents in Shenzhen felt that crime levels had decreased. This finding supports Zhong (2009a) who reported that Shenzhen police had been more proactive and that crime rates had started to decline following a peak in 2003. Hong Kong respondents did not believe that bribery was common (only 6.5 per cent of Hong Kong businesses believed it was compared with an average of 14 per cent in the mainland), but they estimated that extortion was more common than did mainland respondents.

Perceptions of obstacles to doing business—including crime and corruption but also other issues such as lack of consultation, taxes, and regulations in respect to labour, export/import and safety—provide a measure of the salience of crime and corruption as obstacles relative to other problems. Crime and corruption were ranked as important issues and often ahead of other problems such as labour and tax regulations. Overall, corruption was perceived as a moderate to serious obstacle by more than half of businesses (52 per cent), followed by crime and insecurity (49 per cent) and lack of consultation (42 per cent). Lack of government consultation with business was at the forefront of obstacles faced by Hong Kong respondents, followed by crime and insecurity. In contrast, among mainland businesses, corruption was ranked first, followed by crime and insecurity, and lack of consultation with business. Respondents in Shenzhen were the most concerned by crime and insecurity (57 per cent) and those in Shanghai (27 per cent) were the least concerned, which is consistent with Shenzhen's higher risk of crime. Generally, Hong Kong businesses were more negative than mainland businesses about most issues. A striking finding was that the impact of crime victimisation tended to taint perceptions negatively not only about crime and insecurity but across all the potential obstacles.

Comparisons with Other Surveys

Rates of common crime victimisation were considerably lower in China than in both Western and Eastern Europe. The Central Eastern Europe ICBS (1999) found that overall 27 per cent (compared with 6.7 per cent in China) of businesses had been the victims of common crimes, but as in China, the risk there was greater for larger businesses. The 1994 sweep of the ICBS revealed that businesses in Western Europe and Australia were up to 10 times more likely than Chinese businesses to be victimised by common crime. Lower rates of common crime were also recorded in the China ICBS than in the Nigerian CCBS. Comparisons with the UNICVS are consistent with previous research and show that businesses were at much greater risk of break and enter or burglary offences than households. The relative risks of vehicle-related theft and robbery were similar for businesses and households, but the risks of assault were almost double for individuals than for those in business. As with common crime, risks of fraud were lower in China than in Western Europe, Eastern Europe and Nigeria. Incidents of bribery and extortion, however, were more frequent in China than in Western Europe and Australia, but less frequent than in Eastern Europe. The prevalence of crime against business in mainland China was also lower than in the emerging economies of Brazil, Russia and India.

In short, China's transition has not been overly burdened with runaway crime and corruption, although both of these 'distortions' (or side effects of major economic restructuring) are capable of disrupting economies. In this snapshot of crimes against business, the rate of crime reported by Chinese business was relatively modest compared with other transitional economies. The fact that this transition was planned (Messner et al. 2007a) and the ideological importance of order and stability supported by authoritarian forms of campaign policing might have contributed to the containment of common crime. In Shenzhen, however, runaway crime and corruption have been grave enough to threaten the capture of key institutions in the municipality. The presumed crime-control benefits of the long-established 'rule of law' in Hong Kong when compared with the mainland cities was neither as dramatic nor as consistent in respect to crime against business as we might have originally assumed.

All the business surveys we considered showed similar reporting patterns to the China ICBS. Chinese respondents, however, especially in the mainland, were much more likely to report to police than Central Eastern European businesses. Reporting rates were broadly similar in Western nations and in China. Yet, we found that businesses (in Hong Kong and mainland cities) were much more likely to report burglary, vehicle-related theft, robbery and assault than Hong Kong households or for that matter the average households in all the 33 capital cities surveyed by the UNICVS.

Theoretical Perspectives

In the Introduction, we outlined some of the theories that have been used to explain trends in crime in transitional economies. We suggest that these theories, applied at three distinct but related levels of analysis—macro, meso and micro—adequately explain our data. At the macro level, we draw from Durkheim's notion of anomie, Shelley's perspective on modernisation and urbanisation, and Messner et al.'s concepts of institutional anomie and planned transition. At the meso level, we draw from Cohen et al.'s (1980) and Clarke's (1997) opportunity theory, and at the micro level, from Felson's routine-activity approach.

Macro Level

The data from the ICBS provide a snapshot of the extent and nature of crime against business, but on their own do not permit us to analyse changes over time and test either Durkheim's perspective on anomie or Shelley's perspective on modernisation. The literature on crime in China, however, which has shown that crime levels have risen over the past 40 years since the economic reforms, is congruent with Durkheim's association of crime rise with rapid and significant societal change. The fact that economic crime in the form of non-conventional crime rose at a much faster rate than common or street crime (Dutton 2006; Keith and Li 2006; Liu 2005) supports Shelley's hypothesis about the growth of property crime associated with modernisation and urbanisation. Our data show that across the four Chinese cities business victimisation by non-conventional crime was more frequent than victimisation by common crime, which included both property and violent offences. This was also the case in Eastern Europe but not in Western Europe and Australia where an opposite pattern was observed. Although van Dijk and Terlouw (1996) in their European survey did not report the combined rate for each type of crime, we can use the highest rate of common crime (theft by customers, reported by 59.7 per cent of respondents) as a proxy for common crime and sum up the rates of fraud by outsiders and employees (25.2 per cent) as a proxy for non-conventional crime. If we divide the rate of non-conventional crime by that of common crime, we find a ratio of 0.42 (that is, the rate of non-conventional crime was more than half that of common crime). The Eastern Europe ICBS found a total rate of common crime of 27 per cent. Again, summing up the rates of fraud by employees and by outsiders (38 per cent), we find that the rate of non-conventional crime was 1.4 times that of common crime. The same process produces a ratio of 1.8 for the whole Chinese sample.

These differential ratios between non-conventional and common crime in long-established Western market economies compared with societies that only recently moved from command-and-control to market economies support Durkheim's concept of anomie related to changes in values. In both mainland China and Eastern Europe—although the change has been more abrupt in the latter—the communist values associated with a command-and-control economy and the virtue of collective property have been replaced with new values supporting a market economy, private property and the pursuit of individual wealth. Both common and non-conventional crimes have increased, but the anomic effect has predominantly affected economic values so that economic crimes have risen more sharply, and represent a large proportion of crimes against business. In contrast, in 'old' Western capitalist economies, which experienced changes in (economic) values in the eighteenth and nineteenth centuries, the initial rise in economic crime has now stabilised to a level where non-conventional crime represents only a fraction of the total amount of crime. Of course, related factors, discussed below, such as the presence of stronger commercial regulatory and enforcement frameworks in Western countries, affect the ratio between common and non-conventional crimes.

Some differences in the ratio of non-conventional to common crimes are observed between the four Chinese cities: in Hong Kong and Shanghai, fraud was 1.6 times more frequent than common crime; in Shenzhen, 1.7 times; and in Xi'an, 2.3 times. Although Hong Kong has run a capitalist economy based on the free market for a long time, its common/non-conventional crime ratio is relatively similar to that of the other cities. Much of Hong Kong's economic activity, however, occurs with the mainland, with many entrepreneurs on both sides of the border running cross-border operations; therefore, mainland anomic effects are likely to have an impact. In Xi'an, the rate of fraud is 2.3 times that of common crime, which is consistent with a more recent breakdown in the old collective values of economic order and a rise in anomie; Xi'an is probably the city currently experiencing the transition from old to new values and resulting anomie more strongly than Shenzhen and Shanghai. It is a traditional stronghold of the Communist Party, with a high proportion of SOEs and has only recently opened to foreign investment and global trade. Both the new economic values and business structures would increase licit and illicit commercial opportunities that Mertonian 'innovators', from the public and private sectors, seize by embracing the new slogan that 'being rich is glorious'.

Shelley (1981) argues that modernisation and urbanisation involve large-scale migrations from rural to urban areas, which in turn leads to a rise in violent and property crime because opportunities for property crime increase and traditional rural violence is transported to urban areas. In time, when rural migrants settle in their urban lifestyle, violent crime decreases but not property crime and what remains of violent crime is essentially acquisitive (for example, robbery). In the mainland cities, particularly Shenzhen, the 'floating population' of rural migrants has been linked to increases in street crime. In Shenzhen— Deng Xiaoping's laboratory for 'market socialism'—the rate of urbanisation and industrialisation has been phenomenal: from a fishing village of 30 000 inhabitants in 1979, it had grown to a commercial and industrial centre of 8.28 million by 2005. The population growth has been fuelled by the influx of unregistered rural workers from China's interior attracted by the prospect of low-skilled jobs in the city. Official crime data for Shenzhen presented by Zhong (2009a) show not only a general increase in crime since 1980, but also that the nature of crimes has changed. In the recent period, economic crimes in Shenzhen represent a higher share of the total burden of crime and the share of non-acquisitive violent crimes has diminished. For example, in 1981, homicide represented 1.1 per cent of all reported crimes and rape 3.5 per cent. By 2006, homicide was only 0.4 per cent of all crimes and rape 0.7 per cent. The share of robbery (acquisitive violent crime) went up from 2.5 per cent in 1981 to 6.7 per cent in 2006, and the share of grand larceny (that is, theft valued at more than US$370) grew from a low 1.9 per cent in 1981 to 23.1 in 2006. These trends are consistent with Shelley's hypothesis about the impact of early and later stages of urbanisation on crime patterns. The overall volume of all crimes has increased in Shenzhen, but non-acquisitive violent crime has slowed and plateaued after 30 years of urbanisation and modernisation, while property crime has continued to rise.

Results from the ICBS in Shenzhen add further support for Shelley's argument. Shenzhen recorded higher levels of violent crimes against business (robbery, assault and extortion/intimidation) as well as theft by employees and outsiders, vehicle theft, vandalism, fraud and IP infringement than the other cities. Rapid urbanisation, which in Shenzhen was characterised by a dramatic growth in business and commercial activity and attracted a large number of peasant workers bringing their 'rural manners' and traditional violence to the city, has resulted in a higher rate of violent crimes against business. Shanghai and Xi'an have long been urbanised, and they have also experienced a growth in commercial activity and an influx of rural workers, but not to the same extent as Shenzhen. In addition, Shenzhen was the first mainland city to engage in 'market socialism' and served as an experimental ground from which other modernising Chinese cities have been able to learn what not to do, especially in respect to the key issue of political stability. Yet, even though Shenzhen had to contend with both the Durkheimian anomic consequences of modernisation and the effects of urbanisation hypothesised by Shelley, the rates of crime against business are lower than those recorded in Western Europe in 1994 (van Dijk and Terlouw 1996) and in Central Eastern Europe in 1999 (Alvazzi del Frate 2004). This important finding suggests that other mechanisms have acted as buffers against the criminogenic impact of rapid modernisation and urbanisation.

Messner (1982) argued that in times of rapid change, a lag between socioeconomic transformations and institutional adaptations to these transformations (institutional anomie) was likely, and as the experience of the former Soviet Union has demonstrated, this could even lead to total institutional collapse. On the other hand, he and his colleagues (Messner et al. 2007a) also proposed that institutional collapse could be avoided when the economic and social transitions were planned and managed by a strong authoritarian state such as the PRC. The ICBS data illustrate both aspects of Messner et al.'s argument. Shenzhen stands out as the city that has generally experienced higher levels of crime than other cities in our survey, and thus also stands out as the 'litmus test' of the institutional anomie theory. In Shenzhen, institutional anomie occurred during the city's phenomenal expansion: while hundreds of thousands of rural migrants constructed and laboured in Shenzhen's newly established factories, the *hukou* system failed to provide adequate social services or basic social security to the huge 'floating' population. Police resources and regulatory reforms increased at a much slower pace than the population and the changes brought about by market socialism, and were unable to cope with the soaring rate of violent and property crime and the associated triad-related groups who had extended their activities from Hong Kong and Taiwan to Shenzhen. Despite several strike-hard anti-crime campaigns, the effectiveness of the police was limited by 'technical' deficiencies and compromised by high-level corruption in its own ranks and among other officials. The prevalence of most of the common and non-conventional crimes was higher in Shenzhen than in the other cities we surveyed. Extortion and intimidation were on par with Hong Kong and likely due to the same perpetrators.

Yet, if we compare the rates of crime against business in Shenzhen with those of both the 'old' stable Western countries and transitional Eastern European countries, we find that Shenzhen has a lower prevalence of both common and economic crimes. In addition, the majority of Shenzhen's respondents seemed confident that crime problems had stabilised and one-third thought things had started to improve and crime was diminishing. These findings do not suggest that an institutional collapse has occurred, but rather that if social and policing institutions had been slow to come to grips with Shenzhen's experimentation in unregulated marketisation, they are now catching up. Across the three mainland cities, the prevalence of crime, particularly common crime, is lower than elsewhere in the world for which comparable data are available. The PriceWaterhouseCoopers Global Economic Crime Survey also indicated that fraud against business was less frequent in mainland China than in the new economies of Brazil, India and Russia. While the marketisation of the Russian economy has been mostly unregulated and apparently infiltrated by criminal organisations, the democracies of Brazil and India (following Nehru's legacy) have been able to plan, steer and regulate their growing economies, but not to the extent of the Chinese Government.

Consistent with Messner et al.'s (2007a) notion that an interplay of 'master forces' (forces of change) and 'pathway forces' (forces of control) helps to maintain a relatively effective framework of formal and informal social-control mechanisms, our survey suggests that the strong authoritarian Chinese state has been successful (most of the time) in curbing institutional anomie. Nevertheless, the much higher prevalence of non-conventional crime compared with common crime in the ICBS points to some deficiencies in fighting large-scale economic crime and coordinating public and private security services. This finding and interpretation are consistent with Trevaskes's (2010a) argument that the Chinese

Government, through its periodic hard-hitting *yanda*,[11] has kept common crime to low levels, but, we suggest, at the expense of non-conventional crime. Here, institutional anomie—in the sense of lagging institutional reforms in the presence of new challenges—might have manifested in the absence of policing apparatus specialised in economic crime. If a strong authoritarian state is, on the one hand, more capable of controlling institutional anomie than a weak state, on the other hand, the absence of independent oversight and checks and balances can facilitate corrupt practices by party members and officials, particularly in SOEs. For example, corruption was more frequently reported in the mainland than in Hong Kong, and especially in Xi'an where state-owned businesses and traditional party control are still prevalent.

Our reading of the survey results suggests that current countermeasures and policies aimed at mitigating crime against business have failed. Although public police have been able to contain common or street crime, they have not yet transformed into policing agencies with a capacity to differentiate between kinds of criminals and common and economic crimes, and to focus on crimes against business, which are both highly attractive to a new breed of criminals and harmful to society. The lag in implementing crime-proofing strategies, especially by large businesses that are at greater risk of victimisation, is apparent in their slow adoption (in terms of competence and effectiveness) of private security. In short, identifying the 'new enemies of the state' has become much harder than in the past when simple categories—class enemies, 'rightists', feudal remnants and the like—could be readily distinguished and demonised. Economic criminals, it seems, are hard to distinguish from valued entrepreneurs, business leaders and officials of SOEs who gamble with venture capitalists and fall for fanciful and fraudulent innovators.

Meso and Micro Levels

Independent of the criminogenic impact of modernisation and urbanisation observed by Durkheim and Shelley, the growth in economic activities and consumerism also increases opportunities for property crime. As Cohen et al.'s (1980) opportunity theory argued, based on the trends in property crime in post–World War II North America, economic development and the availability of consumer goods led to an increase in property crime. The opening up of the Chinese economy and the implantation of new commerce and industries have produced both an increase in consumer goods (more opportunities for common crime) and an increase in business and commercial activities (more

---

11   A Chinese word meaning 'strike-hard', referring to campaign-style policing.

opportunities for non-conventional crime). In this medium-range theoretical perspective, larger businesses are more at risk of victimisation because they offer more attractive targets than smaller ones.

Related to opportunity theory but at a more micro level of interpretation, our analysis of the risk factors supports our introductory proposition that routine activity theory is relevant because the criminogenic elements highlighted by the theory—criminal opportunity, absence of competent guardianship and target attractiveness—are the key drivers of risk of victimisation for business. Chinese businesses thus suffer similar risks to those found elsewhere and could benefit from many of the measures recommended by situational crime-prevention approaches. Hardening attractive targets (making them more difficult to steal or trade in illegal markets) and improving the effectiveness of capable guardians both actual and virtual (for example, by increasing the capacity of police to 'catch and convict' and improving regulatory frameworks) can reduce the risk of theft and fraud. For example, we found that businesses located in serviced buildings, which offer a higher level of security, suffered relatively less victimisation than those located in shopping areas. The role of prevention is recognised by business and is reflected in the rapid growth of private security and guarding services in China, but their coordination and utilisation could be improved. The recent demise of campaign-style policing and the shift to a prevention focus rather than reliance on crude general deterrence and brutalising punishments will also help in redefining what constitutes serious harm (for example, Bakken 2004; Trevaskes 2010a, 2010b). If these changes release police resources for greater specialisation in complex crime such as fraud and enable better crime proofing of SOEs and other businesses then the costs of serious fraud, IP crime and corruption might be contained. Large-scale businesses usually make investments in crime prevention to protect assets and prevent theft. Smaller businesses have fewer resources and can be more vulnerable, even if they constitute less attractive targets than larger businesses. Collective action by businesses in concert with public police to develop effective countermeasures is vital and can help minimise the problem of crime displacement. Displacement of crime occurs when an industry or business in a particular location takes steps to minimise the risk of crime, often by increasing the role of guardians and reducing the opportunities for theft, but in doing so makes other businesses who invest less in crime prevention (by choice or circumstance) more vulnerable.

Limitations and Development of the Protocol

Our study was the first attempt at measuring the prevalence of crimes against business in China, and a good deal has been learned about how to make the ICBS a more effective instrument. In hindsight, our experience suggests that reducing the number of questions about the business itself—especially whether it was foreign owned, a joint enterprise or an enterprise involved in export/import—had implications for our interpretation of some forms of fraud, and might represent a crucial distinction for risks of IP crimes. Our failure to ask whether or not the business was an SOE was also an omission we later found frustrating; manufacturing, science-based and extraction businesses are often SOEs in mainland China and their extent varies across cities and provinces.[12] It is probable that SOEs are more likely to report crime and to be victimised in different ways than private commercial operations and that this status impacts on their attitudes to obstacles such as corruption. In addition, our standpoint was overly Hong Kong oriented and we should have asked questions about mainland businesses that were operating in Hong Kong because they might face equal if not greater risks than Hong Kong businesses operating in the mainland. We did ask Hong Kong businesses about the obstacles they faced operating in the mainland, but we did not ask the one in eight mainland businesses operating in Hong Kong what obstacles they faced in Hong Kong.

We consider that the current design fully stretches the capacity of telephone interviews and we think that face-to-face interviews might be the only way to achieve further depth and reliability. A related problem was the failure to enlist more business managers and to entice more businesses to participate, and this reflects the limitations of telephone-contact methods. Revision of the protocol should help to reduce overall respondent burden, and the possibility of using a split-sample procedure (that is, two versions of the questionnaire each covering the same core questions but sharing fewer questions from the list of crimes) could be considered for cities such as Hong Kong and Shanghai where survey fatigue might be more of an issue.

A large-scale victimisation survey provides a tool for theoretical analyses and comparative examination of potential risk factors and opportunities for prevention, but is meaningful only if it is reasonably representative of the population of interest. We were hampered by incomplete census data about the number and nature of the business/enterprise population in mainland China. With a clearer idea of the population of businesses, we would have been able to stratify our sample (for example, by sector, size and income) and produce a more representative survey. Sampling options were tested in the pilot surveys, and in Hong Kong randomly dialling telephone numbers from the Yellow Pages (that is, a commercial business telephone directory) yielded a satisfactory distribution of

---

12   The National Economic Census released in 2005 reported that the proportion of SOEs among all businesses was 7.5 per cent, but it increased to 24.6 per cent if collective enterprises (those that are owned as cooperatives or joint state/collective entities) are included. The proportion of SOEs also varied across the cities, with 27 per cent of Shanghai businesses estimated to be SOEs compared with (provincial data in the absence of city data) 55 per cent of businesses in Shanxi (Xi'an) and 30 per cent of business in Guangdong (Shenzhen).

broadly defined business activity compared with the official data about business size and sector. In the case of mainland cities, we also used the available business telephone directories but were not able to assess representativeness.

The main challenge for surveys of crimes against business is to increase participation while retaining a comprehensive picture of the crimes encountered. The literature notes that business crime surveys report generally lower response rates than omnibus victim surveys (for example, KPMG Forensic 2003; Smith and Urbas 2002; Taylor 2002; van Dijk and Terlouw 1996).[13] Overall, the *completed* response rate in our survey was 28 per cent, and well below our initial expectations, with a further 12 per cent who only partially completed the questionnaires. Thus, 2110 businesses that we contacted withdrew at some point during the interview, often stressing time constraints. Although partially completed surveys usually included all the obstacle questions but not the victimisation questions, we chose not to include such data because we thought victimisation was likely to be a key factor in both attitudes to crime and obstacles to business. The 18 per cent response rate for Hong Kong was well below the 2003 pilot survey response rate of 28 per cent,[14] and this might be due to the problem of survey fatigue. In Hong Kong, official, marketing-based or industry-linked surveys are increasingly conducted and there are generally no restrictions on them. Early in the process, we realised that prearranged interviews were a useful option and we made additional call-back and 'booked' interviews, which helped increase response rates to about 41 per cent across the mainland cities. In addition, 17 per cent of mainland contacts partially completed the questionnaires, which suggests that the demanding nature of the survey was a significant factor in depressing the response rate. Shenzhen produced the highest response rate, of 54 per cent (with a further 18 per cent partial completion), followed by Xian with 39 per cent (and 19 per cent partially completed) and Shanghai, 34 per cent (plus 14 per cent partially completed). We have argued that differential response rates might reflect the salience of the crime issue; Shenzhen's high response rate and Hong Kong's low response rate are entirely consistent with these cities' relative experience of crime victimisation.

Hopkins (2002) analysed the results of major surveys conducted in the United Kingdom and remarked that categorising the companies surveyed into broad business sectors (for example, retail, manufacturing) can be misleading because specific types of businesses within the same broad sectorial categorisation might be more prone to certain types of crime than others. For example, in the United Kingdom, off-licence premises and hardware stores were more likely to be

---

13 A large-scale survey of selected crimes against business conducted by KPMG Forensic (2003) yielded an effective response rate of 18 per cent but drew upon its client base to boost the response rate.

14 Note that in the small pilot for Shenzhen, 35 per cent of contacts responded fully and a further 8 per cent indicated that they would be willing to undertake a booked interview.

burgled than other retail shops. If sample size permits, it would be better to use a great number of discrete categories, which can then be combined if required. Alternatively, qualitative questions about the nature of the business might help to better describe it. A self-description of the business would provide functional criteria to better categorise businesses (better identification of types of retail or trading operations such as different types of shops, hotels, tourist/travel services; catering; entertainment; social welfare/community-oriented business) and thus yield the specificity suggested by Taylor, and with it the detailed information necessary to improve police responses and crime prevention. In the ICBS, the question about the business sector of activity should be replaced with the original two-part question that seeks first to identify a single main sector then follows up with a question about involvement in other sectors. There was also confusion between sector of activity and type of business operation (as in headquarters, branch, and so on). Because a further question asked whether the business was a branch in a chain, it would have been better to first query the sector (for example, manufacturing, retail, and so on) and then ask whether it was a shop, headquarters, factory, logistics operation, and so on. It also might be more effective to canvass different questions for different business sectors— for example, customer theft will be prevalent in retail but not so much in other sectors.

Further development of the new questions introduced in the survey and relating to IP infringement, cyber crime and credit-card fraud is needed. Surveying the prevalence of IP theft was an important addition since it is a growing source of concern, according to the more recent industry surveys (Economist Intelligence Unit 2010; PWC 2007a, 2009), and its costs were significant for our respondents; however, the lack of follow-up questions was an omission that arose from an underestimation of the scale of IP crime in China. Intellectual property theft should be included as a non-conventional crime (rather than a common crime) so in-depth questions can be asked about monetary losses, reporting to police and police response.

Cyber crime questions did not work well in part because they were borrowed from the Hong Kong UNICVS and were originally designed for individuals. Whatever advantages a comparison between business and household might bring were outweighed in our view by the poor fit to computer-security incidents in large companies and the growing role of e-commerce. First, there was confusion with the filtering questions in respect to cyber crime: 1) do you have access to a computer; 2) is it connected to the Internet? Many respondents said yes to the first question and no to the second, but then reported cyber victimisation that could happen only if they were connected to the Internet (for example, spam via email or fraud while purchasing online). The first question regarding access to a computer was redundant. There should be only one question—'in your business activities, do you use the Internet?'—with follow-up cyber crime questions then asked to those who answer yes. More importantly, apart from Internet fraud, the questions addressed relatively minor crimes, which occur frequently and do not specifically target businesses (for example, spamming). For example, the Hong Kong UNICVS found that 48.8 per cent of Hong Kong respondents had been victims of malicious attacks on their computer, and 40.6 per cent had received unwanted communication. It is unlikely that respondents will be aware of all such incidents that occurred in their company. They are likely to report incidents that happened to them personally, rather than give a complete picture of cyber victimisation for the whole company.

Questions concerning the types of cyber attacks were too technical for this survey. It is doubtful that many respondents, except perhaps systems or computer specialists, knew the difference between virus, malware and adware. It was enough to ask about viruses or malware in general—that is, something alien that disrupts or prevents the computer from working. As Richards (2009) notes, distinguishing technical failures from criminal acts and recognising how identity fraud in turn might be used to commit online fraud are complex matters even for experts. Cyber crime also raises the complex issues of multiple victimisations and the overlapping nature of crimes against business and crime by business especially in the e-commerce setting since in some cases both can take place in the same event. For example, Alibaba, China's eBay-like e-commerce platform, fell victim to an internal scam based on the integrity of its endorsement of the 'China Gold Supplier' platform, which assured buyers of honest transactions by trustworthy sellers (traders paid fees for independent verification, which was in some cases dubiously acquired). The 'golden status' was a mark of supposed integrity, but 2236 'gold' dealers subsequently defrauded buyers, some of whom were other business, costing the company US$1.7 million in compensation to 2249 buyers. The average compensation claim from victims of the scam was about US$1200 in 2009—similar to the average losses reported by the businesses who had been the victims of cyber crime in our survey (*The Economist* 2011a).

Questions about cyber crime needed to be more specific to a business context—that is, hacking the business network system, spamming using the business's domain email address, shutting a web site down, the use of 'botnets', phishing and so on, but again these are quite technical concepts. Choo (2011) notes that some sectors might be at more risk of insider misuse and fraud, but knowledge about such events is dependent on a capacity to detect computer security breaches. Our experience with introducing questions on cyber crime in the ICBS suggests that the amount of information gathered from these questions was not worth the additional respondent burden. We conclude that measuring both the prevalence of cyber crime and assessing related risk factors would be best served by a specialist survey, targeted at systems and security managers, rather than an omnibus survey (for example, see Richards 2009; Richards and Davis 2010).[15]

In addition, the inclusion of cyber crime items forced us to omit other questions, which, in hindsight, were important. For example, some of the original follow-up questions on bribery—deleted from the China ICBS—inquired about the amounts actually paid and the role of secret commissions. In the context of China, these questions were highly relevant. Questions on bribery also should distinguish between cases where managers or employees receive bribes to do something for someone outside the company and cases where the company is asked for bribes to get something done or obtain a contract with the Government or another business. So the lead question (that is, did anyone try to bribe you, other managers, your employees, or obtain bribes from the company in relation to its activities) requires broader probing than is provided currently by the follow-up questions, which addressed only the case where the company was asked to pay a bribe to get something.

Although the CATI system allowed for the text entry of additional comments made by respondents, there was a lack of attention to the recording of any additional information that respondents gave when opting to choose 'other reasons'. Often the follow-up probes appeared to have been neglected, perhaps due to the pressure by interviewees to curtail the survey. A good example of this was in respect to the question about who actually extorted business; here further details of what constituted the 'others' category would have been helpful. Another instance of the need for further details was in relation to reasons for reporting or not reporting to police. The original research design included the intention to undertake face-to-face follow-up interviews of the respondents who reported extortion and bribery; however, funding limitations did not permit such follow-ups. These follow-up interviews would have been a valuable addition providing a clearer idea of the situational risks faced by businesses and helping to better understand the impact of organised crime. The questions about cooperation and crime prevention were too general, although the survey showed that there is ample scope to develop collective responses. In this respect, we suggest adding a question on whether businesses engaged their own security guards or employed a corporate or private security service.

---

15   The Australian business telephone survey of computer crime reported by Richards (2009) achieved a 29 per cent response rate (N = 4000 business) and reported that 20 per cent of businesses detected at least one computer security incident in a one-year period (financial year 2006–07). The mean loss from these incidents was A$4467, with larger businesses more at risk, but significant differences between sectors were not observed and only 8 per cent reported incidents to the police. Expenditure on computer security and sector (except the financial sector) were not related to the detection of computer security incidents but the number of employees and whether security was outsourced were relevant to detection (Richards and Davis 2010).

Surveys such as the ICBS provide tools to further the study of comparative criminology, which is increasingly relevant in a globalised world. We hope that this work will stand as a benchmark for further surveys and that the challenges we have identified offer some guidance to those that might follow.

Conclusion

This survey enhanced our understanding of the nature of crimes against business, and their impact on business costs and confidence in China. We observed the extent and tolerance by businesses of crime and corruption, but also the high level of concern expressed by respondents about the impact of crime on business. This study enabled comparison of the crime risk of business relative to market development and the effectiveness of law enforcement, and could lead to improved crime-prevention practices and policies. In our view, the development of crime-prevention partnerships between business and police can have a significant impact on crime reduction and diminish the perceived and observed risks of crime and bribery.

An important element in crime prevention is to promote collective action by victims and potential victims in concert with police often in partnership with industry or business-sector associations. A key criterion for collective action is informing others about the crime and usually that requires reporting the event to police. A significant proportion of crimes against business, however, including relatively serious crime, are *not reported* to police. An exception is the case of vehicle theft where mandatory insurance is required and insurers will deal only with claims reported to police. Without the lifeblood of such information to police, follow-up action to identify the frequency of different types of crime (and/or criminals) and, in particular, the methods that the offender used to complete the crime is hampered. Without knowledge of the nature, frequency and location of crime, prevention strategies and countermeasures are compromised. As our survey shows, the willingness of businesses to report crime to police varies substantially by type of crime, business sector, location and size. We noted that mainland businesses had high rates of reporting of common crime (those clearly targeted by *yanda*) compared with Hong Kong and the 'old' democracies of the West, but this did not extend to fraud and other non-conventional crimes. In this sense, Chinese businesses tended to share the same scepticism about the utility of public policing as elsewhere—namely, that often police could do little or would not be interested.

The survey results raise more general questions—in particular, about the oft-quoted assumption that the 'rule of law' provides an advantageous context for business, and enables some evaluation of policing and efforts to curb corruption.

Given the very large differences between Hong Kong and the other cities in China on the World Bank's governance indicators,[16] we expected that there would also be large differences in crime victimisation and that Hong Kong, because of its rule-of-law advantage, would have a lower risk of crimes against business. Apart from the lower level of bribery reported in Hong Kong, however, overall differences between Hong Kong and the mainland were relatively modest. Indeed the size of the business—irrespective of where it was located—was the most important predictor of crime risk. Furthermore, the greater propensity of mainland businesses to report both common and non-conventional offences (albeit to a lesser extent) to police compared with Hong Kong would suggest, on the surface at least, that they too have a high degree of confidence in police. It is possible that the higher reporting rates in the mainland partly reflect the extent that many businesses are state owned and their discretion to report or not might be limited. This being said, it also suggests that the association between effective legal and law-enforcement institutions and a successful climate for business is sufficiently functional in contemporary China to provide the social order and predictability necessary for the expression of capitalist markets. Thus, the assumption that the British legacy of a 'rule of law' culture provides a substantial commercial (competitive) advantage for Hong Kong might be exaggerated, at least in the context of risks of crimes against business. This exaggerated assumption might stem from an underestimation of the rapid development of commercial and contract law in China, especially in practice in Shanghai—the commercial hub of China, where business activity has been the engine of its economic revival. Yet, it is also clear that Hong Kong has been able to curb bribery among both officials and businesses to a much greater extent than mainland Chinese cities. Given the concern about corruption among businesses in China, Hong Kong's reputation for clean and effective government is a credible example of what can be achieved. As noted in the Introduction, however, in practice, clean governance might not provide the arch advantage supposed, and collusion with powerful officials might actually make business sense if indeed competitors also seek 'under the table' assistance.

This study has hopefully enlarged, however modestly, the still too limited picture of attitudes to or perceptions of crime and corruption among businesses in China and contributed to the small body of studies that addresses public perceptions about crime and its salience compared with other issues. It was intriguing to see that in the National Sense of Security survey, the fear of crime in mainland households—which had grown from one in five in the late 1980s to

---

16   On all six World Bank measures of good governance, Hong Kong substantially exceeds mainland China. For example, in 2005 in Hong Kong for the variable 'control of corruption', the value was 1.8 compared with –0.74 for China; 'rule of law', 1.56 versus –0.42; 'regulatory quality', 1.88 versus –0.20; 'government effectiveness', 1.57 versus –0.21; political stability and absence of violence/terrorism, 1.11 versus –0.36; and 'voice and accountability', 0.6 versus –1.52 (the scale varies from –2.5 to 2.5) (for further details, see Appendix A; World Bank n.d.).

one in two in the early 1990s (at the height of the economic transformation)—had declined to less than one in 10 in the period 2003–07, which was a level very similar to that reported for Hong Kong. This pattern might be explained by the control of institutional anomie provided by the policies of the planned transition. The question format used in the survey, however, appeared to be designed to manipulate a more positive response and the improvements might be more artefact than real. Even if it was the case, it remains that many businesses—notably in Shenzhen—felt that crime was in decline, although on the whole mainland businesses rated crime and corruption as serious obstacles. We conclude by arguing that if the extent of crimes against business in China is substantially exceeding that of ordinary households, it has not reached the levels experienced in other developing and developed economies, and that a planned rather than a laissez-faire transition was instrumental in this outcome.

Appendix A.
World Governance Indicators

The following tables, compiled by the World Bank, list aggregate indicators of six dimensions of governance for a selected number of countries. These indicators have been constructed using a statistical compilation of responses on the quality of governance given by a large number of enterprise, citizen and expert survey respondents in industrial and developing countries, as reported by a variety of survey institutes, think tanks, non-governmental organisations and international organisations.

The six governance indicators are measured in units ranging from about −2.5 to 2.5, with higher values corresponding to better governance outcomes. The standard errors have the following interpretation: there is roughly a 70 per cent chance that the level of governance lies within plus or minus one standard error of the point estimate of governance.

Details on the concepts measured by each indicator, its components and the interpretation of the point estimates and standard errors can be found in Kaufman, Daniel, Kray, Aart and Mastruzzi, Massimo 2010, *The Worldwide Governance Indicators: A Summary of Methodology, Data and Analytical Issues*. World Bank Policy Research, available at <www.govindicators.org>

Table A.1 Six Government Indicators: Mainland China, Hong Kong, Macao and Taiwan, 1996–2009

Variable	Country/year	2009	2008	2007	2006	2005	2004	2003	2002	2000	1998	1996
Voice and accountability	CHINA	-1.65	-1.68	-1.72	-1.68	-1.52	-1.46	-1.53	-1.58	-1.29	-1.38	-1.66
	HONG KONG SAR, CHINA	0.54	0.49	0.51	0.57	0.60	0.54	0.31	0.11	0.00	-0.12	0.21
	MACAO SAR, CHINA	0.57	0.14	0.11	0.35	0.40	0.12	0.64	0.40	0.22	0.23	..
	TAIWAN, CHINA	0.85	0.74	0.72	0.73	0.93	0.86	0.97	0.93	0.78	0.81	0.59
Political stability & absence of violence/terrorism	CHINA	-0.44	-0.39	-0.39	-0.46	-0.36	-0.21	-0.38	-0.18	-0.22	-0.16	-0.35
	HONG KONG SAR, CHINA	0.93	1.05	1.00	1.06	1.11	0.95	0.73	0.72	0.82	0.57	-0.01
	MACAO SAR, CHINA	0.57	0.46	0.41	1.00	1.28	1.33	1.07	0.46	0.42	0.19	..
	TAIWAN, CHINA	0.54	0.71	0.46	0.54	0.54	0.50	0.59	0.65	0.37	0.72	0.81
Government effectiveness	CHINA	0.12	0.15	0.21	0.03	-0.21	-0.05	-0.10	-0.05	-0.13	-0.33	0.04
	HONG KONG SAR, CHINA	1.76	1.79	1.83	1.79	1.57	1.67	1.50	1.28	1.08	0.90	1.12
	MACAO SAR, CHINA	1.25	1.03	0.99	1.00	1.27	1.10	1.31	0.84	0.62	0.39	..
	TAIWAN, CHINA	1.06	0.92	0.92	1.01	0.89	1.08	0.99	0.84	0.74	0.64	1.23
Regulatory quality	CHINA	-0.20	-0.15	-0.18	-0.28	-0.20	-0.24	-0.35	-0.49	-0.28	-0.26	0.20
	HONG KONG SAR, CHINA	1.83	1.99	1.96	1.95	1.88	1.94	1.86	1.65	1.70	1.71	1.52
	MACAO SAR, CHINA	1.28	1.00	0.85	1.09	1.09	1.53	1.14	0.68	0.50	0.53	..
	TAIWAN, CHINA	1.14	1.09	1.00	0.96	1.12	1.22	0.99	1.03	1.13	1.04	0.86

Variable	Country/year	2009	2008	2007	2006	2005	2004	2003	2002	2000	1998	1996
Rule of law	CHINA	-0.35	-0.33	-0.45	-0.52	-0.42	-0.35	-0.43	-0.34	-0.44	-0.37	-0.20
	HONG KONG SAR, CHINA	1.49	1.52	1.55	1.58	1.56	1.44	1.36	1.11	0.82	0.95	0.97
	MACAO SAR, CHINA	0.68	0.45	0.35	0.52	0.78	1.39	1.20	0.69	0.18	0.20	..
	TAIWAN, CHINA	0.93	0.78	0.77	0.78	0.98	0.96	0.96	0.93	0.92	0.88	0.90
Control of corruption	CHINA	-0.53	-0.46	-0.60	-0.52	-0.74	-0.62	-0.38	-0.47	-0.23	-0.26	-0.20
	HONG KONG SAR, CHINA	1.84	1.93	1.91	1.88	1.80	1.71	1.59	1.53	1.06	1.10	1.41
	MACAO SAR, CHINA	0.40	-0.03	0.45	0.41	0.47	1.37	0.83	-0.06	0.44	0.47	..
	TAIWAN, CHINA	0.57	0.51	0.54	0.65	0.84	0.83	0.76	0.68	0.84	0.74	0.57

Table A.2 Six Government Indicators for Selected Countries in Africa, America, Asia, Europe and Oceania, 2005–06

COUNTRY/VARIABLE	Voice and accountability		Political stability & absence of violence/terrorism		Government effectiveness		Regulatory quality		Rule of law		Control of corruption	
	2006	2005	2006	2005	2006	2005	2006	2005	2006	2005	2006	2005
CHINA	-1.68	-1.52	-0.46	-0.36	0.03	-0.21	-0.28	-0.20	-0.52	-0.42	-0.52	-0.74
HONG KONG SAR, CHINA	0.57	0.60	1.06	1.11	1.79	1.57	1.95	1.88	1.58	1.56	1.88	1.80
MACAO SAR, CHINA	0.35	0.40	1.00	1.28	1.00	1.27	1.09	1.09	0.52	0.78	0.41	0.47
TAIWAN, CHINA	0.73	0.93	0.54	0.54	1.01	0.89	0.96	1.12	0.78	0.98	0.65	0.84
NIGERIA	-0.52	-0.78	-2.06	-1.80	-0.90	-0.82	-0.96	-0.86	-1.14	-1.39	-1.14	-1.28
SOUTH AFRICA	0.76	0.71	0.20	0.04	0.67	0.81	0.63	0.55	0.24	0.15	0.45	0.58
BRAZIL	0.47	0.43	-0.11	-0.08	-0.05	0.01	-0.02	0.07	-0.41	-0.45	-0.15	-0.18
CANADA	1.41	1.50	1.05	0.90	1.88	1.81	1.54	1.52	1.75	1.63	1.91	1.83
UNITED STATES	1.09	1.33	0.45	0.04	1.53	1.52	1.62	1.59	1.57	1.49	1.26	1.49
INDIA	0.45	0.43	-0.85	-0.65	0.02	-0.07	-0.20	-0.21	0.19	0.19	-0.22	-0.41
JAPAN	0.93	1.00	1.06	1.01	1.53	1.32	1.23	1.20	1.35	1.24	1.35	1.23
FRANCE	1.30	1.47	0.58	0.54	1.50	1.66	1.22	1.17	1.41	1.37	1.48	1.36
GERMANY	1.41	1.51	1.01	0.88	1.58	1.52	1.52	1.44	1.69	1.61	1.77	1.82
ITALY	1.06	1.00	0.59	0.55	0.50	0.71	0.91	0.92	0.31	0.49	0.35	0.29
UNITED KINGDOM	1.37	1.47	0.65	0.36	1.69	1.72	1.82	1.57	1.70	1.52	1.78	1.86

COUNTRY/VARIABLE	Voice and accountability		Political stability & absence of violence/terrorism		Government effectiveness		Regulatory quality		Rule of law		Control of corruption	
	2006	2005	2006	2005	2006	2005	2006	2005	2006	2005	2006	2005
BULGARIA	0.60	0.50	0.46	0.24	0.06	0.26	0.56	0.65	-0.13	-0.10	-0.02	0.12
GEORGIA	-0.16	-0.16	-0.84	-0.63	-0.19	-0.37	-0.20	-0.54	-0.41	-0.63	-0.09	-0.33
POLAND	0.80	0.96	0.43	0.43	0.57	0.61	0.74	0.83	0.39	0.47	0.25	0.33
RUSSIA	-0.93	-0.65	-0.73	-0.89	-0.43	-0.36	-0.49	-0.26	-0.93	-0.84	-0.78	-0.75
UKRAINE	-0.10	-0.42	0.05	-0.24	-0.54	-0.46	-0.46	-0.41	-0.81	-0.73	-0.62	-0.65
AUSTRALIA	1.38	1.52	0.94	0.94	1.73	1.77	1.61	1.58	1.73	1.67	1.91	1.87

Appendix B.
Review of Business
Victimisation Surveys

This table has been constructed from data provided in AIC (2004) and the authors' own research. It includes surveys and studies available in English and is presented in chronological order.

Survey/citation[a]	Year of data collection	Location	Crimes surveyed[b]
Crime against Small Business (McDevitt et al. 1990)	1989	US, Boston	Assault, burglary, theft, robbery, vandalism
Dutch Commercial Crime Survey (Eijken and Meijer 1995)	1989, 1992, 1993	Netherlands	Assault and threats, burglary, theft, vandalism and malicious damage
Crimes on Industrial Estates Study (Johnston et al. 1994)	1990	UK, Northern England	Assault, burglary, theft, theft of and from vehicle, vandalism and malicious damage
Safer Cities Small Business Crime Surveys (Tilley 1993)	1990, 1992	UK	Burglary, robbery, theft and shoplifting
Commercial Robbery: National Robbery Registration System (Eijken and Meijer 1995)	1990–93	Netherlands	Robbery
Ernst & Young Global Fraud Survey (Ernst & Young 2010)	Biennial since 1990	Global, 36 countries in 2010	Fraud among large corporations
National Retail Security Survey (Hollinger 2010)	Annual since 1991	US	Assault, burglary, extortion, fraud, robbery, theft, vandalism (retail sector only)
Crime against Small Holiday Accommodation Units (Gill et al. 1993)	1992	UK	Assault, fraud, theft, vandalism and malicious damage
Study of Employee Injuries and Convenience Store Robberies (Amandus et al. 1996)	1992–93	US	Robbery
National Crime Victimisation Survey (Warchol 1998)	1992–96	US	Robbery, theft, workplace violence
AIC Crimes against Business Survey (Walker 1995)	1993	Australia	Bribery, burglary, extortion, fraud, robbery, theft of and from vehicle, theft, vandalism, workplace violence

Survey/citation[a]	Year of data collection	Location	Crimes surveyed[b]
British Retail Consortium Survey (BRC 2010)	Annual since 1993	UK	Burglary, fraud, robbery, theft, vandalism and malicious damage (retail sector only)
KPMG Fraud and Misconduct Survey (KPMG 2010)	Biennial since 1993	Australia, New Zealand	Asset misappropriation, corruption, credit-card fraud, theft
Violent Victimisation in Retailing Survey (Beck et al. 1993)	1993	UK	Assault, threats, verbal abuse at work (retail sector only)
Commercial Victimisation Survey (Shury et al. 2005)	1994, 2002	UK	Assault, bribery/extortion, burglary, fraud, theft of and from vehicle, theft, robbery, vandalism (retail and manufacturing sectors)
Crimes against Business Survey (Aromaa and Lehti 1994)	1994	Finland	Bribery, burglary, extortion, fraud, theft of and from vehicle, theft, robbery, theft, vandalism and malicious damage, workplace violence
International Commercial Crime Survey (ICCS) (van Dijk and Terlouw 1996)	1994	Czech Republic, France, Germany, Hungary, Italy, Netherlands, Switzerland, UK	Assault, bribery and corruption, burglary, extortion and intimidation, fraud, robbery, theft of and from vehicle, theft, vandalism
CSI/FBI Computer Crime and Security Survey (Computer Security Institute 2011)	Annual since 1995	US	Computer-related crime affecting enterprises
Small Business and Crime Initiative Study (Wood et al. 1997)	1995–96	UK, Leicester	Burglary, fraud, robbery, theft, vandalism, workplace violence
British Forum of Private Business Survey (Gill 1998)	1996	UK	Burglary, fraud, physical abuse, robbery, theft, vandalism and malicious damage, vehicle theft
Crime against Small Business in the Midwest Survey (Fisher and Looye 2000)	1996	US, 6 Midwest States	Assault, burglary, fraud, theft, vandalism
European Union Survey on Living and Working Conditions (European Foundation for the Improvement of Living and Working Conditions 1997)	1996	European countries	Workplace violence

Survey/citation[a]	Year of data collection	Location	Crimes surveyed[b]
Global Fraud Survey (Association of Certified Fraud Examiners 2010)	Various years since 1996	US only until 2008; global in 2010	Asset misappropriation, corruption, financial statement fraud committed by employees
International Crime Victims Survey (Chappell and Di Martino 1999)	1996	32 developed and developing countries	Workplace violence
Crime against Small Business Study (Kuratko et al. 2000)	1997	US, Midwestern and south-eastern regions	Burglary, fraud, robbery, theft
Crimes against Business Survey (Aromaa 1999)	1997	Estonia	Bribery, burglary, extortion, fraud, robbery, theft of and from vehicle, theft, vandalism, workplace violence
Home Office Construction Plant Theft Study (Smith and Walmsley 1999)	1997	UK	Theft
Retail Crime and Safety Survey (Crime Prevention Unit 1998)	1997	Australia, South Australia	Burglary, fraud, robbery, theft, vandalism, workplace violence
Australian Chamber of Manufacturers Survey (Alexander 1998)	1998	Australia	Fraud, vandalism
British Oil Security Syndicate Survey on Petrol Station Crime (British Oil Security Syndicate 2010)	Annual since 1998	UK	Assault, burglary, credit-card fraud, fraud, robbery, theft, vandalism
National Business Crime Survey (Small Firms Association 2010)	Biennial since 1998	Ireland	Assault and harassment, burglary, credit-card/cheque fraud, extortion, fraud, robbery, theft, vandalism and criminal damage
National Pharmaceutical Association Crime Survey (NPA 2000)	1998	UK	Assault, burglary, vandalism
South Africa National Commercial Crime Survey (Naudé et al. 1999)	1998	South Africa	Bribery, burglary, extortion, fraud, robbery, theft of and from vehicle, theft, vandalism, workplace violence
Crimes against Small Business Survey (Perrone 2000)	1999	Australia	Assault and threats, bribery, burglary, credit-card fraud, extortion, fraud, robbery, theft of and from vehicle, theft, vandalism

Survey/citation[a]	Year of data collection	Location	Crimes surveyed[b]
International Crime against Business Survey (ICBS), Central Eastern Europe (Alvazzi del Frate 2004)	1999	Albania, Belarus, Bulgaria, Croatia, Hungary, Lithuania, Romania, Russia, Ukraine	Assault, bribery and corruption, burglary, extortion and intimidation, fraud, request for protection money, robbery, theft of and from vehicle, theft, vandalism
Retail Theft and Security Survey (Grocers' Review 2000)	1999	New Zealand	Burglary, fraud, theft, vandalism (retail)
Scottish Business Crime Centre Survey (Burrows et al. 1999)	1999	Scotland	Assault and threat, burglary, fraud, theft, robbery, vandalism
Airline Fraud Survey (Deloitte 2006)	2000, 2006	Global	Fraud, theft (airline industry)
Global Retail Theft Barometer (Bamfield 2010)	Annual since 2001	Global, 42 countries in 2010	'Shrinkage' in large retail corporations due to customer and employee theft and supplier fraud
Retail Security Survey (RCC 2009)	Annual since 2000	Canada	Fraud, theft
PriceWaterhouseCoopers Global Economic Crime Survey (PWC 2009)	Biennial since 2001	Global, 54 developed and developing countries in 2009	Accounting fraud, asset misappropriation, corruption/ bribery, insider trading, IP infringement, money laundering
Federation of Small Businesses Biennial Survey (FSB 2008)	Biennial since 2002	UK	Assault and threats, burglary, credit-card fraud, e-crime, fraud, robbery, theft, vandalism
KPMG Fraud and Misconduct Survey (KPMG 2009)	2003, 2008–09	US	Asset misappropriation, corruption, credit-card fraud, fraud, theft
KPMG Fraud and Misconduct Survey (KPMG 2007)	2003, 2006	Hong Kong	Corruption, fraud, Internet-related fraud, IP theft
British Chambers of Commerce (Elliott 2008)	2004, 2008	UK	Arson, burglary, e-crime, personal injury or violence, robbery, theft, vandalism
Organized Retail Crime Survey (National Retail Federation 2009)	Annual since 2005	US	Fraud and theft as part of criminal enterprise activities (retail sector)
Port Moresby Business Crime Victimisation Survey (PNG Justice Advisory Group 2005)	2005	PNG, Port Moresby	Assault, bribery and corruption, burglary, extortion and intimidation, fraud, robbery, theft of and from vehicle, theft, vandalism

Survey/citation[a]	Year of data collection	Location	Crimes surveyed[b]
Telecom Fraud Survey (Communications Fraud Control Association 2009)	2005, 2008	Global	Fraud in telecommunication industry
International Crime and Corruption Survey (Alvazzi del Frate 2007)	2006	Cape Verde	Assault and threats, bribery and corruption, burglary, extortion and intimidation, fraud, robbery, theft of and from vehicle, theft, vandalism
The Australian Business Assessment of Computer Users Security (ABACUS) Survey (Richards 2009)	2006–07	Australia	Computer security incidents
International Crime and Corruption Business Survey (Nigerian National Bureau of Statistics 2009, 2010)	2007	Nigeria	Assault and threats, bribery and corruption, burglary, extortion and intimidation, fraud, robbery, theft of and from vehicle, theft, vandalism
Kroll Global Fraud Survey (Economist Intelligence Unit 2010)	Annual since 2007	Global	Bribery and corruption, fraud, IP theft and counterfeiting, money laundering, theft
Study of Encounters of Enterprises with Crime (Ahven et al. 2007)	2007	Estonia	Bribery and corruption, burglary, fraud, robbery, theft, vandalism, workplace violence

Notes: [a] The citation for surveys that have been repeated is that of the most recent sweep; [b] unless otherwise specified, the categories theft and fraud include those acts perpetrated by employees, customers and any other person within or outside the company.

References

Ahven, Andri, Rammer, Andu, Rootalu, Kadri and Murakas, Rein 2007, *Study of Encounters of Enterprises with Crimes*. Talinn: Ministry of Justice, Criminal Policy Department.

Alexander, Donald 1998, A report on the ACM survey into the cost of crime in Australian industry, Paper presented at the Crime against Business Conference, 18–19 June, Melbourne.

Alvazzi del Frate, Anna 2004, 'The International Crime Business Survey: findings from nine Central Eastern European cities', *European Journal on Criminal Policy and Research* 10, 137–61.

Alvazzi del Frate, Anna (ed.) 2007, *Study on Crime and Corruption in Cape Verde*. Cape Verde: Ministry of Justice and United Nations Office on Drugs and Crime.

Amandus, H. E., Zahm, D., Friedmann, R., Ruback, R. B., Block, C., Weiss, J., Rogan, D., Holmes, W., Bynum, T., Hoffman, D., McManus, R., Malcan, J., Wellford, C. and Kessler, D. 1996, 'Employee injuries and convenience store robberies in selected metropolitan areas', *Journal of Occupational and Environmental Medicine* 38(7), 714–20.

Aromaa, Kauko 1999, *Eastern Crime: A Selection of Reports on Crime in the St Petersburg Region and the Baltic Countries*, Helsinki: National Research Institute of Legal Policy.

Aromaa, Kauko and Lehti, Martti 1994, *The security of Finnish companies in St. Petersburg*, Research Communication 16, National Research Institute of Legal Policy, Helsinki.

Association of Certified Fraud Examiners 2010, *Report to the Nations on Occupational Fraud and Abuse*. Austin, Tex.: Association of Certified Fraud Examiners.

Australian Institute of Criminology (AIC) 2004 *Crimes against business: a review of victimisation, predictors and prevention*, Technical and Background Paper No. 11, Australian Institute of Criminology, Canberra.

Bamfield, Joshua 2010, *Global Retail Theft Barometer 2010*. Nottingham, UK: Centre for Retail Research.

Beck, Adrian, Gill, Martin, Sampson, Mary and Willis, Andrew 1993, *Violent Victimisation in Retailing: A national survey*. Leicester, UK: Centre for the Study of Public Order, University of Leicester.

British Oil Security Syndicate 2010, *Forecourt Crime Increases During 2009*. UK: British Oil Security Syndicate, <www.bossuk.org/Statistics-pg18.html>

British Retail Consortium (BRC) 2010, *Retail Crime Survey 2010*. London: British Retail Consortium.

Burrows, John, Anderson, Simon, Bamfield, Joshua, Hopkins, Matt and Ingram, Dave 1999, *Crimes against Business in Scotland*. Edinburgh: Scottish Business Crime Centre.

Chappell, Duncan and Di Martino, Vittorio 1999, 'Violence at work', *Asian-Pacific Newsletter on Occupational Health and Safety* 6(1) (April), <www.acosomoral.org/pdf/violwk.pdf>

Communications Fraud Control Association 2009, Communications Fraud Control Association (CFCA) announces results of worldwide telecom fraud survey, Press release, 26 June, Phoenix, Ariz.

Computer Security Institute 2011, *2010/11 CSI/FBI Computer Crime and Security Survey*. New York: Computer Security Institute.

Crime Prevention Unit 1998, *Retail Crime and Safety Survey 1998*. Adelaide: Crime Prevention Unit, South Australia Attorney-General's Department.

Deloitte 2006, *Airline Fraud Survey 2006: A report looking at fraud in the airline industry*. London: Deloitte.

Economist Intelligence Unit 2010, *Global Fraud Report 2010/11*. New York: Kroll.

Eijken, T. W. M. and Meijer, R. F. 1995, 'Prevalence and prevention of crime against businesses in the Netherlands', *Security Journal* 6, 37–46.

Elliott, Gareth 2008, *The Invisible Crime: A business crime survey*. London: British Chambers of Commerce.

Ernst & Young 2010, *Driving Ethical Growth—New markets, new challenges: 11th Global Fraud Survey*. London: Ernst & Young.

European Foundation for the Improvement of Living and Working Conditions 1997, *Violence at Work*. Dublin: European Foundation for the Improvement of Living and Working Conditions.

Federation of Small Businesses (FSB) 2008, *5th Biennial Survey*. London: Federation of Small Businesses.

Fisher, Bonnie and Looye, Johanna W. 2000, 'Crime and small businesses in the Midwest: an examination of overlooked issues in the United States', *Security Journal* 13(2), 45–72.

Gill, Martin 1998, 'The victimisation of business: indicators of risk and the direction of future research', *International Review of Victimology* 6, 17–28.

Gill, Martin, Salmon, Mary and Hill, Julie 1993, *Crime on holiday*, Research Paper, Crime Order and Policing Series, Scarman Centre for the Study of Public Order, University of Leicester, Leicester.

Grocers' Review 2000, 'Retail crime one of the top 10 industries in New Zealand', *Grocers' Review* (April), pp. 24–5.

Hollinger, Richard 2010, *National Retail Security Survey Final Report*. Gainesville, Fla: Department of Sociology and Center for Studies in Criminology and Law, University of Florida.

Johnston, Valerie, Leitner, Maria, Shapland, Joanna and Wiles, Paul 1994, *Crime on industrial estates*, Crime Prevention Unit Series Paper No. 54, Police Research Group, Home Office, London.

KPMG 2007, *Fraud and Misconduct Survey in Hong Kong: 2006 findings*. Hong Kong SAR: KPMG.

KPMG 2009, *Fraud Survey 2009*. New York: KPMG.

KPMG 2010, *Fraud and Misconduct Survey 2010 Australia and New Zealand*. Melbourne: KPMG.

Kuratko, Donald, Hornsby, Jeffrey, Naffziger, Doublas and Hodgetts, Richard 2000, 'Crime and small business: an exploratory study of cost and prevention issues in US firms', *Journal of Business Management* 38(3), 1–11.

McDevitt, Jack, Pattavina, April, Miliano, Robyn and Pierce, Glenn 1990, *The Impact of Crime on Small Business Viability*. Washington, DC: National Institute of Justice, US Department of Justice.

National Pharmaceutical Association (NPA) 2000, 'Crime is on the up, but so are the deterrents', St Albans, UK, <www.atalink.co.ul/npa2000/html/p227sensormatic.htm>.

National Retail Federation 2009, *2009 Organized Retail Crime Survey*. Washington, DC: National Retail Federation.

Naudé, C. M. B., Prinsloo, J. H. and Martins, J. H. 1999, *Crimes against the South African Business Sector*. Pretoria: University of South Africa.

Nigerian National Bureau of Statistics 2009, *NBS/EFCC Business Survey on Crime & Corruption and Awareness of EFCC in Nigeria, 2007: Summary report*. Abuja: National Bureau of Statistics, <www.nigerianstat.gov.ng/ext/latest_release/NBS_EFCC%20Survey.pdf>

Nigerian National Bureau of Statistics 2010, *NBS/EFCC Business Survey on Crime and Corruption and Awareness of EFCC in Nigeria, 2007: Statistical report*. Abuja: National Bureau of Statistics.

Perrone, Santina 2000, 'Crimes against small business in Australia: a preliminary analysis', *Trends and Issues in Crime and Criminal Justice* No. 184. Canberra: Australian Institute of Criminology.

PNG Justice Advisory Group 2005, *Port Moresby Business Crime Victimisation Survey 2005*. Port Moresby: Justice Advisory Group, PNG Law and Justice Sector.

PriceWaterhouseCoopers (PWC) 2009, *The Global Economic Crime Survey: Economic crime in a downturn*. London: PriceWaterhouseCoopers.

Retail Council of Canada (RCC) 2009, *Canadian Retail Security Survey 2008*. Toronto: Retail Council of Canada.

Richards, Kelly 2009, *The Australian business assessment of computer user security: a national survey*, Research and Public Policy Series No. 102, Australian Institute of Criminology, Canberra, <www.aic.gov.au/publications/current%20series/rpp/100-120/rpp102.aspx>

Shury, Jan, Speed, Mark, Vivian, David, Kuechel, Alistair and Nicholas, Sian 2005, *Crimes against Retail and Manufacturing Premises: Findings from the 2002 Commercial Victimisation Survey*. London: Home Office.

Small Firms Association 2010, 'SFA 7th National Business Crime Survey reveals...', *BackBencher* 31 (June).

Smith, Alaster and Walmsley, Ruth 1999, *The nature and extent of construction plant theft*, Police Research Series Paper No. 117, Policing and Reducing Crime Unit, Home Office, London.

Tilley, Nick 1993, *The prevention of crime against small businesses: the safer cities experience*, Crime Prevention Unit Paper No. 45, Home Office, London.

van Dijk, Jan and Terlouw, Gert 1996, 'An international perspective of the business community as victims of fraud and crime', *Security Journal* 7, 157–67.

Walker, John 1995, *The First National Survey of Crimes against Businesses.* Canberra: Australian Institute of Criminology

Warchol, Greg 1998, *Workplace violence, 1992–96*, Bureau of Justice Statistics Special Report: National Crime Victimization Survey, US Department of Justice, Washington, DC.

Wood, Jeremy, Wheelwright, Gillian and Burrows, John 1997, *Crime against Small Business: Meeting the challenges.* Swindon, UK: Crime Concern.

Appendix C.
Media Sources Used in Chapter 2: Crime and policing in Shanghai, Shenzhen and Xi'an

Asian Wall Street Journal 2004, 'Shanghai tycoon draws three-year jail sentence', *Asian Wall Street Journal*, 2 June.

Barboza, David 2008, 'Former party boss in China gets 18 years, *The New York Times*, 12 April.

BBC Monitoring Service Asia Pacific 1994, 'New police patrol system allows rapid response, "tight grip" on public order', *BBC Monitoring Service Asia Pacific*, 7 March.

BBC Monitoring Service Asia Pacific 1995, 'Shanghai to fight economic crime by officials', *BBC Monitoring Service Asia Pacific*, 20 January.

BBC Monitoring Service Asia Pacific 1999, 'Shanghai security chief reports move to accurate crime records', *BBC Monitoring Service Asia Pacific*, 2 April.

BBC Monitoring Service Asia Pacific 2003, 'China: former Shenzhen Deputy Mayor Wang Ju faces corruption charges', *BBC Monitoring Service Asia Pacific*, 6 November.

BBC Monitoring Service Asia Pacific 2006, 'Supermarkets in China's Shenzhen receive bomb threats', *BBC Monitoring Service Asia Pacific*, 18 January.

Cao, Hai-dong 2004, 'Xi'an founded the system of "outsourcing public security to individuals"', *Economy* 2004(10), 2023.

Chen, Hong 2006, '"Police bible" to upgrade security force', *China Daily*, 20 February.

Chen, Qide 1999, 'Fight reduces crime rate: 12,900 criminals put in prison', *Shanghai Star*, 5 February.

Cheung, Agnes 1996, 'Shenzhen anti-crime crusade', *South China Morning Post*, 10 April.

Chow, Chung-yan 2004, 'More police promised as crime rate soars 57pc in Shenzhen', *South China Morning Post*, 14 January, p. 1.

Chow, Chung-yan 2005, 'Police winning battle for Shenzhen streets', *South China Morning Post*, 23 August, p. 4.

Earnshaw, Graham 1996, 'China steps up fight on financial graft', *Reuters News*, 5 March.

Emerging Markets Report 1995, 'China: Shanghai financial crime up: report', *Emerging Markets Report*, 10 July.

Financial Times 1998, '"Country cousins" take the rap for mounting level of crime in Shanghai', *Financial Times*, 8 August, p. 2.

Leu, Siew-ying 2003, 'Crime in Shenzhen is cut by 30pc in four weeks', *South China Morning Post*, 27 November.

Leu, Siew-ying 2004, 'Shenzhen nabs 10,000 in crime crackdown; number of cases drops 39pc after police get tough in bid to clean up city's image', *South China Morning Post*, 14 June, p. 1.

Lu, Chang 2000, 'Police on road to reducing street crime', *China Daily*, 29 December.

Ma, Lie 1999, 'Financial crimes rise in Xi'an', *China Daily*, 3 December, p. 3.

Mufson, Steven 1994, 'Economic crime explodes as China prospers', *Washington Post*, 3 October, p. 12.

Ngai, Agatha 1997, 'Shenzhen in crime purge', *South China Morning Post*, 25 April.

QQ.com 2009, 'Xi'an declared "the best city for public security governance"', *QQ.com*, 19 May, <xian.qq.com/a/20090519/000005.htm> [in Chinese].

Reuters News 1995a, 'Shanghai securities crime soaring', *Reuters News*, 4 January.

Reuters News 1995b, 'Shanghai crime statistics show surge in early 1995', *Reuters News*, 3 April.

Reuters News 1996a, 'Shanghai launches anti-crime sweep', *Reuters News*, 23 May.

Reuters News 1996b, 'China prosecutors vow to nail police crimes', *Reuters News*, 26 December.

Shaanxi Daily 2006, '"Two decreases and one increase": innovation in dealing with homicide for Xi'an City Public Security Bureau', *Shaanxi Daily*, 24 August, <xlsvshi.net/xingfa/law06/381.html> [in Chinese].

Shanghai Daily 2002, 'Hard times for criminals', *Shanghai Daily*, 28 October.

Shanghai Daily 2004a, 'Shanghai crime rate rises in 2003', *Shanghai Daily*, 9 January.

Shanghai Daily 2004b, 'Shanghai crime reductions', *Shanghai Daily*, 21 April.

Shanghai Daily 2004c, 'Shanghai city to strengthen police force', *Shanghai Daily*, 19 November.

Shanghai Daily 2006, 'Police to report on crime rates', *Shanghai Daily*, 1 January.

Shenzhen Daily 2003, 'Shoplifting causes a dilemma', *Shenzhen Daily*, 27 October, <www.chinadaily.com.cn/en/doc/2003-10/27/content_275932.htm>

So, Irene 1995, 'Police to hit the streets', *South China Morning Post*, 6 September.

Sohu.com 2006, 'Xi'an safe place to live', *Sohu News*, 14 September, <news.sohu.com/20060914/n245333473.shtml> [in Chinese].

Sohu.com 2009, 'Xi'an government targets loss of government-owned assets', *Sohu News*, 16 July, <news.sohu.com/20090716/n265255694.shtml> [in Chinese].

South China Morning Post 2004, 'Soaring crime rate dims Shenzhen's lustre', *South China Morning Post*, 17 January, p. 12.

South China Morning Post 2005, 'Police struggle to cope with Shenzhen crime wave: party secretary orders officials to make the streets safe again', *South China Morning Post*, 30 December, p. 8.

South China Morning Post 2010, 'Crime-buster given a suspended death sentence for graft', *South China Morning Post*, 25 August, p. 10.

Wan, Xiao 1999, 'Swindler cheats 17 banks of $35 million', *Shanghai Star*, 16 July.

Wang, Yiqing 2010, 'The economic roots of China's crimes', *China Daily* [Hong Kong edition], 4 March, p. 9.

Xinhua News Agency 2002, 'Shenzhen improves investment environment', *Xinhua News Agency*, 22 January.

Appendix D.
Hong Kong ICBS Pilot Survey, 2003

The Hong Kong ICBS Pilot Survey was conducted in July 2003 and referred to victimisation that occurred from 1 January to 31 December 2002. The response rate was 28 per cent, producing a sample of 612 businesses. More than three-quarters of the respondents (78.4 per cent) were the owners or managers/executives of the company. Retail was the major business sector represented in the sample (22.7 per cent, including non-food, 15.2 per cent, and food, 7.5 per cent), followed by manufacturing (19.1 per cent), services, trading, restaurants and hotels (16.5 per cent), and wholesaling/distribution (13.1 per cent). Community, social and personal services (4.7 per cent), construction (3.1 per cent) and transport, storage and communication (2.3 per cent) contributed smaller proportions to the sample. More than 80 per cent was involved in a single sector of activity, but 29 per cent had premises other than those surveyed. Foreign investments were present in 10 per cent of the businesses surveyed, and 35 per cent were conducting import/export.

Not surprisingly, it was difficult to obtain data on the businesses' turnover, with only 45 per cent answering the question. The majority of respondents (66.3 per cent), however, came from their company's management stratum, including business owners, managing directors, chief executives, and finance and production directors, and another 7.5 per cent was responsible for the company's security. We can therefore assume that our respondents had good knowledge of crime and security issues in their company. Most of the businesses surveyed were very small, with three-quarters employing 10 or less employees. Only 2.2 per cent had more than 250 employees.

Results of the Hong Kong Pilot

Table D.1 presents the findings of the Hong Kong pilot in relation to victimisation and reporting to police. For conventional crime, 11.8 per cent of surveyed businesses reported at least one victimisation incident in the past year. Theft by customers and theft by outsiders were the most commonly mentioned crimes (5.7 per cent and 5.1 per cent respectively), followed by burglary, cited by 4.7 per cent of respondents. Although the sample was small, the pilot survey found a significantly higher level of crime than previous household victimisation surveys in Hong Kong (for example, Census and Statistics Department, Hong

Kong 1999). The proportion of respondents who were victimised by conventional crimes, however, appeared lower than that reported in the ICBS conducted in Central Eastern European capital cities in 2000 (Alvazzi del Frate 2004).

Significant levels of non-conventional crimes, such as fraud, cyber crime, bribery and extortion, were identified. Rates of bribery (4.6 per cent) and extortion (4.6 per cent) in the Hong Kong pilot were about half those recorded in the Central Eastern Europe ICBS (9 per cent offered bribes, 19 per cent asked for bribes, and 9 per cent experienced extortion). The level of fraud by outsiders was particularly high (16.7 per cent), although not as high as that reported in Eastern European countries (26 per cent). Fraud by outsiders was most prevalent in the restaurant/hotel/transport sector (28.8 per cent), followed by wholesale (23.8 per cent) and retail (23 per cent), and manufacturing (17.1 per cent).

The rates of reporting to police varied by types of offences, but were consistently higher for conventional crimes than non-conventional crimes. Of all businesses that reported the conventional or non-conventional victimisation to the police, 18.4 per cent did so out of a sense of duty ('crimes should be reported') and/or to recover property or get compensation from the offender. Sixteen per cent reported to stop the crime from happening again. One-third of respondents who did not report the incident to the police said it was because it was not serious enough. About 15 per cent did not report because of lack of evidence, and a similar proportion thought the police would not do anything about it. On average, about two-thirds of those who reported (64 per cent) were satisfied with the way in which the police dealt with their complaint, although the rate of satisfaction with the police response was only 48 per cent for fraud by outsiders.

For the respondents' perception of potential obstacles to doing good business in Hong Kong, the survey identified crime, corruption and lack of consultation with the business sector as moderate to strong obstacles (Table 4.2). Concern about corruption and crime was higher than concern about conventional 'impediments' to business such as tax regimes, import/export controls, and labour, safety and environmental regulations, which was an unexpected finding given Hong Kong's well-regarded and efficient anti-corruption and enforcement capabilities.

The majority of Hong Kong business respondents believed that bribery/corruption and extortion were not common practices in their line of business. Most (88.9 per cent) perceived that crime problems had remained stable over the past two to three years, and only 6.4 per cent believed they had increased. About one in five businesses surveyed was involved in some type of collective crime-prevention initiative.

Table D.1 Business Victimisation in Hong Kong, 2002: Victimisation by type of crime and reporting to police (per cent)

Type of victimisation	Percentage victimised, 2002 (N = 612)	N victimised, 2002	Reported to police %
Conventional crimes	11.8	72	-
Theft by customers	5.7	35	40
Theft by outsiders	5.1	31	45
Burglary	4.7	29	93
Vandalism	2.0	12	75
Theft by employees	1.1	7	14
Vehicle theft	0.5	3	100
Theft from vehicle	0.3	2	50
Assault	0.3	2	50
Robbery	0.2	1	100
Non-conventional crimes			
Fraud by outsiders	16.7	102	24
Cyber crime[a]	7.7	47	4
Bribery	4.6	28	7
Extortion/intimidation	4.6	28	46
Fraud by employees	3.8	23	17
IP infringement[a]	3.4	21	n.a.
Credit card-related fraud by outsiders[a]	2.5	15	n.a.
Credit card-related fraud by employees[a]	0.2	1	0
Other crimes	2.1	13	61

Notes: [a] New types of crime surveyed in Hong Kong for the first time; cyber crime includes attacks on computers through virus or malware, online fraud, software copyright violation, and unwanted (spam) or lewd communication.

Table D.2 Obstacles to Doing Business in Hong Kong, 2002: Proportion of respondents who perceived these obstacles as moderate or strong (N = 612)

Potential obstacle	Percentage moderate obstacle	Percentage strong obstacle	Total moderate & strong
Corruption	27.3	27.8	55.1
Crime and insecurity	36.9	17.7	54.6
Lack of consultation with business sector	38.2	15.7	53.9
Changes in law	35.0	13.9	48.9
Labour regulations	34.3	10.5	44.8
Tax regulations	29.4	13.4	42.8
Safety & environmental regulations	31.0	7.2	38.7
Import/export regulations	27.5	8.2	35.7

Appendix E.
Schematic Overview of the ICBS China Questionnaire, 2004–05

Table E.1 Crimes against Businesses

	Victimised in the past 12 months?	How many times in the past 12 months?	Reported to the police?	If reported, why?	If reported, satisfied with police?	If not satisfied with police, why not?	If not reported, why not?	Value of damages or loss
Burglary	✓	–	✓	–	–	–	–	–
Vandalism	✓	–	✓	–	–	–	–	–
Theft of vehicle	✓	–	✓	–	–	–	–	–
Theft from vehicle	✓	–	✓	–	–	–	–	–
Theft by customers	✓	–	✓	–	–	–	–	–
Theft by employees	✓	–	✓	–	–	–	–	–
Theft by outsiders	✓	–	–	–	–	–	–	–
Robbery	✓	–	–	–	–	–	–	–
Assault	✓	–	–	–	–	–	–	–
Intellectual property infringement	✓	–	–	–	–	–	–	–
Other (to be specified)	✓	–	–	–	–	–	–	–
Most serious of above incidents	–	–	✓	✓	✓	✓	✓	✓
Fraud by employees	✓	✓	✓	✓	✓	✓	✓	✓
Credit-card fraud by employees	✓	✓	–	–	–	–	–	–
Fraud by outsiders	✓	✓	✓	✓	✓	✓	✓	✓
Bribery	✓	✓	✓	✓	✓	✓	✓	–
How common is practice?								
Who was involved?								
Intimidation/ extortion/protection money	✓	✓	✓	✓	✓	✓	✓	–
What happened?								
Methods used in committing offences								
Any weapons?								
Who was involved in committing offences?								
Cyber crime	✓	–	✓	✓	✓	✓	✓	✓
Computer usage								
What kind of cyber crime?								

Table E.2 Respondent Attitudes on Crime Prevention and Police, Obstacles to Doing Business, and Description of Surveyed Business

Action against crime and corruption	Any cooperative action in the area with other businesses Would you be interested in such action Contact with local council about crime prevention Contact with local police about crime prevention
Satisfaction with police	How satisfied with how police deal with crime facing businesses If dissatisfied, why
Retail business	Types of goods sold
Obstacles to doing business	
Within Hong Kong	Export/import regulations Labour regulations Tax regulations Safety and environmental regulations Changes in laws and regulations Lack of consultation with business sector Crime and insecurity Corruption
Within China	Export/import regulations Labour regulations Tax regulations Safety and environmental regulations Changes in laws and regulations Lack of consultation with business sector Crime and insecurity Corruption
Description of the surveyed business	
Type and size of business	Business sector Main activity of company How many employees Annual turnover
Location	China only/Hong Kong only/both China and Hong Kong Geographical location (town, etc.) Business location (shopping centre, industrial estate, etc.) Part of a chain of shops

Note: Design of the table adapted from van Dijk et al. (2007:195–6).

Appendix F.
ICBS China Questionnaire,
2004–05: Hong Kong version[1]

Good morning/afternoon/evening. I am an Interviewer of the University of Hong Kong. We are conducting a survey about the problem of crime. Your company has been selected at random from the telephone directory to participate in the survey.

The survey is part of an international project, which is being done in four Chinese cities. The aim of the research is to get information about the patterns of crime against businesses, in order to assess how businesses can best avoid being victims of crime. Your answers will, of course, be treated confidentially and anonymously.

I need to address a few questions to the manager responsible for these premises. Can you please ask him/her whether he/she is willing to come to the phone?

INT.: IF MANAGER AVAILABLE: Go to question 15 and continue with 15A

INT.: IF MANAGER NOT AVAILABLE: Can you tell me at what time I have the best chance of getting him/her on the phone? < NOTE TIME FOR CALLBACK >

INT.: IF MANAGER NOT AVAILABLE ANY TIME: Could you please put me in contact with the best person/a colleague to answer these sorts of questions? < Go to question 15 and continue with 15A >

NOTE: 1) MANAGER

       2) COLLEAGUE

15.   CONTACT WITH RESPONDENT < INT.: If person other than first contact, repeat introduction >

16.   SEX OF RESPONDENT < INT.: Note sex of respondent without asking >

    1)   Male

    2)   Female

---

1 We present the Hong Kong version because it contains extra questions to Hong Kong businesses about their experiences (for those with premises in the mainland) and their perceptions of doing business in the mainland.

SECTION 1A: BACKGROUND

I'd like to start by asking you some questions about your company. I must emphasise that all the questions in the survey refer to your company's activities at and from these business premises.

101.   In which business sector is your company now operating at your present premise?

102.   What is the MAIN activity of your company at these premises? (multiple options)

      1)   Manufacturing

      2)   Retail/non-food

      3)   Retail/food

      4)   Wholesaling/distribution

      5)   Head office/headquarters

      6)   Sub-branch/chain shop

      7)   Financial service (eg., banking)

      8)   Professional service (eg., medical profession)

      9)   Other, namely (SPECIFY)_____

      10)   Refusal

103.   How many paid employees—both full-time and part-time—work at or from these premises at present, including yourself?

<INT.: IF RESPONDENT DOES NOT KNOW EXACT NUMBER, ASK FOR AN ESTIMATE>

1)	1 employee	11)	11–19 employees
2)	2 employees	12)	20–49 employees
3)	3 employees	13)	50–99 employees
4)	4 employees	14)	100–250 employees
5)	5 employees	15)	251–500 employees
6)	6 employees	16)	500–750 employees

7)	7 employees	17)	751–1000 employees
8)	8 employees	18)	more than 1000 employees
9)	9 employees	19)	don't know
10)	10 employees	20)	refused

104.   What is your position in the company?

1)   Managing director, chief executive, owner

2)   Main manager of these premises

3)   Security director/manager/advisor

4)   Finance director

5)   Production manager

6)   Company secretary

7)   Other, namely…(SPECIFY) _____

105.   What is the approximate annual turnover of your establishment?

_____

106.   Are these premises located…<INT.: READ OUT>

1)   In a town or city centre

2)   In a built-up area outside a city centre

3)   Countryside

4)   Or somewhere else?

5)   Don't know

6)   Refusal

107.   Are these premises located in: <INT.: MORE THAN ONE RESPONSE POSSIBLE>

1)   An industrial estate or business park

2)   An indoor shopping precinct

3)   An outdoor shopping precinct

4)   A main shopping street

5)   An out-of-town commercial area

6)   A serviced building for small businesses

7)   Or at another location (SPECIFY) _____

8)   Don't know

9)   Refusal

108.   Does your company only do business at these premises, or does it have other premises? (Multiple options allowed)

1)   Only at these premises

2)   Other premises in Hong Kong

3)   Other premises in mainland

4)   Refusal

109.   Are these premises part of a chain of shops?

1)   Yes

2)   No

3)   Don't know

4)   Refusal

SECTION 1B: OBSTACLES TO DOING BUSINESS

110.   In your opinion to what extent are the below listed representing obstacles to doing good business within Hong Kong?

	1) No obstacle	2) Moderate	3) Very strong	4) DNK	5) Refusal
Export/import regulations					
Labour regulations					
Tax regulations					
Safety and environmental regulations					
Changes in laws and regulations					
Lack of consultation with business sector					
Crime and insecurity					
Corruption					

111.   In your opinion to what extent are the below listed representing obstacles to doing good business within China?

	1) No obstacle	2) Moderate	3) Very strong	4) DNK	5) Refusal
Export/import regulations					
Labour regulations					
Tax regulations					
Safety and environmental regulations					
Changes in laws and regulations					
Lack of consultation with business sector					
Crime and insecurity					
Corruption					

SECTION 2: VICTIMISATION

201.   The following questions concern crimes which have occurred at your premises, including crimes against employees or crimes against visitors.

In general, have crime problems for your company increased, decreased or remained the same over the last two to three years?

1)   Increased

2)   Decreased

3)   Remained the same

4)   Don't know

5)   Refusal

202.   I'd now like to ask you about specific types of offences. I am interested only in offences which happened in the last calendar year; that is between 1st January and 31st December 2004.

In 2004, did any crime occur at your premises?

1)   Yes

2)   No

3)   Don't know

4)   Refusal

<IF ANSWER IS EQUAL TO CODES 2 OR 3, THEN CONTINUE WITH QUESTION 301. OR ELSE CONTINUE WITH QUESTION 203>

203. Which from the following list? <MULTIPLE ANSWER POSSIBLE— EXCLUDE REFERENCES TO REQUESTS FOR BRIBE/CORRUPTION, FRAUD AND INTIMIDATION/EXTORTION>

	1) Yes	2) No	3) DNK	4) Refusal
1) Burglary				
2) Vandalism				
3) Theft of vehicles				
4) Theft from vehicles				
5) Theft by customers				
6) Theft by employees				
7) Theft by outsiders				
8) Robbery				
9) Assault				
10) Intellectual property infringement*				
11) Other (specify_____)				

* illegal copying and counterfeiting, patents/trademarks/copyrights/designs owned by your company have been used by others without your permission

204. (The last time) did you or anyone else from the company report the incident(s) to the police?

	1) Yes	2) No	3) DNK	4) Refusal
1) Burglary				
2) Vandalism				
3) Theft of vehicles				
4) Theft from vehicles				
5) Theft by customers				
6) Theft by employees				
7) Theft by outsiders				
8) Robbery				
9) Assault				
10) Intellectual property infringement*				
11) Other (specify_____)				

* illegal copying and counterfeiting, patents/trademarks/copyrights/designs owned by your company have been used by others without your permission

205.   Taking everything into account, which was the most serious for you and your business? <INT.: NOTE ONLY ONE INCIDENT>

1)   Burglary

2)   Vandalism

3)   Theft of vehicles

4)   Theft from vehicles

5)   Theft by customers

6)   Theft by employees

7)   Theft by outsiders

8)   Robbery

9)   Assault

10)   Intellectual property infringement

11)   Other (specify _____)

12)   Don't know

13)   Refusal

<CHECK AT QUESTION 204 WHETHER <<MOST SERIOUS CRIME>> WAS REPORTED TO THE POLICE. IF REPORTED, CONTINUE WITH QUESTION 206—IF NOT REPORTED GO TO QUESTION 209>

206.   (If reported) Why did your company report it? < MULTIPLE RESPONSE >

1)   To recover property

2)   For insurance reasons

3)   Crimes should be reported/serious event

4)   Wanted offender to be caught/punished

5)   To stop it happening again

6)   To get compensation from the offender

7)   Other reason

8)   Don't know

9)   Refusal

Continue with question 207

207.   On the whole, were you satisfied with the way the police dealt with your report?

1)   Yes (satisfied)

2)   No (dissatisfied)

3)   Don't know

4)   Refusal

If answer is equal to code 1 or to code 4, then continue with question 210

If answer equal to code 2 then continue with question 208

208.   For what reasons were you dissatisfied? You can give more than one reason.

< INT.: MULTIPLE ANSWERS ALLOWED >

1)   Didn't do enough

2)   Were not interested

3)   Didn't find or apprehend the offender

4)   Didn't recover property (goods)

5)   Didn't keep us properly informed

6)   Didn't treat us correctly/were impolite

7)   Were slow to arrive

8)   Other reasons

9)   Don't know

10)   Refusal

Continue with question 210

209.   (If not reported) What were the main reasons for not reporting such incident to the police? < INT.: MULTICODING ALLOWED >

1)   Not worth reporting, not serious enough

2)   Police wouldn't have done anything/wouldn't have been interested

3)   Police wouldn't have been able to do anything/slight chance of success

4)   Involving the police was not appropriate/it was an internal matter

5)   Fear of reprisals

6)   Fear of negative publicity

7)   Didn't bother because no insurance claim was involved

8)   Lack of time/too much trouble

9)   Not company policy

10)   Lack of proof/evidence/witnesses

11)   Other reason, namely…(SPECIFY_____)

12)   Don't know

13)   Refused to answer

Continue with question 210

210.   What was the total value of any damage caused by these incidents, at these premises in 2004? For instance, were there any costs due to thefts, broken windows or other damages?

Please exclude money recovered from the insurance company.

If you don't know exactly, please estimate as exactly as possible.

< INT.: WRITE DOWN AMOUNT IN LOCAL CURRENCY, WITHOUT ANY POINTS OR COMMAS >

MAXIMUM = …

DON'T WANT TO SAY = 8888888 (7x8)

DON'T KNOW = 9999999 (7x9)

Continue with question 211

211.   Are you insured against loss or damage to the contents (including goods, equipment, etc.) of the premises caused by crime?

1)   Yes

2)   No

3)   Don't know

4)   Refusal

SECTION 3: FRAUD BY EMPLOYEES

301.   In 2004 was your company a victim of fraud committed by any EMPLOYEE based at these premises? That is, did anyone, while working for your company cheat the company in terms of diverting funds, goods or services to their own purposes?

1)   Yes

2)   No

3)   Don't know

4)   Refusal

302.   How many incidents of fraud by EMPLOYEES based at these premises occurred in 1992?

< INT.: A SERIES OF SIMILAR INCIDENTS OF FRAUD COMMITTED BY THE SAME PERSON OR GROUP OF PEOPLE COUNTS AS ONE INCIDENT. > If you don't know exactly, please estimate as exactly as possible.

1)   Less than 5 times

2)   Between 5 and 10 times

3)   Between 10 and 20

4)   More than 20

5)   Don't want to say

6)   Don't know = 9999

303.   What was the total value of the incidents of fraud by employees which occurred in 1998? If you don't know exactly, please estimate as exactly as possible.

> < INT.: WRITE DOWN AMOUNT IN LOCAL CURRENCY, WITHOUT ANY POINTS OR COMMAS >
>
> DON'T WANT TO SAY = 8888888 (7x8)
>
> DON'T KNOW = 9999999 (7x9)

304.   Do you know whether all incidents were reported (this incident was reported to the police), most incidents, just some incidents or none were reported to the police?

1)   All (yes, the incident was reported)

2)   Most

3)   Some

4)   None (no, the incident was not reported)

5)   Don't know

6)   Refusal

305.   (If reported) Why did your company report it? < MULTIPLE RESPONSE >

1)   To recover property

2)   For insurance reasons

3)   Crimes should be reported/serious event

4)   Wanted offender to be caught/punished

5)   To stop it happening again

6)   To get compensation from the offender

7)   Other reason

8)   Don't know

9)   Refusal

306.   On the whole, were you satisfied with the way the police dealt with your report?

1)   Yes (satisfied)

2)   No (dissatisfied)

3)   Don't know

4)   Refusal

307.   For what reasons were you dissatisfied? You can give more than one reason.

< INT.: MULTIPLE ANSWERS ALLOWED >

1)   Didn't do enough

2)   Were not interested

3)   Didn't find or apprehend the offender

4)   Didn't recover property (goods)

5)   Didn't keep us properly informed

6)   Didn't treat us correctly/were impolite

7)   Were slow to arrive

8)   Other reasons

9)   Don't know

10)   Refusal

308.   What were the main reasons for not reporting such incident to the police?

< INT.: MULTICODING ALLOWED >

1)   Not worth reporting, not serious enough

2)   Police wouldn't have done anything/wouldn't have been interested

3)   Police wouldn't have been able to do anything/slight chance of success

4)   Involving the police was not appropriate/it was an internal matter

5)   Fear of reprisals

6)   Fear of negative publicity

7)   Didn't bother because no insurance claim was involved

8)   Lack of time/too much trouble

9)   Not company policy

10)   Lack of proof/evidence/witnesses

11)   Other reason, namely…(SPECIFY)

12)   Don't know

13)   Refused to answer

309.   Apart from the incidents already covered, we want to ask about any fraud by employees using corporate payment/credit card.

In 2004, was your company a victim of corporate payment/credit-card fraud committed by any employee?

1)   Yes

2)   No

3)   Don't know

4)   Refused

310.   How many incidents of your employees using corporate payment card/ credit card for things for their personal purpose without proper approval occurred in 2004? A series of similar incidents of fraud committed by the same person or group of people counts as one incident. If you don't know exactly, please estimate.

1)   Less than 5 times

2)   Between 5 and 10 times

3)   Between 10 and 20

4)   More than 20

5)   Don't want to say

6)   Don't know = 9999

FRAUD BY OUTSIDERS

401.   In 2004 was your company at these premises the victim of fraud committed by any OUTSIDER, such as a customer, distributor or supplier?

1)   Yes

2)   No

3)   Don't know

4)   Refusal

402.   How many incidents of fraud by OUTSIDERS, including customers, suppliers and distributors, occurred at these premises in 2004? If you don't know exactly, please estimate as exactly as possible.

1)   Less than 5 times

2)   Between 5 and 10 times

3)   Between 10 and 20

4)   More than 20

5)   Don't want to say

6)   Don't know = 9999

403.   What was the total value of the incidents of fraud by OUTSIDERS in 2004? If you don't know exactly, please estimate as exactly as possible.

< INT.: WRITE DOWN AMOUNT IN LOCAL CURRENCY, WITHOUT ANY POINTS OR COMMAS >

MAXIMUM = ...

DON'T WANT TO SAY = 8888888 (7x8)

DON'T KNOW = 9999999 (7x9)

404.   Do you know whether all incidents were reported (this incident was reported to the police), most incidents, just some incidents or none were reported to the police?

1)   All (yes, the incident was reported)

2)   Most

3)   Some

4)   None (no, the incident was not reported)

5)   Don't know

6)   Refusal

405.   (If reported) Why did your company report it? < MULTIPLE RESPONSE >

1)   To recover property

2)   For insurance reasons

3)   Crimes should be reported/serious event

4)   Wanted offender to be caught/punished

5)   To stop it happening again

6)   To get compensation from the offender

7)   Other reason

8)   Don't know

9)   Refusal

406.   On the whole, were you satisfied with the way the police dealt with your report?

1)   Yes (satisfied)

2)   No (dissatisfied)

3)   Don't know

4)   Refusal

407.   For what reasons were you dissatisfied? You can give more than one reason.

< INT.: MULTIPLE ANSWERS ALLOWED >

1)   Didn't do enough

2)   Were not interested

3)   Didn't find or apprehend the offender

4)   Didn't recover property (goods)

5)   Didn't keep us properly informed

6)   Didn't treat us correctly/were impolite

7)   Were slow to arrive

8)   Other reasons

9)   Don't know

10)   Refusal

408.   What were the main reasons for not reporting such incident to the police?

< INT.: MULTICODING ALLOWED >

1)   Not worth reporting, not serious enough

2)   Police wouldn't have done anything/wouldn't have been interested

3)   Police wouldn't have been able to do anything/slight chance of success

4)   Involving the police was not appropriate/it was an internal matter

5)   Fear of reprisals

6)   Fear of negative publicity

7)   Didn't bother because no insurance claim was involved

8)   Lack of time/too much trouble

9)   Not company policy

10)   Lack of proof/evidence/witnesses

11)   Other reason, namely...(SPECIFY)

12)   Don't know

13)   Refused to answer

BRIBERY

501.   I would now like to ask you about bribery. By bribery I mean

- bribing managers or employees from your company
- being asked or expected to pay a bribe to government officials or politicians
- being asked or expected to pay a bribe to managers or employees of other companies.

Do you believe such practices are common in your line of business? Are they…

1)   Extremely common

2)   Fairly common

3)   Not very common

4)   Not common at all

5)   Don't know

6)   Refusal

502.   Did anyone try to bribe you, other managers, your employees, or obtain bribes from the company in relation to its activities?

1)   Yes

2)   No

3)   Don't know

4)   Refused to answer

503.   (IF YES): Was it < INT.: READ OUT, MORE ANSWERS ALLOWED >

1)   Legislative Council Members

2)   Government Officials

3)   District Board Members

4)   Customs officials

5)   Police officers

6)   Tax/revenues officials

7)   Officials in courts

8)   Managers or employees from other companies

9)   Don't know

10)   Refusal

504.   How many incidents occurred in 2004? If you don't know exactly, please estimate as exactly as possible.

1)   Less than 5 times

2)   Between 5 and 10 times

3)   Between 10 and 20

4)   More than 20

5)   Don't want to say

6)   Don't know = 9999

(INT.: ONCE A MONTH = code 3)

(INT.: ONCE A WEEK = code 4)

505.   Do you know whether all incidents were reported (this incident was reported), most incidents, just some incidents or none were reported to the Public Security Bureau or Anti-Corruption Agency?

1)   All (yes, the incident was reported)

2)   Most

3)   Some

4)   None (no, the incident was not reported)

5)   Don't know

6)   Refusal

506.   (If reported) Why did your company report it? < MULTIPLE RESPONSE >

1)   To recover property

2)   For insurance reasons

3)   Crimes should be reported/serious event

4)   Wanted offender to be caught/punished

5)   To stop it happening again

6)   To get compensation from the offender

7)   Other reason

8)   Don't know

9)   Refusal

507.   On the whole, were you satisfied with the way the Public Security Bureau or Anti-Corruption Agency dealt with your report?

1)   Yes (satisfied)

2)   No (dissatisfied)

3)   Don't know

4)   Refusal

508.   For what reasons were you dissatisfied? You can give more than one reason.

< INT.: MULTIPLE ANSWERS ALLOWED >

1)   Didn't do enough

2)   Were not interested

3)   Didn't find or apprehend the offender

4)   Didn't recover property (goods)

5)   Didn't keep us properly informed

6)   Didn't treat us correctly/were impolite

7)   Were slow to arrive

8)   Other reasons

9)   Don't know

10)   Refusal

509.   What were the main reasons for not reporting such incident to the Public Security Bureau or Anti-Corruption Agency? < INT.: MULTICODING ALLOWED >

1)   Not worth reporting, not serious enough

2)   Police wouldn't have done anything/wouldn't have been interested

3) Police wouldn't have been able to do anything/slight chance of success

4) Involving the police was not appropriate/it was an internal matter

5) Fear of reprisals

6) Fear of negative publicity

7) Didn't bother because no insurance claim was involved

8) Lack of time/too much trouble

9) Not company policy

10) Lack of proof/evidence/witnesses

11) Other reason, namely...(SPECIFY)

12) Don't know

13) Refused to answer

INTIMIDATION/EXTORTION/PROTECTION MONEY

601.   I would now like to ask you about intimidation/extortion. By this I mean

- extorting money from your company
- threatening and intimidating managers and/or employees
- threatening product contamination.

Do you believe such practices are common in your line of business? Are they...

1) Very common

2) Fairly common

3) Not very common

4) Not common at all

5) < DO NOT READ: Don't know >

6) Refusal

602.   Did anyone try to intimidate you, other managers, your employees, or extort money from the company in relation to its activities?

1)   Yes

2)   No

3)   Don't know

4)   Refused to answer

603.   IF YES: Did that include…

< INT.: READ OUT, MORE ANSWERS ALLOWED >

1)   Extorting money from your company

2)   Threatening and intimidating managers and/or employees

3)   Threatening product contamination

4)   Other (SPECIFY)

5)   Refused to answer

What methods were used in committing the offences? < MULTIPLE ANSWERS ALLOWED >

1)   Walk-in into the premises

2)   Face-to-face contact in some other location

3)   Telephone calls

4)   Written communications

5)   Other (SPECIFY)

6)   Don't know

7)   Refused to answer

Were any weapons used at any time? < MULTIPLE ANSWERS ALLOWED >

1)   Yes, firearms

2)   Yes, explosives

3)   Yes, knives

4)   Yes, other weapons

5)   No weapons used

6)   Don't know

7)   Refused to answer

606.   How many incidents occurred in 2004? If you don't know exactly, please estimate as exactly as possible.

1)   Less than 5 times

2)   Between 5 and 10 times

3)   Between 10 and 20

4)   More than 20

5)   Don't want to say

6)   Don't know = 9999

< INT.: ONCE A MONTH = code 3)

ONCE A WEEK = code 4) >

607.   (In your opinion) Who was involved in committing such offences?
< MULTIPLE RESPONSE POSSIBLE >

1)   Local organised crime groups

2)   International organised crime groups

3)   Rival business

4)   Others

5)   Don't know

6)   Refusal

608.   Do you know whether all incidents were reported (this incident was reported to the police), most incidents, just some incidents or none were reported to the police?

1)   All (yes, the incident was reported)

2)   Most

3)   Some

4)   None (no, the incident was not reported)

5)   Don't know

6)   Refusal

609.   (If reported) Why did your company report it? < MULTIPLE RESPONSE >

1)   To recover property

2)   For insurance reasons

3)   Crimes should be reported/serious event

4)   Wanted offender to be caught/punished

5)   To stop it happening again

6)   To get compensation from the offender

7)   Other reason

8)   Don't know

9)   Refusal

610.   On the whole, were you satisfied with the way the police dealt with your report?

1)   Yes (satisfied)

2)   No (dissatisfied)

3)   Don't know

4)   Refusal

611.   For what reasons were you dissatisfied? You can give more than one reason. < INT.: MULTIPLE ANSWERS ALLOWED >

1)   Didn't do enough

2)   Were not interested

3)   Didn't find or apprehend the offender

4)   Didn't recover property (goods)

5)   Didn't keep us properly informed

6)   Didn't treat us correctly/were impolite

7)   Were slow to arrive

8)   Other reasons

9)   Don't know

10)   Refusal

612.   What were the main reasons for not reporting such incident to the police? < INT.: MULTICODING ALLOWED >

1)   Not worth reporting, not serious enough

2)   Police wouldn't have done anything/wouldn't have been interested

3)   Police wouldn't have been able to do anything/slight chance of success

4)   Involving the police was not appropriate/it was an internal matter

5)   Fear of reprisals

6)   Fear of negative publicity

7)   Didn't bother because no insurance claim was involved

8)   Lack of time/too much trouble

9)   Not company policy

10)   Lack of proof/evidence/witnesses

11)   Other reason, namely…(SPECIFY)

12)   Don't know

13)   Refused to answer

CYBER CRIME

Now, about YOUR use of a computer. Please include all computers, laptop, or access to WebTV at home, work, or school for BUSINESS USE or for operating a home business.

701.   During the last 12 months, have YOU used a computer, laptop or WebTV for the following purposes? < INT.: MULTICODING ALLOWED >

1)   Business use at home

2)   Business use at work

3)   Business use at school, libraries, cyber café, etc.

4)   None

5)   Refusal

How many computers? _____

702.   Do(es) the computer(s) you use have software such as a firewall and anti-virus program?

1)   Yes, firewall

2)   Yes, anti-virus program

3)   Both

4)   None

5)   Don't know

6)   Refusal

703.   Is the computer you use connected to the Internet?

1)   Yes

2)   No

3)   Don't know

4)   Refusal

704.   Have you experienced any of the following COMPUTER-RELATED incidents in the last 12 months?

Fraud in purchasing something over the Internet?

1)   Yes

2)   No

3)   Don't know

4)   Refusal

705.   Any attack on your computer from a source such as a virus, spyware, hacker, malware, etc.

> < INT.: MULTICODING ALLOWED >

1)   Virus

2)   Spyware

3)   Hacker

4)   Malware

5)   Others _____

6)   No

7)   Refusal

706.   Threats of harm or physical attack made while online or through email?

1)   Yes

2)   No

3)   Don't know

4)   Refusal

707.   Unrequested lewd or obscene messages, communications, or image while online or through email?

1)   Yes

2)   No

3)   Don't know

4)   Refusal

708.   Software copyright violation in connection with a home business?

1)   Yes

2)   No

3)   Don't know

4)   Refusal

709.   Something else that you consider a computer-related crime?

Please specify _____

710.   Did you suffer any monetary loss as a result of the incident(s) you just mentioned?

1)   Yes

2)   No

3)   Don't know

4)   Refusal

711.   How much money did you lose as a result of the incident?

Enter amount _____

712.   Did you report the incident you just mentioned? < INT.: MULTICODING ALLOWED >

1)   A law enforcement agency

2)   An Internet service provider

3)   A web site administrator

4)   Someone else _____

5)   Not reported

6)   Refusal

713.   Do you know whether all incidents were reported (this incident was reported), most incidents, just some incidents or none were reported to the police or other agency?

1)   All (yes, the incident was reported)

2)   Most

3)   Some

4)   None (no, the incident was not reported)

5)   Don't know

6)   Refusal

714. (If reported) Why did your company report it? < MULTIPLE RESPONSE >

1) To recover property

2) For insurance reasons

3) Crimes should be reported/serious event

4) Wanted offender to be caught/punished

5) To stop it happening again

6) To get compensation from the offender

7) Other reason

8) Don't know

9) Refusal

715. On the whole, were you satisfied with the way the police or other agency dealt with your report?

1) Yes (satisfied)

2) No (dissatisfied)

3) Don't know

4) Refusal

716. For what reasons were you dissatisfied? You can give more than one reason. < INT.: MULTIPLE ANSWERS ALLOWED >

1) Didn't do enough

2) Were not interested

3) Didn't find or apprehend the offender

4) Didn't recover property (goods)

5) Didn't keep us properly informed

6) Didn't treat us correctly/were impolite

7) Were slow to arrive

8) Other reasons

9) Don't know

10) Refusal

717.   What were the main reasons for not reporting such incident to the police? < INT.: MULTICODING ALLOWED >

1)   Not worth reporting, not serious enough

2)   Police wouldn't have done anything/wouldn't have been interested

3)   Police wouldn't have been able to do anything/slight chance of success

4)   Involving the police was not appropriate/it was an internal matter

5)   Fear of reprisals

6)   Fear of negative publicity

7)   Didn't bother because no insurance claim was involved

8)   Lack of time/too much trouble

9)   Not company policy

10)   Lack of proof/evidence/witnesses

11)   Other reason, namely...(SPECIFY)

12)   Don't know

13)   Refusal

MISCELLANEOUS

801.   To your knowledge, have businesses in this area taken any kind of cooperative action against crime and corruption or extortion, such as sharing security patrols, setting up a business watch or ring, phone alarm system, etc.?

1)   Yes

2)   No

3)   Don't know

4)   Refusal

802.   Would you be interested in participating in cooperative action against crime, corruption and extortion in your area such as sharing security patrols, or setting up a business watch or ring, phone alarm system, etc.?

1)   Yes, interested

2)   No, not interested

3)   Don't know

4)   Refusal

803.   Did your business have any contact with the local council about crime or corruption problems or crime prevention in 2004?

1)   Yes

2)   No

3)   Don't know

4)   Refusal

804.   Apart from any crimes you may have reported to the police in 2004, did your business have any contact with the police about crime or corruption problems or crime prevention in 2004?

1)   Yes

2)   No

3)   Don't know

4)   Refusal

805.   In general, how satisfied or dissatisfied are you with the way the police deal with the crime problems facing business in this area? Are you...

1)   Very satisfied

2)   Fairly satisfied

3)   Neither satisfied nor dissatisfied

4)   Fairly dissatisfied

5)   Very dissatisfied

6)   Don't know

7)   Refusal

806.   Why are you dissatisfied with the way the police deal with the crime problems facing business in this area? < INT.: DO NOT READ, MORE ANSWERS ALLOWED >

1)   Police not seen in this area

2)   Police involved in corruption

3)   Take too long to react to incidents

4)   Do not react to alarms going off

5)   Do not catch or prosecute offenders

6)   Give little or no information back on reported crimes

7)   No day-to-day contact with police

8)   Not interested in reported crimes

9)   Too much hassle to report

10)   Other reasons…(SPECIFY)

11)   Don't know

12)   Refusal

Appendix G.
Victimisation by Common Crime by City, Business Sector and Size

Table G.1 Conventional Crime: Rates of victimisation by city and by sector of business (per cent)

	Hong Kong N = 1817	Shanghai N = 1110	Shenzhen N = 1112	Xi'an N = 1078
All common crime				
Manufacturing	5.9	5.7	8.3	5.5
Retail	13.5**	6.9	5.1	4.8
Wholesale/trading	5.6	3.7	2.4	3.6
Financial & professional services	7.0	4.8	10.1	5.9
Other sectors	7.1	0.0	7.7	2.8
Burglary				
Manufacturing	2.6	4.1	5.8	4.3
Retail	4.0	6.2	3.2	4.0
Wholesale/trading	2.7	2.5	0.8	1.3
Financial & professional services	3.4	2.6	6.9	5.0
Other sectors	2.1	0.0	2.6	2.8
Vandalism				
Manufacturing	1.2	1.8	2.3	2.5
Retail	1.6	2.8	3.2	2.2
Wholesale/trading	1.5	0.6	0.0	2.2
Financial & professional services	1.4	0.9	5.3*	1.8
Other sectors	1.4	0.0	1.9	0.0
Vehicle-related crime[a]				
Manufacturing	0.9	0.8	1.4	2.2
Retail	0.4	1.4	1.3	1.5
Wholesale/trading	0.6	0.6	0.0	0.9
Financial & professional services	0.7	2.2	2.7	0.9
Other sectors	1.4	0.0	1.9	0.0

	Hong Kong N = 1817	Shanghai N = 1110	Shenzhen N = 1112	Xi'an N = 1078
Theft by employees				
Manufacturing	2.1	1.6	3.5	1.8
Retail	2.2	2.8	3.2	0.7
Wholesale/trading	0.6	1.2	0.0	0.4
Financial & professional services	1.7	1.3	3.2	1.4
Other sectors	1.4	0.0	3.2	0.0
Theft by customers				
Manufacturing	0.5	0.6	0.6	1.5
Retail	9.2***	3.4**	0.0	1.8
Wholesale/trading	0.6	0.6	0.0	0.0
Financial & professional services	1.2	0.9	1.6	1.8
Other sectors	0.7	1.2	0.6	0.0
Theft by outsiders				
Manufacturing	2.6	2.0	4.8	3.7
Retail	3.6**	5.5*	3.8	4.0
Wholesale/trading	1.2	1.9	0.8	2.7
Financial & professional services	1.9	3.5	7.4*	4.1
Other sectors	1.4	0.0	2.6	2.8
Violent crime[b]				
Manufacturing	0.9	0.6	2.9	0.6
Retail	1.0	0.0	1.3	0.7
Wholesale/trading	0.6	0.0	0.8	1.8
Financial & professional services	0.5	0.0	3.7	1.4
Other sectors	1.4	0.0	3.8	0.0

$* p < 0.05$ $** p < 0.01$ $*** p < 0.001$

Notes: [a] Theft of vehicle and theft from vehicle; [b] robbery and assault.

Table G.2 Common Crime: Rates of victimisation by city and by size of business (per cent)

	Hong Kong N = 1793	Shanghai N = 1035	Shenzhen N = 1040	Xi'an N = 999
All common crime				
Small 1–10	7.3	4.8	5.9	4.1
Medium 11–49	9.7	4.9	5.1	4.9
Medium large 50–250	15.3*	4.2	11.0**	5.6
Large 250 +	36.8***	10.2**	8.2	9.5*
Burglary				
Small 1–10	2.7	3.7	4.1	3.1
Medium 11–49	3.9	3.4	3.0	3.9
Medium large 50–250	8.2**	3.2	6.7*	4.1
Large 250 +	5.3	6.3	5.3	6.3
Vandalism				
Small 1–10	1.2	1.6	2.4	1.6
Medium 11–49	1.9	1.0	1.6	2.1
Medium large 50–250	4.7**	2.6*	3.4	2.6
Large 250 +	0.0	0.8	3.5	4.2
Vehicle-related crime[a]				
Small 1–10	0.6	1.1	0.6	1.3
Medium 11–49	1.2	1.2	1.6	1.0
Medium large 50–250	1.2	0.6	1.8	2.0
Large 250 +	5.3*	2.3	1.8	3.2
Theft by employees				
Small 1–10	1.1	1.6	0.0	0.3
Medium 11–49	3.5*	1.0	1.1	1.5
Medium large 50–250	2.4	1.9	6.1***	1.5
Large 250 +	21.1***	3.1	4.7	2.1
Theft by customers				
Small 1–10	3.1	3.2**	0.6	1.3
Medium 11–49	2.7	1.0	0.3	1.0
Medium large 50–250	2.4	0.6	0.6	1.0
Large 250 +	10.5	0.0	1.8*	4.2**
Theft by outsiders				
Small 1–10	2.1	2.7	4.7	3.4
Medium 11–49	3.1	2.9	3.0	3.3
Medium large 50–250	3.5	1.9	6.4*	4.1
Large 250 +	10.5*	4.7	4.1	7.4*

	Hong Kong N = 1793	Shanghai N = 1035	Shenzhen N = 1040	Xi'an N = 999
Violent crime[b]				
Small 1–10	0.6	0.0	1.8	0.6
Medium 11–49	1.2	0.0	2.4	1.0
Medium large 50–250	1.2	0.3	4.6	1.5
Large 250 +	15.8***	1.6**	1.8	2.1

* $p < 0.05$ ** $p < 0.01$ *** $p < 0.001$

Notes: [a] Theft of vehicle and theft from vehicle; [b] robbery and assault.

Appendix H.
Victimisation by Non-Conventional Crime by City, Business Sector and Size

Table H.1 Non-Conventional Crime: Rates of victimisation by city and by sector of business (per cent)

	Hong Kong N = 1817	Shanghai N = 1110	Shenzhen N = 1112	Xi'an N = 1078
All fraud[a]				
Manufacturing	14.1	10.8	15.5	16.0
Retail	15.3	11.0	12.0	12.1
Wholesale/trading	14.5	9.3	19.7	20.9**
Financial & professional services	11.6	10.8	16.0	8.2
Other sectors	8.6	8.6	14.1	13.9
Bribery				
Manufacturing	5.2**	6.3	8.5	12.6**
Retail	1.0	5.5	7.0	5.1
Wholesale/trading	1.5	4.9	7.9	8.9
Financial & professional services	2.7	6.9	10.6	8.6
Other sectors	4.3	11.1	7.7	8.3
Extortion/intimidation				
Manufacturing	2.8	1.0	3.1	0.6
Retail	4.8*	0.7	3.8	1.1
Wholesale/trading	0.6	0.6	1.6	0.4
Financial & professional services	3.4	1.3	2.7	3.6*
Other sectors	3.6	0.0	4.5	0.0
IP and copyright infringement				
Manufacturing	5.2*	5.1	7.9	8.6
Retail	1.8	2.1 †	7.0	4.4
Wholesale/trading	2.7	6.2	10.2	6.7
Financial & professional services	4.6*	7.4	13.8	10.0
Other sectors	3.6	12.3*	8.3	13.9

* $p < 0.05$ **$p < 0.01$

† $p < 0.05$, rate is significantly lower

Notes: Statistical significance refers to differences between sectors within each city; [a] includes fraud by outsiders, fraud by employees and Internet-related fraud.

Table H.2 Non-Conventional Crime: Rates of victimisation by city and by size of business (per cent)

	Hong Kong N = 1793	Shanghai N = 1035	Shenzhen N = 1040	Xi'an N = 999
All fraud[a]				
Small 1–10	13.4	7.0	13.6	15.7
Medium 11–49	14.0	12.4	16.4	14.7
Medium large 50–250	10.6	9.1	16.8	14.8
Large 250+	31.6*	14.1	12.3	14.7
Bribery				
Small 1–10	2.7	4.3	7.7	5.3
Medium 11–49	3.1	7.5	7.8	10.3
Medium large 50–250	1.2	5.8	9.8	10.7
Large 250+	5.3	10.2	9.9	14.7*
Extortion/intimidation				
Small 1–10	2.6	0.5	1.8	1.6
Medium 11–49	5.4	1.2	1.9	0.5
Medium large 50–250	3.5	0.3	4.3	1.5
Large 250+	10.5*	1.6	5.8*	3.2
IP and copyright infringement				
Small 1–10	3.1	4.8	9.5	4.1††
Medium 11–49	5.1	7.0	7.3	10.0*
Medium large 50–250	5.9	5.2	10.4	9.2
Large 250+	10.5	7.0	11.1	9.5

* $p < 0.05$, rate is significantly higher

†† $p < 0.01$, rate is significantly lower

Notes: Statistical significance refers to differences between business size within each city; [a] includes fraud by outsiders, fraud by employees and Internet-related fraud.

Bibliography

Alvazzi Del Frate, Anna 2004, 'The International Crime Business Survey: findings from nine Central Eastern European cities', *European Journal on Criminal Policy and Research* 10, 137–61.

Alvazzi Del Frate, Anna (ed.) 2007, *Study on Crime and Corruption in Cape Verde*. Cape Verde: Ministry of Justice and United Nations Office on Drugs and Crime.

American Association of Port Authorities 2005, *World Port Ranking 2005*. Alexandria, Va: American Association of Port Authorities, <www.aapa-ports.org>

Anderson, Jack 2009, 'Tax misery and reform index', *Forbes Magazine*, 13 April, <www.forbes.com/global/2009/0413/034-tax-misery-reform-index.html>

Aromaa, Kauko and Lehti, Martti 1994, *The security of Finnish companies in St Petersburg*, Research Communication 16, National Research Institute of Legal Policy, Helsinki.

Asian Development Bank (ADB) 2007, *Inequality in Asia: Key indicators*. Manila: Asian Development Bank.

Associated Press 2010, 'Tainted milk shows China's safety challenges: despite stricter regulations enforcement is weakened by local governments', *Associated Press*, 2 April, <www.msnbc.msn.com/id/35233791/ns/health-food_safety>

Australian Institute of Criminology (AIC) 2004, *Crimes against business: a review of victimisation, predictors and prevention*, Technical and Background Paper No. 11, Australian Institute of Criminology, Canberra.

Ayling, Julie, Grabosky, Peter and Shearing, Clifford 2009, *Lengthening the Arm of the Law: Enhancing police resources in the twenty-first century*. New York: Cambridge University Press.

Bakken, Børge 2000, *The Exemplary Society: Human improvement, social control and the dangers of modernity in China*. New York: Oxford University Press.

Bakken, Børge 2004, 'Moral panics, crime rates and harsh punishment in China', *Australian and New Zealand Journal of Criminology* 37(4), 67–90.

Bakken, Børge 2005, 'Comparative perspectives on crime in China', in Børge Bakken (ed.), *Crime, Punishment, and Policing in China*, 64–99. Oxford: Rowman & Littlefield.

Bamfield, Joshua 2009, *Global Retail Theft Barometer 2009: Monitoring the costs of shrinkage and crime in the global retail industry*. Nottingham, UK: Centre for Retail Research,

Bamfield, Joshua 2010, *Global Retail Theft Barometer 2010*. Nottingham, UK: Centre for Retail Research,

Bernburg, Jón G. 2002, 'Anomie, social change and crime: a theoretical examination of institutional anomie theory', *British Journal of Criminology* 42(4), 729–42.

British Chambers of Commerce 2004, *Setting Business Free from Crime: A crime against business survey*. London: British Chambers of Commerce.

Broadhurst, Roderic and Lee, Kingwa 2009, 'The transformation of triad "dark societies" in Hong Kong: the impact of law enforcement, socio-economic and political change', *Security Challenges* 5(4), 1–38.

Broadhurst, Roderic, Bacon-Shone, John, Bouhours, Brigitte, Lee, Kingwa and Zhong, Lena 2010, *Hong Kong, The United Nations International Crime Victim Survey: Final report of the 2006 Hong Kong UNICVS*. Hong Kong and Canberra: The University of Hong Kong and The Australian National University.

Broadhurst, Roderic, Lee, Kingwa and Chan, Chingyee 2007, 'Crime and violence in Hong Kong, China', in United Nations Human Settlements Programme (ed.), *Enhancing Urban Safety and Security: Global report on human settlements 2007*, pp. 306–7. London: Earthscan.

Broadhurst, Roderic, Lee, Kingwa and Chan, Chingyee 2008, 'Crime trends in Hong Kong', in Wing Lo and Eric Chui (eds), *Crime and Criminal Justice in Hong Kong*, pp. 45–68. Cullompton, UK: Willan.

Brody, Richard and Luo, Robert 2009, 'Fraud and white-collar crime: a Chinese perspective', *Cross Cultural Management* 16(3), 317–26.

Brunetti, Aymo, Kisunko, Gregory and Weder, Beatrice 1997, *Institutional Obstacles for Doing Business: Data description and methodology of a worldwide private sector survey*. Washington, DC: The World Bank, <siteresources. worldbank.org/INTWBIGOVANTCOR/Resources/wps1759.pdf>

Cai, Fang and Wang, Meiyan 2010, 'Urbanisation with Chinese characteristics', in Ross Garnaut, Jane Golley and Ligang Song (eds), *China: The next twenty years of reform and development*, pp. 319–40. Canberra: ANU E Press.

Cao, Li and Zheng, Yijia 2007, 'Shanghai ports see rise in crime rate', *China Daily*, 18 July, p. 5.

Carach, Carlos and Makkai, Toni 2002, *Review of Victoria Police Crime Statistics*, Research & Public Policy Series No. 45. Canberra: Australian Institute of Criminology.

Census and Statistics Department, Hong Kong 1999, *Crime and Its Victims in Hong Kong in 1998*. Hong Kong SAR: Census and Statistics Department.

Census and Statistics Department, Hong Kong 2005, *Hong Kong Annual Digest of Statistics 2004*. Hong Kong SAR: Census and Statistics Department.

Census and Statistics Department, Hong Kong 2006, *Hong Kong Annual Digest of Statistics 2005*. Hong Kong SAR: Census and Statistics Department.

Census and Statistics Department, Hong Kong 2007a, *Crime and its victims in Hong Kong in 2005*, Thematic Household Survey Report No. 31, Census and Statistics Department, Hong Kong SAR.

Census and Statistics Department, Hong Kong 2007b, *Hong Kong in Figures, 2007 Edition*. Hong Kong SAR: Census and Statistics Department.

Census and Statistics Department, Hong Kong 2007c, *Key Findings of the 2006 Population By-Census*. Hong Kong SAR: Census and Statistics Department.

Centre for Retail Research 2000, *UK Retail Crime Statistics: The National Survey of Retail Crime and Security*. London: Centre for Retail Research, <www.retailing.uk.com/report1.html>

Central Intelligence Agency (CIA) 2005, *The World Factbook*. Washington, DC: Central Intelligence Agency, <https://www.cia.gov/library/publications/download/download-2005/index.html>

Chan, Kin-man 2001, 'Uncertainty, acculturation, and corruption in Hong Kong', *International Journal of Public Administration* 24(9), 909–28.

Chan, Kin-man and Buckingham, Will 2008, 'Is China abolishing the *hukou* system?', *China Quarterly* 193, 586–606.

Chang, Yaru 1990, 'Research on fear of crime in China', *Police Studies: The International Review of Police Development* 13(1), 125–7.

Chappell, Duncan and Di Martino, Vittorio 1999, 'Violence at work', *Asian-Pacific Newsletter on Occupational Health and Safety* 6(1), <www.acosomoral.org/pdf/violwk.pdf>

Chen, Xiangming 1987, 'Magic and myth of migration: a case study of a special economic zone in China', *Asia-Pacific Population Journal* 2(3), 57–76.

Chen, Xiangming 2009, 'A globalizing city on the rise: Shanghai's transformation in comparative perspective', in Xiangming Chen (ed.), *Shanghai Rising: State power and local transformations in a global megacity*, pp. xv–xxxv. Minneapolis: University of Minnesota Press.

Chen, Yu 2009, 'Migrants in Shanghai's manufacturing companies: employment conditions and policy implications', *Journal of Asian Public Policy* 2(3), 279–92.

Cheung, Tai Ming 1996, 'Guarding China's domestic front line: the People's Armed Police and China's stability', *China Quarterly* 146, 525–47.

Chin, Kolin and Godson, Roy 2006, 'Organized crime and the political–criminal nexus in China', *Trends in Organized Crime* 9(3), 5–42.

China Business World n.d., 'The life of Deng Xia Ping', *China Business World*, [Online publication], <www.cbw.com/asm/xpdeng/life.html>

China Daily 2005a, 'A world without thieves? A "thief map" helps', *China Daily*, 24 January, <www.chinadaily.com.cn/english/doc/2005-01/24/content_411732.htm>

China Daily 2005b, 'Bank of China fights fraud with review', *China Daily*, 5 April, <www.china.org.cn/archive/2005-04/05/content_1124764.htm>

China Daily 2005c, 'Counterfeit medicines taken off shelves', *China Daily*, 18 July, <www.chinadaily.com.cn/English/doc/2005-07/18/content_460997.htm>

China Economic Review 2011, 'IBM settles China bribery case', *China Economic Review*, 21 March, <www.chinaeconomicreview.com/industry-focus/latest-news/article/2011-03-21/IBM_settles_China_bribery_case.html>

China Internet Information Center News 2005, '18,130 trademark infringement cases dealt with', *China Internet Information Center News*, 12 July, [Online publication].

Choo, Kim-Kwang R. 2011, 'Cyber threat landscape faced by financial and insurance industry', *Trends & Issues in Crime and Criminal Justice* 408, Australian Institute of Criminology, Canberra.

Chow, Chung-yan 2004, 'More police promised as crime rate soars 57 pc in Shenzhen', *South China Morning Post*, 14 January, p. 1.

Chu, Yiu Kong 2005, 'Hong Kong triads after 1997', *Trends in Organized Crime* 8(3), 5–12.

Clarke, Donald C. 2007, 'The Chinese legal system since 1995: steady development and striking continuities', *China Quarterly* 191, 555–66.

Clarke, Ronald 1995, 'Situational crime prevention', in Michael Tonry and David Farrington (eds), *Building a Safer Society: Strategic approaches to crime prevention*, pp. 91–150. Chicago: University of Chicago Press.

Clarke, Ronald 1997, *Situational Crime Prevention: Successful case studies*. Albany, NY: Harrow and Heston.

Clarke, Ronald and Felson, Marcus (eds) 1993, *Routine Activity and Rational Choice*. New Brunswick, NJ: Transactions Publishers.

Cohen, Lawrence and Felson, Marcus 1979, 'Social change and crime rate trends: a routine activity approach', *American Sociological Review* 44, 588–608.

Cohen, Lawrence, Felson, Marcus and Land, Kenneth 1980, 'Property crime rate in the United States: a macrodynamic analysis, 1947–1977', *American Journal of Sociology* 86, 90–118.

College for Criminal Law Science of Beijing Normal University 2011, Symposium on Amendment (VIII) to the Criminal Law of the People's Republic of China, 5 March, Beijing, <www.criminallawbnu.cn/english/showpage.asp?channelid=100&pkid=325>

Crossland, John 1987, 'The Xi'an incident, 1936', *History Today* 37(7), 10–17.

Dai, M. L. 2010, 'Exploring the connection between organised crime and corruption: a case study on "Chian-LI"', *Public Security Science Journal— Journal of Zhejiang Police College* 3, 66–8, [in Chinese].

Dai, Yisheng 2001, 'Minister declares war on crime and secret societies', *Crime and Justice International* 17(57), [Online publication], <www.cjimagazine.com/archives/cji73ca.html?id=166>

Dasgupta, Saibal 2010, 'China's stock fraud totals $30 billion', *TheTimes of India*, 27 November, <articles.timesofindia.indiatimes.com/2010-11-27/india-business/28257324_1_insider-trading-stock-markets-capital-market>

Deng, Xiaoping 1994, *Selected Works of Deng Xiaoping (1982–1992)*. Beijing: Foreign Languages Press.

Doerner, William G. and Lab, Steven 1998, *Victimology*. Cincinnati, Ohio: Anderson Pub.

Durkheim, Émile 1964 [1895], *The Rules of Sociological Method*, George E. G. Catlin (ed.), Sarah A. Solovay and John M. Mueller (trans). New York: Free Press.

Durkheim, Émile 1997 [1893], *The Division of Labor in Society*, Lewis A. Coser (trans.). New York: Free Press.

Dutton, Michael 1997, 'The basic character of crime in contemporary China', *China Quarterly* 149, 160–77.

Dutton, Michael 2005, 'Toward a government of the contract: policing in the era of reform', in Børge Bakken (ed.), *Crime, Punishment, and Policing in China*. Oxford: Rowman & Littlefield, pp. 189–233.

Dutton, Michael 2006, *Policing Chinese Politics: A history*. Durham, NC, and London: Duke University Press.

Economist 2011, 'Bamboo capitalism: China's economy', March 10, p. 13, www.economist.com/node/18332610.

Economist Intelligence Unit 2010, *Global Fraud Report 2010/11*. New York: Kroll, <www.kroll.com/about/library/fraud/Oct2010/>

Eigen, Peter 2002, Corruption is unsustainable, Statement by the Chairman of Transparency International on the launch of the Corruption Perception Index 2002, Transparency International, Berlin, <www.transparency.org/policy_research/surveys_indices/cpi/2002>

Ernst & Young 2010, *Driving Ethical Growth—New markets, new challenges: 11th Global Fraud Survey*. London: Ernst & Young.

Evans, Richard 1997, *Deng Xiaoping and the Making of Modern China*. London: Penguin.

Fan, Maureen and Eunjung Cha, Ariana 2008, 'China's capital cases still secret, arbitrary', *Washington Post*, 24 December, p. A01.

Fay, Joe 2009, 'China executes securities trader over $9.52m fraud', *The Register*, 8 December, <www.theregister.co.uk/2009/12/08/china_execution>

Felson, Marcus 1998, *Crime and Everyday Life*. Thousand Oaks, Calif.: Pine Forge Press.

Felson, Marcus and Clarke, Ronald V. 1998, *Opportunity makes the thief*, Police Research Series, Paper 98, Home Office, London.

Fu, Hualing 1990, 'Patrol police: a recent development in the People's Republic of China', *Police Studies: The International Review of Police Development* 13(1), 111–17.

Fu, Hualing 2003, 'Zhou Yongkang and the recent police reform in China', *Australian and New Zealand Journal of Criminology* 38(2), 241–53.

Garver, John W. 1991, 'The Soviet Union and the Xi'an incident', *Australian Journal of Chinese Affairs* 26, 145–75.

Gill, Martin 1998, 'The victimization of business: indicators of risk and the direction of future research', *International Review of Victimology* 6, 17–28.

Golley, Jane and Song, Ligang 2010, 'Chinese economic reform and development: achievements, emerging challenges and unfinished tasks', in Ross Garnaut, Jane Golley and Ligang Song (eds), *China: The next twenty years of reform and development*, pp. 1–18. Canberra: ANU E Press.

Gong, T. 2004, 'Dependent judiciary and unaccountable judges: judicial corruption in contemporary China', *The China Review* 4(2), 33–54.

Gong, T. 2008, 'The party discipline inspection in China: its evolving trajectory and embedded dilemmas', *Crime, Law and Social Change* 49, 139–52.

Gong, T. 2010, 'An institutional turn toward rule-based integrity management in China', *Conference Proceedings, Centre for International Corruption Studies, HKSAR ICAC, September 16–18*.

Government of People's Republic of China 2005, 'More private companies in China: census', *GOV.cn*, 8 December, <www.gov.cn/english/2005-12/08/content_121412.htm>

Government of Shenzhen 2006, Shenzhen Government Online,

Government of Xi'an 2006, *Xi'an Statistical Yearbook 2006*, <English.xa.gov.cn> [Lennon Chang (trans.)].

Guang, Yang 2002, *Shanghai's Economic Development: Its opportunities and challenges in the 21st century*. Washington, DC: Global Urban Development, <www.globalurban.org/GUD%20Shanghai%20MES%20Report.pdf>

Guo, Yong 2006, *Country Study Report: China 2006*. Berlin: Transparency International.

Hang, Ma 2008, Villages in Shenzhen: typical economic phenomena of rural urbanisation in China, Paper presented at Forty-Fourth ISOCARP Congress, 19–23 September, Dalian, China.

Hawksworth, John, Hoehn, Thomas and Gyles, Meirion 2007, 'Which are the largest city economies in the world and how might this change by 2020?', in PriceWaterhouseCoopers, *UKEconomic Outlook March 2007*, pp. 15–26. London: PriceWaterhouseCoopers.

He, Ni and Marshall, Ineke 1997, 'Social production of crime data: a critical examination of Chinese crime statistics', *International Criminal Justice Review* 7, 46–64.

Henderson, Keith 2007, 'Corruption in China: half-way over the Great Wall', in Transparency International (ed.), *Global Corruption Report 2007: Corruption and judicial systems*. Berlin: Transparency International.

Hill, Gayle 2000, *Australian Laws Prohibiting Foreign Bribery: An overview and practical guide to compliance*. Sydney: Australian Mining and Petroleum Law Association Limited, <www.transparency.org.au/documents/Australian%20Laws%20Prohibiting%20Foreign%20Bribery.pdf>

Hollinger, Richard 2010, *National Retail Security Survey Final Report*. Gainesville, Fla: Department of Sociology and Center for Studies in Criminology and Law, University of Florida.

Hong Kong Police Force 2009a, *Crime Statistics in Details*, <www.police.gov.hk/ppp_en/09_statistics/csd.html>

Hong Kong Police Force 2009b, *Hong Kong Police in Figures*, <www.police.gov.hk/info/doc/2009_police_in_fig.pdf>

Hopkins, Matt 2002, 'Crimes against businesses: the way forward for future research', *British Journal of Criminology* 42, 782–97.

Human Rights in China, 2005, 'The Wuhan Court bribery case', *China Rights Forum* 1, 30–2.

Independent Commission Against Corruption (ICAC) 2006, *ICAC Annual Survey 2006 Executive Summary*. Hong Kong SAR: Independent Commission Against Corruption, <www.icac.org.hk/icac/stat/asurvey06_e.pdf>

Innes, Martin 2005, 'Why soft policing is hard', *Journal of Community and Applied Social Psychology* 15, 159–69.

Innes, Martin and Roberts, Colin 2008, 'Reassurance policing, community intelligence and the co-production of neighbourhood order', in Tom Williamson (ed.), *The Handbook of Knowledge-Based Policing: Current conceptions and future directions*, pp. 241–61. London: John Wiley & Sons.

Jacobs, Andrew 2010, 'Rampant fraud threat to China's brisk ascent', *The New York Times*, 6 October, <www.nytimes.com/2010/10/07/world/asia/07fraud. html>

Jeffery, C. Ray 1971, *Crime Prevention Through Environmental Design*. Beverly Hills, Calif.: Sage.

Jiang, Zhuqing 2004, 'Economic crimes rise, disturb social order', *China Daily*, 28 May, <www.chinadaily.com.cn/english/doc/2004-05/28/content_334742. htm>

Johnson, David T. and Zimring, Franklin 2009, *The Next Frontier: National development, political change, and the death penalty in Asia*. New York: Oxford University Press.

Jones, Francis C. 1939, *Shanghai and Tientsin, with Special Reference to Foreign Interests*. San Francisco: American Council, Institute of Pacific Relations.

Karstedt, Susanne 2003, 'Legacies of a culture of inequality: the Janus face of crime in post-communist countries', *Crime, Law & Social Change* 40, 295–320.

Kaufman, Daniel, Kraay, Aart and Mastruzzi, Massimo 2009, *Governance matters III: individual governance indicators 1996–2008*, Policy Research Working Paper No. 4978, The World Bank, New York.

Kaufman, Daniel, Kraay, Aart and Zoida-Lobaton, Pablo 2000, 'Governance matters: from measurement to action', *Finance and Development* 37(2), 10–13.

Keith, Ronald and Li, Zhiqui 2006, *New Crime in China: Public order and human rights*. London: Routledge.

Klein, Malcolm and Gatz, Margaret 1989, 'Professing the uncertain: problems of lecturing on Chinese social control', in Ronald J. Troyer, John P. Clark and Dean Rojek (eds), *Social Control in the People's Republic of China*, pp. 169–87. New York: Praeger.

KPMG Forensic 2003, *ANZ Fraud Survey 2002*. Sydney: KPMG Australia.

KPMG Forensic 2004, *ANZ Fraud Survey 2004*. Sydney: KPMG Australia.

Ledeneva, Alena and Kurkchiyan, Marina (eds) 2000, *Economic Crime in Russia*. New York: Kluwer.

Lei, Chun Kwok and Yao, Shujie 2008, 'On income convergence among China, Hong Kong and Macau', *World Economy* 31(30), 345–66.

Lethbridge, Henry J. 1985, *Hard Graft in Hong Kong: Scandal, corruption and the ICAC*. Hong Kong SAR: Oxford University Press.

Levi, Michael, Burrows, John 2008, 'Measuring the impact of fraud: a conceptual and empirical journey', *British Journal of Criminology* 48(3), 298–318.

Levi, Michael, Burrows, John, Fleming, Matthew and Hopkins, Matthew 2007, *The Nature, Extent and Economic Impact of Fraud in the UK*. London: Association of Chief Police Officers, <www.cardiff.ac.uk/socsi/resources/ACPO%20final%20nature%20extent%20and%20economic%20impact%20of%20fraud.pdf>

Lewis, Leo 2011, 'Mistakenly-released report reveals embarrassing extent of Chinese corruption', *The Times*, [Republished in *The Australian*], 17 June, <www.theaustralian.com.au/news/world/accidentally-released-report-reveals-embarrassing-extent-of-chinese-corruption/story-e6frg6so-1226076938605>

Li, Deshui 2006, 'China's economic census', *Statistika—Journal for Economy and Statistics* 3, 252–60.

Li, Qiufang 2010, 'Probity culture of public officers and the construction of an integrity system', *Conference Proceedings, Centre for International Corruption Studies, HKSAR ICAC, September 16–18*.

Liu, Jianhong 2004, 'Social transition and crime in China: an economic motivation thesis', *Australian and New Zealand Journal of Criminology* 37(4), 122–38.

Liu, Jianhong 2005, 'Crime patterns during the market transition in China', *British Journal of Criminology*, 45, 613–33.

Liu, Jianhong 2006, 'Modernization and crime patterns in China', *Journal of Criminal Justice* 34, 119–30.

Lo, T. Wing 1993, *Corruption and Politics in Hong Kong and China*. Buckingham and Philadelphia: Open University Press.

Lo, T. Wing 2003, 'Minimizing crime and corruption in Hong Kong', in Roy Godson (ed.), *Menace to Society: Political–criminal collaboration around the world*, pp. 231–56. London: Transaction Publishers.

Lo, T. Wing 2010, 'Beyond social capital: triad organized crime in Hong Kong and China', *British Journal of Criminology* 50(5), 851–72.

Lu, Jianping 2011, The crimes of private enterprise in China in transformation, Paper presented at the Sixteenth Congress of the International Society of Criminology, 5–9 August, Kobe, Japan.

Mako, William 2006, *China: governance, investment climate, and harmonious society: competitiveness enhancements for 120 cities in China*, Report No. 37759-CN, The World Bank, Washington, DC, <siteresources.worldbank. org/INTCHINA/Resources/318862-1121421293578/120cities_en.pdf>

Marks, Stephen R. 1974, 'Durkheim's theory of anomie', *American Journal of Sociology* 80(2), 329–63.

Merton, Robert 1938, 'Social structure and anomie', *American Sociological Review* 3(5), 672–82.

Merton, Robert 1968, *Social Theory and Social Structure*. New York: Free Press.

Messner, Steven 1982, 'Societal development, social equality and homicide: a cross-national test of the Durkheimian model', *Social Forces* 61, 225–40.

Messner, Steven and Rosenfeld, Richard 2009, 'Institutional anomie theory: a macro-sociological explanation of crime', in Marvin D. Krohn, Alan J. Lizotee and Gina P. Hall (eds), *Handbook of Sociology and Social Research*, pp. 209–24. New York: Springer.

Messner, Steven, Liu, Jianhong and Karstedt, Susanne 2007a, 'Economic reform and crime in contemporary urban China: paradoxes of a planned transition', in John Logan (ed.), *Urban China in Transition*, pp. 271–93. New York: Wiley-Blackwell.

Messner, Steven, Lu, Zhou, Zhang, Lening and Liu, Jianhong 2007b, 'Risks of criminal victimization in contemporary urban China: an application of lifestyle/routine activities theory', *Justice Quarterly* 24(3), 496–522.

Mon, Wei Teh 2003, 'What does the crime victimization survey reveal about victims and responses of police: Taiwanese experience', *Journal of Asian Association of Police Studies* 1(1), 17–21.

Nalla, Mahesh K. and Hoffman, Vincent J. 1996, 'Security training needs: a study of the perceptions of security guards in Singapore', *Security Journal* 7(4), 287–93.

National Bureau of Statistics (NBS) 2003, *Statistical Communiqué on Public Sense of Security Survey in 2003*. Beijing: National Bureau of Statistics of China, <www.stats.gov.cn/tjgb/qttjgb/qgqttjgb/t20040315_402136312.htm>

National Bureau of Statistics (NBS) 2004, *Statistical Communiqué on Public Sense of Security Survey in 2004*. Beijing: National Bureau of Statistics of China, <news.xinhuanet.com/zhengfu/2005-02/04/content_2546996.htm>

National Bureau of Statistics (NBS) 2005a, *ChinaFirst National Economic Census*. Beijing: National Bureau of Statistics of China, <unpan1.un.org/intradoc/groups/public/documents/apcity/unpan022709.pdf>

National Bureau of Statistics (NBS) 2005b, *Shenzhen: First economic census of Guangdong Province*. Beijing: National Bureau of Statistics of China, <www.stats.gov.cn/zgjjpc/cgfb/t20051230_402299384.htm>

National Bureau of Statistics (NBS) 2005c, *Statistical Communiqué on Public Sense of Security Survey in 2005*. Beijing: National Bureau of Statistics of China, <www.stats.gov.cn/tjgb/qttjgb/qgqttjgb/t20050203_402300332.htm>

National Bureau of Statistics (NBS) 2005d, *Xi'an:First economic census of Shaanxi Province*. Beijing: National Bureau of Statistics of China, <www.sei.gov.cn/ShowArticle2008.asp?ArticleID=81237>

National Bureau of Statistics (NBS) 2006a, *China Statistical Yearbook 2006*. Beijing: National Bureau of Statistics of China, <www.stats.gov.cn/tjsj/ndsj/2006/indexeh.htm>

National Bureau of Statistics (NBS) 2006b, *Statistical Communiqué on Public Sense of Security Survey in 2006*. Beijing: National Bureau of Statistics of China, <www.stats.gov.cn/english/newsandcomingevents/t20070126_402382822.htm>

National Bureau of Statistics (NBS) 2007, *Statistical Communiqué on Public Sense of Security Survey in 2007*. Beijing: National Bureau of Statistics of China, <www.stats.gov.cn/was40/gjtjj_en_detail.jsp?searchword=public+security&channelid=9528&record=3>

Naudé, C. M. B., Prinsloo, J. H. and Martins, J. H. 1999 *Crimes against the South African business sector*, Draft report, University of South Africa, Pretoria, <www.victimology.nl/onlpub/otherdocs/vicsurveys.html#Naudé1>

Newman, Graeme (ed.) 1999, *Global Report on Crime and Criminal Justice*. New York: United Nations Office for Drug Control and Crime Prevention.

Newman, Oscar 1972, *Defensible Space: Crime prevention through urban design*. New York: Macmillan.

Nielsen, Ingrid and Smyth, Russell 2005, *Who fears crime? Perceptions of public security and attitudes to migrants among China's urban population*, ABERU Discussion Paper No. 8, Monash University, Melbourne.

Nielsen, Ingrid and Smyth, Russell 2009, 'Perceptions of public security in post-reform urban China: a routine activity analysis', *Asian Criminology* 4, 145–63.

Nigerian National Bureau of Statistics (Nigerian NBS) 2009, *NBS/EFCC Business Survey on Crime & Corruption and Awareness of EFCC in Nigeria, 2007: Summary report*. Abuja: National Bureau of Statistics, <www.nigerianstat. gov.ng/ext/latest_release/NBS_EFCC%20Survey.pdf>

Nigerian National Bureau of Statistics (Nigerian NBS) 2010, *NBS/EFCC Business Survey on Crime & Corruption and Awareness of EFCC in Nigeria, 2007: Statistical report*. Abuja: National Bureau of Statistics, <www.nigerianstat. gov.ng/ext/latest_release/NBS_EFCC%20Survey.pdf>

Pei, Minxin 2007, *Corruption threatens China's future*, Policy Brief 55, Carnegie Endowment for International Peace, Washington, DC.

People's Daily Online n.d., 'Deng Xiaoping', *People's Daily Online*, <english. peopledaily.com.cn/data/people/dengxiaoping.shtml>

Perrone, Santina 2000, 'Crimes against small business in Australia: a preliminary analysis', *Trends and Issues in Crime and Criminal Justice* No. 184. Canberra: Australian Institute of Criminology.

PriceWaterhouseCoopers 2007a, *Economic Crime: People, culture and controls—The 4th biennial Global Economic Crime Survey*. London: PriceWaterhouseCoopers.

PriceWaterhouseCoopers 2007b, *Economic Crime: People, culture and controls—The 4th biennial Global Economic Crime Survey Hong Kong*. Hong Kong SAR: PriceWaterhouseCoopers.

PriceWaterhouseCoopers 2009, *Economic Crime in a Downturn*. Moscow: PriceWaterhouseCoopers.

PriceWaterhouseCoopers 2010a, *Economic Crimes Survey, Brazil 2009*. Sao Paulo: PriceWaterhouseCoopers.

PriceWaterhouseCoopers 2010b, *Fraud: The Enemy Within*. Mumbai: PriceWaterhouseCoopers.

Qi, Lei and Lu, Bin 2008, Urban sprawl: a case study of Shenzhen, China, Paper presented at the Forty-Fourth ISOCARP Congress, 19–23 September, Dalian, China.

Qiu, G. 2008, 'From "protective umbrellas" to "gang bosses"', *Fanzui Yanjiu*, 13–16 [in Chinese].

Richards, Kelly 2009, *The Australian business assessment of computer user security: a national survey*, Research and Public Policy Series No. 102, Australian Institute of Criminology, Canberra.

Richards, Kelly and Davis, Brent 2010, 'Computer security incidents against Australian businesses: predictors of victimisation', *Trends & Issues in Crime and Criminal Justice* 399, Australian Institute of Criminology, Canberra.

Roberts, Kenneth D. 2002, 'Rural migrants in urban China: willing workers, invisible residents', *Asia Pacific Business Review* 8(4), 141–58.

Rock, Paul 2002, 'Sociological theories of crime', in Mike Maguire, Rod Morgan and Robert Reiner (eds), *The Oxford Handbook of Criminology*, pp. 51–82. Oxford: Oxford University Press.

Sainsbury, Michael 2010, 'Rio Tinto's Stern Hu jailed for 10 years', *The Australian*, 29 March, <www.theaustralian.com.au/business/mining-energy/rio-tintos-stern-hu-jailed-10-years/story-e6frg9df-1225847088979>

Sergeyev, Victor 1998, *The Wild East: Crime and lawlessness in post-communist Russia*. Armonk, NY: M. E. Sharpe.

Seymour, James 2005, 'Sizing up China's prisons', in Børge Bakken (ed.), *Crime, Punishment, and Policing in China*, pp. 141–67. Oxford: Rowman & Littlefield.

Shahid, Alam 1991, 'Some economic costs of corruption in LDCs', *Journal of Development Studies* 27(1), 89–97.

Shanghai Municipal Statistics Bureau 2006, *Shanghai Statistical Yearbook 2006*. Shanghai: Shanghai Municipal Statistics Bureau, <www.stats-sh.gov.cn/2004shtj/tjnj/tjnj2006e.htm>

Shanghai Municipal Statistics Bureau 2010, *Shanghai Statistical Yearbook 2010*. Shanghai: Shanghai Municipal Statistics Bureau, <www.stats-sh.gov.cn/> (in Chinese).

Shaw, Victor 2006, 'China under reform: social problems in rural area', *China Report* 42(4), 341–68.

Shelley, Louise 1981, *Crime and Modernization: The impact of industrialization and urbanization on crime*. Carbondale: Southern Illinois University Press.

Shelley, Louise 1995a, 'Post-Soviet organized crime', *European Journal on Criminal Policy and Research* 3–4, 8–25.

Shelley, Louise 1995b, 'Privatization and crime: the post-Soviet experience', *Journal of Contemporary Criminal Justice* 11, 244–56.

Shenzhen Daily 2003, 'Shoplifting causes a dilemma', *Shenzhen Daily*, 27 October, <www.chinadaily.com.cn/en/doc/2003-10/27/content_275932.htm>

Sheu, C., Chen, Y., Mong, W., Tsai, T., Huang, L., Huang, C., et al. 2005, *2005 Taiwan Areas Criminal Victimization Report. Volumes 1 and 2*, [in Chinese]. Taipei, Taiwan: National Police Agency.

Shover, Neal and Hochstetler, Andy 2006, *Choosing White-Collar Crime*. New York: Cambridge University Press.

Shury, Jan, Speed, Mark, Vivian, David, Kuechel, Alistair and Sian, Nicholas 2005, *Crimes against Retail and Manufacturing Premises: Findings from the 2002 Commercial Victimisation Survey*. London: Home Office.

Smith, Russell and Urbas, Gregor 2002, *Controlling fraud on the Internet: a CAPA perspective*, Research and Public Policy Series No. 39, Australian Institute of Criminology, Canberra.

Stone, David 2011, 'Three dead in the latest Chinese milk scare', *Food Magazine*, 11 April, <www.foodmag.com.au/news/three-dead-in-the-latest-chinese-milk-scare>

Sun, Ivan Y. and Wu, Yuning 2009, 'The role of the People's Armed Police in Chinese policing', *Asian Criminology* 4, 107–28.

Sun, Liping, Guo, Yuhua and Shen, Yuan 2010, 'Tsinghua report—new thinking on stability maintenance: long-term social stability via institutionalised expression of interests', *Lingdao Zhe* [*Leaders*] 33, 11–24 [in Chinese].

Tan, Xiuzheng and Xue, Kexuan 1997, 'The thinking concerning the strengthening of police force under the new situation', *Shenzhen Political and Legal Yearbook 1997*. Shenzhen: Haitian Press.

Tan, Y. and Yang, G. 2009, 'An empirical study on organizations with characters of black society in north-west region', *Legal System and Society* 12, 113–14 [in Chinese].

Tanner, Murray 2005, 'Campaign-style policing in China and its critics', in Børge Bakken (ed.), *Crime, Punishment, and Policing in China*, pp. 171–88. Oxford: Rowman & Littlefield.

Tanner, Murray and Green, Eric 2007, 'Principals and secret agents: central vs. local control over policing and obstacles to "rule of law": in China', *China Quarterly* 191, 644–70.

Taylor, Natalie 2002, 'Reporting of crime against small retail businesses', *Trends & Issues in Crime and Criminal Justice* 242, Australian Institute of Criminology, Canberra.

Taylor, Natalie and Mayhew, Pat 2002, 'Patterns of victimisation among small retail businesses', *Trends & Issues in Crime and Criminal Justice* 221, pp. 1–6, Australian Institute of Criminology, Canberra.

The Economist 2011, 'An online-fraud scandal in China: Alibaba and the 2,236 thieves', *The Economist*, 22 February, <www.economist.com/blogs/newsbook/2011/02/online-fraud_scandal_china>

The Economist 2011, 'China boosts spending on welfare—and on internal security, too', *The Economist*, 10 March, <www.economist.com/node/18335099>

The Lancet 2010, 'Scientific fraud: action needed in China', *The Lancet* 375(9709), 9, 94.

The Standard 2003, 'Cop infiltrates treads to smash racket', *The Standard*, 22 September.

Trevaskes, Susan 2010a, *Policing Serious Crime in China: From 'strike hard' to 'kill fewer'*. London: Routledge.

Trevaskes, Susan 2010b, 'The shifting sands of punishment in China in the era of "Harmonious Society"', *Law & Policy* 32(3), 332–61.

Truman, Jennifer and Rand, Michael 2010, *Criminal Victimization, 2009*. Washington, DC: Bureau of Justice Statistics, US Department of Justice.

Tuchman, Barbara W. 1971, *Stillwell and the American Experience in China*. New York: Macmillan.

UN-HABITAT 2008, *States of the World Cities 2008/2009*. Nairobi: United Nations Human Settlements Programme.

United Nations Office on Drugs and Crime (UNODC) 2004, *United Nations Surveys of Crime Trends and Operations of Criminal Justice Systems, covering the period 1990–2000*. Vienna: United Nations Office on Drugs and Crime, <www.unodc.org/unodc/en/data-and-analysis/United-Nations-Surveys-on-Crime-Trends-and-the-Operations-of-Criminal-Justice-Systems.html>

United Nations Office on Drugs and Crime (UNODC) 2007, *Responses by Country to Selected Indicators to: Questionnaire for the Ninth United Nations Survey of Crime Trends and Operations of Criminal Justice Systems, covering the period 2003–2004.* Vienna: United Nations Office on Drugs and Crime, <www.unodc.org/documents/data-and-analysis/CTS9_by_country_public.pdf>

United Nations Secretariat 2006, *World Urbanization Prospects: The 2005 revision.* New York: Department of Economic and Social Affairs, Population Division, United Nations, <www.un.org/esa/population/publications/WUP2005/2005wup.htm>

United Nations Secretariat 2007, *World Population Prospects: The 2006 revision.* New York: Department of Economic and Social Affairs, Population Division, United Nations, <www.un.org/esa/population/publications/wpp2006/English.pdf>

United Nations Secretariat 2008, *World Urbanization Prospects: The 2007 revision.* New York: Department of Economic and Social Affairs, Population Division, United Nations, <www.un.org/esa/population/publications/wup2007/2007WUP_Highlights_web.pdf>

United Nations Statistics Division 2008, *Demographic Yearbook 2005.* New York: United Nations, <unstats.un.org/unsd/demographic/products/dyb/dyb2005.htm>

van Dijk, Jan 1997, 'Introducing victimology', *The Victimologist* 1(1), 1–5.

van Dijk, Jan 1999, 'Criminal victimization and victim empowerment', in Jan Van Dijk, Ron van Kaam and Jo-Anne Wemmers (eds), *Caring for Crime Victims*, pp. 15–39. New York: Criminal Justice Press.

van Dijk, Jan 2000, 'Criminal victimisation: a global view', in Anna Alvazzi del Frate, Oksanna Hatalak and Ugljesa Zvekic (eds), *Surveying Crime: A global perspective. Proceedings of the International Conference, Rome, 19–21 November 1998*, pp. 63–95. Rome: National Institute of Statistics.

van Dijk, Jan and Terlouw, Gert Jan 1996, 'An international perspective of the business community as victims of fraud and crime', *Security Journal* 7, 157–67.

van Dijk, Jan, van Kesteren, John and Smit, Paul 2007, *Criminal Victimisation in International Perspective: Key findings from the 2004–2005 ICVS and EU ICS77* [*Onderzoek en beleid*, No. 257]. The Hague: Ministry of Justice, WODC.

van Kesteren, Jan, Mayhew, Pat and Nieuwbeerta, Paul 2000, *Criminal Victimisation in Seventeen Industrialised Countries*. The Hague: WODC/NSCR.

Wakeman, Frederic 1995, *Policing Shanghai 1927–1937*. Berkeley: University of California Press.

Walker, John 1995a, 'Crimes against businesses in Australia', *Trends and Issues in Crime and Criminal Justice* 45, Australian Institute of Criminology, Canberra.

Walker, John 1995b, *First Australian National Survey of Crimes against Business*. Canberra: Australian Institute of Criminology, <www.aic.gov.au/events/ aic%20upcoming%20events/1994/~/media/conferences/business/walker. ashx>

Walmsey, Roy 2005, *World Prison Population List*, [Sixth edn]. London: International Centre for Prison Studies.

Walmsey, Roy 2006, *World Prison Population List*, [Seventh edn]. London: International Centre for Prison Studies.

Wang, Guangze 2007, 'The mystery of China's death penalty figures', *China Rights Forum* 2, 39–43.

Wang, H., Zhou, X. and Jiang, T. 2003, 'Penetration into Guangdong by triads from Hong Kong, Macau and Taiwan and its prevention and crackdown countermeasures', *China Criminal Police* 15(3), 63–71 [in Chinese].

Wang, Ya Ping, Wang, Yanglin and Wu, Jiansheng 2009a, 'Housing migrant workers in rapidly urbanizing regions: a study of the Chinese model in Shenzhen', *Housing Studies* 25(1), 83–100.

Wang, Ya Ping, Wang, Yanglin and Wu, Jiansheng 2009b, 'Urbanization and informal development in China: urban villages in Shenzhen', *International Journal of Urban and Regional Research* 33(4), 957–73.

Wedeman, Andrew 2004, 'The intensification of corruption', *China Quarterly* 180, 839–921.

Wedeman, Andrew 2006, 'Anticorruption campaigns and the intensification of corruption in China', *Journal of Contemporary China* 14(41), 93–107.

Wedeman, Andrew 2008, 'Win, lose or draw? China's quarter century war on corruption', *Crime, Law and Social Change* 49, 7–16.

Wilder, Martijn and Ahrens, Michael 2001, 'Australia's implementation of the OECD Convention on Combating Bribery of Foreign Public Officials in International Business Transactions', *Melbourne Journal of International Law* 22(2), 568–83.

Wittebrood, Karin and Nieuwbeerta, Paul 2000, 'Criminal victimization during one's life course: the effects of previous victimization and patterns of routine activities', *Journal of Research in Crime & Delinquency* 37(1), 91–122.

Wong, Kam C. 2001, 'Community policing in China: philosophy, law and practice', *International Journal of the Sociology of Law* 29(2), 127–47.

Wong, Kam C. 2002, 'Policing in the People's Republic of China: the road to reform in the 1990s', *British Journal of Criminology* 42, 281–316.

Wong, Kam C. 2004, 'Govern police by law in China', *Australian and New Zealand Journal of Criminology* 37(4), 90–106.

Wong, Kam C. 2011, *Police Reform in China: A Chinese perspective*. New York: Taylor & Francis.

World Bank n.d., *GNIPC Income Measures*. Washington, DC: The World Bank, <siteresources.worldbank.org/DATASTATISTICS/.../GNIPC.pdf>

Wu, Yuning and Sun, Ivan Y. 2009, 'Citizen trust in police: the case of China', *Police Quarterly* 12(2), 170–91.

Yan, Zhongmin 1984, 'Shanghai: the growth and shifting emphasis of China's largest city', in Victor F. S. Sit (ed.), *Chinese Cities: The growth of the metropolis since 1949*, pp. 94–127. Oxford: Oxford University Press.

Yu, Olivia 2008, 'Corruption in China's economic reform: a review of recent observations and explanations', *Crime, Law and Social Change* 50, 161–76.

Yu, Olivia and Zhang, Lening 1999, 'The under-recording of crime by police in China: a case study', *Policing: An International Journal of Police Strategies and Management* 22(3), 252–63.

Zhao, Suisheng 1993, 'Deng Xiaoping's southern tour: elite politics in post-Tiananmen China', *Asian Survey* 33(8), 739–56.

Zhong, Lena Y. 2009a, *Communities, Crime and Social Capital in Contemporary China*. Cullompton, UK: Willan.

Zhong, Lena Y. 2009b, 'Community policing in China: old wine in new bottles?', *Police Practice and Research* 10(2), 157–69.

Zhong, Lena Y. and Grabosky, Peter 2009, 'The pluralisation of policing and the rise of private policing in China', *Crime, Law, and Social Change* 52, 433–55.

Zhu, Hongde, Wang, Lixian, Lu, Jialun, Guo, Jianan and Zhou, Lu 1995, '1992 Beijing crime victim survey', in Ugljesa Zvekic and Anna Alvazzi Del Frate (eds), *Criminal Victimisation in the Developing World*, UNICRI Publication No. 55. Rome: United Nations.

Zhu, Ling, Yan, Ran and Cai, Rongwei 2002, 'New regulations on employment contracts in Shanghai', *China Law and Practice*, February, <www.chinalawandpractice.com/Article/1693823/Channel/9931/New-Regulations-On-Employment-Contracts-in-Shanghai.html>

Zhuo, Yue, Messner, Steven and Zhang, Lening 2008, 'Criminal victimization in contemporary China: a review of the evidence and challenges for future research', *Crime, Law, and Social Change* 50, 197–209.

Zhuqing, Jiang 2004, 'Economic crimes rise, disturb social order', *China Daily*, 28 May, <www.chinadaily.com.cn/english/doc/2004-05/28/content_334742.htm>

Zou, Keyuan 2000, 'Towards rule of law in China: experiences in the last two decades', *China Report* 36(4), 491–509.

Zvekic, Ugljesa and Alvazzi del Frate, Anna 1995, *Criminal Victimisation in the Developing World*. Rome: United Nations Interregional Criminal Justice Institute.

www.ingramcontent.com/pod-product-compliance
Lightning Source LLC
Chambersburg PA
CBHW061243270326
41928CB00041B/3380